The Opium Business

The Opium Business

A HISTORY OF
CRIME AND CAPITALISM
IN MARITIME CHINA

Peter Thilly

STANFORD UNIVERSITY PRESS
STANFORD, CALIFORNIA

Stanford University Press
Stanford, California

Printed in the United States of America on acid-free, archival-quality paper

ISBN 9781503628861 (cloth)
ISBN 9781503634107 (paper)
ISBN 9781503634114 (electronic)

Library of Congress Control Number: 2022005932

Library of Congress Cataloging-in-Publication Data available upon request.

Cover design: Michel Vrana
Cover photo: Archival photo of Amoy (Xiamen) outer harbour, seen from the beach at Ē-mn̂g-kang. ID DA26/2/2/1 at Cadbury Research Library, Special Collections, University of Birmingham

Typeset by Elliott Beard in Adobe Garamond Pro 11/14

Contents

Illustrations

Acknowledgments

I am full of gratitude for the guidance of Melissa Macauley, Peter Carroll, Deborah Cohen, Amy Stanley, and Laura Hein, as well as help and feedback from classmates at Northwestern including Keith Rathbone, Marlous van Waijenburg, Michael Martoccio, Alexandra Lindren-Gibson, Teng Li, Yanqiu Zheng, Austin Parks, and many others. At the University of Mississippi, I have benefited from the feedback and support of colleagues including Mikaëla Adams, Jesse Cromwell, Darren Grem, Joshua Howard, Zachary Kagan Guthrie, Theresa Levitt, Marcos Mendoza, Eva Payne, Jarod Roll, Anne Twitty, Jeff Watt, Noell Wilson, and many others. In my prior lives at the University of Chicago and Wesleyan University, I was lucky enough to receive guidance and mentorship from Zhu Xiaomiao, Guy Alito, Steve Angle, Prasenjit Duara, and Vera Schwarcz.

Through the years of research and writing, the following kind souls have offered help, comments, feedback, and volunteered sources. They are listed in no order, and, of course, have no responsibility for this book's contents: Stacie Kent, Wes Cheney, Maura Dykstra, Bryna Goodman, Wen-hsin Yeh, Pär Cassell, Philip Thai, Xing Hang, Fei-Hsien Wang, Cheng-Heng Lu, Eugenio Menegon, Tina Chen, Lincoln Paine, Boyi Chen, Aminda Smith, Ulf Engel, Geert Castryck, Eric Tagliacozzo, Taisu Zhang, Michael Szonyi, John E. Wills, Jacob Eyferth, Johanna Ransmeier, Alexander Cook, Doug Fix, James

Lin, Jake Werner, Guo-Quan Seng, John Cheng, and Amitav Ghosh. Thanks also to David Ambaras, Kate McDonald, Sakura Christmas, Evan Dawley, Weiting Guo, and Nate Isaacson. Thanks to everyone else not named who also put care and labor into helping me become a better historian.

In the research and writing of this book, I received crucial support from the Northwestern Graduate School and History Department, the Buffett Institute for Global Studies, the Renmin University of China, the Fulbright Foundation, the Institute for Historical Research in London, the Mellon Foundation, the Social Science Research Council, the University of Mississippi Department of History, the Harvard-Yenching Library, and the Henry-Luce / ACLS Postdoctoral Fellowship in Chinese Studies. A special thanks to Lian Xinhao at Xiamen University, the Institute for Qing Studies at Renda, the staff of the Number One Historical Archives of China, the Fujian Provincial Archives, the Xiamen Public Library, the SOAS University of London Special Collections, the Cambridge University Library, the British National Archives, Jacques Oberson at the League of Nations Archive, Li Qunying at the Northwestern University Library, and the librarians at the University of Mississippi. Earlier and alternate drafts of chapter 1 have appeared in *Late Imperial China* and *Bodies and Structures: Deep Mapping Modern East Asian History*, and a previous version of part of chapter 5 has been published in *Cross-Currents: East Asian History and Culture Review*. Thank you also to Marcela Maxfield, Dylan Kyung-lim White, Sunna Juhn, the two anonymous readers, and everyone else at SUP. Thank you to Bill Nelson for preparing the maps.

This book exists only because of the support of all of my families, friends, and communities. Thank you to the Pensuwaparp family, Seth and Jamie Lochen, Sara and Nat Love, Ben Keleny, Bean Gepner, John Burr, Ben Weismer, Bryan Koenig, Joaquin Cotler, Lindsay Dula, Krishna Andavolu, Emma Alpert, Carl and Kidist Cervone, Ethan Leinwand, Matt Colvard, Julia Cohen, Katie Shepherd, Mike Kerns, Mark Hatch-Miller, Ariel Lewiton, Ben Goldwasser, David Macnutt, Andrew Vanwyngarden, Noah Nattell and Katie Schoendorf, John Molfetta, Memento Mori F.C., ATNFL, Mahitsara Thibodee 6/1, and family dinner. Thank you to my parents, Mary and Roy, and to Helen, Owen, Beth, Walter, Scott, Alex, Olympia, Sue, Rick, Anina, Jimmy, John, Mike, Herb, Marcia, Barbara, and Bob. Thank you most of all to Rebecca Marchiel, and to my children Bruce and Maggie, whom I love very much.

Note on Currency and Exchange Rates

Currency and Measurements

> One picul (*dan*) = 133.3 pounds (the approximate weight of one
> chest of raw opium)
> One catty (*jin*) = 1.33 pounds
> One tael (*liang*) of silver = 1.3 ounces of silver (until 1933)
> One tael of silver = between 1,300 and 2,200 copper cash (*wen*)
> (until 1911)

During the later years of the Qing dynasty when the first chapters of this book take place (1832–1911), the exchange rate between silver taels (*liang*) and copper cash (*wen*) fluctuated between 1,300 and 2,000 copper cash per tael. In Fujian province, where this book takes place, currency use was highly diverse and variable over time, including gold, silver sycee, Spanish and Mexican silver dollars, Dutch guilders, rupees, and other forms of currency and treasure. In the final decades of Qing rule, the Chinese Maritime Customs assessed the value of foreign trade and levied taxes according to an abstract silver-based currency called the Haikwan Tael (HK Tl.), weighing on average slightly more than the other silver taels in circulation.

The use of the dollar sign ($) in this book, when referring to currency used during the years before 1933, refers to the Mexican silver dollar, the most widely circulated currency in the region. For the period after 1933, the dollar sign ($) is also used as a symbol for the yuan, or the currency of the Nationalist government.

Price Index

In 1840s Fujian, carpenters, masons, smiths, and tailors in the provincial capital earned between 100 and 200 wen per day. A catty (1.33 pounds) of pork cost 80 wen, and a pair of plain blue trousers cost 580 wen. Opium imported into the province in 1847 sold for between $590 and $700 per chest, and a sailor on the British opium ships earned $9 per month.

In 1930s Fujian, a stevedore in the Xiamen harbor earned around $30 per month and paid union dues of $0.2 per month. A picul of rice (133 lbs.) cost between $8 and $9, and a catty of pork (1.33 lbs.) cost $0.5. The cheapest passenger steamship ticket from Xiamen to Shanghai cost $7, to Hong Kong $2, and to Singapore $60. Between 1934 and 1937, legal Guomindang monopoly opium was retailed by the prohibition bureau in Fujian for around $2.40–2.70 per ounce, illegal Persian opium cost on average about $1 more per ounce, and Taiwanese heroin cost $1.30 per ounce.

Coastal Southern Fujian

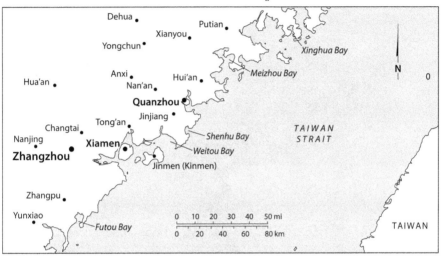

Maritime Fujian

The Opium Business

The Opium Business in Chinese and World History

In the autumn of 1840, as British and Qing forces squared off in what would become known as the "Opium War," a gang of a few dozen men set out into the mountains with a modest cargo of opium hidden in their bundles. The drugs had been cultivated and manufactured in India, transported over the ocean on British clipper ships, and unloaded in clandestine transactions to importers on the Qing empire's southeast coast. The gang purchased the opium wholesale in a bustling maritime port city, concealed it within their clothing and among their supplies, and set out walking for thirteen days from the coast up into the mountainous regions of inland Fujian province towards neighboring Jiangxi. Their leader was a seasoned opium dealer, his second-in-command a locally renowned martial artist. The opium dealer had paid a generous sum for the company of the martial artist, knowing that the mountainous upland districts were teeming with bandits, soldiers, and competitors.[1]

Along the way, all through the final months of 1840, the gang grew in number. Wandering, unattached men and small-time opium dealers threw in their lot with the travelers. Most were surely drawn in by the lure of profit. Some might have joined out of addiction or craving for opium. The personal charisma of the martial arts virtuoso must also have inspired confidence among some of the more vulnerable travelers who joined up. The archive conceals exactly how the group expanded from a few dozen to over a hundred men in just a few months. What we do know is that by the time autumn turned to winter, the ranks of this opium gang had swelled. The two leaders worried that they were becoming too conspicuous. They needed a plan.

The opium dealer and the martial artist created a uniformed, confederated, opium army. They split the large and disorganized gang into ten teams, bringing in people with an existing capacity to capitalize on opium as team leaders and subsidiary investors. For the privilege of working within the organization, team leaders were required to pay steep fees on the opium that they handled. Members referred to these payments with the term *lijin*, drawing on a vocabulary of transit surcharges levied by prominent brokers or industry leaders, often through a tax farming relationship with the local state.[2] At the top of the organization, the founders kept daily ledgers and entered each team's membership, productivity, and lijin contributions into a central register. The teams themselves were made up of small-time bandits, boat paddlers, and rootless rascals, whom the leaders paid a porter's daily fee for carrying and protecting the opium and supplies.[3] The founders gave each team a code name and a red flag, issuing members a small swatch of red cloth to hang on their clothing for mutual recognition. Together, they were known as the Red Society (*honghui*).

The Red Society was a short-lived regional operation with just a small archival footprint, but the case narrative offers tantalizing clues about the economic life of the opium trader. The founders of the Red Society were ambitious rural opium dealers who set out to connect inland consumers with the coastal import market, and who strove to edge out or subsume their competition with a territorial transport and distribution monopoly. They rose to prominence by creating a hierarchical shareholding enterprise: two founders who received profits on all opium sold by the organization, presiding over a small group of investor-salesmen who managed teams of transporters and retailers and passed a cut of their sales up to the founders. They institutionalized the organization with a language of merchant surcharges that has deep roots in late imperial systems of revenue extraction and market regulation.

The people who operated the opium business along China's southeast coast in the nineteenth and twentieth centuries drew upon a variety of local, regional, and global profit-seeking techniques and economic traditions. The

Red Society's business strategy, practices, and terminology embody a particular cluster of those techniques, which echo throughout this book in the tax farms and prohibition agencies that emerged in later decades. Like the leader of the Red Society, many of the people who achieved success in the opium business in this region did so by assembling a small group of investors and then establishing a monopoly over the transport and distribution of opium within a territory. Like with the Red Society, groups of investors in this region often grew and protected their market share by hiring low-wage teams of the laboring poor to put on uniforms, carry weapons, transport drugs, and enforce monopolistic terms of trade and transport.

There was a broad confluence of forces that shaped the opium business in late imperial and Republican China: patterns and practices of lineage organization, flexible citizenship, bribery, subterfuge, jurisdictional arbitrage, and creative accounting. Here, at the beginning of the story, I introduce the Red Society as an early example of what became the hallmark institution of the modern Chinese opium business: a joint-investment corporation that maintained a discrete territorial control over the regulation and taxation of opium's transport and distribution.

———

This book investigates how people in southeast China bought and sold opium: how their businesses interacted with the state, how the most successful opium traffickers accumulated profit and exercised power, and how these practices and patterns changed over time from the 1830s to the 1940s. It starts from the premise that opium was first and foremost a commodity: an important item of exchange and consumption in the late imperial and then modern world economy. The drug was shipped and warehoused with other items. Opium capital was entangled in businesses like cotton, tea, and sugar. Those commodities have inspired scholars to write rich global histories, and as items of production, trade, and consumption, they are less problematic objects of study for historians of global capitalism.[4] Opium was in the same world as those other mass-produced agricultural products: it was in the same boats, the same banks, and it was bought, sold, and consumed by many of the same people. But opium was "special," because it was often illegal, and it was always transgressive. Because of the regulatory and moral context surrounding the drug, opium traders developed a particularly thorny relationship—antagonistic and yet codependent—with the people and institutions of state power.

Opium first became a major industry in China during the early nineteenth century when the drug was a contraband item with a huge market. In those freewheeling years, opium traders partnered with local officials to formalize fees and bribes on the drug's sale, and together they created the first local opium taxation systems. The industry expanded horizontally and vertically across mid-nineteenth-century China, responding to new tensions, new opportunities, and new technologies. When the drug became de facto legalized around 1860, the people at the heights of the opium business worked with officials to determine tax rates and quotas. They made themselves indispensable as sources of state revenue, leveraging their essential contributions to state finances for ever greater privileges. The opium business, as it came to evolve in the age of legal opium, took shape through its interactions with a state that was beset with problems, but which was also determined to protect its borders and build up military capacity.

Opium revenue became a cornerstone of the fiscal basis of the militarizing late Qing state.[5] This was not unique in the region: opium revenue was integral to late-nineteenth-century state finances across Chinese, British, Dutch, and French jurisdictions in Asia.[6] Qing officials taxed opium's circulation after import through farming, or subcontracting the rights to taxation and market regulation to people within the opium business. This too was not unique and mirrored policy in French Cochinchina (until 1881), French Indochina (until 1899), the Netherlands Indies (until 1904), and the British Straits Settlements (until 1909). China's largely unsuccessful move towards prohibition after 1906 was also not unique. It was part of a regionally "shared turn" towards prohibition, and one that in many of China's neighbors also involved the perpetuation of a state-sponsored opium trade into the 1930s.[7] What was unique in China—the story told in this book—is how opium tax farming relationships and practices developed in the nineteenth century then persisted into the prohibition era after 1906, through the Yuan Shikai and warlord years after 1911, and withstood the centralizing efforts of the Nanjing government into the late 1930s. The people who bought and sold opium, in China, maintained their positions at the nexus of profit and power much longer than in neighboring states.

This book takes its journey through opium's modern history from the vantage of the Zhangzhou-Quanzhou littoral in southern Fujian: a region with a dual identity as a volatile maritime frontier and a bustling Mediterranean hub.[8] The Qing invaders who had consolidated rule in the region during the seventeenth century did so with extreme violence. Coastal Fujian was a slow and painful conquest, and the Qing only reopened residence along the coast in 1683 and then further loosened maritime trading restrictions in 1727.[9] As the maritime trade industry revived, investors commissioned ships and dispatched sons and nephews to help build the family fortune in places like Batavia, Tianjin, Manila, Shanghai, Singapore, Macao, and Penang. [10] The most powerful built up large territorial lineages, sometimes fortified with walls, gun towers, and cannon.[11] Sworn brotherhood organizations flourished inland along the coast and among the diaspora, providing mutual aid and community for unattached males, often cultivating a set of rituals and iconography focused around restoring the Ming dynasty and destroying the Qing.[12] Confederated piratical fleets dominated the waters around the turn of the nineteenth century, just as opium was becoming a staple of the regional economy.[13] Year after year, teams of migrant laborers, merchants, and displaced farmers loaded onto boats bound for Taiwan and Southeast Asia.[14]

The extensive trading and diasporic network emanating from the region structured the evolution of the opium business. In the formative years, Fujian's maritime traders and their British partners turned the coastline into a vital offshore import market for the Qing empire, second in volume only to the Pearl River Delta in neighboring Guangdong. Diasporic information networks connecting Fujian to places like Macau and Singapore helped merchants understand price differences and take advantage of market irregularities. Money, people, and commodities continued to flow back and forth between Fujian and Southeast Asia, on sailboats as before, but also on new steamship lines, breaking the older seasonal limitations of trade and migration and increasing opportunities across the board. By the end of the century a new trend had emerged: opium's reverse course. Where the opium business during its rapid expansion in the 1830s–1870s was characterized by the flow of drugs from India to China, the global swirl of drugs after the 1880s or so became more convoluted. In Fujian, there was a steady expansion of local opium poppy cultivation and production in rural areas—often with the encouragement and taxation of local authorities—much of which was being smuggled out of China and into colonial jurisdictions in Southeast Asia to compete with government monopoly opium. By the 1920s, the diaspora maintained a constant and illicit flow of opium (as well as cocaine, morphine, and heroin) from Fujian into places like Manila, Batavia, Singapore, and Rangoon.

The book follows the engagement of people from southern Fujian in the larger enterprise that was the opium business in Chinese and world history. It is a story of structure and agency, how a fluid and opportunistic transshipment network came to influence and impact the late imperial and then modern Chinese political economy. The people at the helm of the opium business captured the power of the state for their own economic purposes, at the precise moment in time when government was exerting more control over local economic life.

The first three chapters are chronological, framed around changes in the legal context for buying and selling opium in the nineteenth century: from a period of total illegality leading up and into the 1830s (chapter 1), to a period of negotiated illegality in the immediate aftermath of the 1843 Treaty of Nanjing (chapter 2), and then a period of de facto legality that began in the late 1850s and lasted until the Qing state's final decision to prohibit opium once again in 1906 (chapter 3). The second half of the book is then divided into three thematic chapters about the history of the opium business in the early twentieth century: one on prohibition bureaus and poppy tax agencies (chapter 4), another on the export of opium and other narcotics from China to Southeast Asia (chapter 5), and then a final chapter on the decisive role played in the opium business by the Japanese-protected community in Xiamen, culminating in the Japanese occupation of that city after 1938 (chapter 6).

Maritime China and the Rise of the Opium Business

In the eighteenth and early nineteenth century, Indian opium was distributed into China through preexisting shipping operations among the southeast coastal maritime community. Seafaring traders since the reopening of trade in the early Qing empire had developed diversified portfolios based on seasonal and regional production and wind patterns, carrying items like tea, clothing, Taiwanese camphor, and metal cookware from China to Southeast Asia, and returning with aromatics, medicinal items, and rice.[15] These same maritime traders carried the diaspora abroad, and each summer when the southwest monsoon was at its strength, the merchant fleet would set sail on their return voyages home from Singapore or Batavia. Throughout the late eighteenth and early nineteenth century, as they sailed alongside the ships of the British East India Company and "country traders," these merchants also carried opium, the market for which grew steadily across China in the late eighteenth century.[16] When the drug arrived at the Qing empire's southeast frontier, maritime traders from Fujian and Guangdong also dominated the transport of the drug—together with rice, sugar, and Southeast Asian commodities—north up the China coast to ports like Shanghai and Tianjin, returning south with beancake fertilizer for sugar and opium cultivation, Jiangnan cottonwear, and silk for export to Southeast Asia.

In the 1820s and 1830s, the moment when this book starts, opium truly began to flood into China in unprecedented waves. The rapid expansion was fueled by new competition in India on the production end of the business. An emergent group of cultivators in Malwa and shippers in Bombay began to challenge the British East India Company opium shipped out of Calcutta, and as a consequence the company redoubled their opium production efforts in Patna and Benares.[17] Chinese merchants still carried the drug from Southeast Asia, but new clipper ships owned by British, Parsee, and American traders brought opium to China's southeast coast in previously unfathomable quantities, at any time of year, without having to wait for the monsoon. The most prolific of these British participants in the opium trade in China were two firms, Jardine Matheson and Dent & Company.[18] Imports into the Qing empire rose, from several thousand chests per year in the 1820s, up to more than 30,000 chests in 1830, and reaching nearly 40,000 chests per year by 1839 and the eruption of war.[19]

Jardine, Dent, and the other foreign merchants were able to sell off this stunning volume of opium by partnering with powerful maritime lineages in southern Fujian and Guangdong, who managed the opium import and transshipment industry during the period of rapid growth from the 1820s to the 1850s. China's southeast coast is an exceptional place when it comes to family size, and Fujian's lineages might consist of whole cities of tens of thousands of people. As commercial organizations, lineages maintained diversified business interests including agricultural production, handicraft manufacture, retail shops, and maritime trading ventures. Lineage networks helped facilitate mutual aid, trust, and the extension of credit for new business ventures.[20] Landholdings helped lineages fund shipbuilding and maritime trade operations, which in turn funded the further territorial expansion of the lineage in the local arena.[21]

When the drug trade accelerated in the 1830s, the lineage formation offered opium traders an inbuilt structure for capital accumulation, lawbreaking, and jurisdictional arbitrage. Lineages in the region had a long history
of understanding and manipulating regulatory discrepancies in order to
gain advantages over their neighbors.[22] Lineage networks linked smugglers
to the naval garrison or the magistrate's office. When state crackdowns were
coming, government insiders gave advance notice to lineage members and
allowed them to make preparations and limit the damage. Internal hierar-
chies could isolate key players from punishment, and the bodies of poorer
lineage members could be substituted for the actual suspects.[23]

Opium was illegal, and yet the volume of trade was stunning. In order
to maintain this delicate profitability, coastal opium merchants and government officials worked out issues of bribery, taxation, and law enforcement
within the context of long-developing negotiations of power and profit
between the Qing state and the maritime trade industry. In eighteenth-
century Xiamen, the city's cadre of wealthy merchants had systematically
partnered with local officials to provide essential funds for educational
institutions, granaries, soup kitchens, and a variety of local social welfare
institutions.[24] The merchant associations (*jiao*) operating between coastal
southern Fujian and Taiwan likewise contributed to public works and temples, cultivating productive relationships with local officials.[25] When British ships began anchoring near Fujianese ports after 1832, powerful figures
within the maritime trading community stepped in to negotiate a system of
fees and protection. Lineage elders regularly met with local officials to negotiate the payment of bribes in the opium import trade, creating a system
of fees that became normalized and standardized, with widely known rates,
stamps, and inspections. The money was spread around, through the civil
and military bureaucracy, and on at least one occasion earmarked to support the victims of a lineage feud.[26] These local systems of opium revenue
extraction developed in the 1830s provided the most immediate context for
the earliest attempts to formalize opium import and transport taxes in the
1850s.

The extralegal offshore opium import system established before the
Opium War (1839–1842) remained largely in place after the Treaty of Nanjing (1843) opened five ports to British commerce and consular representa-
tion. The treaty did not clarify or regulate the legality of the drug at the
heart of the war that had just concluded, and the opium business continued

to expand in a legal gray area until the late 1850s. Along the maritime frontier, British consuls worked to ensure that opium merchants could import the drug without interference, and they negotiated an extralegal, extratreaty settlement with Qing officials to allow British importers to sell off the drug outside of the physical limits of the treaty ports. The opium trade in the 1840s thus entered over a decade of negotiated illegality: a tolerated offshore contraband import market consisting of foreign importers and local wholesalers, each anchorage with its own system of fees and bribery as negotiated with the relevant officials, dating back in some cases into the early 1830s.

Despite this important continuity—opium's formally illegal status and an extralegal import market scattered across anchorages along the empire's southeast coast—the opium business otherwise experienced a wholesale transformation during the two decades after the opening of the treaty ports in 1843. The quantities of drug imported into China increased every year, even as domestic cultivation of opium poppies within China began to accelerate. With this rise in volume, there was a readjustment in the structure of the opium business: consolidation of markets, in part through new efforts to regulate and tax the drug, but also a broad expansion in the opportunities for people to make a living, or a fortune, in buying and selling opium.

Within Fujian's two new treaty ports—Xiamen (also known as Amoy) and Fuzhou—opium capital was increasingly entangled within the production and circulation of other commodities, while the urban distribution and retail sectors offered a range of new jobs and investment opportunities. In Xiamen, a small group of wholesale brokers with connections to the local banking industry dominated the import trade and gradually came to exclude British and American firms almost entirely. In Fuzhou, American and British tea firms partnered with Cantonese and southern Fujianese brokers to send opium up the Min River to fund tea purchases. In both cities, the growing number of opium dispensaries and dens that popped up year after year were engaged in complex negotiations with municipal authorities over the payment of fees for the support of social services and infrastructure.

Opium Revenue and the Fiscal-Military State

The normalization of opium through regulation and taxation occurred locally in the mid-1850s and was ratified internationally in 1860 when the Treaty of Tianjin placed a uniform and low import tax on the drug.[27]

Fujian's officials first received permission from Beijing to start collecting import taxes on opium in 1857, the same year they also created the empire's first formal opium transport taxes, known as the opium lijin.[28] Opium was taxed on these two basic levels throughout the years of its legalization: the import tax, a low and standardized fee collected by a foreign-staffed Maritime Customs Service (after 1863) when the drug was unloaded from ships in port; and the wide range of municipal-, regional-, or provincial-level tax farms that collected a variety of associated fees, the most widely known of which was the lijin. These two separate taxation regimes worked to restructure the opium business during the age of legal opium, creating a new geography of control and evasion while also tying drug profits to state projects in influential ways.

The opium lijin was a tax farm, wherein provincial, prefectural, county, or municipal authorities contracted with a merchant or corporation for a predetermined quota of taxes on the transport and distribution of opium within a specified territory or at a jurisdictional border crossing. The institution has long roots in the same cluster of taxation and market regulation practices that characterized the mid-Qing long-distance trade industry, and which had inspired the Red Society to use the term *lijin* for their fees.[29] The concept found new life in an era of strapped state finances during the Taiping Rebellion (1850–1864), generating crucial revenue on opium and a range of other commodities at a difficult moment in time for municipal and provincial authorities.[30]

Opium tax farms were familiar to the maritime Fujianese. Elite members of the Chinese diaspora for centuries had maintained similar relationships with local rulers in Southeast Asia to collect taxes on opium, liquor, and gambling among the Chinese diaspora.[31] State tax farming contracts enabled mine and plantation owners to monopolize and systematize the sale of opium and liquor to their employees, who often also paid those same business owners for passage to Southeast Asia from China, as well as letters and remittances home.[32] In the mid-nineteenth century, just as lijin bureaus were emerging in the homeland, members of the Fujianese diaspora abroad were finding ways to maintain their roles as opium tax farmers for the British and Dutch colonial states that had displaced many of the earlier maritime city-states and insular kingdoms.[33] The creation and operation of lijin bureaus for opium in the 1850s should be understood within this broad regional context, wherein neighboring states were all seeking to draw revenue from the opium trade by selling off the responsibilities of taxation, market regulation, and social control to groups of powerful Fujianese and Cantonese investors.

From the perspective of an opium trader trying to expand their business during the period 1857–1887, the prospect of taking over a lijin bureau in Fujian was an enticing but risky opportunity. The territorial control over opium's transport and sale could enable a firm or group of investors to edge out competition and consolidate control over a market, but the cash-starved provincial administrations of the late Qing could make for a dangerous partner. Several of the opium lijin bureaus in 1870s Fujian went bankrupt after the state demanded what turned out to be excessively high rates and unrealistic quotas, spiraling when sales were further undercut by smuggling from neighboring provinces with lower lijin fees.

Officials set the opium lijin in Fujian at such ambitious levels because of their determination to invest in military upkeep and modernization during a dangerous age. In addition to feeding, training, and arming soldiers in Fujian, Taiwan, and the Qing empire's northwestern frontier, Fujian's opium taxes were helping pay for the construction and maintenance of the Fuzhou Arsenal, a state-of-the-art naval yard that was chronically short of the money required to produce and maintain warships.[34] The people who made their living in the opium business were thus embroiled in a collaborative but often antagonistic relationship with the helmsmen officials of the late Qing Self-Strengthening Movement, a reform effort intended to buttress the Qing against further victimization by employing techniques from their imperial rivals.[35] These powerful provincial governors and governors-general were vocal advocates for opium's eventual prohibition, which they believed could be achieved through heavy taxation—money that would also enable them to invest in military capacity and modernization. An unintended consequence of this plan was that opium revenue became ever more important to those same officials, which only further entrenched the opium business at the nexus of power and profit.

Prohibition and the Survival of Tax Farming

In 1906, the Qing court issued a series of edicts announcing the empire's return to a policy of opium prohibition.[36] The plan was developed through negotiations with the British government, which had a vested interest in opium's production and sale, but which was also under increasing pressure from missionaries and other activists to accommodate the Qing state's desire to curb and eventually eradicate opium use. In the end, the British only agreed to reduce imports of Indian opium on the condition that the Qing achieved measurable success in eradicating domestic cultivation of the opium poppy. In Fujian, prohibition efforts therefore involved two very different projects: a primarily urban cluster of programs to license opium shops and smokers and thereby gradually reduce the retail of imported opium, and a rural paramilitary campaign to force poppy farmers to plant other crops.[37] Like many of the political and economic transformations in the early twentieth century, the experience of prohibition varied widely from region to region. In Fujian's provincial capital, Fuzhou, a robust gentry-led movement made real progress in holding the local state accountable to the terms of prohibition during the final years of the Qing.[38] In the more freewheeling port of Xiamen, the transnational opium, morphine, heroin, and cocaine smuggling trades all accelerated precisely at the moment of prohibition's introduction.

In rural Fujian, the effort to permanently uproot poppy cultivation was uneven at best and in many places a complete failure. Farmers in the province had been growing opium poppies since at least the 1830s, often cutting the inferior local product into more expensive Indian opium. The quality gradually improved and cultivation expanded throughout the final decades of the Qing, and when the prohibition edicts were announced in 1906, opium farmers and merchants were not predisposed to give up their livelihood.[39] Long-standing poppy-growing districts like Tong'an and Xinghua maintained production through the more robust prohibition years immediately after 1911. Cultivation then accelerated again during the decade after the province fell into civil war in 1917, as a series of warlords and naval commanders fought over the province while drawing substantial revenue from opium poppy taxes.[40]

Following precedent set during the late Qing, warlords in Fujian farmed out poppy tax collection to people within the opium business. During the mid-1920s, the peak years for poppy cultivation in Fujian, high-level brokers from Xiamen would pay several millions of dollars for state contracts to collect and tax just a single county's annual harvest. Cultivation only slowed down in the 1930s, when the Guomindang leadership in Nanjing came to view Fujianese opium as an unwelcome competitor to the state monopoly opium shipped out of Hankou.

For a person trying to make their way in the opium business during these chaotic years, the only job more lucrative than the management of a poppy tax collection agency was the directorship of an opium prohibition bureau (*jinyan ju*).[41] Prominent traders and shadowy groups of investors sought after these positions from their origin in the final years of Qing rule, through the warlord period, and during the period of Guomindang naval authority after 1924. An opium prohibition bureau, when operated as they were in early twentieth-century Fujian, was a state-enforced licensing system on the wholesale, transport, and retail distribution of opium within a given territory. Like the lijin bureaus of the late Qing, and like the poppy tax agencies, the early twentieth-century opium prohibition bureau was also a tax farm, and the people who purchased the rights to manage the bureaus were themselves prominent opium traders, firms, or representatives of opium trade guilds. A vertically integrated operation like that of the Taiwanese opium magnate Zeng Houkun in the 1920s incorporated contracts to collect the poppy tax in several counties, alongside another handful of municipal or county-level prohibition bureau directorships.

The contracting system that warlord and Guomindang rulers employed in their opium revenue infrastructure meant, in essence, the survival of tax farming within the fiscal and regulatory arm of the modernizing Chinese state. China departed in this way from its neighbors in Southeast Asia, each of whom abandoned opium tax farming in the early twentieth century in favor of centralized state monopolies. The Guomindang monopolies of the 1930s, which sought to centralize control of opium supply and distribution from top to bottom, were nonetheless leased out to local "opium kings" in Fujian. The man who directed the southern Fujian Prohibition Bureau from 1934 to 1937, Ye Qinghe, who was contracted to manage the legitimate sale of state opium shipped out of Hankou, used his position from beginning to end for a wide range of purposes counterproductive to the Guomindang's intention in creating the monopoly system. Among other actions, he repeatedly broke his own monopoly by smuggling in truckloads of Persian opium for manufacture into pills and powder, or to pack into small tins for reexport to Southeast Asia.

Mobility, Citizenship, and the Rise of Japan

The resurgence of the opium business and the proliferation of state opium revenue agencies in warlord and Guomindang Fujian was interlocked with what proved to be a robust market for illicit opium in Southeast Asia. Fujian was a center of opium smuggling into colonial jurisdictions like Singapore, Manila, and Batavia dating back at least to the 1880s, expanding rapidly in the 1920s and extending into the late 1930s. On the supply side, there was an almost unlimited volume of drugs in Fujian, purchasable at cheap prices thanks to the state-partnered poppy tax collectors and prohibition bureaus. On the marketing end, smuggling remained profitable in British, Dutch, and French colonies throughout their own long transformations from tax farming in the nineteenth century to state monopolies in the early twentieth century, and then in the 1930s gradually towards prohibition.[42] The diaspora, central to so many of China's important social and political transformations during the early twentieth century, was instrumental to the reoriented spatiality of the global drug trade in the years after World War I.[43]

Packed alongside the millions of tins of opium being sent out from Xiamen to ports abroad were chests and barrels full of carefully concealed packets of narcotic alkaloids like morphine, heroin, and cocaine. These new, more expensive and compact items were traded through many of the same steamship and smuggling networks as opium, but unlike opium these drugs were produced in laboratories and were supplied for the most part from pharmaceutical companies: first from European drug companies like Merck, and then increasingly from Japanese and local Chinese manufacturers. Fujianese traders carved out prolific roles importing and reexporting these drugs before the fall of the Qing dynasty, but the meeting of the International Opium Commission in 1909, the International Opium Convention of 1912, and the implementation of those agreements through the League of Nations after 1922 severely curtailed the illicit flow of narcotics from Europe to Asia.[44] Still, heroin, morphine, and cocaine smuggling operations from China into Southeast Asia continued into the 1920 and1930s, despite the challenges posed by the new international restrictions. Supply lines were adjusted and expanded: cheap Japanese cocaine from Taiwan, morphine produced with local poppies by rural Fujianese lineages, and heroin from underground laboratories in Shanghai.

The circulation of these new powdered drugs was underwritten by the rising power of Japan and the active participation of Japanese pharmaceutical companies in the manufacture of cocaine, morphine, and heroin, some of which held their operations in nearby Taiwan.[45] The rise of Japan had an enormous impact on the drug trade, both in China and among the diaspora. Xiamen's long-reigning urban lineages ceded their neighborhoods to new street gangs from Taipei, Japanese-protected people with lineage connections to southern Fujian but who were relative newcomers to the city of Xiamen.[46] Tea merchants traveling back and forth from Fujian to the Netherlands Indies came to realize that Japanese citizenship could help them avoid onerous taxes in China and increase their privileges in European colonial jurisdictions.[47] Applications for Japanese imperial citizenship surged among the Fujianese population.[48] Tens of thousands sought protection against local Chinese police and tax collectors from none other than China's most bitter rival. The opium business was central to this phenomenon, as Japanese protection enabled people to defy prohibitions with impunity. By the 1930s, Fujian's warlord and Guomindang rulers almost exclusively contracted with Japanese-protected opium merchants to run prohibition bureaus, with the understanding that this community would need to be given a stake in the system of state opium profiteering if the prohibition infrastructure was going to meet its revenue goals.

Xiamen and the neighboring districts became the frontier of Japanese expansion in south China. The institutionalization of this power began shortly after the Xinhai Revolution of 1911, when the Japanese consul in Xiamen created an independent police force housed within a Taiwanese brothel to try and protect the growing community of Taiwanese migrants in the city. By the early 1920s, tensions between the Taiwanese migrants and locals were fueling street fights, with dramatic shootouts and public beheadings. The Taiwanese police force, staffed with roughnecks from the opium and sex industry, had the backing of the Japanese Navy, and slowly but surely the Taiwanese community and their Japanese support compelled Xiamen's warlord and Guomindang rulers to accept a new status quo, wherein the city's administration would partner with the city's Taiwanese opium traders rather than continue the mutual antagonism.

And so began the rise of "opium kings" like Zeng Houkun, Chen Changfu, and Lin Gun. These were powerful men: opium traders, brothel keepers, and gun runners, but also respected community leaders, presidents of the Taiwan Association, developers who shaped the urban landscape, and chairmen of Tokyo-backed finance associations designed to promote sustainable economic growth for the Japanese-protected community in south China. When the global winds shifted and Japan invaded the port of Xiamen in 1938, the city's long-standing clique of powerful drug traders took over important positions in the new occupation government, blending the opium business with governance in a fever dream of power and profit.

Method and Sources

Opium was everywhere in Qing, warlord, and Republican China. The business was a steady enterprise in every part of the Qing empire during the de facto legal years between 1857 and 1906. Opium was cultivated and prohibited in Yunnan, Sichuan, and Guizhou well before the first Jardine Matheson ships anchored off the Fujian coast in 1832, and farmers grew opium poppies in various parts of China long into the mid-twentieth century.[49] The opium business was in Beijing, Hankou, Tianjin, Chengdu, and of course, Shanghai, where the size of the foreign concessions and the existence of a mixed court created singular conditions for the drug's trade and regulation, quite different from the rest of China. The drug was also in Yan'an, where opium revenue helped the Chinese Communist Party survive war and financial crisis in the early 1940s.[50] With the possible exception of Taiwan, there was no successful, sustained prohibition of opium in any of the former Qing territories until the late 1940s.[51]

Opium was everywhere, and yet it was such a shameful business that its centrality within the local and national political economy has been difficult to acknowledge and assess. The popular presses and academic journals of the late Qing and Republican period did not view opium as a legitimate sector of the economy, but as a criminal, even treasonous enterprise. When the drug was legal, nobody spoke of opium merchants in glowing terms, especially in elite Chinese intellectual circles. The opium industry did not inspire people to study and rethink the political economy. It was never seriously promoted as a potential savior in the nationalist quest for wealth and power. The opium business had nobody like a Wu Jienong, a man whose life's work it was to revive a tea industry held down by foreign imperialism and "backwards" technology and labor practices.[52] A great many people openly reviled the opium business, from beginning to end, and the drug trade remained throughout its history an extraordinarily secretive sector of the economy. Even today opium is a moral touchstone in Chinese and global history, a potent symbol of imperial greed, and an orientalist dog whistle used to signal racist images of fin de siècle degeneracy.

Opium's moral untouchability is reflected in the archive by a source base largely written from the perspective of prohibitionists, and in the wider world by a broad moral consensus about opium's instrumental relationship to British and Japanese imperialism in India and China. Social and cultural histories of opium consumption, now nearly twenty years old, have pushed back against some of the oversimplified narratives about opium use and opium smoking culture in China.[53] Historians of civil society and state prohibition institutions have explained the rise of gentry-led opium prohibition movements and the trajectory and challenges of the Guomindang's approach to opium taxation and prohibition.[54] Still, we have only a limited understanding of the basic mechanisms of the opium business, the evolution of the industry, and its impact on the modern Chinese political economy. This book is the first step towards historicizing the drug within its local economic context from the late Qing to the end of the Japanese occupation in 1945.

Excavating opium's place in local economic life is a challenging proposition, however, due to the drug's particular legal and moral status. The opium business was purposefully shadowy, because of the laws and attitudes that surrounded the drug. This was an industry where bribes slowly became taxes, where business owners paid undisclosed sums to state authorities for the right to collect taxes on the drug, where unnamed investors hid behind teams of uniformed, armed officers. After a decade of working through Chinese, Taiwanese, British, Swiss, and American archives, business records, newspapers, and published sources, I wrote this book as the sum total of what I learned about the people running the trade and the forms and flows of legal and illegal taxation that characterized it.

The first two chapters of the book juxtapose three archives: the records of the Qing territorial government preserved in the First Historical Archives of China, the commercial correspondence of the Jardine Matheson Company held at the University of Cambridge, and the records of the British Foreign Office. The Jardine Matheson sources for this period are some of the only archival sources written by opium dealers in the world and offer reliable information about the volume of the opium business and its geography. They also give little or incomplete information about the Chinese buyers of Jardine Matheson's opium and display sometimes inaccurate understandings of the Qing state. Relevant Qing documents from this period are limited to terse "memorials" about the arrest and punishment of people charged with opium crimes. These provide some small biographical information about the people involved and include data on labor and investment arrangements, but also include a host of inaccurate claims about the volume and nature of the opium business.

In the rest of the book, chapters about the opium business in the late nineteenth and early twentieth centuries, the research involved assembling a more expansive range of sources and confronting a wider range of problems and opportunities. English-language customs records and Chinese newspapers like the Shanghai periodical *Shenbao* signpost major changes in the opium business, but customs officers rarely discussed opium after the moment of import, and *Shenbao*'s reporters were circumspect about revealing the identities of key figures in the drug trade, using terms like "a certain merchant" (*moushang*) rather than giving personal names. In the 1920s and 1930s, however, reporters working at the Chinese-language newspapers in Singapore were thankfully more direct in their reporting on the Fujianese drug trade. Diplomatic records and investigations from the League of Nations Archives in Geneva help identify the export markets and shipping patterns for Fujianese opium and morphine (and cocaine) in the early twentieth century, but reveal little about the people in China who managed the clandestine export of those commodities. Guomindang materials in Chinese and Taiwanese archives clarify the trajectory of opium rules and regulations, but only rarely contain information about implementation and enforcement on the ground. British and American intelligence reports fill in some of this picture, but they too imperfectly capture how the actual business of opium buying and selling worked.

These archival and published sources have also helped me corroborate a set of articles from mostly out-of-print local history collections, known as *wenshi ziliao*. The articles in these collections, purchased in used bookstores in Xiamen and Quanzhou, have cavalier approaches to citation and are often polemical. They are also usually right about the details. One example, the oral history of an anonymous subordinate of the "opium king" Ye Qinghe originally conducted in 1965 by the Xiamen historian Hong Buren, offers a laundry list of enticing tidbits about the opium business in the 1920s and 30s.[55] In the years since I first read Hong's article, I have corroborated almost all of the key details in newspapers, diplomatic records, and business records from the Shanghai Municipal Archives (SMA). Locating the name of Ye's Shanghai accountancy firm in the SMA enabled one of the most significant breakthroughs in "following the money" that this book has to offer. Much of the texture and detail that this book offers about opium trading, economic life, and the on-the-ground experience of political transition in early twentieth-century Fujian is possible because of the Xiamen, Jinjiang, and Quanzhou *wenshi ziliao* publications, and especially the good works of Professor Hong Buren (1928–2019).

CHAPTER I

Local Foundations, 1832–1839

In late February of 1839, a man boarded a small boat and paddled out to a ship anchored near the mouth of southern Fujian's Shenhu Bay. He departed his home in Yakou village and slipped quietly past the fleet of large and small vessels that sailed in and out of the bay each day: fishing and trading boats that carried local seafood, beancake fertilizer from north China, Southeast Asian produce like rice and betel nut, and the cotton handkerchiefs that local seamen wore tied around their heads, imported from Manila and manufactured in England.[1] The man arrived at the edge of the small bay's opening, where two massive ships lay anchored. From shore, a person could see light craft plying back and forth, day and night, between these ships and the villages at the shoreline. Lately it was mostly at night. These were the foreign opium ships, crewed by sailors hailing from across maritime Asia, captained by a small group of mostly British men who doubled as mariners and salesmen, and owned by a collection of mostly British firms with operations in Guangzhou (Canton).

The man boarded the *Lady Hayes* and spent the evening with the ship's captain, watching from a safe distance the violent scene that was unfolding back in his hometown. They saw fires on the docks and in the village. They watched as "a party of soldiers entered Ya Kow with the intention of seizing on some of the brokers" and as "villagers turned out and after a fight succeeded in driving [the soldiers] from the town."[2] The British opium ship captain and his local partner, a leader in the village's opium trading operations, waited out the attack. A few days later, the coalition of opium traders in the bay paid $13,000 in cash to the local "Admiral" and an equivalent amount in opium to another authority known by the British as the *Chu Kang*, "this gentleman preferring opium to cash."[3] In a region where just one Spanish silver dollar was equivalent to several days wages for an ordinary boatman, $26,000 for a bribe was a truly monumental sum. It seems to have done the trick. By early March the transnational network of opium merchants had again resumed sales in Shenhu Bay off Yakou village.

The man who escaped and watched the attack on his village from aboard the *Lady Hayes* was known to his British partners as Shik Po, the "Ya Kow man." He was one of a handful of Chinese opium traders who spent time aboard ships like the *Lady Hayes* and the *Colonel Young*, assisting the Jardine Matheson Company and other foreign opium firms by supplying their crews with food and water and brokering opium deals with local merchants. Yakou (Ya Kow) was the largest of several villages on the inner shoreline of Shenhu Bay, one of three chief import markets for opium on the Fujian coast during the 1830s. The town was a lineage village, dominated even to this day by a single-surname group, the Shi lineage.

The Yakou Shi became notorious in the 1830s for their participation in the opium trade, and lineage members like Shik Po were key agents in the early expansion of the opium business in China. They were maritime traders with operations in Southeast Asia, Taiwan, and Chinese ports to the north. They built up an opium transshipment business on the foundation of these preexisting maritime shipping networks and adapted the lineage structure of local society to maximize their profit seeking and minimize legal culpability. They forged ties and built working relationships with British, American, and Parsee opium dealers. To protect themselves and the increasingly lucrative opium business, they worked to transform the regional political economy, injecting opium capital into the Qing state and pioneering a system of interdependency with willing local officials that would bind their interests up with the people who bought and sold opium.

The Coastal Opium Trade, 1832–1839

The Yakou Shi might have been conspicuous participants in the opium trade, but they were hardly alone. Dozens of maritime lineages along the Zhangzhou-Quanzhou littoral in southern Fujian during the 1830s were able to marshal the boats, people, and money necessary to make it big in the opium business. Opium production in India skyrocketed during the decade, and the drug moved efficiently in state-of-the-art clipper ships, transported from Calcutta and Bombay to Singapore and thence to Lintin Island in the Pearl River Delta near Macao. Firms like Jardine Matheson and Dent & Company brought over half of this opium north to Fujian for wholesale. They stationed a fleet of "receiving ships" at key ports along the Fujian coastline to function as warehouses and sales depots, using smaller vessels to bring opium north from Lintin and carry the cash back south. The region became China's second most important opium import market during the 1830s, just as the volume of trade was reaching unprecedented levels.

British records, written in most cases by the people selling the opium, offer the best remaining evidence about the scale of the offshore opium market in southern Fujian during these years. Jardine Matheson commercial reports for 1835, the most complete year of records, document sales of between 700 and 1,000 chests of opium per month for around $600–800 per chest in southern Fujian, spread across the three main anchorages at Xiamen, Shenhu Bay, and Quanzhou.[4] Based on Jardine Matheson intelligence about their competition, opium sales by their chief competitor Dent & Company in these ports can be safely estimated to be of a similar quantity and at similar prices. By this rough reckoning, the two firms sold between 1,400 and 2,000 chests of opium per month in Fujian that year for a monthly total of $840,000–$1,600,000, or an annual total of 16,800–24,000 chests per year for somewhere between $10,080,000 and 19,200,000.[5] The range is broad, but it represents the realm of possibility in a trade that changed dramatically from month to month and grew each year.[6] Buyers in Fujian plausibly handled somewhere between 64 and 91 percent of the total opium imports to China from India, which between April 1835 and March 1836 was 26,200 chests.[7] This was a lively wholesale import marketplace in the middle of an economic boom that was entirely illegal and unprecedented.

While British records offer the best evidence about how much opium was changing hands along the Fujian coastline, they offer only piecemeal information about who was actually buying their opium. From the Chinese-language sources that do exist—written entirely by people who worked for the Qing state—it is clear that the great seafaring coastal lineages of southern Fujian and eastern Guangdong dominated the opium transshipment industry, buying the drug from British sellers and transporting it north to other parts of the empire. The relatively small collection of Qing criminal cases of people arrested for participation in the opium trade confirms this basic interpretation.[8] Tellingly, in the only real attempt by a Qing official to summarize the participants and geography of the trade—an 1840 investigation by an imperially dispatched censor—the official organized his report according to which lineages were active in the trade (see Map 1.1).[9] The map is a small slice of the regional picture, focused on just one of the many coastal counties in southern Fujian and eastern Guangdong province with its own similar geography of lineages, ship owners, and smugglers.

The Zhangzhou-Quanzhou littoral was a good place to set up an offshore contraband market in opium, because there was a preexisting infrastructure for import, distribution, and reexport. British opium merchants could unload far more product than local consumers demanded, thanks to the mercantile networks and shipping capacity of southern Fujian's lineage merchants. Some of the opium did stay in Fujian, facilitated by Quanzhou dealers who monopolized sales to inland districts in southern Fujian and neighboring Jiangxi. There were also people who specialized in brokering deals for the drug to be shipped up through Fuzhou to supply the highland districts up the river Min.[10] In one 1835 example, a group of opium merchants in Quanzhou pooled investments and commissioned a new ship for the express purpose of running Malwa opium up to Fuzhou from Quanzhou, where the drug could be sold at a profit of $100 per chest.[11] The vast majority of opium that hit the Fujian shoreline, however, was promptly reexported to more distant ports like Shanghai and Tianjin for distribution across the vast Qing empire.

The southern Fujianese were central agents in the wholesale distribution of opium from the southeast coast to the rest of China. As one well-informed local magistrate reported, "As for the opium smuggled into Taiwan, Ningbo, Shanghai, Shandong and Tianjin, most comes from the fishing and merchant vessels of Hui'an and Jinjiang county [in southern

MAP 1.1: Lineage villages and opium anchorages.

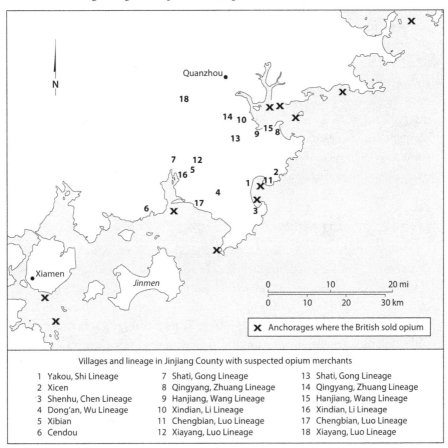

Villages and lineage in Jinjiang County with suspected opium merchants

1	Yakou, Shi Lineage	7	Shati, Gong Lineage	13 Shati, Gong Lineage
2	Xicen	8	Qingyang, Zhuang Lineage	14 Qingyang, Zhuang Lineage
3	Shenhu, Chen Lineage	9	Hanjiang, Wang Lineage	15 Hanjiang, Wang Lineage
4	Dong'an, Wu Lineage	10	Xindian, Li Lineage	16 Xindian, Li Lineage
5	Xibian	11	Chengbian, Luo Lineage	17 Chengbian, Luo Lineage
6	Cendou	12	Xiayang, Luo Lineage	18 Xiayang, Luo Lineage

Source: The British Library, Add MS 16364 A-I CHARTS, Maps drawn by John and Thomas Rees; Huang Juezi, Xu Naiji, and Qi Sihe, Huang Juezi zou shu, Xu Naiji zouyi he kan (Collected memorials of Huang Juezi and Xu Naiji), (Beijing: Zhonghua shu ju, 1959), 102–4; The Jardine Matheson archives (primarily JM B2, In- Correspondence); Yapian zhanzheng zai min tai shiliao xuanbian (Fujian- Taiwan Opium War materials), (Fuzhou: Fujian renmin chuban she, 1982), vol. 4.1, no. 4, 291–95. Hereafter YPZZ–MT.

Fujian]."[12] In Shenhu Bay, local merchants discouraged Jardine Matheson employees from making an exploratory voyage to Shanghai and Tianjin, because the local traders wanted to maintain their own strategic position in those markets.[13] The Shenhu and Quanzhou brokers also controlled the flow of opium into Taiwan, which they supplied with 2,500–3,000 chests per year in the late 1830s.[14] Many of the Shenhu and Quanzhou merchants ran a triangular trade route between Fujian, Taiwan, and Ningbo (in Zhejiang province to the north), carrying opium from Fujian, sugar and rice from Taiwan, and cotton from Zhejiang.[15] For their part, the Jardine Matheson opium ship captains also trafficked in commodities other than opium, such as rice, textiles, saltpeter, and Southeast Asian produce like betel nut.[16] Opium circuits were built onto and integrated into other commodity circuits, and the proliferation of opium-derived capital was extended into other financial circulations.

THE EXPANSION OF THE OPIUM TRADE
INTO FUJIAN AFTER 1832

The Fujian offshore opium trade was an alternate opium ecosystem in the 1830s, expanded from and modeled after the well-known opium marketplace that was developed offshore from Lintin Island in Guangdong province's Pearl River Delta. Lintin had been the epicenter of the Indo-Chinese opium trade since at least the early 1820s. The small island was home to a collection of receiving ships, giant hulks that served as floating warehouses for almost all of the opium imports that came from India. The "Lintin system" was a long-standing, simple, and effective opium smuggling mechanism for transactions between Chinese importers and British sellers. Buyers would go to local banks in Guangzhou to make payment, then take a receipt out to a foreign receiving ship anchored near Lintin to receive their opium. For an extra charge, they could arrange armed escort. Opium traders came from every coastal province, and local officials singled out southern Fujianese merchants as having a particularly large stake in the trade.[17]

In 1832 the British merchants and Fujianese brokers of the Pearl River Delta brought the Lintin offshore receiving ship system north to the coastline of southern Fujian. Networks of Fujianese merchants in Guangzhou had been bringing substantial amounts of opium up to Fujian (and beyond) in smaller sailboats for decades, increasing as the trade expanded.[18] By 1832, the Fujianese were purchasing so much opium that transporting the drug to Fujian in larger, well-armed British ships became for them a sort of economic common sense. It would substantially decrease risk and logistical costs. As one of the most prolific Fujianese brokers explained to his partners at Jardine Matheson in 1834, he "wished to have a ship up every month, as he prefers purchasing from foreign ships than run the risks with their own boats."[19]

Long-standing Fujianese networks in Guangdong facilitated the northward expansion of the trade. Southern Fujianese migrants had a strong presence in the foreign trade networks of the Pearl River Delta, not just as petty traders and boatmen, but as leaders of some of the most prominent firms. Their numbers included the wealthiest and most famous of the merchants in Guangzhou, Howqua (Wu Bingjian), a Quanzhou transplant and close partner to William Jardine, Samuel Russell, and other western merchants. Arranging for southern Fujianese migrants to come on board and act as translators, pilots, and middlemen for a northbound trip would not have been a complicated matter at the wharves in Macao and Guangzhou. There was no shortage of Fujianese who came south looking for work, people with hometown or lineage connections to coastal Fujianese brokers, people could speak enough pidgin to land the job.

The dissolution of the British East India Company's monopoly over the China trade in 1834 also facilitated the expansion of the trade into Fujian, opening the door for private firms to compete with one another for the business of their Chinese partners. During the months leading up to the end of the monopoly, Jardine Matheson and Dent & Company entered into a fierce competition for the business of their Cantonese opium buyers. The leadership of both firms, together with several other influential British merchants in Guangzhou, decided in early 1832 to forestall their competition and together fund an exploratory voyage of a ship called the *Lord Amherst* in preparation for this new period of trade.[20] The ambitious drug importers discovered that Fujian's provincial capital Fuzhou—originally targeted for its proximity to the area of tea cultivation—was well defended, tightly governed, and the approach to the harbor was difficult to navigate. In contrast, the Zhangzhou-Quanzhou littoral in southern Fujian was awash with eager traders located in conveniently secluded bays. And while trade in Fuzhou was closely regulated and the trade there was largely limited to tea and timber, governance in southern Fujian was inherently looser, and local firms there were wealthy and diversified.

The 1832 the *Lord Amherst* expedition laid the groundwork for the next decade of opium trading in Fujian. The ship's officers were charged with finding government officials who might be willing to do business and to establish connections with local merchants. Dent's employee Thomas Rees, the older brother of Jardine Matheson's John Rees, was in charge of the sailing and mapping. His maps became a central tool for opium traders and the British Navy in the years to come, and Rees himself remained on the coast in the *Lord Amherst* (and other ships) as captain until the end of the decade, selling tens of thousands of chests of opium for Dent & Company in Quanzhou, Shenhu Bay, and other Fujianese ports.[21] The head translator of the expedition was the enigmatic Prussian missionary and doctor, Charles Gützlaff, who was proficient in the spoken languages of southeast China as well as literary Chinese. In the event that they were unable to bribe or otherwise come to terms with local Chinese officials along the way, Gützlaff was to deny any connection to the British East India Company and instead offer a cover story of being blown off course by winds en route to Japan.[22] The leader of the expedition described this alibi as "though true in some respects, yet certainly gives no clue for the Chinese to trace the ship."[23] The *Lord Amherst* anchored in both Xiamen and Fuzhou in the spring of 1832 before heading up to Zhejiang, the Zhoushan archipelago, and eventually north China, Gützlaff repeatedly using the alibi in standoffs with local officials along the way.

Jardine, Dent, and their Fujianese partners set up an efficient opium delivery system almost immediately following the *Lord Amherst* voyage. Jardine, in fact, did not even wait for the return of the *Lord Amherst* before dispatching John Rees in the brig *Dansbourg* up the coast in July of 1832. The younger Rees left Lintin with 293 chests of William Jardine's opium along with 174 chests that belonged to a Chinese broker known as Ahant. After a six-week coasting tour, selling modest consignments averaging ten chests per sale over to local smugglers, Rees returned with $131,750.[24] The sales records do not account for the opium delivered on behalf of Ahant, who presumably paid Jardine for delivery of his 174 chests of opium to partners in Fujian. All in all it was a promising start for the new venture.

Within months of these exploratory voyages, Jardine had put into place what came to be called the "receiving ship" system, which would remain in operation for over two decades. After the successful return of the *Dansbourg*, William Jardine sent John Rees, William MacKay, and James Innes north on the *Colonel Young*, *John Biggar*, and *Jamesina*, all large and well-armed ships. Faster boats like the *Sylph* would transport opium up from Lintin to those "receiving ships," which were larger, often older, and not terribly seaworthy vessels anchored in and around Xiamen, Shenhu Bay, and Quanzhou. As evident in Figure 1.1, any ships anchored in Shenhu Bay could not have done so in secret. The Xiamen and Quanzhou anchorages were likewise visible from naval and customs checkpoints.

It is no wonder that local officials in southern Fujian knew all of the pertinent details. As recorded by one of the Quanzhou authorities: "Two smaller lorchas built in a similar way to the big ships and capable of carrying one thousand catties often bring up opium from Guangdong, transfer it to the big ships, and carry the silver from the big ships back down without waiting around."[25] By 1837, there was an average of fifteen foreign receiving ships—owned by Jardine, Dent, as well as a shifting collection of American and Parsee merchants—regularly anchored off the Fujian coast at any given moment.[26]

The successful operation of the receiving ship system depended on local brokers, who could arrange deals between Fujianese buyers and British

FIGURE 1.1: Shenhu Bay, taken from the beach at Yakou Village.

Peter Thilly, 2019.

sellers. After Jardine hired Charles Gützlaff as an interpreter for one of the early opium voyages into Fujian, Gützlaff in September of 1833 sat down with representatives from three major Fujianese merchant houses.[27] One of these firms was San Quan Mao, represented by a man called "Mr. Yabe," a prominent broker in the Fujian trade within the Jardine Matheson records.[28] We meet him again in a letter of Gützlaff's from 1834, wherein Yabe "sighs under the wrath of the Mandarins and does not dare to come on board."[29] A few months later Yabe told Gützlaff "that he has made arrangements with the Mandareens for the next arrival, they will not be troublesome unless some fresh hand come on at the station."[30] Yabe was in hot water again three years later, in April of 1837, trying to negotiate a settlement with local authorities after a government officer was shot while mediating a feud between Yabe's lineage and a neighboring village.[31] When he reappears in 1839, he is again in tense negotiations with the local state: "They are trying to seize Mr. Yabe," writes John Rees, "I believe he is safe and I think they merely want to squeeze him."[32] Among the intermediaries and brokers to be found in the British archives, Yabe's apparent facility with bribery and his tense intimacy with local authorities is representative.

When Qing officials did attack the opium trade, they prioritized the identification of middlemen like Yabe, casting them as troublemakers who "enticed" the British ships to venture north from the Pearl River Delta. The British themselves were out of reach. At very few moments did Qing boats ever fire on the receiving ships and never with any success.[33] And when authorities targeted locals on their way to and from the anchorages, as when the Quanzhou prefect constructed a fleet of thirty-oar longboats in the summer of 1835 in an effort to catch smugglers in the bay, the British opium ships did not hesitate to open fire in protection of their customers.[34] This kind of open violence was the exception. More often, Rees and the other opium ship captains just moved locations when Qing boats were coming, something the brokers in Yakou and elsewhere frequently requested they do in advance of government raids, tours, and inspections.[35] In this context, when a Qing official was appointed to the region with the express purpose of fighting the rise of the opium trade, the area where they could potentially make a difference was on shore, finding and punishing the local people who were working with the British to expand into Fujian.

A man named Wang Lüe was the original scapegoat for the arrival of the British in Fujian, and provincial officials repeatedly used his case to preface memorials on the offshore opium trade for the remainder of the decade.[36] According to Wang's testimony, he was a Jinjiang county native who had originally gone to Macao during the summer of 1825 to live with his father, who worked there as a broker for coastal sailboats looking to purchase opium at Lintin.[37] Growing up in this environment, Wang became fluent in the transnational pidgin essential to doing business in the Pearl River Delta and made contacts within the foreign and domestic merchant communities. In 1831, he brokered a deal for another Jinjiang native to hire an armed foreign vessel in Macao to transport a cargo of opium up to Fujian. Between this time and his arrest, Wang stationed himself on British ships regularly skirting the Fujian coast, brokering sales worth thousands of dollars to the merchants of southern Fujianese ports like Xiamen and Quanzhou. Wang's case stood out from other people caught selling opium because he could be blamed for the arrival of foreign ships on the Fujian coast: he was a middleman, a key agent in connecting the coastal shipping network to the British opium importers.

The Shenhu Bay Opium Network

Like Wang Lüe, a fellow southern Fujianese man named Shi Hou was a few years later also arrested by the Qing state and charged with bringing foreign ships up the coast from Guangdong to Fujian. Much of the remainder of this chapter focuses on the case of Shi Hou and the great Shi lineage of Yakou village more broadly, where local opium traders and their British counterparts John and Thomas Rees came together to establish one of the most prolific opium brokerage systems in the history of the drug trade. The case offers clear evidence about the formative moment in opium's rise: supply-chain relationships, data about labor and investment patterns, and details about the range of interactions between the pioneers of the opium business and the representatives of the Qing state.

When Shi Hou was arrested in early 1837, he testified that he and two of his kinsmen had first entered the opium business in 1832.[38] Shi Hou and Shi Shubao (who was never captured) had traveled that year to neighboring Chaozhou in eastern Guangdong province to sell cloth. The two men traveled together with another lineage member named Shi Gui whom they hired on as a porter. While in Chaozhou, Shi Hou and Shi Shubao encountered a longtime acquaintance who regaled them with stories of the money that could be made in bringing opium from Macao to Fujian. He offered to help them procure the drug, and they agreed. Shi Gui was promptly dispatched back to the Fujian coast to sell the first forty-eight balls of raw opium. Shi Shubao decided to relocate to Macao. He became fluent in pidgin and established a personal relationship with a pair of foreign opium sellers, the "Macao-born foreigners Big and Little Li," also known as Thomas and John Rees.[39] Over the next few years the kinsmen made regular trips to Macao to purchase a chest or two of opium, whereupon Shi Hou and Shi Gui would escort the drug back to Fujian for distribution.

Shi Hou's testimony, as recorded by the Fujian provincial authorities, stated that he and Shi Shubao first devised their scheme to lure British ships north into Fujian during the autumn of 1835, after deciding it was "inconvenient" to continue bringing small amounts of opium to Fujian in small boats or overland. The two men "decided to entice" the foreigners Big and Little Li into bringing a large cargo of opium in a foreign vessel directly to the Shi lineage center of Yakou in Shenhu Bay, where they could broker deals for other local merchants. Shi Hou and Shi Shubao invested $1,600 each to purchase a total of six chests and twenty-seven balls, a symbolic investment of what the British opium captains called "smart money," essentially a minimum guarantee or a down payment. And indeed this was just a fraction of the opium brought to Fujian by Big and Little Li on this pioneering trip up the coast. After the foreign ship's arrival in Fujian, Shi Hou brokered deals for other lineage members and people from neighboring villages. In the most conspicuous example, Shi Hou charged one of his gentry kinsmen (a *jiansheng*, or student of the Imperial College) $600 to act as intermediary in his purchase of opium from the foreigners, a fee of $10 per chest on sixty chests.[40] The wholesale price paid for this opium by the degree-holder Shi Saiguang should have been over $30,000. This is the best evidence about large-scale brokerage in the Qing document on the case, which tallies the other purchases from Big and Little Li's ships during the autumn and winter of 1835–36 at only twenty-seven chests.[41]

Materials from the Jardine Matheson archive demonstrate that the opium market in Shenhu Bay during these years was much, much larger than the officials who wrote the Shi Hou memorial either knew or were willing to admit. The foreign opium merchants Big and Little Li, Thomas and John Rees, sold quantities of opium that far exceed the amounts to which Shi Hou testified. Twenty-seven chests of opium, for the British merchants who sold drugs in Shenhu Bay during the late 1830s, was the work of a slow afternoon. British vessels had also been operating in the Shenhu Bay for several years before Shi Hou supposedly enticed them up. For example, Captain Jauncey of the Jardine Matheson bark *Austen* reported selling 320 chests of Malwa opium in just one day while stationed in Shenhu Bay during August of 1835, several months before Shi Hou purportedly lured Big and Little Li up from Macao.[42] Thomas and John Rees were not brought up to Fujian together by Shi Hou or anyone else. They worked for rival firms. Both men had been operating in Fujian since 1832 out of a handful of ports between Xiamen and Quanzhou, including Shenhu Bay.

INVESTMENT AND LABOR

Although the volume of trade is misrepresented in the Qing memorial on Shi Hou, the record of who was arrested and prosecuted in the case offers important evidence about investment patterns, the distribution of labor, and the character of labor relations in the import and wholesale distribution sector during this early stage of the opium business.[43] The memorial lists a total of 111 people (all men) as arrested or at large and wanted for various crimes associated with the case. Of those named in the memorial, 53 provided labor for other people's businesses, 55 were investors or business operators, and the remaining 3 people started off providing labor for opium investors and subsequently invested their earnings in their own opium.[44] Those labeled as investors are people who contributed money to buy opium, though they may also have provided labor in the form of sales, brokerage, and arranging transportation.

The evidence about investment patterns in the opium trade suggests a commercial milieu in which large-scale brokers worked alongside an army of petty investors, wherein a transport laborer might eventually pool funds with other workers to invest in a small cargo of opium. On the upper end of the trade, wealthy investors frequently pooled huge sums to buy several chests of opium for transshipment to other districts, such as the foursome who pooled together a fund of $4,500 to purchase four chests of opium from the ships at Yakou. More common, however, were smaller-scale group investments like the group of ten Shi lineage members who gathered $200–300 each to purchase a few chests of opium that were then resold along the coast by a team of four laborers, also Shi lineage members. These smaller-scale group investments could be as petty as a few dollars, such as in the case of three men who banded together to purchase and resell a few of balls of opium for a net profit of eight dollars. In another case from the same time and region, a group of five kinsmen pooled capital to invest in a few chests of opium and then turned around and opened an opium den, with four of the investors working as labor within the new business.[45] The opium trade was becoming a viable path to upward mobility for the laboring people and petty traders of the southeast coast.

There were also realistic limits to advancement. Looking at the memorial on Shi Hou, only three people involved in the case began by laboring in the opium trade and transitioned later to become larger-scale investors. The first, Lin Yun, was a boat owner hired by the large-scale broker Lin Ji. Lin Yun was able to muster $36 to purchase three balls of opium after just one stint transporting the drug for another investor. The payment for transporting the drug was hardly enough to form the basis of this investment, and clearly Lin Yun was a person who already possessed adequate funds to become at least a small-scale investor in a few balls of opium. Still, Lin's experience working on the transport end provided him with the confidence that this would be a smart way to invest his modest capital. The second person who transitioned from labor to investment was a man named Shi Kai, who was originally hired by the degree-holder Shi Saiguang to take his boat out to the foreign ships anchored in Shenhu Bay to purchase sixty balls of opium. Shi Kai subsequently pooled together a few thousand dollars with nine other investors to purchase two chests of opium and then hired a group of four laborers to distribute the opium along the coast. In this case, Shi Kai like Lin Yun was a person of middling capital who experimented first with ferrying other people's opium and quickly ascertained that the real money was in investment and sales.

The third, mentioned in his capacity as a broker above, was Lin Ji. Lin is notable for his rapid accumulation of capital. He began as the owner of a small boat, an early hire of Shi Hou's in 1835 who plied his vessel between Shi Hou's storage facility near Yakou and the foreign ships in Shenhu Bay for 3,000 wen a trip. After performing this work for several months, Lin Ji managed to get hired by the foreign opium merchant Qing Si (Captain Jauncey, one of the Jardine Matheson employees who frequented Shenhu Bay) to provide supplies for the receiving ships in Shenhu Bay. Through this work Lin was able to assemble enough funds to buy 120 balls of opium in the autumn of 1836, which he used to open an opium den, eventually hiring his own team of laborers to run the business. Lin began like many people on the littoral—a petty boatman, paid to bring cargo to and from shore—and through his transport work he was able to diversify and expand his business.

The people within the memorial whom I describe as laborers were almost exclusively people who worked on boats: sailors, ferry operators, and pilots. They could earn as little as 300 wen, as in two men who were hired by an investor to transport a single packet (*bao*) of opium from Yakou to a neighboring village. Based on an 1846 survey by the British consul in Fuzhou, carpenters, masons, smiths, tailors, cabinetmakers, rattan weavers, and bricklayers in the provincial capital earned between 100 and 200 wen per day.[46] If that is what people could earn for a relatively safe day of labor, that people accepted 300 wen for a potentially deadly opium run seems unfathomably low and speaks to the reality of life and labor relations on this part of the coast. In contrast, boat owners could earn as much as $5, as in the man hired by a consortium of investors to transport twelve chests of opium from Yakou village in a "white-bottom boat." The most common payment for opium transport services was 3,000 wen per boat, per run, split among the laborers with a larger cut going to the boat owner.

Looking at who was arrested and who escaped prosecution reveals the harshly exploitative side of labor relations in the coastal opium trade. Among the people who invested capital in the opium business, only thirteen were arrested while forty-two remained at large when the Fujian provincial authorities wrapped up the case and forwarded it to Beijing. Among the laborers, only eight remained at large while the remaining forty-five were arrested and prosecuted.[47] The investors had an almost uncanny ability to avoid arrest, as in Wang Zhou, who hired two boatmen to transport him out to Shi Hou's warehouses at Yakou to purchase eight bricks of opium for $100. Wang was never captured while the boatmen he had hired were each sentenced to beatings of one hundred strokes of the heavy bamboo and three years of hard labor. The case includes several variations on this story, as in Lin Xiaojiu, who hired three boatmen to purchase eight balls of opium from the foreign ships in Shenhu Bay and somehow escaped with the opium while his three employees were captured and punished. Likewise, the rising star Shi Kai and his team of nine investors all evaded arrest while the four lineage members they hired to redistribute their opium were all captured and punished. Working as a boatman in an opium operation was a dangerous job with harsh consequences. Investing in opium, on the other hand, was comparatively safe and incomparably remunerative.

STATE-MERCHANT COLLABORATION

The offshore market that the Shi lineage and Rees brothers operated was dependent on securing cooperation and protection from people in the Qing government. Shi Hou charged other local buyers a fee of $10 per chest to act as an intermediary with the foreign ships, according to the Qing memorial on the case. British opium merchants in southern Fujian also discussed a $10 fee at great length, but they generally understood it as a bribe that was being funneled to the local authorities. In one such letter, Captain Jauncey reports that a man with an official "chop" was put on board the ships to receive payment and stamp each chest as having paid the fee.[48] Some of the British merchants were suspicious that the Yakou brokers had claimed the fee was a bribe to the local authorities in order to dupe the British into giving them a monopoly over access to the foreign ships.[49] Captain John Rees, who spent more time in Shenhu Bay than the other Jardine employees, believed that the fee was genuinely being used to secure the protection and cooperation of local officials. He suggested that by refusing to endorse the fee the British were putting the brokers in danger, who "have been in the habit of paying a sum" to local authorities. Rees also noted that he intended to get around the uncertainty by going on shore to pay the relevant official directly.[50]

The matter of the $10 fee in Shenhu Bay was part of a broader pattern of bribery and market regulation developing between the British opium ship captains, the coastal lineages, and the Qing civil and military authorities in Xiamen and Quanzhou. During May and June of 1836, for instance, Captains John and Thomas Rees, representing the rival firms of Jardine Matheson and Dent, entered into negotiations with an official with jurisdiction over Shenhu Bay known in the Jardine sources as "Luo Toa" (*laoda*, local parlance for "elder brother" or "the big man"). In May, John Rees reported having negotiated with his brother to fix prices for the bay and subsequently combine together to offer the Luo Toa an annual fee of $20,000 in order to secure the trade and also "not to allow strangers to trade" (i.e., not allow competing British, Parsee, and American opium ships into the bay).[51] A month later Rees reported that the official had "sent off to say he cannot accept less than $24,000 fees for accommodation for both ships.

For this sum he says he can protect the trade in case strange ships should come in . . . He is certainly authorized to treat with us by the authorities at Chinchew [Quanzhou]."[52] Dent and Jardine captains were in direct negotiation with local authorities on the coast.

The Shi Hou memorial and other similar cases also illustrate how the opium trade created opportunities for people in positions of authority to make money through blackmail and extortion. In the autumn of 1835, when Shi Hou was operating his opium depot out of the Yakou wharves, a Quanzhou prefectural yamen clerk together with an associate threatened to report Shi to the authorities unless he offered a bribe. Shi Hou complied and gave each of the two men a payment of eighty silver dollars to keep quiet. A few weeks later they returned and purchased ten balls of opium.[53] In another case, a Jinjiang county licentiate (*juren*) came across a man on the road whom he suspected of carrying opium on his person and demanded a bribe of 200 wen to stay quiet. Successful, the degree-holder then made a practice of using his status to extort bribes from Jinjiang smugglers for two years, until in 1837 he decided to invest $300 to make a purchase of his own and set up an opium den. The licentiate was arrested in 1838 and promptly hanged himself before trial.[54] In both cases, official functionaries and people of status were drawn into the opium trade by the opportunity for extortion. As people with high social status and official connections, it was easy to frighten opium dealers into offering bribes. Both of these predatory figures also realized that extortion was not nearly as lucrative as direct involvement in the opium trade itself. They became opium dealers, converting their extortion capital into investments.

Reading the Chinese and British documents together, it is clear that the major arrests that took place in Yakou during early 1837 happened as a result of a failed negotiation between the Shi lineage and some local government officials over the payment of an opium import fee. Rees wrote on January 2 of that year that trade was stopped in Shenhu Bay for five days "in consequence of a party having cheated the Mandarines out of their customary fees."[55] The Jardine Matheson employee went ashore himself with a $5,000 bribe prepared and sat in on lineage negotiations with the government officials for three days at the "Consoo house," a term usually connoting a customs outpost. Rees "saluted the mandarins" and made an effort to help his onshore partners secure protection for the trade, but after "severe quibbling" he returned to his ship in frustration and "left them to settle their disputes without paying anything."[56] Then on January 15 a group of government officials descended on Yakou village for the purpose of "recovering their fees" and again stopped all boats from coming out for a period of three days.[57] On January 21 Rees lamented that trade was completely stopped in Shenhu Bay due to the fact that "the Mandarines are about collecting their fees prior to the New Year and I believe are squeezing the brokers that we deal with rather hard."[58]

Shi Hou and the hundred or so people caught up in Yakou during the dragnet of early 1837, it seems, were not arrested for dealing in opium so much as they were arrested for failing to pay state actors their cut. It was the Lunar New Year, a customary time for the settling of debts and not coincidentally the period during which the wave of arrests took place. A month later, after sending a local employee ashore to reconnoiter the situation, Rees reported that a new official stationed near Yakou "had burnt several houses and destroyed some boats . . . in consequence of the brokers not coming to terms with him. They have not paid the Mandarines 1/3 of their fees, and several of the brokers have absconded."[59] The turmoil in the bay after the arrests lasted for months, with the remaining brokers at one point even requesting Rees return to Canton to let things cool down.[60] Eventually, Rees learned that "some of the best and most respectable men" from Yakou were going over the head of the uncooperative local official, seeking help from the provincial authorities in Fuzhou to secure the local officer's removal and replacement so that trade could resume on previous terms.[61] It seems to have done the trick. By July, the Jardine Matheson opium ship captains were once again describing the trade in Shenhu Bay as "brisk."[62]

The opium business evolved through interactions with state authorities. Both Qing and British sources describe a well-established practice of *somebody* in Shenhu Bay charging $10 fees for every chest sold. In the Qing report, the payment is coded as a brokerage fee that captured suspect Shi Hou was charging other Chinese merchants for access to the foreign ships. Such a brokerage fee would not have been totally out of place, but the British opium captains give convincing evidence that the surcharge was actually part of a government protection scheme. Deals were arranged at a high level, lineage elders and high-volume brokers sat down with local officials and naval commanders, occasionally including the British merchants as well. When ambitious new transfers appointed to the region tried to root out the trade or to demand bribes over the acceptable limit, lineage elders would try to go over their heads and make deals with their superior officers. The top British and Chinese opium merchants also competed with one another to be in charge of collecting and paying the fees, and British sources evince a distrustful assumption that their Chinese partners would embezzle the fees rather than pay the state the agreed upon sum. Whether these concerns were founded or not, this was a realm of total illegality. Actors could and did play fast and loose with the rules of trade, seeking out any potential advantage over their rivals and partners.

"Local Customs" and the Opium Business

If you take the region's appointed government officials at their word, Fujian's emergent offshore opium trade in the 1830s was unquestionably built on local foundations. Local and provincial authorities routinely cited "local customs" as the principal reason why the coastal Fujianese were so heavily engaged in opium trafficking. Quanzhou Prefect Shen Ruhan calls the opium smugglers of southern Fujian "fearless ruffians" (*wangming zhi tu*).[63] Censor Du Yanshi, a Quanzhou native with a low opinion of his home region, writes repeatedly that the people are "cunning and fierce" (*diaohan*) and must be controlled with heavy-handed state authority. Lineage braves kill and kidnap each other, and people, feeling that "government is useless," do not dare submit petitions for justice. The pirates of Jinjiang county, Du writes, assemble each night to "filch like rats and snatch like dogs." And when pirates are captured off the coast of other provinces, the ship and crew are inevitably traced back to southern Fujian. Meanwhile, rapacious clerks and runners—the local staff of centrally appointed officials—"work their way into positions of trust in order to deceive officials and chew the commoners into bits."[64]

Qing officials routinely used blanket terms like "treacherous coastal people" (*yanhai jianmin*) as shorthand for the entire population of coastal southern Fujian. The term evokes an explicit contrast with the "inland good people," or "inland commoners" (*neidi liangmin*), and signals the irredeemable deviousness of the coastal population. These ideas read today like stereotype, but to a Qing administrator it was relevant information that people in southern Fujian had a bad reputation. The coastal Fujianese were members of a marginal and predictably depraved social group, officials routinely complained as they faced uncomfortable questions about their own inability to rein in the drug trade. Looking back at these documents almost two centuries after they were written, we can discern fleeting images of the mobile, independent, entrepreneurial, and opportunistic residents of coastal southern Fujian through the haze of stereotype and accusation.

THE LINEAGE STRUCTURE OF LOCAL SOCIETY

The territorial lineage was most important social institution on the southeast coast during the late imperial period. Some of the more powerful Fujianese lineages dominated large swaths of territory and had populations in the tens of thousands, with complex corporate structures and internal class divisions. The maritime lineages of China's southeast coast had important political functions: merging with official systems of taxation, corvée labor (*lijia*), and social order (*baojia*). Lineages also had cultural functions: hiring teachers, promoting candidates for examination, conducting religious ritual, and maintaining a system of traditional values.[65] The territorial lineage, as Zheng Zhenman argues, "provided the model that underlay all other organizations within late imperial Chinese society. Political factions, secret societies, native-place associations and guilds, as well as local militias and joint stock investment corporations, were all constructed out of, or according to the principles of, lineage organization."[66]

The maritime lineages that dominated the region rose to prominence during and after the Qing conquest of the region. When the Ming dynasty (1368–1644) collapsed in the mid-seventeenth century, the Zheng lineage of southern Fujian launched a bureaucratic state nominally dedicated to reviving the Ming and became one of the last holdouts against the Qing conquest.[67] In order to capture the Fujian coastline, the Qing invaders became determined to cut off the Zheng organization from mainland support. In one of the most horrific campaigns of early modern warfare, Qing administrators in Fujian (and parts of Guangdong and Zhejiang) banned maritime trade as well as physical residence along the entire Fujian coast. In Jinjiang county, home to the Yakou Shi, the new state forced residents to abandon at least 110 settlements (including Yakou village), totaling 1,252 acres of cultivated land in an already land-poor county.[68] The consequences were devastating, as Zheng Zhenman and others have shown.[69] The scorched-earth policy moved untold numbers of impoverished coastal residents away from their only source of income and dismantled local economic and social structures.

The repeal of the evacuation policy three decades later seems to have further encouraged the dominance of the region's already powerful territorial lineages. A central figure in the repeal of the evacuation policy was a local naval commander and patriarch of the Shi lineage of Yakou village, Shi Lang (1621–1696). Shi, like many coastal Fujianese, had fought with Zheng Chenggong against the invading Qing army but later defected to become the Qing's first naval commander-in-chief (*shuishi tidu*) in Fujian. Shi Lang helped defeat the Zheng rebels and pacified the Fujian coastal waters, and soon after he began to press the Kangxi emperor for benevolence towards the people of the Fujian coast.[70] Shi's home village of Yakou was among those that the Qing had forcibly evacuated, and he gave a humanitarian case for reopening the ports that ultimately proved convincing. In 1684, the Kangxi emperor lifted the ban on maritime trade, abandoned the destructive policy of coastal evacuation, and eased land scarcity and the food shortage by allowing the coastal Fujianese to colonize and settle in Taiwan. People with connections to powerful men like Shi Lang had an obvious advantage in this context, and accordingly the Yakou Shi were able to (re) claim a choice piece of territory, enjoying a privileged status in the region into the twentieth century.

Powerful lineages like the Yakou Shi became the dominant power brokers in the region and were treated warily by the Qing state. By 1740, the Yakou Shi were attracting negative attention for the size and strength of the lineage and the illegal activity of its members. The Fujian-Zhejiang governor-general reported multiple times that year on his attempts to deal with the powerful lineage. The Shi lineage at Yakou had "10,000 healthy and strong young men," he wrote. "They can gather at the sound of a whistle to engage in armed struggle, to resist arrest and refuse to pay the grain tax, to smuggle and sell private salt, and to rob and plunder merchant ships . . . the local authorities are afraid of them and therefore conceal their crimes. Nobody dares to say a thing."[71] The governor-general summoned ten of the Shi lineage elders to Fuzhou and chastised them, recommending to his superiors in Beijing that a greater government presence ought to be to be established near Yakou. His approach did not work.

By the 1830s, the Yakou Shi were firmly established as one of the most powerful southern Fujianese lineages with maritime interests. They controlled a long stretch of the inner shoreline of Shenhu Bay, an inlet approximately four miles across and strategically situated between the large ports of

Xiamen and Quanzhou. With Xiamen twenty-five miles to the south and Quanzhou fifteen miles to the north, the Shi were far enough away from the seats of local officialdom to avoid constant and direct surveillance, yet close enough to the ports to capitalize on the region's commercial networks. On top of their geographical advantage, the Yakou Shi lineage had the requisite finances, boats, storage space, processing capacity, and connections to move quickly in the early 1830s when British opium merchants first began to express interest in bringing the trade up the coast from Guangdong.

They were also far from unique. The entire region was dominated by similarly positioned lineages with strong numbers, official connections, diversified business interests, boats, weapons, and money. Many of these groups, like the Shi, were formulated out of kinship claims during the chaotic years after the coastal evacuation was lifted. By the time British opium ships began arriving in Fujian, many of these lineages even boasted small coastal fortresses complete with well-stocked batteries to defend their small anchorages and jetties against attacks from the state or other lineages.[72] As noted earlier in this chapter, when imperial investigators reported on the opium trade in 1840, they organized their report around which territorial lineages were the most active in the trade.[73]

Lineage feuds (*xiedou*) were also endemic in the region, and Qing officials perceived a connection between the opium trade and the chronic feuding among lineages. As Harry Lamley argues, lineages in the region had developed a systematized "feud industry," wherein chronic feuding encouraged the development of a professional mercenary class among the otherwise "indigent inhabitants" of the region.[74] Tong'an county, an epicenter of opium trading situated on the coast between Jinjiang county and Xiamen, was by far the worst county for feuds, listed by one imperial investigator as having eight notorious lineages whose fighting resulted in a total of 283 deaths and over 800 houses destroyed during the late 1830s.[75] These Tong'an lineages invested a great deal of money and technology into feuding, and several went so far as to erect illegal cannon fortifications (*paotai*) outside of villages and along prominent roads. Jinjiang county had its own share of feuding lineages, including the Qianpu village Xue lineage, the Cizao Wu, and the Shishi Xu and Cai.[76] The Cai of Shishi village (located only seven miles from Yakou) is also listed as a prominent opium smuggling lineage in Huang's earlier memorial on the opium trade.[77] In the zero-sum competition between lineages for wealth and power, opium became a crucial financial tool.

TRADITIONS OF MARITIME TRADE, SMUGGLING, AND PIRACY

When Qing officials used terms like "treacherous coastal people" to describe the southern Fujianese, they were making an unambiguous reference to the region's long and well-known history of maritime trade, piracy, smuggling, and secret society uprisings. Official stereotypes about the southeast coast quite reasonably perceived a connection between the opium trade and the economic and social patterns that gave the region its difficult administrative reputation. Maritime commerce, not agriculture, is what enabled powerful lineages like the Yakou Shi to grow so large and influential.[78] For people struggling to make ends meet, the sea was the only realistic economic security blanket in this land-poor maritime region. They were fishermen, smugglers, and pirates. The wealthy among them sponsored fleets of sailboats to carry (or plunder) the coastal trade, the Southeast Asia trade, and the Taiwan trade. Families across the region commonly sought out poor male relatives to adopt as sons and dispatch overseas.[79] As early as the fifteenth century, thousands of Fujianese people sojourned and made lives across the oceans.[80]

The arrival of European empires in the greater Indian Ocean and Southeast Asian maritime region shifted the structure of markets and opportunities, ultimately increasing the appeal of overseas trade and migration for the Fujianese. Merchants from Fujian took advantage of their position between China and the Southeast Asian maritime world, importing swallow's nests and other tropical produce of Southeast Asia, exporting cottons, silks, and porcelain.[81] The Ming state banned overseas trade apart from officially sponsored "tribute" ships from places like Ryukyu, Luzon, and Siam, which were allowed to trade in specific items, at specific times, in designated ports, some in Fujian. But, as scholars have demonstrated, the official tribute trade was dwarfed by the illegal "sideline" operations of traders who traveled in convoys with the tribute ships.[82] The Fujianese port of Yuegang in Zhangzhou prefecture near Xiamen was perhaps the most famous illicit entrepôt, a flourishing and entirely illegal center of maritime trade.[83] The smuggling in of globalized commodities was a mainstay of the coastal economy for centuries before the arrival of men like John and Thomas Rees.

The disruptions of the Qing conquest and harsh early-Qing policies against maritime trade only deepened the Fujianese dependency on illegal foreign trade. The coastal evacuation policy and maritime bans of the early Qing effectively made all overseas trade illicit, creating innumerable lucrative smuggling opportunities. Much of the private trade between China and Southeast Asia was effectively legalized after Kangxi lifted the maritime ban in 1685, but as trade and migration increased over the next century, a new trend emerged. The most prosperous years of the Qing empire—the late eighteenth century—were experienced in the South China Sea as a "golden age of piracy," when staggeringly huge fleets of piratical junks raided the coastline and controlled shipping lanes, led by charismatic chieftains like Cai Qian, Zheng Yi, and his widow Zheng Yisao.[84]

Piracy never fully disappeared from the Fujian coast, but its attractiveness as an occupation decreased substantially in the 1820s and 30s with aggressive Qing anti-piracy campaigns and the rise of British naval supremacy in the region. Just as the opportunities to pillage the coastal trade began to decline, the chances of making a quick dollar smuggling opium multiplied exponentially. The infrastructure and skill set were there. Pirates have to be able to fence goods, and smugglers to be able to protect themselves. When the British arrived in coastal Fujian with shiploads of the most sought-after and profitable commodity on the market, the region was flush with boat owners and sailors hungry for profits and schooled in flexible approaches to import laws and taxation.

MARITIME DEFENSE AND THE OPIUM BUSINESS

Because southern Fujian was a maritime frontier with a history of violent resistance, secret society uprisings, lineage feuding, and piracy, the Qing state invested the region with what looks on paper like a formidable maritime defense infrastructure. Xiamen, where Jardine Matheson reported their highest sales, was the seat of the Xinghua-Quanzhou-Yongchun circuit intendant (*Xing-Quan-Yong dao*) and the powerful Fujian admiral (*shuishi tidu*). Jinmen (Quemoy), the dumbbell-shaped island just seawards from the island of Xiamen, was the site of a massive naval garrison and the home base for ships patrolling the coasts of Fujian, Taiwan, and eastern Guangdong. A Fujian sub-statute required the garrison to maintain 266 warships at all times.[85] There was also a dense network of customs checkpoints in the Zhangzhou-Quanzhou region to oversee the thousands of fishing and trading boats in the region, including three offices near the mouth of the inlet into Shenhu Bay and in direct sight of the opium anchorages. So how did the local opium smugglers manage to buy and sell such prolific amounts of the drug?

Fujian was a genuinely difficult place to govern. The provincial government and military were simply unable to prevent lineages like the Yakou Shi from taking up the opium trade. Since their formation in the seventeenth century, the Fujian Navy and inland garrisons had been locked in perpetual struggle with an unending wave of pirate confederacies, secret-society uprisings, and lineage feuds. When faced with such problems in the 1830s, the government's boats were in poor shape, and ammunition costs had made training impossible.[86] The approach of a well-armed British opium ship would have been an ominous event in the life of a Qing naval commander. It could have seemed hardly worth the lives of soldiers or the shame of defeat to start a fight. It was also a trade that many local people supported and depended on, almost certainly including friends and kin of the officers and crew.

The local civil and military administration was not merely revenue-starved, they were staffed by officers who were part of local society and who had mixed loyalty about their various obligations. There was an independent streak among Fujian's coastal administrators, dating back to the enigmatic Yakou Shi lineage patriarch, Shi Lang. Shi and many of his successors in the Fujian Navy were locals, which was taboo for most official positions in the imperial bureaucracy but more common in the naval and customs administration on the maritime frontier. Shi Lang's own son Shi Shibiao was also appointed to the position of naval commander-in-chief (*shuishi tidu*) in 1712.[87] Locals also held positions of power within the Fujian maritime customs and played important roles in the policing of trade.[88] In this context, state-merchant collaboration in opium smuggling is perhaps less surprising.

The Fujian naval commander-in-chief was a middleman between the seagoing merchant houses of Fujian and the Qing government. He represented the authority of the central state, but his men were local, and more than half the money that kept his ships afloat came from local merchant contributions.[89] During the early nineteenth century, the naval fleet was increasingly supplemented with confiscated local pirate boats and crewed by former pirates from the region.[90] Quanzhou native Zhang Ran, for example, achieved the rank of commander (*canjiang*) in the navy after having been captured as a pirate, continuing in the grand tradition of how the Qing state coopted Zhang Bao and the great pirate confederations of the Jiaqing era (1796–1820).[91] This strategy was also occasionally used to combat the opium trade. "The government have unleashed their cruisers," wrote John Rees in 1837, "and employed a great number of the lowest class of fellows, no other than the native pirates, to man fishing boats and cruise about in disguise."[92] The navy in Xiamen was a local institution, reliant on the support of prominent merchants, among whom there was a growing number of opium investors, and staffed by the class of laboring boatmen who would otherwise be doing work that the state considered to be piracy and smuggling.

The lure of opium profits for Qing military and civil authorities beguiled those who were crusading against the drug. While investigating the opium trade in 1838, censor Du Yanshi accused several officials as well as government office clerks and runners of aiding and profiting off of the opium trade. Du argued that corruption among the naval garrisons was the main reason why "treacherous" locals had managed to successfully collude with foreigners to distribute opium with such impunity.[93] He levied numerous indictments of soldiers and officers serving under the naval commander-in-chief. One officer was accused of taking bribes of $400–600 to allow foreign ships to anchor off the coast and of recruiting garrison soldiers for helping distribute the opium. A squad leader (*bazong*) in the navy was discovered selling opium and taking bribes, and patrol boats belonging to the navy were reported to have been used to escort smugglers and assist locals in transporting grain and water to and from the foreign boats.[94] A former Jinjiang county magistrate was accused of having colluded with a Yakou man named Shi Jin to kidnap or purchase women and sell them into sexual slavery aboard the foreign receiving ships (an extremely common practice, according to the censor). Du also believed that the reason why Shi Shubao—the aspiring foreign expert and broker named in the Yakou Shi case of 1837—was never arrested was that the Quanzhou prefect took a bribe of $800 to allow him to escape.

Four months later, another high official named Huang Juezi was sent to investigate each of Du's numerous and inflammatory accusations. The accused naval squad leader was confirmed to have accepted $700 in bribes and was sentenced to immediate hanging. Huang also agreed with Du that a major source of success for smuggling operations was the complicity of naval officers and soldiers, as well as the yamen runners and customs staff. These people, Huang argued, were responsible for the detection and arrest of smugglers but were in fact likely to have lineage connections with the smugglers themselves and could be swayed by family pressures or the opportunities for profit. No wonder, he lamented, are the treacherous people comfortably secure in their crimes, and "we catch only one or two out of a hundred."[95]

Huang also downplayed some of Du's other accusations. The Quanzhou prefect could not have allowed Shi Shubao to escape, Huang argued, because Shi had been a wanted criminal long before the official in question was appointed to Quanzhou.[96] Huang also argued that while Shi Jin may perhaps have sold one woman to the foreigners, this could not have been a common practice. After all, when investigators went to Yakou to look into the matter, there were no official complaints or lawsuits filed. Du countered that the parents of such unfortunate women were highly unlikely to come forward because they could be found guilty of selling their daughters and thereby aiding and abetting foreign bandits. The question was not resolved.

The Crackdown

The governors and governors-general assigned to Fujian in the late 1830s arrived with an imperial mandate to find an expedient solution to the opium problem. Provincial authorities sidestepped corruption issues in order to prioritize symbolic gains, pressuring local authorities to round up as many people and confiscate as much opium as they could manage. In 1836, in a single sustained raid, the Fujian authorities captured 1,119 suspects and confiscated 250 boats.[97] In 1839, local officials captured Yang Awan together with 143 other suspects and over 23,300 catties of processed opium paste.[98] Later that year they captured Zhu Kepei and several Yakou Shi smugglers totaling twenty-seven people, together with opium, silver, and boats.[99] In the first four lunar months of 1840, Fujian Governor Deng Tingzhen reported processing a total of 260 opium cases involving 543 suspects, including the capture of Yakou native Shi Dama with 1,400 catties of opium.[100] That same year, Deng reported that the province had run out of space for housing the prisoners awaiting prosecution and punishment.[101]

Activist officials like Huang Juezi worked tirelessly to harness local systems of social control and make these arrests. Huang was particularly vocal about taking advantage of the *aojia*, a system of mutual responsibility for boat owners, replicating the household registration and mutual responsibility system (*baojia*) operating throughout the Qing empire.[102] The system dated back to the Ming era, and Fujian's provincial government promulgated a new sub-statute on the *aojia* system in early 1836 to introduce a more stringent system of auditing the local officials in charge of monitoring the *aojia* system so as to fight local corruption and the abetting of illegal offshore activity.[103] Huang Juezi wrote in 1840 that regulations needed to be even tighter, because in Fujian "there are seven fishermen for every three farmers." Petty smuggling was not the problem, he continued, rather it was "treacherous people with large investments capable of wholesale purchases, who hire and send people to assist the foreigners on the ocean. These boat owners are occasionally caught, but they are no more than fearless ruffians. Meanwhile the real investors are safely in their villages, unharmed and with no reason to stop their practices, and thus the problem has grown bigger."[104] In response, Huang urged local officials to rein in the *aojia* units and enforce strict inspections of ships' cargo and close adherence to procedure. Any boat staying out longer than a typical fishing voyage was to be considered suspicious. The crew of any boat caught within sight of a foreign receiving ship were to be considered "opium-purchasing traitors" (*maiyan jianmin*) and arrested accordingly.

Fujian's government officials were able to capture thousands of people involved in the trade by employing the aid of knowledgeable locals in the naval garrison at Xiamen and harnessing a system of mutual responsibility to keep track of boats and people. Still, these same institutions could be used to conceal crimes from provincial authorities, allowing for a more systematic and insulated system of smuggling to evolve between opium traders and complicit military and civil authorities. The opium trade did not go away, and it is beyond question that the majority of smugglers—the most successful, one naturally has to conclude—were never captured. Even among the Yakou Shi, it is reasonable to argue that the supposed ringleader Shi Hou might not have been the most important figure. Clearly he was not indispensable to the operation of the trade, which continued on after his arrest and death without interruption. An investigation that took place nearly four years after Shi Hou's arrest repeatedly refers to the Yakou Shi as a prominent smuggling lineage and continues to cite Yakou as a prominent site for foreign receiving ships to unload cargoes of opium.[105] The Jardine Matheson materials confirm this. Shi Hou might have died while awaiting execution, but the business interests of the Yakou Shi do not seem to have suffered.

The persistence of the opium trade in the face of state opposition transformed the coastal defense administration. The systematized bribery negotiated by the Shi lineage and local authorities is an important part of the story of the rise of the opium business, but it is also worthwhile to consider the impact of those officials within the state who did not get roped into the trade. Du Yanshi, Huang Juezi, and other officials invested in improving the military capabilities of the navy's coastal garrisons as a direct response to the drug trade. The inability of the Fujian naval authorities to chase off a few foreign opium ships highlighted problems in both preparedness and technological sophistication. Du complained that while walking on the beach in retirement he had seen the warships lined up, lying "in piles of joints, masts and ropes."[106] Huang was again dispatched to investigate. Du's accusations were not untrue, but the matter was not so simple. The coast is long and jagged, the navy was poorly funded, and smugglers' boats could disappear and reappear at will. Huang knew this, and he was also a pragmatist. Rather than echoing Du's complaints and further alienating local officials and naval officers, Huang smoothed over Du's harsh censure and simply continued to lean on the local administration to make arrests, fix boats, and get busy.

It was an uphill battle, too little and too late. In the early summer months of 1839, the Fujian native and high official Lin Zexu took drastic measures to dismantle the opium trade in Guangdong, confiscating around 2.6 million pounds of opium from Jardine, Dent, and the other British merchants and destroying it in the Canton harbor. The British response was punitive, and the advance of British forces up the coast destroyed much of the Fujian naval fleet just as Huang and others were investing time and resources in reinvigorating the institution. After the war, the people responsible for the direction of affairs in southern Fujian were desperate for funds and unable to give sufficient attention to technological development and training. There was never enough revenue for the local state to adequately police the seas and control maritime trade. Opium revenue, which everyone understood was being informally collected since the 1830s, became an increasingly obvious and enticing solution to the fiscal problems of the Fujian provincial authorities.

Conclusion: Old Foundations, New Beginnings

A few months after the arrest of Shi Hou and his compatriots in early 1837, Captain John Rees sent a letter to William Jardine that explains the aftermath of the raid on Yakou village.[107] In the letter, Rees describes how the conflict in Shenhu Bay continued on after the wave of arrests in February, reescalating when a newly appointed official discovered a missing bribe amounting to $7,000. Over the course of the previous year, Rees and his brother had paid a total of $26,000 in fees "to the [Yakou] authorities (or Elders)." Of this money, Rees was informed that $9,000 had been extended to the "District Mandaren." Another $10,000 of the money was "distributed among the widows and relations of the deceased that fell during a severe battle between other villages in 1835." A sum of $7,000, then, was still missing. Both Rees and the new official assumed it had been embezzled by the lineage elders at Yakou.

Global circulations of opium and capital placed the Shi lineage elders in the powerful position of mediators between the British importers and the Qing state. The lineage became, in a way, tax farmers: collecting standardized fees of $10 on each chest of opium unloaded from the foreign ships, placing a seal or stamps on the tax-paid chests, and paying a quota of this revenue to the relevant local officials. John Rees certainly viewed them as tax farmers, writing that "the fellows on shore have been in the habit of paying a sum much short of what they received from the ships and divide the surplus amongst themselves."[108]

It was not a new phenomenon that Fujian's maritime lineages would take on responsibilities associated taxation, social control, and market regulation. Lineage elders had long acted as legal authorities, managing dispute resolution among members. Lineages also provided funding for education, social welfare, and infrastructure. Merchant organizations likewise have a long regional history of partnering with the state in social welfare projects, including funding the naval garrison in Xiamen, contributing to municipal infrastructure, and building the Dragon King Temple (*longwang miao*) in Xiamen and funding "local temples to seek protection from deities associated with the sea for their maritime trade."[109] What was new in the 1830s, with the rise of the opium business, was the tense illegality of the trade and the amount of money involved.

The path to success in these early years of the opium business required participants to openly break the law. As a consequence, when opium and opium-derived capital became embedded in local government structures, it was done so in a way that lacked regulation, consistency, transparency, and central oversight. Government officials were themselves drawn into the opium business, like the officer known to the British as the Chu Kang who opted to collect his $13,000 fee in opium rather than cash. The Chu Kang used the drug to generate both institutional revenue and personal profit, shipping a portion of the drug up to Fuzhou where prices were high and issuing the rest to his officers to unload locally at $20 per ball, using the drug to supplement the insufficient salaries of his officers and soldiers.[110]

This early history of the opium business therefore demonstrates the early and powerful influence of the industry on the Qing state. The Shi lineage elders achieved incredible leverage vis-à-vis the local government, demanding that $10,000 of the annual $26,000 bribe be earmarked for the victims of a lineage feud that they might have otherwise been seen as culpable for. When a newly appointed official disturbed the flow of drugs and money, "the most respectable men" in the lineage activated their elite contacts in the provincial capital to get the obstreperous official transferred.[111] At those times when negotiations with local officials were ongoing and unresolved, lineage elders were known to fine or confiscate property from unruly brokers who ignored their commands to temporarily cease trade.[112] They were a force to be reckoned with.

The transnational coalition of people who made their living in the coastal opium trade during the 1830s set in motion a broad transformation of the regional political economy, creating a set of local practices that would endure the transformations engendered by the Opium War and subsequent treaty. Fujianese lineages, British and Parsee opium merchants, and Lascar ships' crews inserted opium into local markets and government finance across the realm. They extended and reshaped the culture of state-merchant interaction, funneling huge sums of illicit capital into state finances and the pockets of individuals. This took place in major ports as well as neighboring districts. So long as opium remained illegal—all the way into the late 1850s—the standard practices of this early stage of the opium business would remain largely in place.

CHAPTER 2

Negotiated Illegality, 1843–1860

On a March morning in 1851, Yang Alü was transporting a cargo of opium up the Min River to Fuzhou.[1] Opium imports took place downstream, near a cluster of small islands at the mouth of the river, thirty-five miles from the treaty port and provincial capital (Map 2.1). Just off one of the smallest islands, called Wuhu, lay anchored the same fleet of aging British and American opium hulks that had been stationed along the Fujian coast since the early 1830s. Yang had a contract with one of these ships, probably the Jardine Matheson vessel *Harlequin*, for the exclusive right to deliver opium from the Wuhu anchorage upstream to the warehouses of southern Fujianese and Cantonese opium merchants on Nantai Island, just south of the walled city of Fuzhou.[2]

Yang Alü had acquired the lucrative opium transport contract through intimidation. An outsider in Fuzhou, Yang came north from Jinjiang county to seek his fortune selling firewood in the provincial capital. As he struggled to earn money, Yang "watched with great envy" the profits reaped by a local boat-person (*danmin*) named Lin Wenwen, who had contracted with one of the foreign opium importers to transport opium up to Fuzhou from the Wuhu anchorage at the rate of $12 per month. The contract itself was good money for a transport provider, but the arrangement was particu-

MAP 2.1: Harbor limits in the treaty port of Fuzhou.

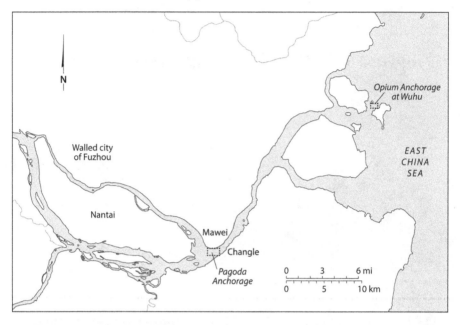

larly desirable because it gave the holder direct access to enormous stocks of
opium. For people like Yang and Lin, a deal with one of these ships meant
first access to an unlimited quantity of the most coveted commodity on the
market.

Yang Alü understood how lucrative the opium business could be, and he
wanted this slice of it for himself. He conceived of a bold plan to acquire a
powerful connection and approached Yang Xiyuan, a Fuzhou native and a
member of the highest level of the degree-holding elite (*juren*), employed as
an instructor at the Confucian academy. The two men were not related, but
they shared a surname. Yang Alü proposed to compensate Yang Xiyuan for
pretending they were kin, requesting that Xiyuan use his status to intimidate the current holder of the opium transport contract, Lin Wenwen, into
giving up his business. The degree-holder agreed to the plan, and it worked.
Yang Xiyuan confronted Lin Wenwen on behalf of his supposed kinsman
Yang Alü, and Lin accordingly ceded his business to the intruders. Yang
Alü then traveled out to the opium anchorage and took over Lin's contract

on identical terms: $12 per month to ferry opium upstream from the ships at the mouth of the river to the merchant community in Fuzhou. Yang Alü paid for the construction of two fast-boats, presumably with help from his benefactor, and hired on a crew of seven. The two conspirators wasted no time. They took advantage of their strategic position vis-à-vis the foreign ships and invested $160 each in a cargo of opium.

Lin Wenwen stewed for months before deciding to reclaim his stake in the opium transport business. He assembled his old crew with a plan to ambush Yang Alü's boats near Luoxing Pagoda, a little more than halfway back to Fuzhou from the opium ships at Wuhu. Lin's plan was to propose a compromise: he would only demand half of his old business back, and the two transport workers could coexist. His backup plan, if Yang Alü refused these terms, was to rob Yang of whatever goods and money were in his possession.

The backup plan turned out to be necessary. When Lin and his crew paddled up to Yang Alü's boats and made their demands, Yang refused to give back any share of the transport business. After exchanging some strong language, Lin's men boarded Yang's vessel. But there was something Lin Wenwen had not counted on. Yang Alü had employed two armed escorts for protection. These were foreign men, so-called "black foreigners" (heiyi), a catch-all term not dissimilar to "Lascar" in its broad application to the seafaring population of the maritime Indian Ocean world. Armed with fowling rifles, the two foreign men gave chase when Lin and his party took off on land with armfuls of stolen property. One of them men shot and killed two people: a member of Lin's party, as well as an innocent bystander. The foreigners were also injured when one of the fleeing men started throwing rocks. It was a messy affair.

Life on the Fujian coast during the intertreaty moment, between the Treaties of Nanjing (1842) and Tianjin (1858), was often messy. It was a period of transition: for the territorial administration of the Qing empire, for the people living in and near the new treaty ports, for the foreign merchants and diplomats who flocked there. For the opium business, this was a moment of both vertical and horizontal expansion: more people were involved in the trade as the drug became normalized, and the vast quantity of money circulating worked its way across industries and into state finances.

The Treaty of Nanjing that concluded the Opium War did nothing to address the opium trade. Instead, the treaty authors focused their energy on opening five treaty ports, placing Hong Kong under British rule, establishing rudimentary rules for consular jurisdiction, and filing a devastating indemnity on the Qing state. The word *opium* does not appear in the treaty text. The people who made their living in the opium business responded to the imperfect treaty with strategic noncompliance. As in the 1830s, most opium imports continued to take place offshore. Foreign importers arranged deals with Chinese brokers aboard foreign-owned receiving ships, and both buyer and seller facilitated and protected their businesses through a combination of bribery and violence. But unlike during the previous decade, the ports near those opium anchorages were now bustling with foreign merchants, new opportunities, and a much more relaxed administrative approach to the opium business. There was also a corps of foreign consuls assigned to the ports, some of whom would claim jurisdiction over Chinese employees of foreign firms and diasporic returnees. There were a host of new conflicts over trade and sovereignty.

The conflict between Lin Wenwen and Yang Alü was a turf battle over the movement of opium between these two jurisdictions: the unregulated opium anchorages and the new treaty ports. The moment of import, when chests of opium crossed into Qing jurisdiction as they were carried from sea to land, often just as the drug passed from foreign to Chinese hands, was a moment of heightened violence, of opportunity and contestation, a moment when bribes and taxes would be paid or not paid, and when competitors could attack the vulnerable. When the ports were first opened, neither Qing nor British officials had clear instructions about how to deal with a booming opium trade, nominally illegal but increasingly looking like the staple of a new coastal economy.

In this absence of centralized policy, drug traders and local administrators forged their own ways of doing business. Importers negotiated ad hoc import fees with local officials, as they had in the 1830s. In the cities, distributors and retailers too began to pay various fees and surcharges to municipal authorities. In response to the central Qing state's unenforced prohibition of the drug, the people who bought and sold opium came increasingly out of the shadows. Opium capital worked its way into local banking institutions, and into the tea, camphor, rice, and cotton trades. As opium became ever more central to the local economy, there was increased contestation among traders and between traders and the state for control over the profits. This tension began to take new forms in the late 1850s with the advent of a halting and uneven, but ultimately unstoppable, movement by the Qing state towards formalizing and taxing the trade.

The Opium Business in Fujian, 1840–1860

The 1840s and 1850s were boom years for the Indian opium trade in China. Annual opium shipments from India had risen from around 4,000 chests at the turn of the century to 35,000 chests at the eve of the Opium War, and jumped to over 40,000 in 1843 when the treaty ports first opened. All the while opium's import, sale, and use remained technically illegal under Qing law, even if officials largely ceased to enforce the prohibition. The people involved in the opium trade took advantage of the administrative silence coming from British consuls and Chinese officials along the coast, and carried their drugs fearlessly into each of the ports now legally open to merchants and consuls from Europe and the United States. Imports continued to increase: to over 50,000 chests of opium in 1849, 65,000 by 1853, and 75,000 by the end of the 1850s.[3]

Because the opium trade was still nominally illegal during this period, local authorities did not register and quantify the trade as they did with other branches of commerce. Information concerning the quantities, people, and practices involved is piecemeal. British consuls interviewed residents and came up with a rough estimate of around 3,000 chests of opium imported into Xiamen each year from 1844 to 1855.[4] The Jardine Matheson Company's ship captains and agents reported a slightly higher amount based on better evidence, having recorded their own sales and estimated the sales of competing foreign firms and Chinese brokers. These records put the average annual sales by all parties in Xiamen from 1853 to 1856 at around 2,500 chests, with another 2,000 chests imported into the Shenhu Bay and Quanzhou markets each year.[5] This estimate suggests that the merchants of southern Fujian were handling around 4,500 chests of Indian opium per year.

Up the coast from Xiamen, Shenhu Bay, and Quanzhou, the opium trade in the provincial capital Fuzhou was also substantial. A British consul in 1845 estimated Fuzhou's annual trade in opium to be worth not less than $2,000,000, or around 4,000 chests. Jardine Matheson records indicate that the annual imports through the foreign receiving ships at Fuzhou were probably closer to 2,000–2,500 chests.[6] The consul's estimate was higher in this case because he included not only drugs imported directly into Fuzhou from the receiving ships at the mouth of the Min River, but also opium brought up on land routes from Quanzhou through networks established in the 1830s before the British started permanently anchoring ships near Fuzhou. Much of the opium imported into Fuzhou was transshipped up the Min River into tea country and the mountainous regions on the Fujian-Zhejiang-Jiangxi borderland.[7]

Within Fujian's two treaty ports, Xiamen and Fuzhou, wholesale distribution and retail of opium was increasingly tolerated, regularized, and indeed taxed. Both cities were important opium transshipment hubs as well as sites of migration and population growth. In Fuzhou during 1845, there were more than 100 opium dens operating within the walled city, a small part of the greater metropolitan area housing the province's most important civil and military offices.[8] One Qing official—according to a visiting British consul—claimed that an estimated 80 percent of the provincial capital's residents were opium smokers, "stopping his ears and shutting his eyes to give effect to his words, they neither see, nor hear, nor meddle with such matters even when brought to their notice by direct information."[9] In Xiamen, according to another consul, the municipal consumption was 150 chests per month. Opium, he writes, "is carried through the streets, and it is reported that the mandarins receive about 5d. sterling per ball."[10] Drugs were flowing into the two cities, and the opium distribution taxes that would come to characterize major Chinese cities in the late nineteenth and early twentieth centuries were beginning to emerge.

Widening the lens to a national scale, Fujian's role in these boom years of the opium trade was not quite as central as it had been during the 1830s, when around half of the opium imported into the Qing empire passed through the hands of southern Fujianese brokers. Consumption increased in Xiamen and Fuzhou as the populations of the new treaty ports bloomed, and the opening of the Fuzhou tea trade increased the quantities of opium shipped up the Min River into upland Fujian. But of the 8,500 odd chests imported into Fujian each year, it is likely that more than half was still destined for reexport to other parts of the Qing empire. Taiwan (administratively a part of Fujian during these years) was still largely supplied with opium by southern Fujianese brokers engaged in the rice, camphor, and sugar trades.[11] The Quanzhou receiving ships—selling around 1,000 chests of opium per year—were almost entirely dependent on northbound vessels for opium sales, the city itself described as having "small local consumption."[12]

Shenhu Bay (Chimmo)—also responsible for importing around 1,000 chests per year—was not even adjacent to a large city that could account for local consumption, and that port's survival into the 1860s as a profitable receiving ship station was entirely dependent on the persistence of the southern Fujianese brokers in supplying ports in Taiwan and to the north.[13] The volume of reexported opium should be larger still if we consider the rise of domestically produced opium, discussed below. No longer fully centered in the empire-wide opium business, merchants in southern Fujian nonetheless carved out sustainable profits.

As the opium business expanded in volume and stature, the people and money involved in the drug trade increasingly overlapped and were entangled with other branches of trade. Opium was a shadow market that existed largely outside of the state infrastructure, but it was thoroughly enmeshed with legal commerce and commercial capital in the treaty ports. Each spring when tea merchants would escort chests full of silver up the Min River to arrange wholesale purchases, firms like Jardine Matheson and Russell & Company in Fuzhou would send hundreds of chests of opium along with the cash, enticing the tea brokers to take the drug instead of silver by offering a discount under the prevailing opium prices in Fuzhou.[14] The relationship between tea and opium also figured into off-season tea sales each winter, as tea merchants haggled over the remaining stocks of the previous year's crop and bartered opium chests, tea, and silver in complex calculations.[15] Shenhu Bay and Quanzhou merchants who transported Taiwanese camphor to coastal Fujian for reexport to Southeast Asia likewise took payment in opium, which they resold in in Taiwan.[16] Textile purchases in Jiangnan funded Quanzhou opium transactions.[17] Local banks in Xiamen responded to market gluts by purchasing up excess opium stocks for transport to inland villages.[18] The drug was becoming a kind of ready capital in an age of increased circulation.

THE SURVIVAL OF THE RECEIVING SHIPS

Even though Xiamen and Fuzhou were open to foreign trade, opium imports took place just outside of the port limits. The opium import business in Fujian during the two decades after 1843 operated largely as a continuation of the offshore receiving-ship system that had migrated up from

Lintin in the early 1830s. It remained as before: a fleet of ships, mostly foreign-owned, anchored in key locations and selling opium to local brokers, and paying systematized import fees to local authorities. As one consul described the situation, there were "British vessels commanded by British subjects, armed to resist all Chinese interference, and openly lying within a few miles of each of the ports at which Her Majesty's Consuls are resident."[19] The letters from Jardine Matheson's agent in Xiamen during this period did not come from an office in the city as they would in later years, but from the cabin of a ship anchored out of sight from the inner harbor, at the old smuggling station near the six islands at the outermost limit of the bay (Map 2.2). In Fuzhou, as noted in the case of Yang Alü, the receiving ships stayed anchored at the mouth of the Min River (Map 2.1), around thirty miles downstream from the provincial capital and treaty port.

By stationing their opium ships outside the ports, drug importers consciously placed themselves outside of the treaty responsibilities of the British consuls. These consuls were responsible for maintaining what proved to be an awkward position, because British opium revenue in India was dependent on marketing the drug in China, but the people marketing the drug in China complicated the consuls' obligation to enforce the new treaty. The consuls were supposed to try and stabilize the Chinese maritime administration in order to increase the prospects of lawful trade, but yet they were also meant to support the people breaking the law. Fuzhou's first consul, Rutherford Alcock, felt it was all deeply unfair: unfair to the opium firms in China whom he viewed as "free from blame," and unfair to consuls like himself who were forced by this circumstance to absorb "no small portion of the odium attaching to the illicit traffic."[20] For consuls like Alcock, the real culprit was the Chinese purchaser and not the British seller. But for local Qing officials, the British investment in perpetuating and protecting the opium trade undermined trust in the fidelity of consuls like Alcock to the terms of the treaty.

The solution eventually agreed upon by the British and Qing officials stationed in the treaty ports was to keep the opium trade separate from the legal trade and restrict it to receiving ships anchored as far away from the inner harbors as possible. As early as 1843, Hong Kong governor Henry Pottinger wrote to the Imperial Commissioner Qiying that he had ordered British opium ships out of the inner harbor at Guangzhou and requested the cooperation of the Chinese authorities to do the same in the other treaty

MAP 2.2: Harbor limits in the treaty port of Xiamen.

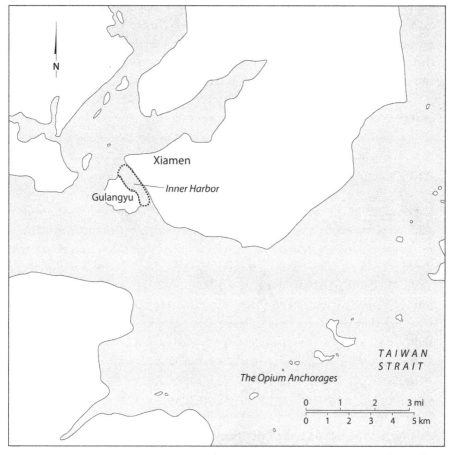

ports. Pottinger's goal, which Qiying supported, was to "separate the legal from the illegal trade," worrying that opium traders would be enticed to smuggle legal goods if they were allowed to smuggle illegal opium within the port limits.[21]

Xiamen's British consul moved against the opium ships on the very day that port was officially opened, "to avoid being the first to break the treaty."[22] He had the officers of the HMS *Serpent* board the three opium ships that had previously lain anchored "unmolested" near the inner harbor of the city and forced them to declare their manifests according to the new treaty system. The three ships, "during the night, ceased to be opium holders and entered the port with nearly empty holds, in order to be made to pay port-charges, and leave again to take back their Opium!"[23] After this point the opium ships in Xiamen anchored much further away and out of sight from the inner harbor in order to avoid this sort of trouble.

Similarly, the consul in Fuzhou issued a proclamation to British merchants in 1845 demanding that their opium trading activities be restricted to the receiving ships outside of the inner harbor. "If smuggling of opium there must be, within the limits of the port," he writes, "the Chinese are ready enough to undertake the risk of infringing their own laws, and I conceive it most important that this very questionable occupation should not be taken out of their hands by British subjects."[24] The Fuzhou receiving ships were to remain at their old station near Wuhu, where the Min River meets the ocean. Chinese transport workers like Yang Alü would shoulder the burden of carrying the drug from the foreign ships upstream to the city.

In Quanzhou and Shenhu Bay, the opium ships faced no such restrictions. Quanzhou and Shenhu Bay were "inland" ports, not treaty ports, meaning that they were only open to domestic shipping. The only oversight was from local officials long experienced in illicitly taxing the trade and minimizing its visibility to the provincial and imperial leadership. After 1843 both the Jardine and Dent firms continued to station permanent receiving ships in Shenhu and Quanzhou, an open treaty violation, in order to cater to the same group of lineage-based brokers discussed in chapter 1, who continued to ply between Fujian, Taiwan, Ningbo, and other ports to the north.[25] The illegal ships would remain there until the summer of 1861.[26]

Chinese and British officials in Xiamen tacitly supported the receiving stations in Quanzhou and Shenhu Bay despite the presence of British ships in those waters constituting a direct treaty violation. The supplementary treaty of 1843 stipulated that Qing officials were "at liberty to seize and confiscate" any British vessels calling at ports outside of the five treaty ports. Additionally, a British Order in Council mandated a fine of £100 or three-months imprisonment for any British subject who called at ports outside of Canton, Xiamen, Fuzhou, Ningbo, and Shanghai. British and Chinese officials alike were empowered and obligated to punish any British ships known to call in Shenhu Bay or Quanzhou.

Still, British ships continued to call at those ports without repercussion. British ships were anchored in Shenhu Bay and Quanzhou, in plain sight, every day for almost twenty years after the treaty was signed. Among the volumes of documents concerning treaty violations in British and Chinese archives, the gross violations of British ships permanently anchored in Quanzhou and Shenhu Bay do not figure into the discussion. When the two nontreaty ports do appear in the records, such as when one foreign seaman murdered and injured several local residents and was detained in a rural village, the presence of the illegal opium ships was not highlighted or questioned.[27] British and Chinese officials in nearby Xiamen seem to have had a mutual understanding that it was to the benefit of law, trade, and taxation in the treaty port to allow the receiving ships to remain at the Shenhu Bay and Quanzhou anchorages.

Two incidents did create some uncertainty for the extralegal opium anchorages. The first was the infamous 1847 "Chimmo" (Shenhu) Bay piracy case, wherein two well-armed lorchas, reportedly Cantonese, attacked the two receiving ships stationed in Shenhu Bay and made off with an estimated $160,000 worth of opium and cash.[28] The Jardine Matheson Company's *Omega* was holding sixty chests of Patna, forty chests of Benares, some small amount of Malwa and Turkish opium, and $40,000 in treasure; Dent's *Caroline* had forty chests of Patna, thirty-nine of Benares, and $19,000 in treasure.[29] Both ships had been sitting in their usual anchorage conducting business when the pirates struck, killing the captains of both crews and twenty-nine sailors.[30] As reported in the Singapore press, Captain Chamberlain was found dead, lying face down on the beach in Shenhu Bay and the *Caroline* was located adrift soon after. Neither Captain MacFarlane nor the *Omega* were seen again.[31]

The attack in Shenhu Bay caused an uproar in the foreign press because of the violence done to the foreign opium traders. At first, it seemed like it could be a harbinger of treaty enforcement when the local authorities in Xiamen initially responded by informing the British consul that the offshore receiving-ship system in Shenhu Bay must come to an end. The Chinese officials on the coast, suggests historian John King Fairbank, "were now ready to sacrifice their interest in the opium trade in order to avoid responsibility for piracies which they could not prevent."[32] A few of the opium ships did in fact retreat into the Xiamen harbor out of a concern for their safety. But the sentiment expressed in the Singapore press—that the core issue was "mismanagement and want of vigilance" on the part of the captains of the victimized ships—cut closer to the truth: the receiving ships had never been dependent on the Chinese authorities for protection from pirates. Perhaps they had simply gotten too complacent. The opium ships re-armed themselves, the Shenhu Bay anchorage was back in full swing by midsummer, and the Xiamen authorities did not see fit to protest the violation again. The piratical attack ultimately had no long-term effects on the import markets in Shenhu Bay or Quanzhou.

The second time the Shenhu and Quanzhou anchorages were threatened with official intervention was in 1855–1856, and it was because of rice smuggling and not opium. Rice was a branch of commerce that was highly sensitive to Qing administrators in southern Fujian, where grain supply was one of the major logistical challenges of governance in the land-poor region, a delicate matter of state security. Brokers in Shenhu Bay and Quanzhou had long worked with the Fujian authorities to import rice from Southeast Asia and Taiwan to help ensure that the overpopulated coastal region would avoid famine. But in 1855 when rice became expensive in ports to the north due to the Taiping crisis, British and Chinese merchants alike realized they could reap good profits by reexporting the rice intended for Fujian.

Jardine Matheson's Captain Fitzgibbon and a Xiamen merchant called Eamak were among the first opium traders to use this circumstance to their advantage, arranging with brokers in Shenhu and Quanzhou to exchange opium for rice, in direct contravention of strict official bans on the transshipment of rice out of the Quanzhou region.[33] Soon after, merchants from Dent, Tait, and other foreign houses were sending boats full of silver and opium up to Shenhu and Quanzhou to try and purchase rice for reexport.[34] Tait's representative paid cash, while Jardine and Dent's agents paid in opium at a discount of $10 per chest.[35] The flurry of activity quickly caught the attention of Xiamen's Maritime Defense sub-prefect, who promptly arrested several Chinese brokers. The same week the arrests took place the price of rice had jumped from $2.00 per picul to $3.30.[36] Authorities who had ignored the illegal anchorage and the illegal opium trade began to intervene over the unauthorized export of grain. But the trend was temporary, a function of Taiping-related grain shortages in the north, and official concern over the foreign ships in Shenhu and Quanzhou again fizzled out.

THE GRADUAL EXCLUSION OF THE BRITISH

British legal trade in the two Fujianese treaty ports after 1843 did not live up to expectations, though there was some mild optimism in British circles that the extralegal opium trade would more than make up for lost profits. When it came to legal imports—cotton goods primarily, but also South-east Asian produce (like swallows' nests and aromatics), ginseng, kerosene, and various metals—China was simply not the inexhaustible market the British had hoped. More to the point, Chinese merchants already had a corner on many of those markets. During 1852, British merchants imported £327,437 worth of legal goods into Xiamen alongside an estimated £451,137 worth of opium. During 1853, when the market was disturbed by the Small Sword uprising, the British imported just £115,108 worth of legal goods, yet managed still to sell off an estimated £315,600 in opium.[37] "It seems very certain," wrote one consul, "that the demand for this drug does at this moment, and probably may always, far exceed that for manufactured goods of every description." [38]

The consul's optimism about the future of the opium trade ignored a visible trend in who was actually importing and profiting from the opium. The British Empire as a totality had much to gain from the increased volume of the opium trade, but a picture of the opium business in intertreaty Fujian suggests that those gains must have been experienced elsewhere. In southern Fujian, firms like Jardine Matheson and Dent clung desperately to a constantly shrinking corner of the market as local Chinese merchants took on greater and greater shares of the opium import business. One slice of evidence to this effect are the mid-1850s business reports of Jardine's agent in Xiamen, recording opium sales and stocks in the port for the five major foreign firms (Jardine Matheson, Dent, Tait, Elles, Nandershaw) and a loose collection of local figures whom he called the "China brokers."[39] Each month, Jardine's employee documented how the "China brokers" outsold their foreign competitors, often by a wide margin.[40] The "China brokers" also controlled the vast majority of opium stocks in the port, such as in August of 1854 when they possessed 630 chests of Benares opium while the next-highest holder was Dent's receiving ship the *Lord Amherst* at just 81 chests.[41] Even in Shenhu Bay and Quanzhou, where foreign receiving ships found enough business to remain in place until the early 1860s, the British faced fierce competition from dealers in Xiamen who consistently undercut their prices.[42]

Other fleeting evidence suggests that a good deal of opium was entering China through channels that were not controlled or even monitored by the British. No data exists that could enable us to accurately estimate the amount of opium brought into Fujian on Chinese shipping from Singapore and other places in Southeast Asia, but it was by all accounts a substantial and mostly unquantified portion of the imports.[43] Jardine's representative mentions offhand in an 1852 business letter, for example, that a local vessel had just arrived in Quanzhou from Singapore with 275 chests of opium for the local Chinese brokers.[44] There was a fleet of Fujianese ships plying between Xiamen and Southeast Asia, carrying commodities and people back and forth. More than 3,000 people traveled on Chinese ships to Singapore each year during the early 1850s.[45] Given this growing traffic between Xiamen and colonial Southeast Asia, it is reasonable to assume that like the 1852 ship noted by the Jardine employee, other vessels too carried opium on their return voyages, as one could purchase the drug more cheaply in Singapore than after its transport to China.[46] Opium does not take up much cargo space in comparison with cheaper items like rice, tea, or textiles, and adding a few balls or chests of opium (or a few hundred) to a ship's cargo would have been a commonsense choice for many of the merchants and migrants traversing annually between China and Singapore.

Import substitution was also beginning to impact the opium business. Opium poppy cultivation in China extends back long before the 1850s, but in the earliest years it happened mostly in the highland southwest frontier.[47] When the opium import and reexport business in southeast China took off during the 1830s–1860s, the residents of Tong'an county and other areas of the littoral also began experimenting in cultivating opium.[48] According to a report from 1850, a collection of thirty to forty villages in Tong'an county produced $2,500,000 worth of opium during the previous year, or the equivalent of 12,500 chests, nearly twice the amount of Indian opium brought into Fujian that year. The local drug was said to induce headaches, but entrepreneurs in Xiamen apparently purchased massive amounts of the Tong'an opium to mix with Indian opium for transport to other parts of China for resale.[49] A shadow market hidden behind a slightly more tangible shadow market, the nature of the domestic opium business in this period is impossible to fully appreciate. What is clear: domestic opium further saturated the market, and it created new and different opportunities for the people who made their living by selling the drug.

LABOR AND VIOLENCE IN THE INTERTREATY
FUJIAN OPIUM TRADE

As the opium business expanded in a realm of negotiated illegality, violence remained a central feature of the commercial landscape. Much of the evidence surrounding the role of labor in the opium trade during these years points towards individuals who were hired to perpetuate or protect against violence, the consequence of a self-inflicted administrative blindfolding. This was an unregulated and extraordinarily lucrative marketplace. Force and intimidation were acceptable methods to grow and protect a business. In later years, as discussed in chapter 3, the shift from prohibition to taxation would not end the violence associated with the trade, as state actors exerted their own violent sovereignty over drug profits and new smuggling opportunities emerged in the moving of opium between tax jurisdictions.

When the treaty port system was first launched, gangs of young men banded together to transport opium from the coast into the interior, often with people hired on specifically for their fighting ability. One of the more well-documented examples of this comes out of an expansive series of arrests that took place in the borderland region connecting Fujian, Guangdong, and Jiangxi provinces.[50] The case, referenced in the opening passage of the introduction to this book, originated when the Jiangxi authorities captured 167 people involved in an opium transport organization called the "Red Society" (*honghui*) in the autumn of 1840. The group was founded by an opium dealer from eastern Guangdong named Jiang Ahua and a renowned Fujianese martial artist named Li Zhengchang, who together organized and armed teams of men in order to monopolize and protect the transport of opium from the coast into the highland districts in the Fujian, Jiangxi, and Guangdong hinterland.

The Red Society is an early example of a formalized, systematized, and violent transport monopoly system for opium. The organization's structure and terminology presage the notorious opium *lijin* institutions that dominated the region in later years (see chapter 3). Other clues from this earlier moment also point to a similar early connection between the labor of opium transport and violence. One British consul, describing the transport of opium overland from the Quanzhou anchorages to Fuzhou, wrote of the need for opium dealers to hire groups of young men to protect the trade against banditry. "When transported overland in any large quantity," he writes, "a company or caravan club together for the purpose and travel well-armed, not from any fear of the Government taking legal measures against them, but on account of apprehended attacks from robbers to whom the value of the drug forms a strong attraction."[51] After the local government in Xiamen formalized an opium tax in 1859 (discussed below), the British consul in Xiamen reprimanded Jardine Matheson for assisting Chinese smugglers in evading the tax by providing them with armed escorts.[52] There was precedent for this kind of arrangement, as in the Yang Alü case that opened this chapter, which involved the hire of foreign gunmen to protect shipments of opium on the Min River.[53]

The foreign receiving ships and the waters around them were also a key site for violence in these years. Pirates hid out near the ships, seeking out opportunities to capture the silver and opium stored below decks. Only occasionally did they attack the receiving ships themselves, as happened in Shenhu Bay during February of 1847. More often, opportunistic parties would focus their attacks on the Chinese purchasers paddling small boats to and from the ships, as in January of 1857 when a "piratical village" on an island near the Quanzhou anchorage launched a flurry of raids on the city's opium brokers, capturing and attempting to ransom twelve men and a chest of opium.[54] The attacks brought competitors together as a unified force, with Dent and Jardine representatives sending joint expeditions into the village to recover the stolen opium and kidnapped boatmen.

Accounts of the receiving ships often shift abruptly between quotidian life and extreme violence. The 1848 travelogue of American dentist B. L. Ball offers a detailed portrait of Fujian's receiving-ship stations. In Xiamen, at the six-islands anchorage on the outer reaches of the harbor, he describes the receiving-ship *Pathfinder* as "like a fine house on shore, instead of a ship in the water," containing multiple staterooms and creature comforts. In Quanzhou the representatives of the competing opium firms lived a pastoral existence. They dined together each night, enjoying evening horseback rides along the beach "for exercise and recreation," hunting fowl and working together to maintain "a small yard, in which they raise livestock for their own use. We looked in, and saw quite a variety; hogs, sheep, goats, geese, ducks, chickens, pigeons, and monkeys."[55] When Ball got chilly, not having packed warm clothes, there was no problem finding a local tailor to come on board and make him some thicker clothing out of the locally popular coarse blue cotton cloth. From these descriptions alone, one would hardly know that this was an illegal anchorage set up for the carrying out of a criminal enterprise.

Yet Ball's account also highlights the heightened role of violence in the receiving-ship life during the intertreaty period. The Shenhu Bay piracy of 1847 was fresh in the minds of all of the opium merchants he encountered. On the *Pathfinder*, Ball was introduced to a sailor who claimed to be the sole survivor of that terrifying episode. Surely trying to impress the reader with the danger he invited by visiting the opium ships, Ball dwells on the military capacity of the receiving ships:

> Several guns are kept on deck, constantly loaded with grape-shot and cannon-balls, and even primed and pointing out of the port-holes. There is also a rack of muskets, swords and hatchets; and the muskets are kept loaded. In each of the tops, some forty feet from the deck, are stands of muskets and ammunition; so that, should they be driven to the rigging during a conflict, the firing may be directed from thence to the deck. Around the outside of the vessel is a rope net-work, to prevent the ship's being boarded in a sudden attack, and to keep out robbers at night.[56]

In Quanzhou, Ball writes how the captain of the *Louisa* conducted regular training exercises, having his men shoot muskets at a bottle thrown in the water, or fire the cannon at a buoy from a few hundred yards.[57] Near Fuzhou, at the anchorage in the mouth of the Min River, he gives an account of a boat trip up the Min from the opium ships to Fuzhou that evokes the same chilling anxiety that caused men like Yang Alü to hire foreign gunmen for their journeys along that river. "Towards dark," he writes, the boatmen "fixed their rough guns and matchlocks into the sides of the boat, and lighted their matches. I could see no reason for this movement . . . but I presumed it was not the sight of pirates, but the anticipation of their sudden appearance."[58]

Of course, the captains and crews of the receiving ships like those that Ball described were also known to perpetuate violence in their own right. In one particularly gruesome case from 1856, a group of sailors on liberty from the opium ship *Independence* wandered into a village near Quanzhou. They got drunk, stumbling into a crowd of locals who were watching an opera, and a fight broke out. A Malay sailor was "thrown into a paroxysm of fury," and "he drew a table knife with which he cut and stabbed at whatever came within his reach."[59] When all was said and done, the sailor had severely injured a man and his child, lightly wounded three others, and a child of just ten years lay dead with stab wounds in the abdomen and hip. Another of the ship's crew had also brandished a weapon, though it seems he did so in self-defense and injured nobody. The village authorities put the two sailors in custody and got word back to Captain Thompson of the *Independence* of the actions of his men. Thompson had been hired by a local businessman known as Amah, owner of the *Independence*. Thompson notified his boss, who promptly traveled to the village and paid $300 for the release of the two sailors.

The Quanzhou anchorage existed outside of the treaty port system, but officials in Xiamen nonetheless sought to exert jurisdiction over the case. Why the *Independence* was illegally anchored in Quanzhou in the first place was a subject that both governments politely ignored. The British consul in Xiamen, about 100 km to the southwest, wanted to visit the village to inspect the wounded parties and collect evidence and requested permission from the circuit intendant (*daotai*) in Xiamen, as British residents of the port were prohibited by treaty from visiting locations in the interior. The circuit intendant refused the consul's request on the grounds that it might be dangerous, but the consul disobeyed him and traveled with Captain Fitzgibbon of the Jardine Matheson opium ship *Harlequin* to the village to investigate. The British consul found no ready witnesses, however, as the villagers had likely understood that the $300 they had been paid for the release of the sailors was hush money. Unable to obtain sufficient evidence to substantiate more than a minor charge, the consul sentenced the sailor to twelve months imprisonment at Hong Kong for "unlawfully and maliciously stabbing and wounding sundry Chinese."[60]

In their efforts to hold the British to the treaty, Chinese officials in Xiamen routinely cited violence as the reason the British should stay within the geographical limits of the treaty port. They sought to convince the British consuls that local people in the surrounding area were dangerous, especially when put into contact with the crew and sailors of the receiving ships. "The people living along our coast are prone to insult and abuse the ignorant," wrote Imperial Commissioner Qiying, over a decade before the stabbing incident near Quanzhou. "Now the black sailors on board your ships are by nature ignorant and fond of liquor, they should in no account be permitted to go on shore to drink and get intoxicated lest they will be ill used by our people."[61] In early 1844 the Xiamen circuit intendant had written to the consul that he was anxious for the safety of British people who might try to connive with the people living along the southern Fujian coast, "being in their nature and customs said to be violent and brave." If foreigners travel to places outside of the treaty port, he suggested, "the villagers may assemble around them and collect together to see them causing uproar and rude assembly . . . [and] stones and tiles may be thrown."[62]

In Fuzhou, there was also a great deal of violence surrounding the opium trade, both on the Min River and in the city itself. Small crews of bandits snaked between the steep mountains crowding the riverbank on both sides, ambushing unsuspecting parties on moonless nights and escaping back to their villages through a maze of creeks and inlets. The attack of Lin Wenwen on the transport operation of Yang Alü is just one of many examples of this. In fact, just weeks before Lin's attempted robbery a pair of foreign clergymen were also ambushed on the Min while traveling in a boat that was carrying fourteen chests of opium and a suitcase of cash. The Swedish missionary A. Elquist made a soggy escape, and his partner Reverend J. C. Fast died after suffering a spear wound to the head.[63]

Within the city, the violence endemic to the opium business was often expressed along the fault lines of native place affiliation, and opium sharpened the already tense divisions between southern Fujianese, Cantonese, and Fuzhou natives. British merchants in the provincial capital of Fuzhou had a more difficult time hiring local translators and other employees than their counterparts in Xiamen, and they usually avoided hiring locals and instead relied on Cantonese and southern Fujianese migrants as translators, compradors, and household staff.[64] In the Yang Alü case, a southern Fujianese migrant battled a group of local *dan* people (a sub-ethnic group who lived on boats in the Min River). Captain Roose of Jardine Matheson reported a similar incident, wherein a recently arrived group of Cantonese merchants started a fight with the "old brokers," in an attempt to chase them out of port and steal their business. Two men were seriously injured, and the local government took steps to banish the offending Cantonese newcomers.[65]

Riots were a regular occurrence during these years on Nantai, the large island in the Min River to the south of the walled city of Fuzhou where the Cantonese, southern Fujianese, American, and British mercantile communities lived and ran their businesses. These riots were often sparked by petty conflicts between the southern Fujianese and Cantonese employees of foreign firms, such as the massive fight that broke out in December of 1855 after a Fujianese carpenter accidentally knocked down a Cantonese employee of Russell & Company, or the brawl of July 1856 that broke out when a Fujianese man picked up a potato spilled from the shoulder-pole of a Cantonese employee of Augustine Heard & Company.[66] In 1859–1860, violence between Cantonese and Quanzhou natives in Fuzhou escalated to a boiling point after a boat collision. The Cantonese coalition brought in over twenty ships to bombard the Quanzhou residences on Zhongzhou Island (next to Nantai), and the local government responded with what Consul Medhurst referred to as the "barbarous execution" of dozens of Cantonese merchants.[67]

Opium Taxation and the Roads Not Taken

From an administrative perspective, violence was not the only problem stemming from the formally illegal status of the intertreaty opium trade. Opium's questionable legality also hindered efforts to tax both the drug itself as well as legal commerce in items other than opium. For example, in early 1845, just over a year after Xiamen was officially opened to British commerce, the Fujian Military Commander (*jiangjun*) reported on possible collusion between dangerous local elements and the foreign ships visiting the newly opened port.[68] These "treacherous" locals had built smuggling boats in advance of Xiamen's opening. When the foreign ships arrived, they arranged offshore meetings to do business tax-free outside of the treaty port.

The report does not mention opium—these were people accused of defrauding the revenue on legal trade—but the trend was a function of the receiving-ship system. By 1850, one British consul estimated that an annual trade in legal items to the value of £100,000–200,000 was smuggled into Xiamen through the opium ships stationed outside of the inner port.[69] Meanwhile, the continued vitality of the Quanzhou and Shenhu receiving-ship stations stemmed in part from their ability to facilitate the transshipment of Taiwanese camphor to Southeast Asia without paying the export tax at Xiamen.[70] Allowing foreign ships to remain permanently stationed outside the treaty ports in order to sell the illegal drug was hindering efforts to tax the trade on legal goods, just as Pottinger and Qiying had worried.

THE BRITISH TAX FARMERS OF XIAMEN

After more than a decade of negotiated illegality, local officials in Fuzhou and Xiamen decided to introduce formal taxes on opium's import into the treaty ports during the summer and autumn of 1857.[71] The process began in Shanghai, where local authorities were the first to openly collect an import tax on opium.[72] The decision in Shanghai set off a chain reaction, and officials in Fuzhou watched to see if the Shanghai authorities would be punished or censured by Beijing for disobeying existing prohibitions on the opium trade. When it seemed safe, the Fuzhou officials too moved to tax the drug. And about six months after Fuzhou's authorities decided to institute an import tax on opium, their counterparts in Xiamen decided it was safe for them to do the same.

The Fuzhou authorities were determined not to include the British in the process of the opium import tax collection. In Shanghai, the decision to openly tax opium happened only after the pilot launch of a foreign-run Maritime Customs had met with some moderate success. An interpreter at the British consulate in Fuzhou, desiring to bring a foreign-run inspectorate of customs to his port, volunteered his services to the Fujian provincial authorities to act as inspector of customs. His supervisor at the consulate repeatedly tried to convince the Fuzhou authorities to accept the proposal, arguing that "they were actually being duped out of an alarming portion of their export revenue [on tea]."[73] But the Qing officials in Fuzhou refused the offer.

Instead, they decided to continue collecting import and export taxes through the existing Maritime Customs infrastructure and would approach the taxation of opium by farming the collection out to the Chinese compradors working for foreign firms on the opium ships. Their plan was to catch the drug while it was still warehoused on the opium hulks, rather than try and track down individual Chinese buyers and ask them to pay the levy. "When distributed from [the opium ships at the mouth of the Min River] to the various Chinese merchants," wrote the superintendent of trade in Fuzhou, "it passes into so many hands and is divided into such small and irregular quantities, that inspection (with a view to the collection of the import) would at that time be attended with great difficulty, and would probably leave the way open for grave irregularities."[74] The British consul in Fuzhou strongly objected to the superintendent's proposal to delegate taxation responsibility to the Chinese compradors, pointing out that the British opium firms "dislike and are disposed to resist any interference with their own servants."[75]

The initial attempts to tax opium in Fuzhou were a complete failure, not necessarily because of the tax farming scheme, but because the superintendent attempted to impose a rate of taxation four times what was being collected in the other treaty ports. He wished to charge $48 per chest in Fuzhou, as compared to $12 in Shanghai and Ningbo. As a British consul protested, with prescience, the "exorbitant rate of $48 per chest will defeat the very object that the Mandarins have in view; and instead of raising a revenue by opium they will drive the trade elsewhere, especially as there are so many points north and south of the river Min, where the drug might be easily imported free of duty."[76] By mid-June of 1857, about a month after the proposed tax was instituted, Jardine Matheson's agent in Fuzhou reported that the Chinese opium brokers had all closed their shops in protest of the high rate of taxation.[77] Two years later, when Beijing finally rubber-stamped the Fuzhou government's proposal to tax opium, the rate increased further to around $90 per chest.[78] As I discuss at length in chapter 3, Fuzhou's unusually high taxes on opium continued into the age of de facto legalization, driving the trade back underground and to other ports.

When the Xiamen authorities dealt with the problem next, they decided to forego Fuzhou's plan to use the compradors and dispatched government officers to collect opium import fees directly from purchasers in the harbor.[79] When the tax was announced in November of 1857, the city's opium brokers immediately began stockpiling the drug in advance of the launch date, as Jardine Matheson and the other firms lowered prices to take advantage of the inflated market.[80] The rush was unwarranted, however, as this first attempt by the Xiamen authorities was toothless and overly complex, and garnered poor results. The plan was for purchasers to first negotiate the price, then go to a government office to report the details of the transaction and purchase a tax stamp, then take the stamp out to the opium ships to affix to the opium as it was unloaded into their possession, which they could then use to pass through government checkpoints.[81] The details are hazy, but it seems as though nobody felt compelled to bother with the new rules. Five months after the tax was inaugurated, the Xiamen circuit intendent issued another proclamation identical to the original.[82] The opium merchants, Chinese and foreign, continued to ignore him.

A plan to rearrange the system of collection and turn the British opium firms into tax farmers began to take shape in the spring of 1859, after over a year of disappointing results for the Xiamen authorities. Xiamen's circuit intendant approached the largest British firms, Jardine Matheson and Dent & Company, and requested they assume the responsibility for the entire community and pay taxes on a monthly quota of 150 chests.[83] Because the monthly imports of the two firms was much greater than this, around 300 chests, Jardine and Dent jumped on the opportunity. It was not to be, however, as the other foreign opium houses in Xiamen—Syme, Tait, Nandershaw, and Elles—protested the plan on the grounds that it "would have the effect of giving to those houses the monopoly of the opium trade at this port, to our manifest detriment."[84] The circuit intendant went back to the drawing board, all the while watching untaxed opium enter his city. In August, he proposed that the six major British opium merchants "should guarantee the payment of the duty ($48 per chest) on 2000 chests per year, or 166 chests per month, they levying the duty on the Chinese purchaser and dividing between them all over the above quantity sold."[85] The British merchants refused outright, but their consul found the proposal intriguing and began lobbying the opium merchants to reconsider.

It took over two months of negotiations for the British merchants to finally work out a tax farming arrangement with the Xiamen circuit intendant. The attraction of the scheme to the opium merchants was that, if the foreign firms collected taxes on every chest sold but only had to pay the circuit intendant on the monthly quota (say 150 chests), then taxes on the remaining chests of opium amounting to an estimated $48,000 could be split among the firms. This is the basic principle of tax farming, and similar arrangements characterized the opium *lijin* farms of the late nineteenth century (see chapter 3), as well as the famous opium farms of colonial Southeast Asia.[86] In this case, the Dent and Tait firms were quickly sold on the idea, but Jardine's Captain Fitzgibbon protested that Chinese, Portuguese, and German merchants would take advantage of the British firms finding their "hands tied with this duty" and would respond by smuggling the drug in tax free.[87] Fitzgibbon's real game, however, was to try and further reduce the quota. By late August Fitzgibbon had the circuit intendant down to 120 chests per month, but he still wasn't satisfied, continuing to insist that there would "be great difficulties in collecting it, and it would lead to smuggling by foreigners and Chinese from the Straits."[88] A week later he wrote, with a certain amount of relish, that "it is hoped that the protracted resistance of the boat people and dealers will induce the authorities to desist in their attempts at levying the tax"[89] The coalition of firms continued to discuss the proposal, however, and by late September they were again trying to negotiate the quota down to 100 chests.[90]

The ultimate proposal was finally drafted in October, and against all odds the British opium merchants of Xiamen became tax farmers for the Qing state, if only for a brief moment. A coalition of the six opium firms—Jardine Matheson, Dent, Tait, Nandershaw, Syme, and Elles—agreed to pay the Xiamen authorities a tax of $48 per chest on no more than 100 chests per month, or $4,800 per month.[91] The agreement empowered the firms to protect the revenue with violence, vesting them "with full power to adopt such measures as may appear to them requisite for the prevention of smuggling," and "prevent smuggling in every way that lies in their power."[92] The Jardine Matheson firm managers in Hong Kong were the last holdouts, and Jardine finally wrote back on October 11 in acquiescence.[93] The three-month trial period began and ended with little fuss.

Xiamen's brief tax-farming arrangement was a historical anomaly, blending together Chinese and British commercial and administrative culture in a way that would look quite different from the foreign-managed Chinese Maritime Customs that took over the opium import tax after 1861. This is not to imply that tax farming was an inherently Chinese practice: after all, the British and Dutch used tax farms extensively in their Asian colonies. The French too had used a tax farming system to handle American tobacco and Indian calico imports during the eighteenth century.[94] But the collusion of British merchants and the Qing state in an opium tax farming system is nonetheless surprising when we look back on the overall trajectory of the British imperial project in China and the eventual role of the Chinese Maritime Customs in creating a centralized bureaucracy for the collection of the opium import tax. This was a road not taken, but to the opium merchants and government officials stationed on the Fujian coast in the late 1850s, for a brief moment it symbolized the future of the opium trade.

THE "INLAND PORTS" AND OPIUM TAXATION

When the Xiamen circuit intendant originally launched that port's opium tax in 1857, he also opened a satellite office to collect the tax on the receiving-ships illegally anchored in the "inland ports" (i.e. nontreaty ports) of Quanzhou and Shenhu Bay. Prior to this order, opium sold from the receiving ships in Shenhu and Quanzhou paid a much lower fee of $1.50 per chest to an unnamed local official, most likely the Quanzhou prefect.[95] This was going to be different: the tax would go to Xiamen, not Quanzhou. The circuit intendant in Xiamen wrote the British consul "to order the masters of foreign ships" in the Quanzhou region "to throw no obstacle in the way of the Inspecting officers, and moreover not to enter into private contracts for the sale or delivery of opium with native dealers."[96] Intriguingly, the opium merchants in Quanzhou ignored the circuit intendant, continuing to pay the Quanzhou prefect instead. In the summer of 1859, the Quanzhou prefect even sent a letter to Robert Jardine praising him for his positive response to the local government's efforts to collect taxes on the drug and granting the firm approval to station ships in the Quanzhou harbor in perpetuity.[97]

The circuit intendant in Xiamen was determined, however, to capture the revenue from the inland ports north of the treaty port. Exactly one month before the Quanzhou prefect wrote his letter to Jardine praising the Quanzhou opium traders and promising their continued access to the harbor, the circuit intendant began pressuring the British consul in Xiamen to order the receiving ships out of Quanzhou. The consul complied and issued a circular stating that the circuit intendant had just informed him (as if both officials were not already aware) that there were British ships anchored in the Quanzhou harbor selling opium and going ashore to hunt and buy supplies. The circuit intendant was now, finally, ordering the ships out of Quanzhou and Shenhu Bay.[98] The pressing issue was not the treaty violation—which had been going on for nearly two decades without protest—but rather his collection of the new opium tax in Xiamen, which was jeopardized by these alternate sites of import.

Nobody was on the same page about what to do. The captain of the Jardine Matheson vessel *Adventure* believed that the provincial authorities in Fuzhou had in fact approved the continuation of the Quanzhou opium trade along previous lines (i.e., with fees going to the Quanzhou prefect). A government officer who had visited the foreign ships wrote "to inform us that by the order of the Viceroy of Foo Chow a duty on opium was to be levied at this place and that boats would be sent out for that purpose today. There are 3 boats now stationed here and are now collecting $27 per chest."[99] Within a week the captain then received contradictory advice about the legality of his position in Quanzhou. First, in early August, the British consul in Xiamen reforwarded his circular from June to the effect that in the Xiamen authorities intended on clearing all British ships out of the Quanzhou harbor, and the British government could offer no assistance to the opium ships if they put up resistance.[100] But the circular was delivered overland, through intermediaries in the Quanzhou prefect's office, who conveyed the message while also reassuring the captain that "the Taotai of Amoy has no control over this place, that whilst we hold their grand chop [the seal of the Quanzhou prefect] no danger can incur the vessels."[101] The Xiamen authorities wanted to end the Quanzhou trade, but the Quanzhou authorities had clearly received support from higher-ups in the provincial government to allow the ships to remain in their anchorages.

The Quanzhou authorities won out in the short term. Neither the British Foreign Office archive nor the Chinese archives mention the Quanzhou opium ships after the 1859 circular demanding their removal, but Jardine Matheson sources indicate that the ships remained on for three more years with a tax officer from the Quanzhou prefect stationed on board to collect an import tax of $40 per chest from the purchaser.[102] In the final Jardine Matheson dispatch from Quanzhou, during April of 1862, the captain reported having sold fifty-seven chests of opium after renegotiating the tax down to $35 per chest.[103] Later that year, Jardine's agent in Xiamen noted that the *Vindix* and three other ships had recently unloaded 130 chests of opium to brokers in Quanzhou.[104] By that point, it seems Quanzhou was no longer a permanent and independent station, but much more of an extension of the Xiamen market.

Fiscal Crisis and the Opium Business in Intertreaty Xiamen

Contestation over opium taxes during this period should be understood within the context of acute financial crisis and domestic unrest. Chinese records suggest that British demands on Chinese officials were, as historian John King Fairbank writes, "far less important than the domestic affairs of an empire heading into a great rebellion."[105] Fairbank's account underplays the devastating effect of the $21 million indemnity foisted upon the Qing state as a result of the Treaty of Nanjing, but he was right to note that administration of the new treaty ports should not be viewed in isolation from the problems generated by rebellion. Unrest elsewhere in the empire (especially the Taiping rebellion 1850–1864) and locally (the Xiamen Small Sword uprising of 1853–1854, and the Lin Jun uprising in Taiwan three years later) created new revenue demands for the already cash-poor Fujian provincial government, further redirecting state resources to quash rebellion.

The Taiping rebellion erupted just as previously reliable sources of revenue disappeared. For local officials in jurisdictions where the primary industry was seafaring, a key revenue source had been the "inland merchant tax" (*neidi shangshui*), a duty on Chinese-owned bottoms (boats) when entering and leaving port. Fujian's officials struggled to meet their quotas on this tax throughout the 1840s and 1850s. In 1843, the Fujian authorities were several thousand taels short of the inland merchant tax quota of 96,549.[106] The following year they came up 19,022 taels short.[107] Such shortages were chronic during these years. New taxes on foreign ships were implemented, but the taxes collected from foreign ships in the treaty ports were forwarded directly to Guangzhou rather than retained locally. When local merchants shipped their cargo on foreign ships, the tax revenue was thus redirected from local administrative budgets to the Maritime Customs headquarters in Guangzhou. For Fujian's officials, the loss of these funds created new constraints in an era of already stretched administrative capacity.

Officials stationed in Fujian were keen to call attention to the challenges they experienced while implementing the new treaty system. In 1844, the new governor-general of Fujian and Zhejiang laid out the reasons for the failures in revenue collection during the first year of the treaty port system.[108] First, he suggested that fighting in Xiamen during the Opium War had taken a serious toll on the local merchant population. The British attackers had destroyed boats, merchants had lost fortunes, and trade patterns remained disrupted as a result. Five years after the war passed through Fujian, Xiamen's merchants possessed just one-tenth of their earlier wealth. Second, he pointed out that the import taxes paid by foreigners were forwarded to Guangzhou. Previously, when Fujian's merchants had imported cotton from Jiangnan and Southeast Asian produce, it had been on Chinese-owned boats and the tax revenue had stayed in local coffers. With the trade now being done on foreign bottoms, the revenue stream was diverted outside of local control.

Finally, the governor-general gave a geographical explanation for Fujian's decline that mirrors my earlier narrative of the decline of Fujian's role in the national opium trade. Before the opening of the treaty ports, tax revenue in

Fujian had benefited from the province's strategic location as a distributing hub for the Canton trade. Southern Fujianese merchants, as discussed in chapter 1, made their living by connecting north and central China with the global marketplace in Guangdong and Southeast Asia. But now, after Ningbo and Shanghai were opened to foreign commerce, Fujianese merchants lost their special geographic advantage. Once Shanghai was open to British shipping, for example, it became much cheaper for merchants in Shanghai to serve a northern port like Tianjin than for Fujianese merchants to take the goods all the way up from the southeast coast.[109]

Fiscal challenges were made worse by the growing reliance on British shipping among Chinese merchants, which further shifted tax revenue out of local government coffers. In 1833 there had been 303 large and small sailboats licensed and operating in Xiamen; by 1850 there were only 83.[110] Chinese merchants were choosing to ship goods in well-armed British ships rather than take the risk of using smaller Chinese-owned boats, thanks in part to a new wave of piracy along the coast. Steamers were also more reliable, not having to rely on the winds. Chinese officials recognized this problem as early as 1851, when Fujian's governor-general suggested that the only way to undercut the growing use of British steam convoys was to invest in the coastal military and improve maritime security.[111]

Tong'an county businessmen Lew She-kwan and Tsing Leen-kwan were two such merchants who, like many of their contemporaries, decided that British shipping was a safer bet. In 1854 they appealed to the British consul in Xiamen for legal assistance when the superintendent of trade in Ningbo caught them transporting sugar out of Xiamen on the British brig *Kitty*. They had paid the foreign trade export tax in Xiamen, instead of the domestic customs tariff they had been accustomed to pay, choosing the British brig because the coast was "still so unsafe from pirates."[112] The growing preference of merchants like Lew and Tsing to use British shipping at the dawn of the treaty port era was to have enormous (though unintended) consequences for local government. The shift to British shipping destabilized local society by removing a key source of revenue for local officials and potentially reducing employment opportunities for coastal Chinese (although many seamen on the steamers were also Chinese).

Local uprisings also decimated Fujian's administrative capacity in the early treaty port era. During the Small Sword uprising, when rebel forces captured Xiamen for around six months in 1853, domestic customs revenue fell to 50 percent short of its quota.[113] Chinese merchants within the port closed their shops and sought refuge in the offices and warehouses of foreign firms, and coastal traders became increasingly prone to avoid the dangerous Taiwan Strait while Fujian's naval garrison was tied up with the rebellion.[114]

In addition to scaring off commerce, the rebels also stole some of the taxes that the Qing state collected. During the summer of 1853, the Small Sword rebels managed to capture around 10 percent of that year's foreign trade tax revenue, $6,648, through raiding customs houses and government offices.[115] By midsummer, the rebels were collecting their own opium tax on imports from the Quanzhou receiving ships.[116] In Xiamen where government offices and the customs house were burned down, the rebels were careful to keep a distance from foreign property.[117] Unable to sell opium once their Chinese buyers had fled the city, the British turned to other trades that summer. "Gunpowder, and saltpeter, also a few large guns, has been disposed of during the month to both imperialists and rebels," wrote Jardine's agent in Xiamen at the height of the occupation.[118] The uprising lasted until early November, effectively cutting off an entire season of revenue for the local government while causing untold damage to commercial and administrative infrastructure.

It makes sense that officials turned more and more to opium as older sources of revenue became depleted and as waves of rebellion shook the foundations of the state and dried up sources of commercial capital. Opium was reliable in an unreliable world. If anything could solve the problems of the embattled Qing territorial administration, it was more money. And here was a lucrative branch of trade, growing each year, impervious to the disruptions of war, rebellion, and piracy, and with a seemingly insatiable market.

Conclusion: The End of an Era

Opium's legalization was a gradual process, a winding collection of pathways that was ultimately paved over by the bold insertion of a provision in the Treaty of Tianjin calling for a tariff convention that would place an import tax on the drug. Local officials in Fujian had been drawing both personal profit and state revenue from the drug for decades, informally before 1857 and after that as a legitimate item of commerce. Part of the value of focusing on Fujian rather than taking a wider view is that offers a sense of how little the grand story of national policy and diplomacy mattered on the ground during these uncertain years. The Arrow War (or second Opium War, 1856–1860) barely registers in the documents from Fujian, where officials had been experimenting with different ways of taxing opium for several years by the time the Treaty of Tianjin was signed and the court authorized the Board of Revenue (*hubu*) to collect an import tax on the foreign drug. The Treaty of Tianjin and the tariff convention that followed did not introduce an opium tax in Fujian, they simply formalized and re-structured the existing one.

The receiving-ship system for importing opium lasted two decades longer than it otherwise might have. It was not until after 1860 that the opium trade fully abandoned the leaky, aging hulks anchored across the south China littoral and found its way into steamships and warehouses in the treaty ports themselves. The de facto legalization of the opium trade after 1860 was of course the most important reason for this, alongside the expansion of a foreign inspectorate of customs to all of the treaty ports and the emergence of steamship dominance over the carrying trade. Just when foreign firms like Jardine Matheson were being encouraged to aban-don their old smuggling stations and enter their drug cargoes into the tax books, the brokers they had been dealing with along the maritime frontier were losing their edge in the transport trade. Opium purchases which had been dispersed among the many ship owners and lineage-based merchants along the coast were becoming increasingly concentrated among large firms based in the treaty ports, and the drug was being shipped in ever-larger consignments in the holds of ironclad steamships.

The brokers that held out in Shenhu and Quanzhou were already becom-ing increasingly marginalized by the 1840s. When British opium merchants first arrived in Fujian, the Shenhu and Quanzhou brokers dominated the opium business, controlling shipments of the drug to ports north of Fujian, places like Ningbo and Shanghai that were in 1843 opened to direct foreign commerce. After the treaty ports opened to direct foreign trade, the coastal transport network that supported the enormous purchases of the Shenhu and Quanzhou brokers did not immediately disappear. Jardine's agent in Quanzhou, for example, reported in August of 1853 that the Shenhu dealers were expected to make a large purchase in the coming weeks, just as soon as their ships returned from Ningbo with funds.[119] Evidence like this suggests that the opium-fueled domestic shipping industry in Quanzhou and Shenhu held out longer than might be expected. But in hindsight there were signs that these politically marginal opium stations might eventually see their business migrate to the treaty ports.

The increasing value of British shipping to Fujian's opium merchants also provides important context for understanding these shifts. During the late 1840s and 1850s, the lineage-based Shenhu and Quanzhou merchants had become dependent on the growing steamer traffic for protection against pirates. They were still sending their sailboats to Taiwan, Ningbo, Shanghai, and Tianjin, but they had begun paying their competition—the foreign-owned steamships—to protect them on the volatile seas. Even this measure did not guarantee safety, as in June 1855 when the well-armed *Thetis* was unable to stop pirates from rendering utter destruction on a fleet of sugar junks accompanied by a British steamer in convoy south from Ningbo.[120] It was only a matter of time before people began shipping their goods and money on the steamers themselves, especially firms in the treaty ports where those steamships could legally call.

But before steamships had fully established their dominance, Chinese opium traders also found value in using the British flag to their advantage. British shipping was not just about deterring pirates; Chinese merchants chose to ship their goods in British ships because it could help them escape Qing intervention into their businesses. Recall the *Independence*, the Quanzhou receiving ship that had employed the sailor whose tragic drunken exploits on shore resulted in the death of a child. The *Independence* flew a British flag, and it was captained by a man named Thompson. But it was not owned by Jardine Matheson, Dent, Augustine Heard, or any of the other foreign opium magnates. It was owned by a man known to the Jardine Matheson captains as "Amah," a Xiamen businessman. By purchasing a vessel from the British and hiring a captain who could fly the British flag, Amah was shielding his business through extraterritoriality. A few years later, another local merchant followed suit and purchased the *Harlequin* from Jardine Matheson, setting it up as a receiving ship in the Xiamen harbor.[121] This was a new strategy, which as we shall see, would become hugely influential in the years to come. Chinese opium traders were discovering how foreign privilege could serve their own interests and help them grow and protect their profits.

CHAPTER 3

Drug Money and the Fiscal-Military State, 1857–1906

If the Shanghai press is to be believed, the hatred that Lin Yi'nen and his family felt towards the Fuzhou Maritime Customs was personal.[1] In the spring of 1875, the Lins were opium smugglers in an age of legalized opium. They made their living by bringing tax-free opium up to Fujian from Hong Kong on passenger steamships and sneaking the drugs past the Customs after arrival in port. The rumor in the press was that the Customs had just recently confiscated a parcel of smuggled opium bound for the Lin family hometown in nearby Changle county, and the large territorial lineage had sworn to exact revenge on the officers who had made the confiscation. One reporter even suggested that the Lins had kidnapped the child of a Customs officer and demanded $1,800 in ransom.[2]

The Lin family did not intend to stop smuggling just because the Fuzhou Maritime Customs had managed to intercept one of their packages. In Fujian's two treaty ports, Fuzhou and Xiamen, opium was taxed far more heavily than in China's other ports. Evasion was common and profitable. The margin on smuggling a single ball of opium past the various tax collectors amounted to the equivalent of a month's wages for a Fuzhou day laborer.[3] So when the SS *Douglass* arrived in port from Hong Kong on

May 26, 1875, a small group of lineage members once again prepared for a midnight rendezvous. They paddled silent longboats through the streams and estuaries, snaking along the Min River towards the Maritime Customs and the deepwater port at Pagoda Anchorage. A co-conspirator on board the *Douglass* was awake, waiting for them with a water-tight, buoyed parcel of opium, ready to throw it overboard at the appointed time.

Someone else aboard the *Douglass* was also awake that night, a young Customs employee from London, and he too was waiting for the arrival of the Lin family's longboats. The man lay out all evening on a sun chair on the upper deck, cradling a borrowed revolver and smoking nervously.[4] Around 1:30 in the morning, a watchman called up to him that a small boat was pulling abreast of the *Douglass*. The man jumped up, spotted the smugglers, and ran along the deck firing wildly into the dark river below, emptying his revolver over the side of the ship. Out of ammunition, the Customs officer leaned over the rail and cut a clear figure against the moonlit sky. He was shot in the chest and died soon after.

This was the unfortunate Frederick Blacklock, a tidewaiter in the Chinese Maritime Customs Service. Blacklock had left the slums of East London years earlier, journeyed to China, and found himself employed by the Qing imperial state. The night he was killed, Blacklock was working the night watch aboard the *Douglass*, assigned to prevent the passengers and crew of the visiting steamship from secretly conveying untaxed opium off the ship during the night. Blacklock's duty was to protect the Qing state's revenue collection on foreign trade and, in particular, to ensure that the empire's most expensive import commodity paid its due taxes.

But Frederick Blacklock did not die because the Lin family was unwilling to pay the import tax that he was nominally protecting. The rate of the import tax was low and hardly worth risking the consequences of killing a government officer. The threat that Blacklock posed to the smugglers, rather, was his role in channeling opium imports into a state-monitored system, wherein it would later be subject to a laundry list of additional fees and surcharges. These included municipal opium paste retail taxes, paid by dispensary operators, as well as an array of taxes on the transport of opium between jurisdictions, the most important of which was called the *lijin*.

The lijin was a transport tax with separate bureaus for opium, salt, and general commodities (*baihuo*). Provincial officials expanded these institutions rapidly in the mid-1850s to help fund counterattacks against the armies of the Taiping Heavenly Kingdom across the mid and lower Yangzi valley. By the 1870s, a decade after the fall of the Taiping regime, lijin bureaus had expanded and formalized across the Qing empire, and lijin fees came to constitute the largest percentage of the total taxes that the Qing state levied on opium.[5] In Fujian, an ambitious governor-general and his successors built a massive naval yard and modern arsenal that would become dependent on the opium lijin for a substantial portion of the funds required for construction and upkeep. To help pay for those warships, and myriad other military expenditures, Fujian's provincial authorities from the 1860s all the way to 1880 set the provincial opium lijin rate around six times more expensive than in the neighboring provinces. The plan, shared among most of the top officials of the era, was to kill two birds with one stone: to raise as much revenue as possible in the short term, while making the trade financially unviable in the long term through overtaxation.[6]

But the opium business did not become unviable. The Treaty of Tianjin guaranteed the British right to import Indian opium into China, and prohibition remained a largely aspirational conversation among high officials like Guo Songtao and Zuo Zongtang. These men sketched out idealistic plans to reduce opium use among officials and to exhort the population into better behavior, but the area where they most acutely impacted the opium business was in their consistent support for taxing the drug. By using taxation to try and disincentivize opium, they created patterns of revenue collection and distribution that empowered the buyers and sellers of opium and entangled their business within various levels of the state.

The revenue from Fujian's opium taxes was spread across provincial and empire-wide investments. This was a decisive moment for Qing territorial sovereignty, and Fujian's opium lijin helped pay to expand Qing rule in Taiwan and to fund the consolidation of Qing power in Shaanxi, Gansu, and Xinjiang in the 1870s. Opium revenue helped China pay off the enormous indemnities owed to foreign states and helped the foreign-managed Customs Service purchase state-of-the-art lighthouses and patrol boats. Wrote Shen Baozhen, the commander of the Fuzhou Naval Yard from 1867 to 1872: "All of a country's expenditures can be reduced, except when it comes to feeding soldiers, erecting defenses, weapons training, and the building of naval steamships."[7] He was not unique in this view, and the powerful regional officials of the late Qing state worked at a fever pitch to raise armies, invest in ships, weapons, and other new technology, and to extend direct rule into places like Taiwan and Xinjiang. Self-Strengthening was expensive, and it was achieved in no small part through a robust taxation of the opium business.

The Lin family's smuggling operation was parasitic towards the state's aggressive program of revenue collection, but other people in the opium business capitalized more directly on the rising status of opium revenue by collaborating with the state to help collect opium taxes, rather than resisting or evading those taxes. The people and firms who grew richest from buying and selling opium during this era competed with one another to purchase state contracts for administering the various opium lijin jurisdictions. The successful among them would pay the state a quota and pocket the surplus, lining their pockets with the proceeds of their competitors. Opium lijin bureaus, at their height in the 1870s and early 1880s, employed hundreds of officers and spies, fleets of boats, and exercised a privatized territorial authority with the force of violence. These institutions were ubiquitous, until British representatives in China forced the Qing state to abolish the tax farming system and centralize the opium lijin under the Maritime Customs in 1887.

In Xiamen and in the counties beyond, local authorities and opium firms looked to continue their productive relationships in spite of the new treaty conditions and revived various fees and surcharges on opium, protested by the British as treaty violations and yet never fully disappearing. These local tax farms, from the urban distribution taxes in Xiamen to the poppy taxes in nearby Tong'an county, demonstrate an institutional continuity between the lijin bureaus of the nineteenth century and the opium prohibition bureaus and poppy tax agencies of the early twentieth century.

The Age of Legal Opium

Upon legalization, opium was instantly the most valuable article of import in China's treaty ports. Between 1863 and 1906, the Qing empire imported an average of 62,826 piculs (8,355,858 pounds) of raw opium every year.[8] The total net worth of the opium trade—the price tag on those millions of pounds of raw drug brought in each year—averaged around 35–40 percent of the total value of foreign goods imported into the treaty ports, far exceeding any other individual branch of commerce. In Xiamen, as in many ports, the next highest-volume import was usually cotton yarn, $599,656 of which was imported in 1873, as compared to $1,836,263 worth of opium that year.[9] Opium imports reached their peak in the late 1870s and early 1880s (82,927 piculs in 1879) and only began to decline slightly in the late 1890s when there were rapid advances in the quantity and quality of opium grown and produced domestically.

The trade networks that sustained the opium business during these years were utterly transformed from the offshore receiving-ship system of the decades previous. Like in the 1840s and 1850s, British-owned vessels still carried Indian opium to Hong Kong for redistribution to the treaty ports, but Jardine Matheson and the other foreign firms were by the 1870s almost entirely cornered out of the import market by Chinese merchants who could buy direct from Hong Kong. For the duration of the 1860s and 1870s, opium imported into the two Fujianese treaty ports arrived on a fleet of six steamships that plied between Hong Kong, Shantou, Xiamen, and Fuzhou—three owned by the Peninsular & Oriental Steam Navigation Company, and three owned by the Hong Kong watchmaker Douglas Lapraik.[10] The competition for profits on the British end of the trade thus migrated to India, where firms like Sassoon & Company gained advantage through strategic relationships with opium producers.[11]

With the opening of new treaty ports after 1860 and the expansion of steam networks into Taiwan, north China, and the upper Yangzi region, Fujian's role in the empire-wide opium trade continued to decline. Back in the 1830s, around 60 percent of the opium that entered China passed through the hands of southern Fujianese opium merchants. This dropped precipitously after the opening of Shanghai in 1843, and even more so after 1860. During the period from 1863 to 1906, Xiamen and Fuzhou together accounted for an average of around 15 percent of the opium imported into China.[12]

Reexports from Xiamen to Taiwan were the only remaining vestige of the region's former opium transshipment industry.[13] For more than a decade after the establishment of treaty ports on the island of Taiwan itself in Tainan and Danshui (Tamsui), merchants from Xiamen continued to supply a sizeable portion of the Taiwanese market by importing the opium into Xiamen and then reexporting it across the strait, "for the purposes of laying down funds to purchase Sugar, &c."[14] In 1874, for example, merchants in Xiamen reexported 1,159 chests of opium to the southern Taiwanese treaty port of Takow.[15] The 1880s also saw the beginning of a new trend in opium exports from Fujian to colonial ports in Southeast Asia, wherein domestic Chinese opium was packaged and smuggled into those jurisdictions (see chapter 5).

In the treaty ports and in the cities and countryside beyond, a wide field of other opportunities arose in connection with the legalization and normalization of the drug. In Xiamen during the late 1840s, local merchants had boiled around 150 chests of opium into paste for sale to consumers in the port each month.[16] The population grew, and opium use continued to increase and reach new levels of social acceptance. By 1886 the consumption in Xiamen had risen to 400–500 chests per month, according to the former lijin monopoly holder.[17] An investigation into opium consumption from 1870 concluded that 15–20 percent of the adult population in Xiamen and the surrounding counties were opium users, 60 percent of whom used very little of the drug, 30 percent who were "habitual" users, and another 10 percent of whom "cannot exist" without a large amount of the drug.[18] In 1881, another commissioner of customs described the rate of consumption in Xiamen as "absolutely astonishing" and reported that the opium shopkeepers in town had estimated that 5 percent of the women living in the treaty port were opium users.[19]

A formal system of regulation and taxation attended the expansion of the drug's presence in the local economy. At the moment of import, the foreign-staffed Maritime Customs tallied and taxed each chest. An army of uniformed (and some clandestine) officers from the lijin bureau then ensured that the drug paid its due transport taxes as it moved from port to city, and then to the districts beyond. In the cities, a prominent merchant or firm worked as the municipal tax farmer, issuing registration fees to opium shops, collecting a scheduled retail tax, and inspecting each shop's receipts. In 1881, Xiamen was home to 420 opium retail businesses (so-called opium dens) that employed 1,440 people, or an estimated 6 percent of the adult male population of the treaty port. The local administration and their tax farmers divided the opium shops of the city into four classes, licensed and taxed based on their daily earnings. These opium den operators produced a combined revenue of around $2,000–$3,000 per day. Among the various expenditures tied to the taxes on opium retail in the port, $1,000 was earmarked for a hospital for orphaned girls.[20]

THE CHINESE MARITIME CUSTOMS AND OPIUM TAXATION

When it formally happened, the Qing court did not have sovereignty over
the terms of opium's legalization. The Treaty of Tianjin and accompanying
tariff agreement placed an import tax on the drug and mandated the rate
of taxation: these were British demands that the Qing court was forced to
accept. This is generally recognized as the de facto legalization of opium in
China, although it was predated by the creation of opium lijin bureaus and
other forms of taxation within the provinces. But while Qing officials could
determine the lijin and retail tax rates according to their own priorities,
the British forced on China a low import tax of 30 taels for every picul of
opium, a picul weighing around 60 kilograms or 133 pounds (approximately
one chest of opium), which in 1863 Fuzhou cost on average $776.[21] The
tax was to be paid immediately upon import—impartial and standardized
across all ports—and then the drug could be sold off to Chinese customers
within the treaty port for transport into the interior. Low as it was, the high
volume of trade meant that the 30-tael import tax on opium brought the
Qing state an average annual import revenue of 1,884,780 taels during the
years 1863–1887 constituting around 10 percent of the total annual revenue
on foreign trade, import and export.[22]

The institution that came to be in charge of collecting the foreign opium
import tax, and which had employed Frederick Blacklock as a tidewaiter,
was the Imperial Chinese Maritime Customs Service.[23] A coalition of foreign diplomats had set up the first iteration of the Customs on an experimental basis in Shanghai during 1854, when the local Qing officials were
otherwise occupied with the Taiping crisis. The Customs was then extended
to the other treaty ports after the Xinyou coup d'état by Prince Gong in
1861. The founding purpose of the Customs was for foreign governments
and the Qing state to jointly assess the amount of taxes that foreign merchants legally owed the Chinese state in a public and transparent way, but
the complicated and intertwined nature of capital and shipping meant that
Customs operations were frequently more complicated than the original
idea of using foreign officers to collect revenue on foreign trade. More often
than not, the Customs was collecting taxes on Chinese-owned goods being
shipped on foreign vessels, and men like Blacklock found themselves policing Chinese people on behalf of the Chinese state.[24] He was shot while
attempting to prevent local smugglers from removing opium from a British-
owned steamship without paying the import tax.

In Fuzhou and Xiamen, long-standing issues with smuggling and navigation compelled the Maritime Customs to invest heavily in outdoor staff and marine departments. The two Customs offices in Fujian were oversized in comparison to other ports, as the officials in charge set about hiring more people and purchasing more technology to surveil and police the waters. In the mid-1870s, the Xiamen Customs had the third largest total staff among the fifteen customs houses, and Fuzhou was fourth largest.[25] Of the nearly 300 marine department employees across China's fifteen treaty ports—engineers, harbor inspectors, river police, lighthouse operators, and signalmen—nearly 20 percent lived and worked in Xiamen or Fuzhou. The relative value of trade in those ports would not seem to substantiate such a large investment in personnel.

Customs officials believed that the difficult topography of the Fujian coast and the long-standing history of smuggling in the region necessitated the robust investment in maritime infrastructure. Fuzhou's first foreign commissioner of customs, F. Nevill May, wrote in 1865 that Fujian's mountains and rivers present "so many obstacles to the construction of canals and railways that they will probably never be introduced into this part of China."[26] When Fuzhou and Wenzhou—a large city in coastal Zhejiang 207 miles to the north—were finally connected by rail in 2003, the construction necessitated the excavation of no fewer than fifty-three tunnels.[27]

Lighthouses were central to the project of coastal surveillance (see Figure 3.1). In both Fuzhou and Xiamen, a jagged coastline abutted with steep mountains prevent easy administrative surveillance over the coastal trade routes and port entrances. The Maritime Customs erected seven lighthouses along the southeast coast during the period 1871–1875, adding three more over the subsequent decades, in order to "render navigation on the Coast as easily as walking down Broadway by gas-light."[28] Historian Eric Tagliacozzo, comparing the island lighthouse to a "floating panopticon," has argued that the advent of coast lighting meant "the state could not only see the periphery, but channel movements," making "the war against smuggling that much easier."[29] The passage in Fuzhou to the anchorage from the sea was especially shallow and dangerous, patched with sandbars. Locals who might plunder grounded ships or evade customs agents found refuge in the basin's labyrinthine waterways and impenetrable mountains. Lighthouses—their upkeep dependent on the profitable taxation of the opium trade—illuminated the maritime thoroughfares, pushing smugglers deeper into the periphery.

FIGURE 3.1: Chapel Island Lighthouse, Xiamen Harbor. Erected 1871.

Source: T. Robert Banister, *The Coastwise Lights of China: An Illustrated Account of the Chinese Maritime Customs Lights Service* (Shanghai: Inspector General of Customs, 1932), 79.

From the perspective of those smugglers, the new Maritime Customs was a formidable threat. The aftermath of the Blacklock case highlights the violence that was just beneath the surface of the interactions between the coastal Fujianese and the Customs. In the days after the gunfight on the *Douglass*, according to one report, "it was openly stated to be [the smugglers'] intention to muster 1,000 men, and then return to the attack of the Custom house."[30] In response to these threats, the Fujian provincial officials summoned 3,000 troops and several gunboats to guard targeted customs employees from the anticipated mass retaliation.[31] As late as September of 1875—nearly four months after the Blacklock incident—Shanghai newspapers were still reporting on the number of troops that had remained to protect the Customs against further attack.[32] Meanwhile, rumors had circulated within the foreign community that the Changle lineage was offering $400 for the head of two foreign customs employees, and $5,000 for Harbor Master Bisbee.[33] The Customs archives seem to confirm that these threats were taken seriously: the two employees named by the newspapers, Bisbee, and the acting commissioner of customs were all transferred to different ports within the month.[34]

FUJIAN'S OPIUM LIJIN FARMS

The other system of opium taxation was the lijin. Lijin was but one of a variety of surcharges on opium and other commodities, but British diplomats tended to use it as a catch-all term to encompass the entire range of municipal and transport taxes collected by the late Qing state, which in the case of opium included fees for intra- or interdistrict transport, as well as retail taxes and business registrations for opium dispensaries and dens. The diversity of practices and considerations involved meant on a basic level that this was not a standardized tax across (or even within) provinces. These were fees set by local officials with their own priorities, farmed out to teams of high-level opium investors on a regional level at the treaty port, and then subcontracted to various firms in other cities and counties.

Fujian's governors created the province's first lijin bureau in 1854 to tax the transport of tea from the highland production districts to the treaty ports in order to supplement military budgets strapped by the Small Sword uprising near Xiamen and years of fighting Taiping forces along the Jiangxi border. Three years later the Fujian authorities created an opium lijin bureau, in 1857, the same year they received permission to begin collecting an import tax on the drug.[35] The amount of money the new opium lijin bureau collected doubled, and then tripled, and by the early 1860s the Fujian provincial authorities were collecting more than 400,000 taels annually in opium lijin. The provincial opium lijin revenue fluctuated over the years as a consequence of disparities between the rate of taxation in Fujian and neighboring provinces, from a low annual revenue of 194,467 taels in 1876 to a peak of 529,695 taels in 1886.[36] For most of the 1860s and 1870s, the rate of opium lijin collection—the amount of tax paid per chest of the drug—was the highest in China and substantially higher than neighboring Guangdong and Zhejiang provinces. This trend later reversed during the period from 1880 to 1886.

In the two treaty ports, opium lijin bureaus set up offices adjacent to the foreign-owned warehouses where importers were required to store their opium after paying the import tax to the Maritime Customs. As a rule, lijin was only levied on Qing subjects, and the logic of the system was that

Chinese buyers would pay the tax upon removing the drug from a foreign warehouse. According to a 1864 consular report, a Chinese merchant importing into Fuzhou would first pay the fixed import of 30 taels to the Maritime Customs, and then on removal from the harbor or a foreign warehouse, they would pay the lijin bureau over 83 additional taels, comprised of eight different surcharges (such as a war tax of 16 taels, and an "extra tax to meet rebel expenses" of 5 taels), as well as various complicated discounts and meltage fees. Writing in the 1930s, historian Luo Yudong summarized the basic structure of Fujian's opium lijin during the 1870s and 1880s as a 66 tael total fee, comprised of 16 taels of transport tax (*lijin*), 30 taels of luxury tax (*huashui*), 5 taels of military contributions (*junxiang*), and 15 taels of a stamp tax (*piaoshui*).[37]

The Fujian Provincial Government sold off opium lijin rights on an annual basis to a merchant or firm, usually a collection of firms.[38] The farms operated along lines of territory and supply chain, with the province separated into two rough halves according to the two treaty ports and the inland counties they supplied with the drug. Xiamen and Fuzhou were the primary focus of the major contracts for opium lijin rights, housing the major lijin offices. In Xiamen, the collection of lijin for opium transported out of the treaty port was operated in connection with the dense network of checkpoints across the counties that make up Quanzhou prefecture. Inland prefectures like Jianning, Tingzhou, and Funing had their own subcontracted lijin bureaus that collected fees on the distribution of the drug to local retailers. Subcontracting firms might also take over the collection of duties on the urban retail of the drug by dispensaries and dens in various county and prefectural cities.

Wealthy opium traders invested in the system as a way to expand their businesses and increase their profits. The people who purchased the lijin farm—usually a coalition of investors, almost never named in any remaining sources—would advance the provincial government taxes on a quota of opium and were then responsible to arrange their own means of collection (or subcontract out these rights) within a given territory. The fundamental principle of tax farming is profit: the quota that a farm pays out to the state must be lower than the actual amount of tax that the farm collects, so that there is a surplus of revenue to pay the farm's employees and profit its owners. Although lijin operations are poorly documented at best, one snapshot from 1870 Xiamen demonstrates an example of a successful operation.

In that year, a coalition of six merchants—local opium firm owners and compradors for foreign firms—purchased the Xiamen opium lijin farm for a quota of 130 chests per month at the rate of 80 taels per chest. The farm's expenses that year were $1,470 (for 260 collectors, watchers, sailors, soldiers, boatmen, etc.) and $330 (for subsistence of certain men in Xiamen and out stations), and the net profit of the farm was estimated at 63,297.5 taels.[39]

Opium tax farming could also be a risky investment. Distant changes in the supply chain, quarreling among investors, new and evolving methods of smuggling, and unreasonable demands from the state could all undermine a farm's profitability. The lattermost of these was hugely influential in Fujian, where cash-poor provincial authorities were reliant on opium revenue and consistently overestimated the capacity of the opium market to continue uninterrupted in the face of higher and higher taxes. This tendency in Fuzhou dates back to the first opium import taxes in 1857, which as noted in chapter 2 were introduced at a much steeper rate than contemporaneous import fees collected in Shanghai and Ningbo. In the year after the founding of Fuzhou Naval Yard, 1867, the opium lijin bureau in Fuzhou collapsed after it had been farmed out that year for 144,000 taels, based on an anticipated import of 4,800 piculs of opium. Local merchants imported just 4,020 piculs, responding to the rise in the amount being demanded per chest, and the farmer fell short 24,000 of his initial investment, still theoretically responsible to pay the salaries of his employees.[40] Bankruptcy was to become a familiar pattern in opium lijin farming during the late nineteenth century.[41]

Fujian's high lijin diverted the trade through ports in neighboring provinces, discussed later in this chapter, and it also incentivized the smuggling of opium direct from Hong Kong. The Blacklock case is a clear example of this, wherein a Fuzhou-area lineage had arranged with a passenger on a steamship from Hong Kong to toss opium overboard to the buyers at night while the ship was anchored in port. As one commissioner of customs reported, the methods of smuggling off the tightly surveilled steamships during this period were varied and ingenious:

> Tin boxes, hermetically sealed and bearing printed labels intact, imitating exactly the homemade boxes of preserved milk, biscuits, meats, matches, etc., and having very nearly the same weight, have been found, in many instances, full of opium. Opium has been discovered in flower-pots with

plants in full bloom; in common market baskets, covered with garlic, onions, and other strong-scented vegetables; and in bamboo broomsticks carefully hollowed out. In most cases, however, the opium has been found concealed under the loose garments of the passengers, who can easily hide half a ball of Patna under each arm, thus avoiding, if not found out, some HK Tls 3 import duty and inland taxes.[42]

With over 10,000 passengers coming through Fuzhou and Xiamen each year on the Hongkong-Shanghai steam route, Blacklock and his fellow tidewaiters in the Customs Service were being tasked with the impossible.[43] In considering the impact on state finances, Maritime Customs officers frequently complained that these chests of opium *would* have paid the 30-tael import tax if it were not for the high lijin rate.[44]

In response to the challenges posed by smugglers, lijin bureaus invested in expanding their regulatory presence and territorial authority during the 1870s and 1880s. In Xiamen, the lijin bureau became huge, employing over 600 "spies and runners" in the lead-up to the reorganization of lijin bureaus in 1887.[45] One of the primary tasks of these men was to closely monitor the foreign-owned warehouses where opium was stored before being transferred to Chinese merchants, as the secret removal of opium from these warehouses constituted one of the easiest and most common methods of lijin evasion.

Lijin bureaus often stirred up diplomatic tensions as a consequence of monitoring these foreign warehouses. In one instance, during November 1886, the British consul in Xiamen discovered that officers from the lijin bureau had secretly hired British consular employees to keep watch at night within the consular compound, where merchants sometimes stored their opium in a bonded warehouse. The spies were discovered when a constable from the consulate caught one of the employees snooping around at night. He went to the quarters of the Chinese staff and found three lijin runners in uniform, delivering the pay of $1.50 a month for spying on British merchants.[46] The duplicitous employees were promptly dismissed.

The private authority exercised by lijin bureau officers combined with their close proximity to a highly profitable commodity introduced a wide range of opportunities for extortion and smuggling on the part of the collectors. In one case, the Xiamen lijin farm hired a former smuggler named Wu Tian to manage a preventive unit, taking charge of a fleet of boats and a small army of collectors. He promptly turned around and used the patrol boats to smuggle opium out of the foreign firms on Gulangyu into the coastal hinterland.[47] Rui Que, a notorious Filipino-Fujianese opium smuggler, also agreed at one point to merge his smuggling forces with the ships and men of the lijin bureau. Like Wu Tian, he too reneged on his promise and resumed smuggling.[48] "It is only [people] of the most ruffianly classes who undertake such duties," wrote one British critic of the lijin farm's army of spies and collectors. "The records of this and other consulates in [Xiamen] show a succession of assaults on foreigners, and many cases of unoffending members of the community being stopped and searched by the runners."[49]

In one such case from 1885, lijin runners stopped a Parsee merchant named Dauver who was crossing the harbor from Xiamen proper to the foreign firms and residences on Gulangyu. Dauver's Chinese employee was walking behind him carrying a leather briefcase that Dauver later claimed was filled with $210, and upon disembarking at Gulangyu, a group of lijin runners armed with knives confronted the two men and departed with the briefcase. When Dauver and his business partner appeared at the lijin office to protest, they were told that the briefcase had been found to have twelve balls of unstamped opium and that Dauver's employee was therefore guilty of lijin evasion. Dauver and the British consul countered that this was a half-baked alibi to try and excuse a robbery. The bag was too small and not sturdy enough to hold that much opium, and in any case Dauver's employee had been in uniform and the opium (which he maintained did not exist) would have been technically in the possession of a foreigner and thus not yet subject to the lijin. "Any Chinese servant carrying his master's effects," wrote the British consul in a letter of protest, "is liable to be robbed in the middle of the port by any person who chooses to call himself a likin runner."[50] Dauver had two decades earlier been convicted by the British consulate in Xiamen for "assault on Chinese revenue officers and connivance at smuggling," but in this later case he succeeded in securing damages from the lijin office for his loss.[51]

FOREIGNERS AND FOREIGN STATUS IN OPIUM TAX EVASION

The opium business in the age of legal opium was mostly dominated by Chinese participants, but certain foreigners like Dauver remained key players in the trade. The foreign ownership of the opium warehouses in the treaty ports was one of the most important ways that opium continued to profit foreigners in China. The warehouses were a legal necessity, as they offered lijin bureaus a way to track and register the imported drug before it was fully in the possession of Chinese merchants. Most of the steamship companies—including the P&O and the Lapraik line that operated between Hong Kong and Fujian—were also foreign-owned.

Tax-evaders and smugglers could also be foreign nationals. During the early 1880s, for example, the British consulate in Xiamen accused an enigmatic photographer named St. Julian Hugh Edwards of opium smuggling.[52] Edwards, according to the accusation, was colluding with Chinese dealers in villages outside of the treaty port to evade the onerous lijin by capitalizing on his foreign status, running shipments out of the foreign warehouses and delivering them to a pharmacist in a nearby county.[53] Edwards would leave in the middle of the night, using a four-oared boat with the opium concealed underneath his photographic equipment. His gang would cross the harbor and drop off the smuggled opium with his Chinese contacts in the villages on trips that took six or seven hours, which allowed Edwards to return to Xiamen in time to show his face at the United States consulate, where he worked as a constable. "Edwards," worried the British official, "who, under pretense of photography, goes about the country fully armed for the purpose of running opium, will be found killed. His existence here is a public scandal."[54]

Within the overlapping administrative complexities of late-nineteenth century maritime Asia, people like St. Julian Hugh Edwards found new ways to seek profit. Edwards could speak multiple languages, including southern Fujianese (Hokkien, or Minnan hua). Born in Malacca in 1843 to an Antiguan father and a Portuguese-Malaccan mother, Edwards grew up in Singapore. In his early twenties, Edwards fled to Xiamen after a failed attempt to scam a distant relative in a land deal. Rather than registering with the British authorities who might send him back to Singapore to face trial, Edwards approached the United States consulate and made a claim for protection, based on the premise that his father had been a freed slave from the state of Maine.[55] The calculated shift of citizenship allowed him to restart in Xiamen with a clean slate.

In Xiamen, Edwards thrived by building a creative résumé around an eclectic assortment of skills. He worked odd jobs for shipping companies and as a linguist and constable in the Spanish and American consulates. Where he really left his mark was in photography (see Figure 3.2). Edwards

FIGURE 3.2: St. Julian Hugh Edwards, "Amoy Races, 1889."

Source: SOAS University of London O501-015. Reprinted with Permission.

is perhaps the most famous nineteenth-century photographer of Xiamen—his work is prominently featured in a recent history of Western photographers in China—and he is believed by historians to have been the first person to ever photograph Taiwan.[56] He was a commercial photographer, he accompanied official expeditions as a translator and photographer, and was a talented artist. He also used his photography as a cover for opium smuggling.

As a consular marshal, an opium smuggler, and a member of a dangerous expedition to Taiwan, Edwards cultivated the image of a person who was capable of violence. His opium smuggling voyages were said to be well armed. He seems to have enjoyed a certain mystique. "I am given to understand," wrote an employee of the British consulate, "that he always carries what might be called a 'pistol-cane' of American invention. It is ostensibly a walking stick, but contains within it a pistol."[57] He instructed his Chinese contacts in the villages around Xiamen to refer to him as the "Singapore Helmsman," an imaginary title that intimated a false connection to the

British government. Others simply called him "black face," which he was said to dislike. "But however they may name him," wrote the consular investigator, the Chinese residents of Xiamen "all agree in saying that he is a very bad man."[58]

Edwards found success in opium smuggling during the 1880s by taking advantage of cracks in the treaty port citizenship regime. Edwards was a savvy—if not always successful—manipulator of consular jurisdiction in Xiamen, dating back to the calculated shift to United States citizenship upon his arrival. A few years after Edwards arrived in China, the US consul Charles Le Gendre arrested him for involvement in the human trafficking business, and convicted Edwards in 1867 of recruiting "coolies" for shipment to Macao and beyond.[59] After a year in the consular prison, Edwards returned to the good graces of the US government and for several years was able to work for their consulate as a constable. But once the British diplomats became interested in Edwards's lijin evasion scheme, around 1884, the US consul became determined to disown the troublemaker. Not wanting jurisdiction over the now notorious Edwards, the consul tracked down evidence that Edwards's father was from Antigua—and not Maine—and the well-known opium smuggler was therefore a British subject.[60] Still, the British government refused to recognize Edwards's citizenship because of his previous affiliation with the US government.

As the extent of Edwards's opium smuggling was becoming public knowledge among the official community at Xiamen, none of the foreign diplomats wanted to claim or arrest him. Meanwhile the Qing authorities in Xiamen were also unwilling to interfere with him, due to the treaty rights of foreigners to extraterritorial protection and the potential diplomatic consequences of arresting a foreigner. After some prodding by the British consul, the furthest the Xiamen Maritime sub-prefect was willing to go was to issue an official proclamation to the local Chinese population, exhorting them that they "must not again have any secret dealings with the Black man named Lu Lien."[61] Temporarily stateless in the land of extraterritoriality, St. Julian Hugh Edwards was free to go about his smuggling.[62]

The participation of foreign merchants like Edwards in the lijin evasion game in Xiamen was not necessarily representative of the demography of the industry, but nonetheless indicates an important truth about opium smuggling during this period: foreign status could be useful. Lijin evasion was by all accounts still a largely Chinese enterprise, but the incentives were attractive enough that it drew in people like Edwards—foreigners with local connections and a willingness to break the rules. In 1886, when Xiamen authorities raised the lijin and consequently lost 2,000-odd piculs of revenue-paid opium to Shantou, the British consul in Xiamen reported the recent arrival of two British merchants, "both of whom I have no doubt have been attracted by the chances offered by successful opium likin evasion."[63] One was an Englishman named Johnstone, described as a "not reputable" merchant. The other was a Singaporean Chinese man named Lam who, since his recent arrival, had already been the subject of a formal complaint for smuggling from the Maritime sub-prefect. The next year, the consul wrote that there had been a steady increase in Parsee and Singaporean opium merchants in Xiamen—people from British colonies who were entitled to British protection in China. "They live mainly by the sale of opium, their profits depending on their success in evading the likin duties."[64]

Foreign status was useful in lijin smuggling for several reasons. Because the lijin could only be levied on Qing subjects, a foreign person was allowed to possess opium on Chinese soil before the tax could be collected.[65] This was how Edwards achieved his position, as a foreigner with access to opium who had paid the import tax but not yet paid any lijin fees. Edwards also benefited from being able to move about Chinese territory without being interfered with by the lijin collectors. Local Chinese smugglers in Xiamen were not blind to this reality, and many began to strategically employ foreign citizenship—whether their own or that of family members—because it made it easier to smuggle. The rising participation of Singaporean firms in lijin evasion as cited by the British consul in 1886 is testament to this.[66] In another case, a Fujianese man named Rui Que who had lived in the Philippines was known to have smuggled over 1,000 chests past the lijin bureau, using Spanish citizenship for protection.[67]

The usefulness of foreign status in this regard was so readily apparent that local smugglers frequently pretended to be foreign in their attempts to evade the lijin. "I am informed," wrote one consul, "that the smugglers when sending opium across the harbour always make use of a foreign-built gig in the stern of which sits a Chinese with a European coat and hat on and a cigar in his mouth."[68] This trend in turn caused the eager cadre of lijin collectors to be on the lookout for false foreigners, which then inspired the consul to express his concerns over the safety of British subjects who walked about after dark on the streets of Xiamen.

Drug Money and the Late Qing State

When the doors swung open and Qing officials were authorized to start taxing opium, the drug business became firmly implanted within the fiscal bedrock of the modernizing Chinese state. Opium was China's largest import sector, and the opium import tax accounted for 51 percent of total import taxes between 1867 and 1900.[69] It was also a domestic cash crop of increasing prominence, and the total domestic opium lijin collection rose from an annual average of 46,214 taels between 1867 and 1881, to an average of 483,236 taels from 1881 to 1904.[70]

Municipal infrastructure and social welfare projects relied on opium revenue to balance their budgets, the imperial court in Beijing got its cut, and so too did the projects that made up what historians refer to as the Self-Strengthening Movement: wide-scale investments in military technology, and communications and transport infrastructure.[71] Ambitious regional authorities like Li Hongzhang, Zuo Zongtang, and Ding Richang built modern naval yards and commissioned steam-powered revenue cruisers; they installed state-of-the-art lighthouses along the coast and strung up telegraph wires between the treaty ports. Many of the state projects funded with both Maritime Customs and opium lijin revenue were, fittingly, geared towards assembling the maritime infrastructure China would need to combat smuggling and thereby protect revenue collection in an era of rapidly advancing technology.[72]

Much of the opium revenue collected by the late Qing state was channeled into the military: whether for general upkeep and training, or for constructing and maintaining expensive new technology. The original expansion of lijin bureaus in the 1850s in Fujian during the mid-1850s happened amidst a threefold military crisis: the Lin Jun uprising in Taiwan, the Small Sword rebellion that erupted across the counties of coastal southern Fujian, and the incursion of Taiping rebels from Jiangxi along the mountainous inland provincial border.[73] This connection between lijin revenue and the budgetary emergencies surrounding provincial military requirements did not disappear after the collapse of the Taiping, and military expenses (*junxiang*) remained a specifically earmarked portion of Fujian's opium lijin throughout the period.[74]

The provincial governors and regional governors-general who were determined to build up regional armies were also responsible for the funding and upkeep of expensive military technology. This began in Fujian during 1866, when Zuo Zongtang hired a French naval expert to construct a naval yard and arsenal at Mawei, several miles downstream from the city of Fuzhou (see Figure 3.3).[75] Across China, powerful regional officials were setting out to build similar shipyards, arsenals, and military training institutions. Zeng Guofan had undertaken a similar project near Shanghai (the Jiangnan Arsenal), and Li Hongzhang would do the same in Tianjin and later, Nanjing. To help pay for these expensive projects they leveraged their access to opium revenue through the lijin bureaus, and they sought out remittances of Maritime Customs funds back to the provinces.[76] Like the Customs, these military investments involved hiring foreign experts and mobilizing new technology to strengthen Qing sovereignty in the face of foreign aggression, and the funding of these projects rested in no small part on the continuance of a robust and thoroughly taxed opium trade.

The Fuzhou Naval Yard came to be one of the most prolific consumers of opium revenue. As historian David Pong has documented, the project's original patron Zuo Zongtang had secured an initial 400,000 taels for construction to be remitted back to Fujian from the portion of the Fuzhou

FIGURE 3.3: The Fuzhou Naval Yard, with Luoxing Pagoda in the background.

Peter Thilly, 2010.

Maritime Customs revenue normally sent to Beijing. The project's monthly operational costs, some 40,000 taels, would be taken from the province's cut of the customs revenue and supplemented as needed by the provincial transport tax (lijin) on opium.[77] By 1870, the opium stamp tax (*piaoshui*) in Fuzhou and Xiamen was also earmarked to supply the naval yard with around 70,000–80,000 taels annually.[78]

Pong's narrative of the naval yard's financial history describes a Sisyphean battle against ever-mounting costs, with none of the help from the governors of neighboring provinces that Zuo had expected would come. Zhejiang and Guangdong had both initially joined in what was to be a joint venture at the outset, but "since Fukien monopolized all the decision-making power, none of the provinces felt obliged to help out."[79] By May of 1872, the naval yard's monthly budget was only able to cover half the cost of steamship maintenance.[80] With few options and a desire to see the project to fruition, Fujian's provincial authorities raised the opium lijin in 1872 and again in 1873 in an effort to fund the expensive project.[81] As discussed later in this chapter, these rate hikes would serve to drive a substantive portion of Fujian's imports into neighboring provinces.

Opium revenue from Fujian also contributed to the late Qing state's violent consolidation of rule in the far northwest of the empire. The same year that Zuo Zongtang began preparations for the Fuzhou Arsenal, he was transferred from the maritime frontier to the edge of the Gobi Desert. As governor-general of Shaanxi and Gansu provinces, Zuo spent the period from 1866 to 1881 engaged in constant warfare across northwest China and central Asia. One of his first measures to address the fiscal challenges of his new post was to ensure a cut of the same source of revenue that had enabled him to build Fuzhou's warships.[82] Between 1866 and 1881, the Fujian Provincial Government sent around 5.5 million taels to supplement military expenses in far-off Gansu. This was not a minor sum, amounting to a yearly average of 339,516 taels, or 15 percent of the province's total lijin revenue.[83] Opium lijin made up a substantive portion of this fund, constituting an average of 21 percent of the province's total lijin revenue from 1856 to 1898.[84]

The opium taxes collected by various levels of the Qing state were thus an essential component of the flurry of local and empire-wide investments in the 1860s and 1880s that historian Stephen Halsey describes as "the most innovative period of state-making in China since the early seventeenth century."[85] Halsey argues that the late Qing state maintained its independence during the peak years of European imperial expansion thanks to the emergence of a strong fiscal-military state piloted by officials with a mercantilist plan to use "commercial warfare" to ensure and enhance Qing sovereignty.[86] Opium, and opium taxes, occupied an awkward space in this plan, because the same people who were the loudest in their advocacy for opium's prohibition were also the most instrumental in embedding opium taxes into the fiscal-military state.

In Fujian, Zuo Zongtang and his successor Shen Baozhen were both prominent anti-opium proselytizers who oversaw projects that relied on opium revenue. Zuo launched the Fuzhou Naval Yard, noted above, and he also arranged for a portion of Fujian's lijin revenue to be transferred across the empire to fund the Xiang Army's campaign across the war-torn central Asian frontier. Zuo did not write in any detail about opium in Fujian, but he was a vocal opponent of opium cultivation in Shaanxi and Gansu, and Zuo's advice to raise opium taxes as a way to ultimately prohibit opium also helped influence the Qing court's position in their negotiations with the British over proposed transformations in opium lijin collection during 1881.[87]

Shen Baozhen was the official charged with taking over the Fuzhou Naval Yard when Zuo departed for the northwest, and then in the early 1870s Shen was transferred across the strait to consolidate Qing rule in Taiwan. Shen was from Fuzhou, a member of the local gentry, and the son-in-law of the famous anti-opium crusader and local hero Lin Zexu. As with Zuo, Shen's published writings from his time in Fujian and Taiwan do not dwell on the sources of the revenue he required for those projects, in large part because his job as an imperial commissioner for naval defense (*zongli chuanzheng dachen*) was to manage expenditures, and other officials within the provincial government were tasked with collecting the revenue he required.[88] Shen's years in Fujian do coincide with the years when the province levied the highest taxes on the drug across China, however, and he frequently references the Fujian opium lijin as a source of revenue without commenting on any tension between this and his support for opium prohibition.[89] He later achieved commendation for his anti-opium reputation during his reign as the governor-general of Liangjiang, when he took steps to shut down opium dens in Nanjing.[90]

Zuo and Shen maintained a general anti-opium stance in their writings that was shared by most of the prominent officials of the Self-Strengthening

Era, such as Zhang Zhidong and the diplomat Guo Songtao.[91] Guo was the most prolific advocate for opium's prohibition within the late Qing state, and he spent over a decade drafting letters and memorials about the social and moral damage caused by the drug, and the plans that the Qing empire should pursue in order to eventually prohibit the drug's sale and production.[92] Expressing desire for opium's eventual prohibition was, in our contemporary language, the politically correct position within late Qing administrative culture.

As such, late Qing officials were rarely anything but circumspect about the complicated relationship between their short-term demand for opium revenue and their long-term desire for prohibition. One uniquely candid acknowledgment of this tension was expressed by the governor-general of Guangdong and Guangxi Liu Kunyi, who in 1877 described one of Guo Songtao's prohibition plans as "totally impossible" (*wan buneng xing*). In Guangdong alone, wrote Liu, the annual combined opium import and lijin revenue was over 1,000,000 taels. This money was used for crucial expenditures in Beijing and to support the Guangdong civil and military officials. What, he asked, is the plan to replace this revenue?[93]

Liu's was a reasonable question, and there was not a good answer. A few years later, when Zuo Zongtang suggested raising opium lijin rates across China as part of a plan to eventually make the drug trade unviable, Liu enthusiastically participated in a discussion about how to successfully implement the proposed tax hike.[94] He was the administrator of a province with massive opium revenue collection operations. For Liu, the "problem" of opium was one of effective revenue collection, and he opposed opium prohibition plans that did not involve further escalation and consolidation of opium revenue.

THE INTERPROVINCIAL OPIUM WAR

Many of the heightened tensions surrounding the opium business-state nexus during these years were structured around a protracted trade war that was fought out during 1865–1886 between the Fujian and Guangdong provincial governments. The governors of the two provinces, under constant pressure to increase revenue, competed for a greater percentage of the regional opium trade by strategically manipulating the lijin rate in order to draw more opium away from the other province and thereby increase local revenue. The most easily recognized manifestation of this interprovincial jockeying is the balance of opium imports into the treaty ports of Shantou in eastern Guangdong and Xiamen in southern Fujian (see Figure 3.4). The two ports are part of the same ethnolinguistic and marketing macro-region and lie just over 150 miles apart (see Map 3.1). As opium distribution centers in the 1870s and 1880s, they were both positioned to supply much of the same territory: the inland districts of southwest Fujian, northeast Guangdong and the bordering districts of Jiangxi province.

In the first thirteen years after the establishment of the Fuzhou Naval Yard in 1867, authorities in Fuzhou and Xiamen charged substantially higher lijin rates than their counterparts in the treaty ports of Ningbo and Shantou in the neighboring provinces of Zhejiang and Guangdong. For most of the years between 1865 and 1879, the total combined lijin fees on a picul of opium in Xiamen was 82 taels, as compared to just 14 taels in neigh-

FIGURE 3.4: Opium imports to Xiamen (Amoy) and Shantou (Swatow), 1863–1890.

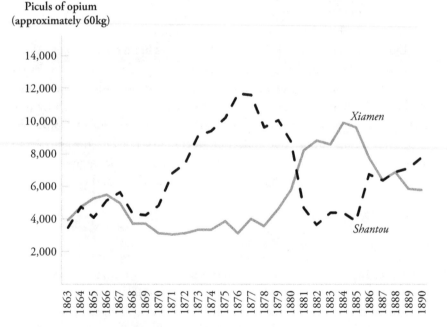

Source: "Analysis of Chinese Commerce, 1865" CMC Film Reel 4; "Analysis of Chinese Commerce, 1866" CMC Film Reel 4; "Annual Report on Trade, 1879" CMC Film Reel 7; Decennial reports on the trade, navigation, industries etc. of the ports open to foreign commerce in China and Corea and on the condition and development of the treaty port provinces, 1882–1891 and 1902–1911, IMC (Imperial Maritime Customs), Reports and Special Series, (Shanghai: Kelly & Walsh).

boring Shantou.[95] As Figure 3.4 demonstrates, this discrepancy pushed a substantive portion of the opium import trade out of Xiamen and into Shantou. Xiamen averaged 3,669 piculs during 1866–1879, down from net imports of over 5,000 piculs in 1864 and 1865. Meanwhile Shantou's imports rose annually, from 3,473 piculs in 1863 to over 11,000 piculs in each of 1876 and 1877. In Fuzhou, where the lijin was two taels higher still than in Xiamen, opium imports dropped from 7,000 piculs of opium in 1864 to an annual average of just 3,995 piculs during 1867–1879.

The consequence of this policy in Fujian was an incentive to smuggle the drug in through the neighboring provinces with lower lijin rates. As early as 1866, Xiamen's commissioner of customs reported that trade in his port was suffering due to a lijin rate that was six times as expensive as in Shantou.[96] "Opium and other foreign commodities," he wrote, were "consequently

MAP 3.1: Xiamen and Shantou.

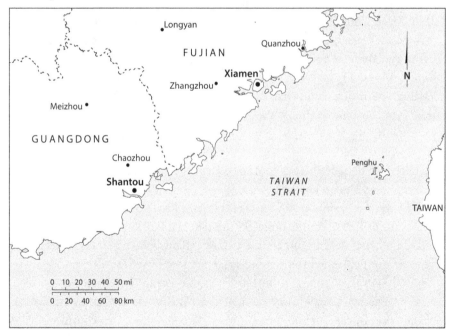

purchasable a few miles inland cheaper than the same can be procured by the retail dealer in [Xiamen]."[97] The importers of these items had paid taxes in Guangdong and clandestinely transported them into Fujian. In 1872, the commissioner of customs estimated that Shantou merchants had brought 1,500 chests of opium worth $975,000 into the Zhangzhou district of Fujian.[98] He also estimated that Xiamen's "excessive" *lijin* was diverting around 800,000 to 1,000,000 taels worth of piece goods from Xiamen to Shantou. The following year, he presented evidence that Shantou opium was being smuggled all the way into Xiamen proper.[99]

The balance of trade shifted back from Shantou to Xiamen around 1880. In Guangdong, the Governor-General Liu Kunyi won a long-standing battle with local interests to increase the opium lijin, just as the Fujian authorities were finally persuaded to lower their rates after so many years of depression.[100] When the tax hike in Shantou was announced at the beginning of 1879, scheduled to be put into place during the summer months, there was a rush to import drug at the old rate while it was still possible. That spring, Shantou's opium merchants imported the vast majority of 1879's 10,063 piculs of opium.[101] Under the new rates prevailing at Shantou, Patna and Benares opium—the varieties preferred by Fujianese smokers—were now taxed 15 taels more than at Xiamen. By 1880 several of Shantou's leading opium merchants had moved their businesses to Xiamen, "so that they may continue to supply the south-western portion of Fukien."[102] That year opium imports into Shantou dropped to 8,760 piculs, and then down to just 4,664 piculs in 1881, the year that Xiamen finally overtook Shantou. In 1884 and 1885, Xiamen imported 9,896 and 9,610 piculs of opium, the two highest years on record.

The Xiamen opium import market managed to retain its advantage over Shantou until 1886. At one point during 1883 the Fujian provincial authorities did try to raise the lijin, but the two merchants who had leased the farm successfully petitioned the state to keep the rate lower than that at Shantou.[103] Fujian's governor and the lijin farmers eventually reached a compromise by creating a flexible rate calculated according to the final destination of the drug. By 1885, opium brought into Xiamen and sold for consumption within the neighborhood of the city paid 80 taels of lijin per picul (thus it was still very profitable for people like Edwards to smuggle the drug into nearby villages), but opium bound for districts on the Guangdong and Jiangxi frontier paid only 33 taels.[104]

Creating this schedule of rates allowed Xiamen's opium lijin farmer to compete with Shantou for business in the interior, while still making good profits on the drug in the vicinity of the treaty port. But the situation changed again in late 1885 when the Shantou merchants who had moved to Xiamen in the early 1880s placed bids to take over the lijin farm in southern Fujian. A man named Cai Wei (also known as Cai Bixi) was the leader, organizing a syndicate of Cantonese merchants to take over the southern Fujian lijin farm at the end of 1885 and again the next year.[105] Cai eventually was able to control both the southern Fujian and Guangdong opium lijin farms and quickly took measures to alleviate the border war by equalizing rates to $72 per chest.[106] As is clear from the quantity of imports in 1886–1887, his plan had the effect of shifting several thousand piculs of opium from Xiamen back to Shantou. He also seems to have succeeded in influencing how provincial authorities set the lijin rate, which the many bankrupted lijin farmers of the 1860s and 1870s had failed to do.

The opium lijin war involved layers of escalating competition for drug profits: between provincial authorities, among merchant syndicates, and between merchants and the state. For Qing officials, a high lijin was presented as a way to both increase revenue and—at least according to the prevailing logic—also make Indian opium more expensive and hopefully start to reduce opium use among the population.[107] The danger of this plan was that the steadily increasing institutional demands for revenue incentivized the growth of the opium industry, rather than its slow death. As historian R. Bin Wong summarizes the dynamic, "the twin goals of creating local order and satisfying state needs for revenues became antithetical from the late Qing through the first half of the twentieth century."[108]

By "local order," Wong was referring to the spreading consumption of opium, but other critics have suggested that the institutional structure of opium taxation also undermined state authority. At the time, British diplomats worried that empowering merchants to collect revenue on their own industry would have dangerous consequences for Qing authority in the region. As one consul argued, local officials should have been more concerned about "the power accruing to a wealthy private body through the possession of well armed junks, and the maintenance of a considerable force of soldiers, sailors, watchers, spies, &c."[109] By contracting the responsibility of opium taxation and regulation to firms outside the government, the Chinese state helped fund competing local power holders at the expense of central control. This worry was embedded within the system as early as 1869, when the Xiamen lijin farmers were suspected of either being in league with or being the actual leaders of a local rebellion.[110] It was echoed again at the close of the era, in 1887, when a British customs official castigated the "evil" system as one which would farmers "would not be over scrupulous" in enforcing regulations and that "disputes, disturbances and fights and their consequent complications will be of frequent occurrence."[111]

THE CHEFOO AGREEMENT AND
THE RESTRUCTURING OF OPIUM TAXATION

The same year that Frederick Blacklock was killed by smugglers trying to evade Fuzhou's singularly high lijin, the murder of another British subject started a twelve-year chain reaction that eventually led to a total restructuring of opium lijin collection in China. This was the demise of one Augustus Margary, a British diplomat whose violent death in Yunnan during February of 1875 nearly sparked a land war between British and Qing forces along the Burma-Yunnan frontier. Strangely, it was this event—600 miles from the nearest customs outpost, under conditions having nothing to do with taxes—that finally empowered the British government to force the Qing state to reform the lijin system. The British government achieved this by attaching an Additional Article to the 1876 Chefoo Agreement, which was implemented in February 1887. The measure addressed lijin fees on the entire range of commodities, and in the case of opium it equalized rates across China, removing the incentive for interprovincial smuggling. It also empowered the foreign-managed Customs to collect the opium lijin together with the import tax, making the notoriously violent and invasive lijin farms redundant and making evasion of the lijin after import impossible.[112] Though the new policy was not a response to Blacklock's death, it directly addressed most of the central reasons for it.

The inauguration of the Chefoo Agreement in Xiamen inspired the kind of short-term opportunism that had become a distinctive characteristic of the opium business. When the changes were first announced in early January of 1887, Xiamen's soon-to-be-extinct lijin bureau immediately lowered its rates in order to induce merchants to bring in as much drug as possible before the launch of the new policy in February.[113] The tax farmer continued to lower his rates all night on January 31, and importers responded enthusiastically. Importers brought in a full quarter of that year's opium in the first month of 1887.[114] Once the new system was in place, the British consul expressed his belief that the policy would bring "the greatest improvement in the peace and good order" to Xiamen.[115] No longer would the city and its harbor be the "battlefield of, literally, hundreds of smugglers and likin runners, between whom there has not been a pin to choose as regards honesty and respectability."[116]

If British authorities were enthusiastic about dismantling the opium lijin bureaus, they were less sanguine about some of the unintended consequences of the Chefoo Agreement, most especially the further marginalization of British firms in the opium trade. British merchants had managed to maintain their position in China in large part by offering secure storage for Chinese buyers within the treaty ports. After the summer of 1887, when the Maritime Customs took over collection of the opium lijin, the Qing state began to provide a bonded warehouse service to the buyers of imported opium at a much lower rate than the British firms ever had. As the Fuzhou commissioner predicted, "It is not unlikely that in no long time it may end in the exclusion of the foreign importer altogether."[117] For other observers, the Chefoo Agreement spelled the end of the Indian opium trade itself. "Indian opium is dying an easy but sure death," wrote the British consul in Xiamen during 1888.[118] Smuggling was all but impossible under the new system, and yet *less* opium was being imported into Xiamen than during the years when smuggling was "rampant." How was this possible?

In the consul's view, the change in rules had incentivized the cultivation of domestic opium, which was gaining on Indian imports each year. Previously, when the opium lijin was leased to a Chinese firm, a substantive portion of the revenue remained local: lijin farmer, local magistrate, and provincial authorities were all cut in on the cash flow. But when the Maritime Customs started collecting the lijin in 1887, the system was revised to prioritize the channeling of funds to Beijing. "The state of affairs will of course greatly promote the growth of native opium," the consul concluded, "on which the local officials can impost what tax they like, without being accountable to the imperial government for it."[119] As evidence for his argument, he cited reports from Tong'an and Anhai counties, where the total value of opium cultivated and processed locally rose from $140,000 to $200,000 between 1887 and 1888.

If local officials in poppy-growing counties were happy to tax the drug for local budgetary reasons, as the consul suggested, many of the central-

izing officials at helm of the late Qing state were also becoming interested
in systematizing the taxation of domestic opium. It was not an easy task,
especially compared to the taxation of imported opium. Domestic opium in
China could come from any of a dozen provinces, and within those provinces, a vast number of counties. It was not something funneled into China
through the treaty ports. In Fujian, the provincial officials formalized a tax
on domestic opium in 1887 called the *tuyao lijin* (domestic opium lijin),
which in 1887–1890 amounted to a total of 17,739 taels on domestic opium,
by Luo's estimation.[120] This revenue was split between local Fujianese-
produced opium, taxed at just 0.3 taels per picul, and opium shipped in
from Yunnan and Sichuan, taxed at 35 taels per picul.[121] After 1890, revenue
collection on opium cultivated in Fujian expanded to include a *miaojuan*,
or poppy tax, which is a term and practice that would persist in Fujian
into the 1930s, as discussed in chapter 4. There was no consistency about
domestic opium taxation across the Qing empire, until in 1897 the Board
of Revenue recommended centralizing the collection of a domestic opium
lijin along the lines of the imported opium lijin, advocating for a standardized and high rate of 60 taels per picul, employing the increasingly
common logic of raising taxes in order to ultimately suppress the trade,
while maximizing revenue in the short term.[122] No formal central policy
on domestic opium taxation was enacted until the summer of 1906, when
eight provinces banded together in a united opium paste distribution tax
system during the final months before the Qing court decided to commit
to prohibition.[123]

Like their rural counterparts, municipal officials in the treaty ports were
also challenged by the centralization of opium lijin collection in 1887. In
Xiamen, the implementation of the Chefoo Agreement had a direct and ad-
verse effect on social services within the city, where a portion of the opium
lijin had previously been devoted to an assortment of public goods. These
were not projects earmarked within the new centralized opium lijin budget,
and so the elimination of the municipal tax farming arrangement served to
cut off an important revenue source for the Xiamen Examination Hall, the
Home for Female Foundlings, and two temples that provided alms for the
poor. The Xiamen circuit intendant wrote to the British consul about this
situation in July 1888, stating that local opium merchants had "voluntarily"
contributed under the earlier system, and these opium dealers were now
petitioning the circuit intendant to implement an additional fee on opium

sales so that they could continue to support these services. A deputy at the circuit intendant's office had "called together the owners of all the opium shops, and they thoroughly discussed [the circuit intendant's] instructions, collectively deciding that they were willing to pay, by an extra charge on opium, since it was a question of charity."[124] In a terse response, Consul Forrest wrote merely that the rules of the Chefoo Agreement are clear: no additional taxes can be levied on opium. "I am consequently quite unable to consent to the additional tax . . . I must ask you promptly to suppress its collection."[125]

The circuit intendant did not heed the consul's demand, and authorities in the city continued to enforce various surcharges on opium distribution up to and after the prohibition edicts of 1906. In 1889, for example, the British consul complained that Xiamen was once again losing opium imports to Shantou, because the Xiamen circuit intendant was illegally collecting a $1.70 surcharge on each chest of imported opium.[126] After the consul had refused to allow the circuit intendant to collect the tax through the Maritime Customs, the Chinese official had accomplished his goals by reviving the old tax farming system. He leased out the surcharge to a local firm, the Taiji Company, who agreed to pay the circuit intendant for $1.70 on 500 chests of opium per month and was responsible for organizing its own means of collection.

When the tax ended up driving trade out of Xiamen and into Shantou, the Taiji Company found itself short of taxes on an average of 135 chests of opium each month. The circuit intendant sought to punish the firm for coming up short by imposing a fine of $4,000, which led to a series of legal appeals, and eventually, a raid on the Taiji firm's headquarters by troops sent by the governor-general of Fujian and Zhejiang. Undaunted, the circuit intendant turned to the guild of opium shop owners in Xiamen and demanded that they organize among themselves, "choose a headman," and figure a way to pay the additional tax (now reduced to $1.50, but still on a quota of 500 chests per month).[127] The lijin system was resurfacing. The British government finally convinced the Qing Ministry of Foreign Affairs (zongli yamen) to order the circuit intendant to stop collection of the surcharge in October of 1890, but this too seems to have been a futile effort. In a petition from 1910, Xiamen's opium den operators stated that the Xiamen Maritime sub-prefect had for several decades been collecting a surcharge on opium's retail in the city at a quota of 850 taels per month, called the opium paste "donation" (*juan*) to be used as an "administrative fee" (*xingzheng jingfei*).[128] Officials in Xiamen and elsewhere would periodically farm out a range of fees onto opium sales until, and after, the drug's prohibition.

Conclusion: A Shared Regional History

Because of opium's particular history in China, it can be difficult to remember that the late Qing state was but one of a large handful of governments in late-nineteenth-century Asia that made opium taxation a central part of their fiscal infrastructure. A Fujianese investor in the 1880s would have known this and would have likely viewed the opium lijin bureau in Fujian as one of many similar opportunities available in places like Hong Kong, the Philippines, French Indo-China, Siam, the Netherlands Indies, and the British Straits Settlements. In all of these places, states farmed out opium distribution and retail taxes to Chinese firms, many of which were members of the southern Fujianese diaspora.[129] In Java during these same decades, for example, coalitions of the powerful Hokkien (southern Fujianese) merchants promised tens of millions of Dutch guilders to the colonial state for territorial opium taxation rights, purchased at highly competitive auctions.[130] In Singapore, where the British state was even more reliant on opium revenue, contracts for the opium farm were extraordinarily lucrative.[131] And where in Java the competition for opium profits operated along family or surname lines, in Singapore the bidding for opium tax farming rights was often fought out along native-place lines between Hokkien firms and their Teochew rivals (Teochew or Chaozhou is in eastern Guangdong, home to the treaty port of Shantou).[132]

Like the competition for state opium contracts in Singapore, the Fujian-Guangdong opium lijin war analyzed in this chapter was a forum for the global competition for wealth and power between the populations of southern Fujian and eastern Guangdong. These two population groups composed a majority of the Chinese diaspora in the nineteenth century, and native-place associations from southern Fujian and Chaozhou were central forces in the most lucrative branches of trade in most of China's major cities. Their commercial and territorial competition spanned the entire globe and shaped the urban history of Shanghai and Singapore, among other global cities.[133] Hokkien and Teochew communities lived in cities and ports from Paris and London to San Francisco and Seattle, from Bombay and Calcutta through Singapore, Saigon, Hong Kong, Taiwan, and Shanghai. The evidence from this chapter brings that competition back home, examining how late Qing opium revenue policies fueled a trade war between those districts.

Viewed in the long history of the opium business on the southeast Chinese maritime frontier, the legal years of the opium business saw the crystallization of practices that would become fundamental to the operation of the drug trade in the early twentieth century. Chinese smugglers learned the utility of foreign citizenship and tested the limits of their rights as foreign subjects. This was a transitional moment in the evolution of Fujianese approaches to the jurisdictional complexity of their maritime world, when the advantages of foreign citizenship became so obvious that dressing up in a jacket, hat, and holding a cigar became a common ruse among the legions of opium smugglers in Xiamen. Meanwhile, the foreigners who remained involved in the drug trade—like St. Julian Hugh Edwards and the growing number of Singaporean and Parsee merchants that the British consul bemoaned—were increasingly drawn to illegal methods of securing profit. The detail that Edwards's opium buyer in the hinterland was a pharmacist is also worth pausing to consider, as it presages the role that pharmacists would play in the global drug networks of the twentieth century.

The evolution of lijin bureaus were fundamentally influential on the political economy of the drug trade in later years. In Southeast Asia, the turn of the century saw many of the old tax farming systems die out in favor of new centralized state opium monopolies, or in the case of the Philippines, outright prohibition. As China pursued its own path towards prohibition after 1906, the drug's special significance as a symbol of national victimization and humiliation meant that a centralized state opium monopoly was ultimately not a politically viable option. Instead, the consensus plan was to entirely uproot the opium business, which in Fujian would involve transitioning municipal opium surcharge institutions into prohibition bureaus (*jinyan ju*) and eliminating poppy taxes altogether.

In practice, prohibition meant the repackaging of late-nineteenth-century opium taxation institutions. The people running the new prohibition bureaus would be independent contractors, coalitions of professional investors from within the opium business just like their predecessors in the lijin bureaus. These independent contractors used their position to stimulate the drug trade and maximize revenue extraction. By the 1920s, as examined in the next chapter of this book, the opium business in Fujian would reach unprecedented new heights.

"Opium Kings" and Tax Farmers in the Age of Prohibition, 1906–1938

In September of 1910, the Xiamen Maritime sub-prefect posted a controversial public notice about changes in the regulation of opium. He was announcing the launch of a new system of opium licensing and taxation, in conjunction with the city's embattled Anti-Opium Society. All shops selling opium paste—opium dens and dispensaries—would now be required to pay a tax of $3 per tael on opium smoked in house and $5 per tael on opium carried out of the shop to be smoked elsewhere. Additionally, the shops would be required to submit their account books to the Anti-Opium Society for auditing. Soldiers and inspectors from the society were authorized to enter all licensed opium establishments every five days to collect the fees. Violators would be fined ten times the tax they were determined to owe and lose their operating licenses.[1]

Xiamen's opium shopkeepers were unhappy with the measure. They sent a collective petition to the port's British consul, not as his constituents but because he was duty-bound to uphold Britain's treaty rights as regarded the taxation of Indian opium. The opium merchants pointed out to the consul that the British government had diplomatic grounds to demand that the local authorities withdraw the plan, based on a clause in the Sino-British Chefoo Agreement (signed 1876, implemented 1887) prohibiting additional taxation on imported opium.[2] They added the obvious implication—that the tax was a threat to British profits—and warned the consul that Indian opium imports into Xiamen might cease altogether if the new impost were to continue unimpeded. Consul B. G. Tours responded positively to the petition and lodged a complaint with the Xiamen authorities that cited each of the arguments suggested by the coalition of opium paste merchants.[3]

Four years into the late-Qing prohibition era, officials and investors in Xiamen were adapting preexisting taxation and regulatory structures to increase revenue and profits in the new context of opium prohibition. The opium merchants stated in their petition that they had for several decades paid the maritime sub-prefect an opium paste retail tax at a monthly quota of $850. What they were protesting, then, was not the existence of a tax, although that was the premise of their approach to enlisting the British consul's support. Rather, this was a group of powerful opium merchants expressing their opposition to a hostile takeover of the preexisting system of fee collection, which would entail the increase of their long-standing monthly quota on opium retail surcharges from $850 to $1,000.[4]

Beyond the rise in the quota, which was unwelcome, the new system would place the Anti-Opium Society as an intermediary between the opium merchants and the maritime sub-prefect. Where previously the city's officials had farmed the tax directly to the opium retailers, now the Anti-Opium Society would be the agency to arrange for opium's regulation and taxation. The man behind the plan was Shi Shijie, the president of the Xiamen Anti-Opium Society and a person the opium merchants referred to in their petition as a "gentry bully" (lieshen). According to the US consul, Shi was "not a popular man in the Association."[5] A few months after the launch of the new scheme, outraged members of the Anti-Opium Society forced Shi's dismissal for having "associated with a court runner in farming the monopoly of the prepared opium tax."[6]

The opium dealers' petition offers a rare glimpse into the institutional and commercial history of the transition from a legal opium regime to one of prohibition. Shi used his position as the director of the Anti-Opium Society to raise revenue (and by implication, personal capital) by demanding a higher per-piece retail tax and consequently a higher monthly quota of opium retail fees. He did this by coopting a preexisting "administrative fee" on opium paste dispensaries in the city, one which predated the prohibition edicts, and he sold off the collection of this now reorganized impost along with the authority to enforce it. Shi Shijie was consolidating the opium business under the moral and institutional auspices of prohibition, while retaining the tax farming relationship within this new infrastructure.

Tax farming survived within the modern Chinese opium revenue and prohibition institutions. This commercial and institutional continuity helps explain how the Opium prohibition bureaus (*jinyan ju*) of warlord and Republican China came so notoriously to serve the exact opposite purpose of their titular role. Prohibition bureaus were created in the final years of the Qing and incorporated formally into nearly every Republican and warlord government after 1911 as a signal of dedication to nationalists at home and moralizers abroad that the Chinese state was determined to curtail and eventually eliminate opium use. In much of China, and indeed especially in Fujian, the directorship of an opium prohibition bureau was an office that state actors contracted out to private entities. Among the many investors who purchased these positions, the most powerful were people who were already involved in the opium business, and they used the opportunity of state affiliation to expand their businesses. The practice dates to the first prohibition institutions in late Qing Fujian and would survive every political upheaval until the late 1940s.

Continuities in local commercial and tax farming practices also structured the rapid expansion of poppy cultivation in Fujian during the height of the warlord years, between 1917 and 1928. Southern Fujian's militarists in these years operated opium prohibition bureaus in the cities to handle the drug's distribution and retail, while simultaneously collecting millions of dollars worth of poppy taxes in the countryside. Rural lineages who had fought tooth and nail to protect their poppies against prohibitionists in the final years of the Qing were in the early 1920s asked to increase opium production, even as farmers of other crops were pressured, coerced, and according to some accounts, forced to grow the opium poppy. Large wholesale buyers of the local drug stepped forward to partner with the warlords, promising quotas in the millions of dollars for the sole right to purchase a county or territory's opium production (and in so doing, tax the farmers). Vertically integrated investors would seek to overlap poppy tax contracts and opium prohibition bureau directorships. These opium experts shifted nationality and political allegiance with effortless grace, weathering each revolutionary storm and reemerging to sign multimillion-dollar contracts with the region's new authorities.

This chapter builds on earlier historiography of opium prohibition in China by offering the local story from the perspective of the people invested in the trade, highlighting continuities in personnel and tax farming relationships throughout this period.[7] Opium prohibition bureaus and poppy taxes were not simply installed. These were institutions with local roots. The dominant opium investors of the era stood their ground, through waves of collapsing warlord regimes and through a succession of increasingly muscular national opium plans emanating from Nanjing. Retelling the history of poppy taxes and opium prohibition bureaus as one of negotiations between powerful drug traders and the state illuminates the remarkable consistency that drug traders achieved during these years—in terms of profits, personnel, and practices—and suggests that we should endeavor to take seriously their impact on the political economy of early twentieth-century China.

Prohibition and Profit in Southern Fujian, 1906–1911

During the autumn of 1906, the Qing court issued a series of edicts designed to suppress and ultimately eliminate the opium trade in China. The plan was set out in eleven steps, the most urgent of which was the prohibition of poppy cultivation within China over a period of no longer than ten years.[8] Stopping Chinese domestic opium production was first on the list because it was the precondition for British promises to reduce and eventually stop imports from India. The plan also provided for a licensing system to enroll smokers and dealers with the goal of gradually reducing their number. It mandated the total prohibition of opium dens within six months, and smokers who were too old or too addicted to quit immediately would be issued permits to purchase opium paste from licensed dealers and smoke at home. There were also provisions for research into medicine designed to help smokers quit, strict prohibition of opium use among the official population, and the establishment of rehabilitation clinics. Provincial officials were to encourage the nonofficial gentry population to set up Anti-Opium Societies in all the major cities.

The global opium economy had changed a great deal since the last time the drug was illegal in China. Some of China's opium was still coming from India, but the market share of Persian, Turkish, and especially domestically produced opium had grown exponentially. Chinese opium eclipsed imports around 1870, and by 1906 only one-tenth of the opium consumed in China was still coming from India.[9] Morphine, heroin, and cocaine use were also on the rise, and new transnational networks had risen up to connect Chinese buyers with suppliers in Germany, France, England, and Japan. China had also become an exporter of opium, after Southeast Asian colonial governments from the Philippines to Burma began tightening their grip over the opium trade and made it lucrative to smuggle the drug illegally into those places. The United States and Mexico also emerged as major destinations for Chinese opium during these years.

The prohibition edicts went largely unimplemented in southern Fujian. While other ports with more robust prohibition movements clamped down on drug flows, Xiamen began to reassume its earlier status as an important hub in the global opium trade (see Figure 4.1). As the commissioner of customs wrote of the years 1902–1911, "When it is considered that Amoy supplies the wants of a comparatively limited area, the relatively large quantity of opium and its derivatives imported through this port is perhaps without a parallel in any other province in China."[10] Opium imports to China from India were finally beginning to decrease, and yet imports of the drug into Xiamen continued apace. In 1911, when opium imports finally dropped over 1,000 piculs under the average for the decade (a consequence of the Xinhai

FIGURE 4.1: Opium imports into Xiamen as a percentage of the national total, 1904–1911.

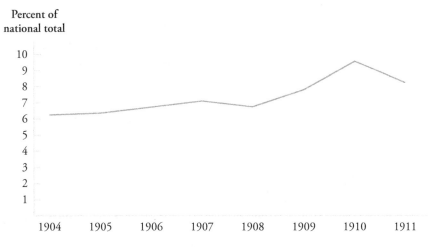

Source: IMC (Imperial Maritime Customs), "Decennial Report for Amoy, 1902–11," in Vol. II, *Southern and Frontier Ports* (Shanghai: Kelly & Walsh, 1912), 102, 344.

Revolution, which disrupted trade during the autumn months), the port still accounted for a substantially higher percentage of the national opium trade than in any year between 1863 and 1906.

Skyrocketing opium prices underwrote the resurgence of the regional opium business. The average price of a chest of Patna opium imported into China rose from 394 taels in the 1890s to 1,008 taels during the first decade of the twentieth century. In Xiamen, where the escalation in opium prices was even more dramatic, a chest of Patna in 1911 cost an average of 2,800 taels and the more popular Benares variety cost 3,230 taels, more than three times the national average.[11] The British consul believed that a few of the larger dealers involved in this flurry of speculation earned as much as $2,000,000 each during the summer of 1911.[12] Sichuan and Yunnan opium, carried to Xiamen by steamer via Shanghai or overland routes from Hunan, saw a similar trend: the cost of a picul rose from 330 taels at the turn of the century to 2,060 taels in August of 1911, when the governor-general ordered the prohibition of domestic opium imports.[13] At the height of the price surge, a single chest of Benares opium was worth more than 60,000 kg of rice. [14]

The Fujianese opium transshipment industry, which was undercut in the mid-nineteenth century by the opening of the treaty ports and the legalization of the opium trade, was experiencing a resurgence. The final decades of the Qing saw a rapid uptick in opium smuggling from Fujian into various jurisdictions across colonial Southeast Asia, as is examined in chapter 5 of this book. The high price of Benares in Xiamen, just noted as three times the national average, came from that variety's status as a luxury brand in Fujian and among the overseas Chinese in Southeast Asia. It was something not legally available in French, Dutch, or American colonial jurisdictions, and buyers in Xiamen were willing to put down huge sums to ensure what could be their final opportunity to package and sell the most sought-after brand name.

Local consumption, increasingly regulated and taxed through the opium prohibition infrastructure, was also part of the reason for the continued strength of the trade. Four years into the prohibition era there were still over 100 opium dens remaining in Xiamen, divided into three groups. The largest dispensaries could boil down and sell seven to eight balls worth of opium per day, with the middle ones selling paste derived from four to five balls, and the smallest one to two balls. In their petition to the British consul for assistance when the maritime sub-prefect raised taxes on their business, the coalition of opium paste dispensaries estimated the city's daily consumption at around seven to eight chests of foreign opium per day, or close to 3,000 chests per year.[15] Because the petition was addressed to a British official about imported Indian opium, their accounting purposefully did not include domestic Chinese opium, which by most estimations had a much higher market share. Total consumption in the city during 1889 was around 6,000 chests per year. By 1910, four years after the prohibition edicts, this number would seem to have increased.

Farmers were also reluctant to give up poppy cultivation in rural Fujian. The 1906 edicts had made eradication of poppy cultivation the first priority in the imperial effort to suppress the opium trade. In Fujian, where cultivation had expanded dramatically during the late Qing, this was a tall order. Between 1899 and 1901, domestic opium production in Fujian increased by an estimated 33 percent, from 6,000 piculs per year to 8,000.[16] By 1907, the undoubtedly conservative Qing official estimate was that there was 37,000 *mu* (approximately 6,094 acres) of land solely dedicated to poppy cultivation in the province.[17] In August of that year, the Fujian and Zhejiang Governor-General Songshou issued the first of several unheeded orders to local officials across the province for total eradication of the poppy. All fields planted with the poppy were to be uprooted and replanted with foodstuffs; violators were to be subject to land confiscations.[18]

Farmers, lineages, and local officials invested in the cash crop were not so easy to convince. The British consul in Xiamen derided the local officials' reception of Songshou's orders, arguing that "the area under poppy cultivation in this district does not yet show any signs of decrease, actual or impending, though official statistics may show the contrary, by classifying under rice or wheat land which is really devoted to the papaver somniferum."[19] After Songshou's two-month deadline passed without any progress in the districts with entrenched cultivation, the governor-general granted the Quanzhou prefect another six months to carry out his orders.[20]

Two years later, in December of 1909, a team of soldiers sent into Tong'an county to order farmers to cease growing the poppy were met with violence. The Tong'an magistrate had dispatched a commander to negotiate with the leadership of the powerful Hong lineage and sought to convince the elders to order their lineage members to uproot their poppy crops. When the rest of the lineage got wind of the reason for his visit, a mob assembled and people began shooting rifles over the heads of the small group of soldiers and scouts. When one of the soldiers was shot and killed, a protracted gunfight ensued. The advantage was clearly in favor of the enraged Hong lineage members, and the soldiers retreated to Xiamen. Within the week a new unit of 1,000 soldiers from the Xiamen garrison entered the village and—according to a Shanghai newspaper report—"subdued" (*jiao*) the troublemakers.[21] The story was repeated in newspapers across the world, including the *New York Times*.[22]

As activists and some officials sought to enforce an agenda of prohibition, lineages along the southern Fujian littoral were investing more land and capital than ever in the opium trade. Guns and ammunition flowed into the poppy districts of southern Fujian, where the long-standing pattern of lineage feuding was fueled by the surge in poppy cultivation during the final decade of Qing rule. In 1903, the Maritime Customs intercepted a huge shipment of weapons and matériel bound for a dealer supplying the feuding lineages of Zhangzhou prefecture, including over 520,000 copper pipes for gun manufacture and 4,800 artillery shells.[23] Just a few months later a bloody, gun-fueled feud between two coastal lineages in Quanzhou prefecture spilled over into dozens of other villages, making the whole Jinjiang county coastline unsafe for travel.[24] In 1908, the Maritime Customs intercepted a shipment of over 9,000 foreign manufactured guns being smuggled in from Taiwan, bound for the villages of coastal Quanzhou prefecture "for the purposes of supplying those villages engaged in lineage feuding."[25] In coastal Hui'an, one of the epicenters of poppy production, British missionaries commented on how lineages were rebuilding old "fighting towers" from the seventeenth century due to a "boom" in lineage feuding.[26]

In Xiamen, long-standing urban lineages also structured and limited the work of prohibitionists. The Chen, Wu, and Ji families were the port's largest and most powerful lineages in the late Qing and Republican period, maintaining control over a wide range of occupations and territories within the city itself and neighboring Tong'an county.[27] These three families controlled stevedore work and inner harbor transport, hotel management, and rice distribution in the city. Many members of the Wu, Ji, and Chen lineages also owned neighborhood institutions for gambling, prostitution, and opium smoking.[28]

In their role as the dominant power players in stevedore work and harbor transport, the Chen and Wu lineages often feuded over smuggling and transport operations, such as in 1911 when members of the Chen lineage captured one of the Wu family's small steamships. The incident involved two kidnappings and a pitched battle on the beach.[29] A Shanghai newspaper described the three lineages of Xiamen as serious problems for local government: "All of them are armed with an arsenal of foreign rifles and machine guns, as a means to engage in feuding, to kidnap people and earn money."[30] The unsuccessful solution proposed by the circuit intendant was to have a respected gentry figure request that all three groups hand over their weapons.

Lineage power determined the extent of government power in the city, a sphere of self-regulation that generally served to resist against centralizing impulses. Sometimes the power and autonomy of urban lineages stemmed from long-standing tax farming relationships, such as those members of the Chen family who had operated the region's lucrative salt tax monopoly during the late Qing. Other times lineages influenced the local government through bribery, as when a notorious smuggler from the Wu lineage hosted a lavish banquet for the Tong'an county magistrate. Historian Zhou Zifeng uses this incident to demonstrate how courting government officials was a means by which lower-status lineage members who struck it rich in unlawful occupations could increase their social standing and help ensure protection in the event of trouble.[31] In 1910, a prominent member of the Chen lineage was widely rumored to have bribed the local judicial officials to abstain from holding an inquest after public suspicion was aroused when his future daughter-in-law was found murdered.[32] These were the city's power brokers.

Opium prohibition in Xiamen was implemented through the city's new police force, and policing would depend on cooperation and support from the lineages that ruled over neighborhood life and occupational security in the city. Until Xiamen's three lineages would face the existential threat of Taiwanese encroachment on their territory in the late 1910s (see chapter 6), they did not support the police. In 1905, for instance, the Chinese detectives hired by the Gulangyu Municipal Council were refusing to work. "They frankly confess that they are afraid to do so," wrote one foreign diplomat, "they say their families will get killed if they get anyone convicted."[33] When the Qing government set up the city's first municipal police force in Xiamen in 1906, the circuit intendant tried to avoid the problem of indirect retaliation against police family members by recruiting his patrolmen and officers from the floating population of impoverished migrants from the highland districts of inland Fujian.[34]

It did not help. In December of 1906, just a few months after the force was established, a mob surrounded and killed one of the new police officers.[35] A few years later, when an ambitious new maritime sub-prefect arrived in Xiamen and attempted to close the city's brothels as part of an effort to rid the district of all locations with opium smoking divans, a group of local soldiers became enraged and "promptly proceeded to smash everything in the vicinity, including some of the [Inspection Office] policemen."[36] In 1914, the circuit intendant shut down his new police school after filling only 20 of 120 positions. He gave up on recruiting locally and sent off for 300 "Northern Police."[37] Prohibition was already an unpopular policy among the many who consumed the drug or made their living by its production and distribution. The waves of outsiders that municipal authorities imported to do the work of policing was a symptom of a local state with a lack of local control.

THE XIAMEN ANTI-OPIUM SOCIETY

The Xiamen Anti-Opium Society was established in 1908 as an afterthought.[38] This institution was meant to be the primary engine of prohibition, linking up powerful gentry figures with the local government in pursuit of the task, but the Xiamen branch never operated in the same way as the provincial headquarters in Fuzhou. That organization, the Fujian Anti-Opium Society, had been founded by a group of prestigious literati figures during June of 1906, led by the great-grandson of the Opium War crusader and nationalist symbol Lin Zexu. The Fujian Anti-Opium Society, according to historian Joyce Madancy, "proved itself a savvy manipulator of nationalistic symbolism, cognizant of the need not only to appeal to provincial loyalties but also to cement the approval of the central state and co-opt its symbolic and legal authority."[39] Madancy's research demonstrates how the Fuzhou activists actually made tangible progress towards prohibition, against all odds. The Fujian Anti-Opium Society was formed out of a core group of die-hard supporters with government connections and symbolic stature. In contrast, Xiamen's poorly funded group came together belatedly, a half-hearted response to pressure from the fervent activism in the provincial capital.[40]

The Xiamen Anti-Opium Society was held back by a lack of continuity in leadership, funding, and general public support. During the three-year span from 1908 to 1911, the society elected at least six different presidents, one of whom was later described by a British consul as "a disreputable person" who "had previously been engaged in smuggling cocaine," and another who, as detailed in the opening passage to this chapter, was forced to resign following criticism for farming out a new distribution tax.[41] For someone genuinely committed to prohibition, the post would have been quite frustrating. The Xiamen Anti-Opium Society was forced to partner with local officials who were at best reluctant about the cause. Whereas government officials in Fuzhou were under the constant surveillance of the Fujian Anti-Opium Society for opium use, officials in southern Fujian were often described as notorious users of the drug, according to one US consul, and "thus their edicts have little effect."[42] When the leader of the provincial anti-opium movement came from Fuzhou to inspect the progress of Xiamen's Anti-Opium Society during mid-1910, the Xiamen circuit intendant complained at length to him about the hardships associated with prohibition and begged that Xiamen "be left alone by the opium crusade."[43] The visitor from Fuzhou was so enraged that he telegraphed Beijing and got the reluctant official dismissed. After four years of national prohibition policy and two years of the Anti-Opium Society's existence, the most powerful local officials in Xiamen remained generally unsupportive of prohibition.

The symbolic nadir of the Xiamen Anti-Opium Society's influence took place at a banquet held in June of 1911. During the festivities—a joint celebration of the Anti-Opium Society and the Athletic Society—two men began smoking opium in plain view of all of the leaders of the prohibition group. Detectives from the Anti-Opium Society walked across the hall and tried to arrest the two men, and a fight broke out. When the dust settled, one of the smokers stated that he was a Taiwanese (and therefore Japanese) citizen, and the offending duo was able to resist arrest by enlisting the support of the Japanese consulate. The Xiamen Anti-Opium Society, after five years of prohibition, was unable to enforce opium regulations even in their own dining hall.[44]

Prohibition and Profit after the Xinhai Revolution

When the Qing dynasty finally collapsed, the institutions of prohibition were thrown deeper into flux. The Xinhai Revolution took Xiamen at eleven p.m. on November 5, 1911, when the circuit intendant fled his office and took refuge in the Mixed Court Municipal Jail in the foreign concession on Gulangyu. The next morning the British consul and the commissioner of customs placed the harried official on the customs cruiser *Pingcheng* and sent him out on the water to keep safe. The former Qing representative took to the sea, as revolution waved over the city. "Thus," wrote the consul, "the Chinese government has ceased to exist in Amoy."[45]

A group of local revolutionary activists, including the alleged cocaine smuggler and "loud-mouthed patriot" Huang Tingyuan, subsequently posted a manifesto around the city declaring the beginning of a new era.[46] Unbeknownst to them, the new revolutionary governor who came to power in Fuzhou was in the process of trying to telegraph Xiamen's former circuit intendant in order to encourage him to "carry on the government as heretofore." The governor did not know that the man had absconded in the *Pingcheng*. When the missing official finally did return to try and assume the responsibility, he ended up in a bloody conflict in front of the government building with another hopeful to the job.[47] This was a moment of instability, violence, and opportunism.

Early enthusiasm about prohibition work in Xiamen after the Xinhai Revolution was ultimately overwhelmed by the continued profitability of the opium business. In the summer of 1912, a group of officials and activists calculated that prior to 1911 local prohibitionists had managed to reduce the number of opium dens in Xiamen from over 800 to just 105. The number had risen back up to over 300 in the chaos following the political upheaval, and the new authorities decided to immediately reduce the number of opium dens to a more manageable 135.[48] The Anti-Opium Society divided the 135 remaining opium dens into ten categories, with licensing fees ranging from $5 to $50 per month.[49] Each month one of the ten categories would be shut down, and after ten months there would be no opium dens left in Xiamen.

It was an ambitious plan, and police and constables accompanied by the maritime sub-prefect in person traveled through the eighteen wards of the city to shut down unlicensed opium dens and notify the local population of the plan. The US consul was impressed by what he viewed as the newfound dedication of Xiamen's officialdom to the cause, stating that before the revolution local officials only supported prohibition "in a more or less half-hearted way," whereas now they "have been using their best endeavors to see that the regulations are carried out."[50] Less than a year later, Xiamen's anti-opium commissioner was caught in the act while smoking opium and arrested.[51]

Foreign diplomats stationed in Fujian frequently obstructed the work of prohibitionists. In June 1913, for example, the British and French consuls in Xiamen defeated a proposal by the mixed court magistrate to implement Chinese prohibition laws within the foreign concession on Gulangyu. "There seems," wrote the American consul, "to be a disinclination on the part of my colleagues to take any action towards suppressing the opium evil unless the Legations in Peking or the Consular Body in Shanghai take the initiative."[52] Opium smokers were ferrying over to the foreign concession in Gulangyu rather than staying in Xiamen proper where they risked arrest in unlicensed dens or being entered into the system as a registered smoker, which entailed being photographed and restricted to buying more expensive opium in licensed dens. Smokers could also indulge without repercussion by doing so on any of the myriad boats within the Xiamen harbor flying foreign colors. "Along the busy southern coast of this province where vessels ply in great numbers," wrote the inspector general of the Opium Administration for South Fujian, "passengers, sailors and servants of the vessels often smoke opium on board, openly and boldly."[53] Outside of the foreign concession, in Xiamen proper, the Japanese and French consuls raised objections whenever local authorities raided unlicensed opium dens and arrested smokers with claims to foreign protection.[54]

British support for prohibition in China, never full-throated to begin with, deteriorated further after the Xinhai Revolution. In 1913, just as the British government was set to cease imports of Indian opium into China, the minister in Beijing decided that remaining stocks of Indian drug could continue to be sold into Fujian, after he received numerous reports indicating that cultivation was still common in the province, and also that domestic opium from other provinces was being brought in.[55] As part of his evidence for this decision, the minister cited a letter from the Shanghai merchant, Edward Ezra, whose Fujianese contacts in the Shanghai opium trade stated that they "positively declare that not only have large crops been harvested [in Fujian], but also that native opium is freely obtainable. They declare emphatically that the farmers have made good profits this year on their crops . . . and up to the present beyond issuing proclamations [local officials have] took no steps to interfere with the harvesting or sale of the crops."[56] Ezra was the chairman of the Shanghai Opium Combine, and his interest in forwarding such a report to the British government was to give evidence that would allow him to continue selling Indian opium into the province.[57]

In advance of that decision, Fujian's Anti-Opium Society had lobbied consuls in the ports to report positively on prohibition work in the province. In one letter to a newly appointed British consul in Xiamen, the society claimed that "complete success" had been achieved in eradicating cultivation. The consul, perhaps a bit naïvely, responded with effusive praise. "The whole world admires the loftiness of the meritorious desire to set in order the evil customs of an abuse," he wrote, "to get rid of those who have wandered from the path and are on the 'black list,' to change a fiery pit into a lotus field, to remove a dreadful poison and reform its victims."[58] This unusual support from a British diplomat inspired the Fujian Anti-Opium Society to preemptively declare to Beijing that the British government "had recognized that complete success had been attained as regarded the prohibition of opium cultivation in the province." This declaration in turn prompted a reader at the British legation in Beijing to scribble angrily in the margin of the document that "it was quite unnecessary [for the consul] to have written this letter which is embarrassing at the present juncture."[59] It was not the position of the ministry that Fujian's provincial authorities had achieved success in eradicating opium poppy cultivation.

The Fujian Anti-Opium Society wrote a scathing letter of protest in response to the British Minister's 1913 decision to continue to allow the sale of Indian opium into Fujian. The authors asked for the British to empathize with impoverished Fujianese cultivators, who were being forced to give up an important cash crop during a period of economic uncertainty. The letter singled out the Xinghua district near Quanzhou as the primary holdout in favor of continuing poppy cultivation, where locals felt "that to suppress the cultivation before suppressing the import was merely robbing the farmers of their livelihood to fill the pockets of the foreign merchants."[60] The letter's authors then go on to suggest that the British consider the human cost of the Fujianese prohibition effort. "It is certainly the first time in the history of any of the provinces that an enormous income has been thrown away and the lives of the people regarded as of no more value than dirt," they wrote. "We beg that you will press for the early prohibition of import, so as to grant us liberty in suppressing opium, and enable us to pass safely over these dark waters."[61] The minister did not appear to give any credence to the notion that continuing Indian imports into Fujian might be one of the reasons why prohibitionists had found it difficult to eradicate poppy cultivation in the countryside.

POPPY TAXES AND THE WARLORD-ERA
PRODUCTION BOOM, 1917–1926

Farmers had been cultivating opium poppies in southern Fujian since the
early nineteenth century, taxed in formal and informal ways up to the time
of the prohibition edicts, which delegitimized all formal taxation of domestic opium. After 1911, when the new revolutionary government tried to seize
the moment and eradicate poppy cultivation in southern Fujian, counties
like Tong'an and Xinghua held out and continued to produce large crops.
A Hong Kong opium firm estimated the 1912 crop in southern Fujian to be
worth $20,000,000.[62] By 1914, the British consul in Xiamen reported that
there were sufficient stocks of locally produced opium in Tong'an county
alone to supply the entire province's opium smokers for three to four years.[63]
"It is reported," wrote an American observer, "that the stronger clans have
been able to prevent any very active operations in the districts where they
are growing their crops. While some actual destruction has taken place,
the percentage is said to be small."[64] In Xinghua prefecture, a man named
Huang Lian spearheaded a popular uprising, capitalizing on rural resent-
ment about anti-opium policies, Christian missionaries (themselves closely
allied with the prohibitionists), and high taxes.[65] Huang's uprising was
funded through a widespread protection scheme, wherein he collected a
poppy tax at the rate of $6 per acre to fund a militia to resist the provincial
governor's attempts to uproot the crop.[66]

Poppy taxes like the one Huang Lian collected snowballed across southern Fujian in 1917, after Chen Jiongming's Cantonese forces attacked the
Beiyang military commander Li Houji. When Chen Jiongming's forces
conquered a district, they immediately installed an opium tax, called the
"field tax," and used troops to go around collecting the levy.[67] It was a clever
strategy, thought one British consul, because farmers in districts that had
grown the poppy during the late Qing had "suffered a great deal economically through the eradication of the poppy."[68] Recalling the Tong'an riots of
1909—when powerful lineages fought tooth and nail with prohibitionists
who sought to uproot their poppy crop—the aspiring militarists of the late
1910s adopted a strategy to secure alliances among the rural lineages of
southern Fujian by ensuring that poppy cultivation would go unpunished,
if not untaxed. As the British consul put it, "Both the authorities and the
people profited by such action."[69]

Li Houji and the Beiyang forces followed suit. In Putian county, an area controlled by Li's armies, the total crop of opium produced during 1919 was worth an estimated $5–10 million.[70] The tax revenue from this was substantial. By 1921 Li had systematized his taxation of the poppy crop, collecting it in three installments during the harvest (March–April) with troops under the command of Shi Tingyang, Li Houji's cousin and the commissioner of defense for Xiamen, Quanzhou, and Zhangzhou.[71] When confronted by the Fujian Anti-Opium Society in the provincial capital, Li Houji confirmed that "it was an established fact" that the poppy was being grown in huge quantities, but claimed that it was "being planted contrary to his commands" and that "any drastic action on his part would only result in those concerned turning bandits and so increase the confusion of affairs and difficulty of government." Next year, Li pronounced with little enthusiasm, "the province would be clear of the foul weed."[72] He appointed a Quanzhou man named Wang Dazhen to serve as special deputy of opium suppression that autumn, and shortly after that the Fujian Anti-Opium Society accused Wang of "secretly joining with the military officials in order to divide the taxes obtained from the poppy fields."[73]

Farmers who lived in districts that passed back and forth between rival warlords were placed in constant danger by the heightened value of the poppy tax to warlord finances. In Jinjiang county's Yakou Village, home of the powerful Shi lineage who had dominated the opium import business nearly a century previous (see chapter 1), villagers found themselves in a terrifying position when control over their district shifted from one warlord to another. In early 1919, a Shi lineage elder entered into a poppy tax agreement with the Jingguo Army's commanding officer in the region. Shortly after this, the southern part of Jinjiang county was taken over by a Cantonese unit dispatched north by Sun Yatsen. Accordingly, the Shi lineage elders were forced to enter into a new agreement with the resident Cantonese army captain, who collected a poppy tax on what proved to be a bumper harvest.

A few months later, disaster struck when the Cantonese forces departed from Jinjiang county and the Jingguo Army reassumed control. As one Shi lineage member recollected in the early 1960s, the Jingguo officers were furious with the Yakou residents for handing over their poppy tax to the Cantonese forces. In retaliation, the commanding officer rejected the lineage elders' offer to take over a local temple, instead demanding to house his soldiers in people's homes. The Yakou Shi called together a village militia to resist the depredations of the occupying soldiers, and months of armed conflict ensued.[74]

Despite occasional resistance, the tactic of encouraging and taxing opium cultivation proved highly effective and was emulated by subsequent military commanders and power holders in Fujian. Zhang Zhen, Xu Chongzhi, Wang Yongquan, Cang Zhiping, Chen Guohui, Sun Zhuanlao, and Zhou Yinren, to name the most notable figures in Fujianese warlord-era politics, all came to rely heavily on the poppy tax to keep their regimes solvent.[75] As the International Anti-Opium Association wrote in 1924, "practically the whole province is under compulsory cultivation and its attendant heavy taxation. In every instance the compulsion is military and the taxes seized by the Armies."[76] A *New York Times* article from that same year asserted that, in Fujian, "about 70,000 soldiers, under five principal Generals, together with the navy and the marines, are being supported by opium taxation."[77]

Some of Fujian's military figures even framed poppy cultivation as a matter of patriotic necessity. In one instance, the military commander of southern Fujian went so far as to issue instructions to farmers on how to cultivate the poppy, which included an official proclamation "urging the people to plant the poppy in order to defeat the efforts of the Japanese to introduce opium from Formosa; in other words, to encourage home industries!"[78] Warlords affixed a creative assortment of euphemisms to poppy cultivation: "love the nation and benefit the people" (*aiguo limin*); "revitalize the employment sector" (*zhenxing shiye*); "recover the sources of wealth" (*wanhui liyuan*); "resist against foreign products" (*dizhi waihuo*); and "protect the vessel from leakage" (*busai louzhi*).[79] Customs officials began to take note of a constantly increasing amount of imported bean cake, a common fertilizer used in poppy cultivation.[80]

To collect the poppy tax, warlords turned to familiar practices and contracted the responsibility out to prominent opium merchants for exorbitant sums. Cang Zhiping, a commander with support from Zhejiang who took control of Xiamen in 1922, farmed out the annual poppy tax collection rights in Maxiang for $400,000; in Tong'an he charged $450,000, Lianhe $50,000, Jinmen $130,000, and in Anhai he demanded a quota of $600,000.[81] By the end of 1923 Cang had earned an estimated $2,800,000–3,000,000 through the collection of these quotas from his various poppy tax contractors.[82] In Tong'an county, Cang sold the poppy tax rights to a

Taiwanese businessman named Zeng Houkun, a multiterm president of the city's Taiwan Guild (*Taiwan gonghui*), urban developer, and large-scale opium investor.

Zeng's affiliation with the Tong'an county poppy tax dated back at least as far as 1921, when he was the sole licensed dealer for buyers of Tong'an opium in Xiamen.[83] Through his position as an investor who organized large-scale transactions in domestic opium, Zeng eventually transitioned to a role as a state contractor for collecting poppy taxes, a job that entailed buying up a territory's opium and subtracting the poppy tax from the amount paid to each farmer for their crop. He then lost his control over the Tong'an poppy tax when a group of generals from the Zhili faction of the Guomindang (GMD) took the county out of Cang Zhiping's control in late 1923. Through their own contractor, the new rulers collected $2,700,000 in tax revenue on opium cultivation in that single season.[84] Zeng Houkun bounced back. By 1926, he had purchased the rights for collection of the poppy tax in three of the most productive southern Fujianese counties by paying out $1,000,000 to Fujian's military governor Zhou Yinren. Tong'an county that year produced $2,000,000 in poppy taxes, collected by a pair of local "Poppy Kings."[85]

Poppy taxes declined as a practice in Fujian after the Guomindang more or less came to control the province during the Nanjing Decade (1927–1937). Guomindang opium policy evolved over time, but each new iteration of their prohibition and monopoly plans over these years was increasingly designed to control China's opium supply by offering only opium produced in various western provinces and shipped out of Hankou.[86] As such, Guomindang authorities in Fujian were never supposed to encourage poppy cultivation or collect poppy taxes.

But there was a lack of consistency in Fujian on this point. Xiamen's civil administration was entirely under the control of the navy, under the leadership of Lin Guogeng, from 1924 into the late 1930s.[87] The navy in Xiamen operated with a degree of independence, and the expedient option of collecting poppy taxes to supplement strapped budgets often superseded policy requirements sent down from Nanjing. In Fuzhou, the GMD military governor Zhou Yinren was also farming out a poppy tax as late as 1928, in direct contravention of central policy. That year, the Guomindang estimated that 21 percent of Jinjiang county's acreage and a full 50 percent of the acreage in Nan'an county were dedicated to growing the poppy.[88] In 1931, Guomindang officials from Nanjing expressed concern over continued poppy cultivation encouraged by the province's military authorities.[89] A year later four officials in the province were censured for allowing and taxing opium poppy cultivation.[90]

Smaller warlords also captured control over various rural areas throughout the Nanjing Decade, rising on the crest of poppy tax finances. Ye Dingguo in Tong'an, for example, was reported in the Singapore press to have amassed $45,000,000 in 1932 through a combination of poppy taxes and distribution monopolies.[91] Chen Guohui, who controlled large areas of Quanzhou and Yongchun prefectures between 1929 and 1932, imported huge shipments of poppy seeds from Burma when he took over the region in order to better facilitate a lucrative harvest.[92] On the eve of his eviction by the Nineteenth Route Army in late 1932, Chen's personal wealth had grown to an estimated $66,000,000.[93]

PROHIBITION BUREAUS, DISTRIBUTION MONOPOLIES

Like the poppy tax, the prohibition bureaus of the early twentieth century involved a confluence of new politics and familiar economics. Directorship of a prohibition bureau, like the poppy tax collection rights discussed above, was an office that state agents farmed out to men like Zeng Houkun, none other than the most successful opium businessmen of the age.

This dynamic goes as far back as the earliest prohibition bureaus of the late Qing. When the new prohibition policies were first launched in Fujian during 1907, there was a bidding war over the rights to operate the licensing scheme that was supposed to have been an institutional way to curb opium use. In this case, an unnamed local gentry figure was outbid by an overseas Chinese businessman who paid 300,000 yuan to the Fujian provincial government for the sole rights to licensed opium paste distribution.[94] Like the lijin bureaus of the late nineteenth century, large-scale regional or provincial prohibition bureaus had local subcontractors, and big cities like Xiamen and Fuzhou had their own systems. In Xiamen, as illustrated in the opening story of this chapter, one of the first iterations of the prohibition bureau phenomenon occurred when a "gentry bully" took over a preexisting opium distribution tax through the auspices of the Anti-Opium Society, and contracted with a handful of firms to implement the restructured licensing and taxation system.[95]

The spread of local prohibition bureaus in the increasingly decentralized atmosphere after the Xinhai Revolution deepened the connection between prohibition and profit. "The sale of office by opium inspectors is sufficient indication of the lucrative nature of that occupation," wrote one British investigator in 1914.[96] The sale of licensed opium was good money, but there were innumerable other opportunities to profit from the infrastructure of prohibition. Confiscating and reselling nonmonopoly opium was probably the most important of these, and the same British investigator suggested that as much as one half of all confiscated opium was funneled into the stocks of the monopoly holder rather than burned publicly, as it was supposed to be. He also claimed that local municipalities were charged exorbitant amounts of money ($1,700 for one night, in the Zhangpu county case he cites) by the prohibition bureau for receiving the bureau's inspectors on their tours around the province.[97]

When civil conflict escalated in 1917, the warlord contenders for southern Fujian set up opium prohibition bureaus alongside their new poppy tax agencies, moving to suppress unauthorized opium while encouraging opium use within approved channels. Each time, these militarists used the mantle of prohibition to frame their administration's relationship to opium revenue. When Cang Zhiping captured the city of Xiamen during the early 1920s, for example, he declared that the creation of a "special bureau" would be "a good scheme to stop the evil by taxation."[98] Using the familiar local model, Cang's "special bureau" divided up the various opium establishments into four classes, with taxes ranging from $5 to $20 per lamp, per month.[99] The income Cang received by farming out this bureau to the local opium merchants was then supplemented by monopolizing the opium supply with another agency that would purchase opium for $1.50 per ounce and resell it to the city's licensed opium dens at the rate of $4 per ounce. The League of Nations estimated that Cang's government earned upwards of $500,000 per month through the regulation and taxation of opium.[100] In neighboring Zhangzhou, Cang contracted with the Lisheng Company to manage the operation from top to bottom, collecting licensing fees from the city's opium dens and bringing an estimated 15,750 taels of opium into Zhangzhou from Xiamen each month to sell to the licensed shops.[101] When Cang re-auctioned the Xiamen opium paste monopoly in early 1924, two prominent bankers and a notorious local opium smuggler purchased the rights for a steadily increasing quota over the first four months of the year, with the goal of eventually plateauing at a quota of 45,000 yuan per month.[102]

Like the poppy tax, distribution monopolies funded all of Fujian's military regimes in the 1920s. In 1923, when a new group took over Zhangzhou and Quanzhou prefectures, they stated their plans to raise $15,000,000 from the creation of a new opium licensing system.[103] When Haicheng county just south of Xiamen shifted hands in 1924, two parties who each believed they had exclusive rights to tax opium and gambling in the district ended up in a bloody conflict near the south market of the county seat.[104] When the navy ousted Cang Zhiping from Xiamen in 1925, Admiral Yang Shuzhuang took immediate steps to take over Cang's opium revenue infrastructure. This required protracted negotiations with the city's chamber of commerce, where Xiamen's long-standing opium investors wanted to maintain some local control over market regulation and tax collection. Yang at one point unsuccessfully bluffed that he had received a competing offer for the city's opium paste distribution monopoly at twice the quota suggested by the chamber of commerce. In the end, Yang capitulated and sold off the distribution monopoly according to the chamber of commerce's original offer of $20,000 per month.[105] He also farmed out the rights to distribution on the island of Jinmen just outside the Xiamen harbor to a joint stock company of officials and gentry for the annual sum of $200,000, the greatest shareholder of which was the local magistrate.[106]

Map 4.1 offers a partial snapshot of opium taxation midway through the Guomindang's conquest of the province in 1925–1926. For the purposes of disaggregating the complexities of these flows of money, I have divided the locations on the map into three types. Indicated on the map as black squares, Xiamen and Jinmen were under the control of the Xiamen naval garrison, which farmed out distribution in Xiamen for $20,000 per month and in Jinmen for $200,000 per year. The black diamonds on the map are a collection of counties and cities controlled by the provincial governor, Zhou Yinren. In Jinjiang, Hui'an, and Nan'an, Zhou farmed the poppy tax to the Taiwanese businessman Zeng Houkun for $1,000,000. In Tong'an he farmed out the poppy tax to two local representatives to the provincial assembly for $2,000,000, and in Maxiang the poppy tax went to the head of the local chamber of commerce for $800,000.[107] In the cities of Fuzhou (Nantai), Quanzhou, and Zhangzhou, Governor Zhou empowered local opium dealers to set up distribution monopolies under the auspices of prohibition similar to what the navy operated in Xiamen.[108]

The locations indicated as white diamonds represent counties not fully controlled by Governor Zhou or the Xiamen naval garrison, locations controlled by minor warlords, or that were in the process of shifting hands

MAP 4.1: Opium taxation in Fujian, 1925–1926.

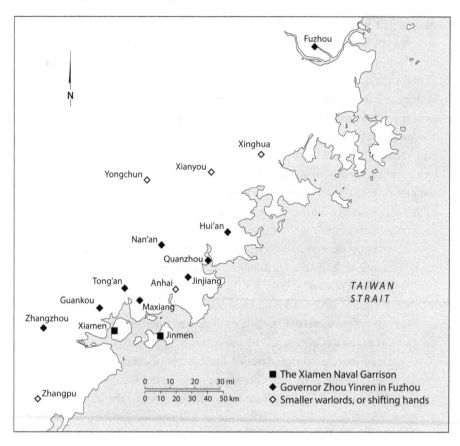

Source: LON 1919–1927, Box R759, Sec 12A, Doc 20286, Dossier 20286, "Opium Cultivation and Traffic in China: An Investigation in 1925–1926 by the International Anti-Opium Association, Peking."

during 1925–1926. In the far southern county of Zhangpu, the League of Nations estimated $1,000,000 in poppy taxes during 1926, collected at $3–4 per family or as much as $80 per working man. Anhai and Yongchun, longtime poppy-producing counties, were said to have sporadic and uneven taxation during those uncertain years. In Xianyou and Xinghua, League of Nations informants described the poppy crop as "enormous," and that "70–90% of the fields are planted with the poppy."[109]

After the Guomindang military rose to power in Fujian during 1925–1926, distribution monopolies under the auspices of prohibition assumed a proportionally greater importance to government finances than the poppy tax. This was due to the Guomindang's reliance on revenue derived from the control of Yunnan, Sichuan, and Shaanxi opium shipped out of Hankou, where Chiang Kai-shek's government collected an estimated $100,000,000 per year during the early 1930s.[110]

In the Heshan district of Xiamen, during the autumn of 1934, the county government issued stern warnings against the cultivation of poppies at the precise moment that they were launching a new distribution monopoly. "Why," asked one newspaper editorialist, "isn't the selling of opium subject to this kind of prohibition?"[111] The answer was that Nanjing was profiting from state monopoly opium sales, and this local production cut into their revenue. If Fujian's military rulers were going to rely on opium distribution monopolies, those monopolies were going to have to enforce the prohibition of local opium cultivation and purchase opium that profited the central government. Still, as the Guomindang would learn the hard way, farming these regulatory and taxation institutions out to opium dealers meant risking the possibility that they would bend the rules on sourcing their opium.

THE OPIUM KING OF FUJIAN:

YE QINGHE AND THE YUMIN COMPANY, 1934–1937

In 1933, the prodigal "opium king" of Fujian returned home from a ten-year sojourn in Shanghai. Ye Qinghe had left his home in Xiamen as a petty opium smuggler in his early twenties and was returning as a powerful man. In the interim, he had shuffled through Chinese, Chilean, and then Portuguese citizenship, been convicted twice for various drug crimes by the Shanghai courts, and become a morphine, opium, and heroin supply coordinator for Du Yuesheng, the boss of the Shanghai Green Gang and president of the Guomindang National Board of Opium Suppression Bureau. In Shanghai, Du had pioneered a new level of collaboration between state-run prohibition institutions and the underworld of narcotics distribution. In 1928, Du appointed Ye to serve in the role of "Assistant Section Chief" (*fu kezhang*) of the Jiangsu Opium Prohibition Bureau, and it was there that Ye learned firsthand how lucrative the state prohibition infrastructure could be.[112]

Ye was determined to return to Fujian to apply Du's Shanghai model and establish himself as the dominant force in the provincial drug trade through government contracts. The shifting map of warlords and their attendant poppy taxes and distribution monopolies were a potential gold mine, and Ye was always ready in an opportune political moment. His first attempt was in 1931, when he partnered with Zeng Houkun and several other Taiwanese businessmen in Xiamen to purchase the new Guomindang opium distribution monopoly in southern Fujian.[113] That plan was aborted when opium laws and regulations were again reshuffled in the city a few months later, but in 1932–1933 Ye found another opportunity to return home during the "Fujian Rebellion," a declaration of independence by the Nineteenth Route Army (*Shijiu lujun*), who had determined to separate themselves from Chiang Kai-shek's forces and take over the province as an independent territory.[114] The Nineteenth Route Army had a reputation for suppressing poppy cultivation in Fujian, but high-level officials in the regime also took steps to use the new government's prohibition infrastructure for revenue and profit.[115]

Ye's relationship with the Nineteenth Route Army predated his arrival in Fuzhou in 1933. The star-crossed unit had disobeyed Chiang Kai-shek's orders to stand down when the Japanese invaded Shanghai in January of 1932, and the Nineteenth Route Army had spent three months resisting Japanese forces together with urban guerilla fighters and ammunition supplied by Ye Qinghe's boss and ally Du Yuesheng.[116] Chiang transferred the Nineteenth Route Army to Fujian after the Shanghai debacle, to occupy the southeastern front of the Guomindang's encirclement of the Jiangxi Soviet. In Fujian, the Nineteenth Route Army rapidly expanded their power vis-à-vis the Guomindang, even engaging in independent negotiations with the leadership of the Chinese Communist Party. Their expansion in Fujian was funded, at least in part, by the purchase of large stocks of Persian opium.

Ye Qinghe was the middleman in these opium deals, serving as the connection between a renegade Shanghai military unit and his native Fujian. The first evidence of this comes from July of 1932, shortly after Chiang Kai-shek transferred the Nineteenth Route Army to Fujian, when a Maritime Customs cruiser out of Fuzhou attempted to capture a "suspicious launch" and found themselves overpowered by a machine gun concealed within.[117] The boat was said to be carrying eighty cases of raw Persian opium, each weighing 160 pounds, worth a total of at least $1,000,000. An informant to the customs claimed it was being delivered by Ye Qinghe to the Nineteenth Route Army in southern Fujian. At the time of the failed seizure, Ye was under investigation in Shanghai after a raid on a morphine factory uncovered several documents linked to Ye and the United Dispensary (*guomin yaofang*), an institution he founded under his alternate name Ye Zhensheng for the purpose of importing the equipment and ingredients necessary to the manufacture of morphine and heroin.[118]

Sentenced to a four-year jail term and a $5,000 fine, Ye evaded arrest by hiding out in the Sino-Foreign Clinic in the French Concession.[119] At that same moment, the United States government was also pursuing Ye in Shanghai in connection with the arrest of Judah and Isaac Ezra in San Francisco, who Ye had been supplying with opium and heroin through a fictional tea company called Dah Loong.[120] Things were getting hot in Shanghai, and the deal to supply the Nineteenth Route Army with Persian opium would function as an escape route. Ye jumped bail and evaded both his Shanghai jail sentence and American investigators, returning to a home newly conquered by Du Yuesheng's erstwhile allies, and began a new partnership.

Ye arrived in Fuzhou in early 1933, not long after the Nineteenth Route Army had established themselves as an independent government. He linked up with a high-ranking officer who offered the protection necessary to continue importing Persian opium for sale in the licensed opium dens operated by the newly independent Fujian government. With the support of his ally, Ye launched a new business in Fuzhou called the Wufeng Firm to handle the distribution of the Nineteenth Route Army's monopoly opium through the new government's opium prohibition bureau. They were to sell Persian opium: the shipment Ye had arranged in 1932, and subsequent stocks including some 1,911 chests (around 150 tons) of Persian opium sent up to the highland tea districts in Yanping prefecture.[121] To fund the enterprise, Ye partnered with a coalition of Xiamen's most powerful Taiwanese businessmen: Shi Fanqi, Zeng Houkun, and Chen Changfu, established opium investors who would all serve as presidents of the Xiamen Taiwan Guild. Wufeng also set up a satellite office in Xiamen inside of one of the buildings owned by Zeng Houkun, which was insulated from potential intervention by both the GMD and the Nineteenth Route Army by Zeng's Japanese citizenship.

The Fujian Rebellion was short-lived, but Ye Qinghe and his partners in the Wufeng Firm survived the province's transition from a rebellious military colony to a (mostly) incorporated province of the Guomindang national polity with astonishing facility. In January of 1934, a year after Ye's arrival in Fuzhou, Chiang Kai-shek's forces descended on Fujian and quickly wiped out the Nineteenth Route Army's Fujian People's Government. The night before Guomindang troops were to enter Fuzhou, Ye Qinghe and his associates evacuated their office and hightailed it south with a massive cargo of opium in a convoy of seventy trucks. They hid the opium in a small village in Hui'an county before bribing the Tong'an county warlord Ye Dingguo to escort them into Xiamen, now controlled by the Guomindang.[122] Undaunted by his association with the rebellious unit only just deposed, Ye approached the new authorities with a proposal.

By September of 1934, after a few months of wrangling and uncertainty, Ye Qinghe had maneuvered his way into control over the Guomindang opium prohibition infrastructure for the southern half of Fujian. He would hold that position for more than two years, selling a stunning volume of drugs within and outside the system. When Ye first arrived in Xiamen during January of 1934, he sent for the stores of Persian opium that he had purchased for the Nineteenth Route Army and stashed in Hui'an county on his flight south from Fuzhou. Ye paid taxes on the drug to the local Guomindang representatives and acquired government monopoly stamps, thereafter founding a new opium business called the Lutong Company, again with investments from several figures in Xiamen's notorious Taiwanese underworld, including Lin Gun and Chen Changfu, as well as the president of the Xiamen Merchant's Bank (*Shangye yinhang*).[123] The United States attaché in Shanghai believed that Ye and Chen had bullied the Guomindang into accepting their offer to manage the new opium monopoly by threatening to unload their stocks of Persian opium at low prices if they were not granted control over the distribution system.[124]

After acquiring the state contract, Ye Qinghe set about divvying up and farming out the city's districts and surrounding counties. The Lutong Company sold off neighborhood monopolies to a collection of Taiwanese opium merchants, setting a quota of 12,000 taels per month in Xiamen proper and 4,000 taels per month in the Heshan district just east of the city center.[125] Lutong's operations grew rapidly and soon after reorganized into a new company, called Yumin, and hired over 100 employees. By the following spring they had subdivided Heshan into nine districts, controlling the four most lucrative for themselves and tendering the remaining five districts to (primarily Taiwanese) opium merchants.[126]

Ye Qinghe's Yumin Company was a huge success between 1934 and 1936. Historian Alan Baumler credits the company with breaking the power of

Fujian's military garrisons over the opium trade and bringing retail more fully under central government control, thereby reducing the problem of smuggled imports.[127] The rapid expansion of the company was the product of a cozy relationship with powerholders in the Guomindang, just as Ye's old boss Du Yuesheng had achieved in Shanghai. They hired on the brother of the naval commander in southern Fujian, Lin Guogeng, and paid monthly bribes to various members of the navy, public security bureau, as well as Xiamen's Mayor Li Shilin, Police Captain Shen Jinkang, and other prominent officials. This was all on top of the 70,000 yuan per month paid to the Xiamen office of the Fujian Provincial Government for the rights to the monopoly.[128] Subsidiary companies were farmed out to local warlords, bandits, and gentry members in Jinmen, Longxi, Haicheng, Yongchun, Quanzhou, Dehua, Xianyou, Nan'an, Hui'an, Tong'an, and Anxi.

The Yumin Company, though founded on the capital of an original cache of illicitly acquired Persian opium, was legally mandated by Nanjing to sell only domestic Chinese opium (from Shaanxi, Sichuan, and Yunnan, primarily), shipped out of Hankou. A representative of the Yumin Company, usually Ye Qinghe's nephew, would travel up to Hankou and escort shipments of around 1,000 chests of opium down to Fujian via steamship. The Yunnan opium was packaged in round balls and packed in bamboo husks, resembling "cow dung." The Shaanxi opium was packaged into 50-tael bricks. Both types were stamped with "special product" labels, to match the euphemistic title the Guomindang had granted to the state-managed opium sales infrastructure.[129] Payment was facilitated, as historian Edward Slack has demonstrated, by the Farmer's Bank, which operated several locations across Fujian to transmit payments to Hankou.[130] By 1936, an estimated 150,000 ounces of national monopoly opium was consumed in Fujian each month.

The system did not achieve total control over the market, however, and monopoly opium was just a fraction of what was produced, imported, and consumed in the province. According to a Minnesotan journalist who reported extensively on the drug trade in Fujian, there was an additional 200,000 ounces of Persian opium and 182,000 ounces of domestic Fujianese opium consumed each month outside of the state monopoly infrastructure.[131] On the question of local opium, a Shanghai publication asserted that the monopoly was selling opium sourced from Xianyou, Hui'an, and Tong'an counties, relying on subcontractors in those regions to provide quotas of the raw drug.[132] As regards Persian imports, in 1936 the Lutong Company requested help from the British government in Hong Kong to put a stop to the smuggling of Persian opium into Xiamen from Hong Kong and the British government responded promptly, reporting twelve separate seizures of the drug on steamships from Hong Kong to Xiamen in February and March of that year.[133] Smuggling was clearly still a problem.

Some of the smuggling was undoubtedly conducted by Ye and his associates themselves. The Yumin monopoly employed a diverse range of profit strategies beyond selling approved opium through approved channels. Historian Hong Buren argues that Ye used the cover of his monopoly to oversee numerous other unauthorized drug operations. This included smuggling "red pills" (a smokable concoction of morphine and other drugs) into rural Fujian from Hong Kong. Ye's 1932 prosecution in Shanghai was publicly connected to the manufacture of red pills, and he had experience in the business.[134] After he moved back to Fujian, Ye brought the pills into Xiamen on British steamships, and when the steamer would enter the port, a group of monopoly employees armed with pistols and carrying Xiamen Guomindang Public Security Bureau licenses would ride up to the steamer on a motorboat and load the drugs directly from the ship.[135] In early 1937, *Shenbao* reported that Ye was also using his Japanese connections to bring unauthorized drugs into Fujian from Manchuria.[136] Ye and other Yumin operators were also known to purchase large quantities of domestic opium from rural Fujian to manufacture into opium paste for export from Xiamen. None of this activity fell within the legal authority granted to Yumin through the opium prohibition infrastructure, and it undercut the purpose of the Guomindang opium revenue and regulatory system.

Ye's relationship with the Guomindang soured during 1936. The shaky foundations of the relationship had already been apparent to Ye, when a year earlier he bribed the Japanese consul in Xiamen to acquire Taiwanese (and thus Japanese) citizenship.[137] But then in mid-1936 the Guomindang signed onto the Geneva Opium Accord and soon after announced a six-year plan to completely monopolize opium's production and distribution with a final goal of prohibition.[138] Ye was kept on in his position within the opium prohibition infrastructure, for a time, despite the new rules and his having long played fast and loose with the Guomindang requirement to sell only opium shipped from Hankou was also at the heart of the matter. But by late 1936, the military governor in Fuzhou became concerned that Ye was obviously prone to cut the state out of the profits and dispatched an officer down to Xiamen to try and take down the Yumin Company.

Matters came to a head in Fuzhou during June of 1937, when the provincial authorities invited Ye to attend a meeting and he found himself spirited out of Fujian into a Guomindang prison in Hankou.[139] As the authorities in Nanjing came around to understanding what had transpired in Fujian, they reacted with shock that Fujian's authorities would contract with Japanese nationals to oversee opium prohibition duties.[140] With war on the immediate horizon, the Guomindang ignored Ye's claims to Japanese protection and sentenced him to five years in prison for breaking his "special product" contract and also illegally using violence. He escaped after a month, in August of 1937, while being transferred out of Nanjing on a steamship that was attacked by Japanese bombers. The child of Gulangyu island leaped into the Yangzi River, swam ashore, and eventually found his way to Hong Kong.[141]

Conclusion: An Intractable Fiscal Consensus

The particular combination of prohibition and profit in Fujian had its distinctive characteristics, but opium prohibition and state revenue have similarly intertwined histories across China and most of Southeast Asia. In colonial Indochina and Malaya, opium monopolies nominally dedicated to long-term reduction in opium use accounted for as much as 50–60 percent of state budgets in the late 1910s, and continued to collect substantive revenue into the 1930s even as the great powers were reaching a global consensus on prohibition.[142] In China, an open transition towards a monopoly system (even one nominally geared towards reducing use) was without political traction during the final years of the Qing, when patriotic youth and entrenched political elites alike viewed opium as a reason for China's victimization by foreign power, and as an impediment to China's modernization into a power that could resist such victimization in the future.

But alongside this moral consensus about opium's undesirability, there was across China what proved to be an intractable fiscal consensus that opium was a profitable business, and as such, a ready-made opportunity for state revenue. The Qing state was still unable to quit opium revenue when it collapsed, and the warlord governments that followed along with the Guomindang and the Chinese Communist Party all operated opium monopolies to supplement military and administrative budgets.[143] In Fujian, there was also what might be called an institutional consensus, about what kinds of systems and practices could be used to regulate and control the drug. Prohibition bureaus, from the beginning, took over preexisting institutions and systems of opium den registration, classification, and taxation. Like the nineteenth-century lijin bureaus in Fujian and the opium farms in Southeast Asia, these prohibition bureaus were contracted out to coalitions of wealthy opium investors seeking an edge over their competition. With the help of men like Ye Qinghe and his Taiwanese associate Zeng Houkun, the Guomindang and warlord rulers of Fujian after 1911 embedded opium tax farming within the modern Chinese state.

In the final years of the Qing dynasty, few would have guessed that the end of dynastic rule would involve such a stunning recrudescence of the opium business. But indeed there was more opium coming in and out of southern Fujian during the 1920s and 1930s then at any other point in the province's history. Opium was being grown in unprecedented quantities, not only in places like Tong'an and Hui'an counties where cultivation had been taking place since the early nineteenth century, but also in places that had never seen opium poppies. In Xinghua district just north of Quanzhou, an investigator from the International Anti-Opium Association in 1934 reported that 70–90 percent of the fields were planted with the poppy. In the words of the investigator: "I have seen square miles of white flowers and the atmosphere is heavy with the scent." The local population, he asserted, were commonly heard saying that "the people must now eat opium instead of grain."[144]

Where was it all going? Who was smoking all of this opium? The export orientation of the Fujian opium economy during these years—intimately tied to the revenue and regulatory structures surrounding opium discussed here, as well as the rapid growth in domestic production and the import of vast quantities of Persian opium—is the subject of the next chapter.

CHAPTER 5

New Spatialities in the Global Drug Trade, 1890s–1940s

In November of 1924, customs officers in Hong Kong boarded a steamship arriving from Xiamen and discovered 704 tins of prepared opium hidden in a consignment of cargo bound for Singapore. Seizures like this happened all the time, but the customs agent who drew up the report on the case was intrigued by several stamps affixed to each of the opium tins, and so he removed samples of each stamp, translated the stamps into English, and forwarded the evidence to the League of Nations Opium Advisory Committee in Geneva, Switzerland. These stamps remain in Geneva today and can be viewed by researchers in the United Nations Archives. Pictured here in Figure 5.1, they are five- and ten-cent tax receipts from an agency called the "Head Management Association," with the inscription "Xiamen Examination Bureau, Export Stamp."[1]

Opium was not a legal item of export from China. Nor was Chinese opium a legal item of import in Singapore. But yet this type of smuggling had become so systematized that someone in Xiamen was collecting an export tax on the drug. In late 1924, when the opium was seized in Hong Kong, Xiamen was under the control of Admiral Yang Shuzhuang, who had ousted the city's erstwhile warlord during the previous April. Like his

FIGURE 5.1: Opium export tax stamps from 1924.

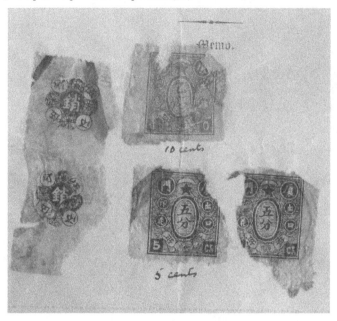

Source: United Nations Archive at Geneva. Reprinted with permission.

predecessors in Xiamen and his neighbors across the districts of southern Fujian, Yang supported his military rule by taxing opium. In the city of Xiamen, he farmed out an opium inspection office (a distribution monopoly under the mantle of prohibition) through the city's chamber of commerce for $20,000 per month. In neighboring Jinmen—a long-time naval stronghold—Yang collected $200,000 per year for the rights to the opium monopoly. This was all good revenue to be sure, but it cannot have escaped Yang how much more drug money was circulating through his neighborhood. Poppy taxes in the neighboring counties were not controlled by Admiral Yang, instead farmed out by the military governor in Fuzhou.[2] Poppy tax contracts for major poppy-producing counties like Tong'an, Nan'an, Jinjiang, and Hui'an were worth millions of dollars. Once the drug was harvested and processed, poppy taxes paid, a vast quantity of it was sent into Xiamen for export.

The tax stamps pictured above are perhaps the only archival information on the institutional framework for the opium export industry in Xiamen during these years. All of the drugs discussed in this chapter—millions of tins of opium paste and raw opium unearthed in donkey boilers and baskets of fruit in Manila, Surabaya, Singapore, and Rangoon, shipped alongside countless packets of morphine and cocaine—had at one point been clandestinely loaded onto steamships in the port of Xiamen. Yang Shuzhuang had found a way to profit from this, by creating a bureau that issued five- and ten-cent export stamps for the tins of opium being funneled through his port from factories in the countryside onto steamships bound for Southeast Asia. Admiral Yang was likely not alone among the warlords and military rulers of Fujian in attempting to profit from the moment of export. He was, however, the only one who left behind receipts.

Southern Fujian and the Export-Oriented Phase of the Chinese Opium Business

The surging volume of opium produced in and circulating around early twentieth-century Fujian enabled the resumption of the opium transshipment business in the region. Like in the early days of the opium trade, a century before, Fujianese migrants and travelers were once again pioneering new ways to bring illicit drugs across jurisdictions. Local consumption in Fujian was by all accounts still substantial—the value of the prohibition bureau opium monopolies discussed in chapter 4 is testament to this—but the ramped-up production and continued import of the drug was filling more pipes than could have possibly been smoked within the province. The rising fortunes of men like Ye Qinghe, Zeng Houkun, Chen Changfu, and the other warlord- and Guomindang-affiliated opium magnates were ultimately built on supplying an increasingly lucrative export market in the colonial ports of Southeast Asia (see Map 5.1). This chapter documents this transformation of the global narcotic economy and the attendant rise of the morphine and cocaine trades, highlighting a collection of structural transformations that enabled the population of southern Fujian in the 1920s–1930s to assume a prominent role within in a reoriented and newly diversified global drug trade.

Fujian's narcotics transshipment industry experienced this resurgence during a period of rapid acceleration in passenger steam traffic and mass migration between southern China and Southeast Asia. The port of Xiamen was for centuries a point of departure for an endless stream of ships full of

MAP 5.1: Southeast Asian markets for smuggled opium from Fujian.

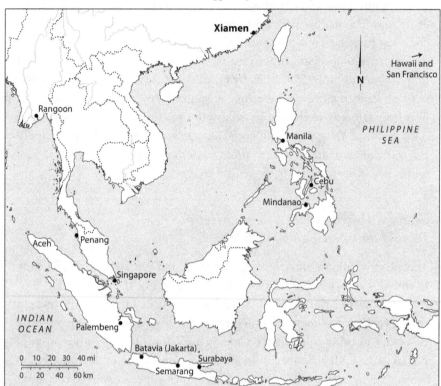

sojourning merchants and laborers bound for Singapore, Batavia (Jakarta), Rangoon, Penang, and Manila. Passenger steamship connections between China and Southeast Asia were first launched in the 1870s, and by the first decades of the twentieth century there were millions of migrants and travelers moving back and forth each year.[3] In 1904, 61,566 people left Xiamen on ships bound for the Straits Settlements and the Netherland Indies; in 1907 the number was 74,532.[4] In 1914, when the war cut off immigration into the Straits Settlements during the second half of the year, there were still 54,561 people who journeyed to those ports from Xiamen.[5]

Traffic between Xiamen and the Philippines was also extensive. The Chinese population in the Philippines came almost exclusively from a collection of four counties in Quanzhou Prefecture near Xiamen, and there remain close connections between the Philippines and coastal southern Fujian today.[6] In 1918 there were over 43,000 Chinese nationals living in the US Philippine Islands, despite US immigration restrictions, along with a much larger population of naturalized migrants and their descendants.[7] Around 160,000 letters and packages sent to and from Southeast Asia passed through the central branch of the Xiamen Post Office during each month in 1933.[8]

The passengers and crews departing Xiamen for Southeast Asian ports embarked on their journeys from a city with a diverse and tempting drug market. Fujian province was oversaturated with opium throughout the early twentieth century, thanks to warlord-encouraged poppy cultivation, Guomindang opium monopoly projects that mandated the shipment of opium from Hankou to Fujian, and the illicit import of Persian opium by people like Ye Qinghe. Within this buyer's market, opium investors carried out rapid advancements in the commodification and commercialization of the drug. Factories in Fujian began in the early 1920s to produce dozens of brands of tinned opium paste for export.[9] Many of these companies sourced their opium locally, such as the Stork, Deer, and Fig Tree & Deer brands, which drew upon raw stocks cultivated in Tong'an, Hui'an, and Nan'an counties to produce one-tael tins of opium marketed within Xiamen for between $3 and $4. These brands were routinely discovered in the Philippines and the Straits Settlements, as well as far-off San Francisco. The Unicorn and Two Peach brands produced a wider range of options—0.5, 1, 2.5, and 5-tael tins—sourced from opium poppies grown under warlord supervision in Tong'an, Guankou, Maxiang, and Anhai districts in Fujian. These tins went to the Straits Settlements and the Philippines too, as well as French Indochina and parts of north China. The highly expensive Cock brand of opium paste—the "most famous on the market"—was boiled down from Benares opium imported from Calcutta but had inspired local knock-offs, one using Yunnan opium and another drawn from opium cultivated locally in southern Fujian. These too were found in places from Rangoon to San Francisco.

The tightening of opium controls across Southeast Asia during this period encouraged people in Fujian to invest in opium and seek out ways to spirit the drug into those locations through the passenger steamships. Opium smuggling was profitable, whether the destination was a colony that pursued absolute prohibition, like the Philippines, or a place with a state opium monopoly, like French Indochina, the British Straits Settlements, and the Netherlands Indies.[10] In all of these places, there was a long-term tightening of state and interstate restrictions on drug flows that happened over the course of the early twentieth century.[11] This regulatory environment served as a menu of opportunities for people in Fujian, where the drug could be purchased and resold for as much as a 600 percent profit margin in the colonial markets.[12] All that was needed were people bold enough to test customs officers, clever enough to conceal the drugs properly, and connected enough to find buyers.

Alongside these migratory, political, and regulatory transformations, technological advancements in drug production and new international systems of drug control also served to enhance Fujian's prominence within the global drug trade of the early twentieth century. On the technological side, the rise of new trades in morphine, heroin, and cocaine were interlocked with the reorientation of the global opium trade. Opium users in China and across the world were transitioning to powders and pills manufactured in laboratories, which were both easier to conceal and promised faster, stronger psychoactive effects. These new drugs originally found their way to China from Europe, but by the 1920s the League of Nations and cooperating states had largely cut off illicit movements of the drug from Europe to Asia. Businesspeople in Fujian took advantage of these shifting winds by rapidly expanding local operations in the production and distribution of heroin and morphine, while also capturing control over a major segment of the global cocaine trade by connecting producers in Japan and Taiwan with consumers in Singapore, Burma, and India. Like the story of opium, the history of these new manufactured narcotics also revolves around parallel advancements in commodification, branding, and marketing.

SINGAPORE AND THE STRAITS SETTLEMENTS:
FROM FARM TO GOVERNMENT MONOPOLY

The history of Singapore is rooted in the port's role in the transshipment of Indian opium to China. But beginning in the final decades of Qing rule, the British colonies in Singapore and Malaya emerged as markets for illicitly imported opium sent back westward from China. The opium trade was reversing course, and smuggled Chinese opium would plague British revenue collectors in Southeast Asia for a half century. As early as 1889, the Singapore Opium Farm was advertising rewards for information concerning opium smuggling from the southeastern Chinese ports of Xiamen and Shantou.[13] One newspaper article from that year argued that the smuggling was a product of "the extensive coolie immigration and the close commercial connection between Chinese firms and agents in Singapore and the coolie and general trade agencies at these Chinese ports [i.e., Xiamen and Shantou]."[14] Later that year, revenue officers in Penang boarded a German steamer arriving from Xiamen and discovered among the passengers' luggage a water tub containing thirty-one tins of opium and a basket of eight puddings also containing opium, all told $1,300 worth of the drug.[15]

Opium revenue in Singapore, a port founded on the principle of free trade, was exclusively derived from the urban distribution of the drug. As Diana Kim writes, the relative lack of Maritime Customs revenue meant that vice taxes and especially opium taxes were "generally accepted as an inevitable condition of the colony."[16] From the early nineteenth century all the way until 1910, the British government employed a tax farming system to collect this money. The colonial authorities set up competitive auctions for the rights to collect revenue and enforce opium regulations, and groups of Fujianese and Cantonese investors competed with one another for the privilege. These "farmers" paid huge sums for these contracts, and for their part the British authorities milked the system for all that they could. One former managing partner of the Singapore Opium Farm stated in 1904 that the price paid to the government by the farm rose from $118,000 per month to $465,000 during his tenure.[17] The competitive bidding system, according to the farm's former prosecuting agent, created a strong incentive for the operators to try and increase opium use among the population.[18]

Because the opium tax farms in Singapore and Malaya were intended to turn a profit, prices remained high enough that smuggled opium from China could provide valuable returns for migrants and sailors bold enough to test the colony's revenue authorities. The Singapore Opium Farm was not usually in danger of going bankrupt like the opium lijin bureaus of southern Fujian in the 1870s–1880s, but as one of the farm's inspectors admitted, still "there [were] a great many prosecutions" for violations of the monopoly. [19] Newspaper articles suggest that the main culprits were new arrivals from southeast China, describing frequent and steady seizures of "Amoy *chandu*" (Xiamen opium paste) by the Singapore customs and police.

Many of the seizures in Singapore consisted of small cargoes concealed in personal baggage, although others are indicative of a highly organized and monetized smuggling trade. In 1904, for example, the crew of a Chinese steamship arriving in Singapore from Shantou was charged with smuggling $3,900 worth of opium into Singapore. The drug, which the farm's tester determined to have originated in Xiamen, was concealed in an empty bunk in the crew's quarters.[20] In October of 1907, the Singapore customs confiscated a total 164 tins of opium worth $4,740 from a pair of steamships arriving from Xiamen and levied fines on the captains of each vessel for failing to prevent smuggling on board his ship.[21] An editorial appeared in the Singapore press later that week, lamenting the "revival of serious opium smuggling from China in the ships trading from Amoy to this port." The author suggested that decreasing opium production in India would only further exacerbate the problem.[22]

The dismantling of the tax farms in Singapore and the Straits Settlements during 1909–1910 did not decrease opium use or curb smuggling, as was the nominal purpose of the policy shift. Instead, the new government bureaucracy created to enforce a state monopoly on sales of the drug became an essential source of state revenue, an institution that indeed encouraged opium use. Carl Trocki has estimated that the annual revenue from the Straits Settlements colonial opium monopolies was as high as $29 million in 1920.[23] In 1929, after a decade of new international restrictions on the opium trade and increasing pressure from the League of Nations on Britain and the other colonial powers to clamp down on opium flows, and four years after the colonial government set up a $30 million fund to compensate for the loss of revenue that would accompany eventual abolition of opium use in the Settlements, the Straits monopoly still managed to earn $8 million for the British crown.[24] Consumption in Singapore would not seriously drop until the 1940s.

Opium remained a government-protected market in British colonial Southeast Asia, which created opportunities for smugglers from places with access to cheap opium. The state monopoly charged higher retail prices than the preceding tax farms had charged. Meanwhile, there was a steady decline in opium's regulation in Fujian, especially after 1917 when opium poppy cultivation accelerated during the province's warlord conflicts. By 1924, the Singapore monopoly reported that of the 29,438 taels of opium seized that year, there was "but little" that did not come from Xiamen.[25] The officers added to their report the obvious point that the amount of opium smuggled past authorities was likely much higher than the amount seized. Among the rare victims of large-scale seizures were a group of seamen on a Chinese steamship who were caught smuggling 16,860 taels of Fujianese opium paste worth an estimated $100,000 from Xiamen to Singapore.[26] Later that year, the Hong Kong Customs found another 7,000 taels of opium paste from Xiamen concealed in the donkey boiler, bound for Singapore.[27]

Opium smuggling from China into the British colonies in Southeast Asia continued even into and after the global depression, when the Straits Settlements' opium market entered its final downward spiral.[28] In 1930, the Straits Settlements reported seizures of 2,161 kg of prepared foreign opium. "Except in a few isolated instances," the authorities there reported, "the raw and prepared opium came from China."[29] The next year, the number went up further: 416 kg of raw opium and 2,278 kg of opium paste, 90 percent of which was the Red Lion brand from Xiamen.[30] In 1934, the Singapore preventive service searched several baskets of fruit being transported across the harbor in a motorized sampan and discovered 344 taels of opium paste—mostly Red Lion brand—worth $2,320. The arrested suspect stated that he had been paid 40 cents per tael for smuggling the opium to Singapore from Xiamen.[31] The brand retained a robust market in Singapore throughout the decade. A photograph from 1938 shows the Singapore customs displaying the seizure of Red Lion brand *chandu* concealed in drums of caustic soda (Figure 5.2).[32]

THE NETHERLANDS INDIES OPIUM RÉGIE

Opium from Fujian also poured into the Netherlands Indies, sometimes arriving direct but more often transshipped in Singapore. Dutch colonial rulers in what is now Indonesia had preceded the British in transforming from a tax farming system to a government-controlled monopoly (the *régie*, modeled after the French system in Indochina), which they had done in the 1890s. One contemporary observer claimed that the Dutch régie served to increase opium use, in part because the government monopoly was willing to open special opium dens for women whereas the previous Chinese tax farmers had only sold the drug to men.[33] An official in the Netherlands, as noted by historian James Rush, concluded of the régie in a 1910 report that "there is no indication whatsoever that anyone strives to reduce the use of opium."[34] Like the British in Singapore, the Dutch in Java were formalizing opium distribution monopolies within the modernizing colonial state.

The transition from tax farming to a state monopoly cut the island's ethnic Chinese population out of most of the legal occupations associated

FIGURE 5.2: Red Lion opium smuggled in drums of caustic soda. Singapore, 1938.

Source: United Nations Archive at Geneva. Reprinted with permission.

with the opium business. In the second half of the nineteenth century, groups of elite Hokkien (Southern Fujianese) businessmen had achieved immensely lucrative and powerful positions as opium farmers for the Dutch colonial state. As James Rush argues, "The demise of the farms meant not only that the Chinese were kept from the legal opium trade and its vast profits but also that the former opium-farm Chinese lost their organizations as a force in the countryside, and, as a result, their controlled access to Java's rural markets."[35] Still, as demonstrated in the subsequent pages, there was no shortage of people moving between Java and China that would step in to take advantage of cracks in the new system. In both Singapore and Java, the colonial state's increasing dedication to extracting revenue from opium and regulating the trade created opportunities for people with connections to the opium market in southeast China. By 1900, only one sixth of the opium consumed in the Netherlands Indies was estimated to be legal régie opium, and the remaining five-sixths was smuggled in via Singapore.[36]

Throughout the first several decades of the twentieth century, opium from Fujian would continuously supply markets in the Dutch colonial sphere. In one example from June of 1925, the steersman of the S.S. *Tjik-arang* on the Java-China-Japan route was found with 12 kg of opium split up into 286 small copper boxes marked with a winged horse and the words "Lie Seng, [Xiamen]." Two months later an employee of a Chinese Hotel in Batavia was arrested by the Dutch police with 10 kg of opium split into 278 small copper boxes, each of which was wrapped in a piece of paper bearing the words "Tay Yoe Kongsi, [Xiamen]."[37] People trading grocery items and other goods between Java and Fujian were concealing modest cargoes of opium in their otherwise innocent consignments. It was a sound profit strategy, and this pattern repeated throughout the 1920s, such as in February 1929 when a steamship arriving in Batavia from Singapore was discovered to be carrying 400 small boxes of Red Lion brand opium from Xiamen, weighing 14 kg.[38] A few months later, Dutch police in Semarang raided a Chinese grocery and found a cargo of opium hidden in 195 tins of cucumbers, beans, and pickles from the China Canning Company of Xiamen.[39] That year the Netherlands Indies reported to the League of Nations on 495 individual seizures of non-monopoly foreign opium weighing 306 kilograms, almost exclusively from Xiamen.[40] Tins of Fujianese opium confiscated in the Netherlands Indies are pictured in Figure 5.3.

During the 1930s, Fujian's political upheavals brought about a new trend in the Netherlands Indies, wherein smugglers were increasingly found to trade in raw Persian opium rather than tins of prepared Fujianese opium paste. In just the last four months of 1934, the Dutch East Indies reported a total of 184 kg of raw Persian opium bearing the stamp of the "A&B Monopoly."[41] In January and February of the next year, Dutch authorities seized another 166 kg and then another 208 kg between April and June of 1835.[42] These large-scale seizures were all the result of routine searches of the Dutch-owned fleet of steamships running the Java-China-Japan line, calling at Kobe, Taipei, Xiamen, Hong Kong, Singapore, and Netherlands Indies ports. The drug seized in these cases was almost exclusively raw Persian opium packaged with a stamp from the A&B Monopoly (see Figure 5.4), a stamp that sometimes also bore the Chinese characters for Fujian.[43]

The circulation of Persian opium from Fujian into the Straits Settlements and the Netherlands Indies was a direct result of the ongoing conflict and collaboration within the province between government agencies and

FIGURE 5.3: Tin of Red Lion brand opium (left) and Tin of Fu (Luck) Brand opium (right), from the Fusheng Company in Xiamen. Confiscated in the Netherlands Indies in 1930.

Source: United Nations Archive at Geneva. Reprinted with permission.

FIGURE 5.4: A&B Monopoly stamps.

Source: United Nations Archive at Geneva. Reprinted with permission.

men like Ye Qinghe. The League of Nations had evidence of several immense shipments of opium from Bushehr organized out of Shanghai, the cargoes of which were often split between a group of locations including Hong Kong, Xiamen, Taipei, Tianjin, Dalian, and Vladivostok.[44] As discussed in chapter 4, Ye Qinghe was a prominent figure in the organization of these shipments of Persian opium, having once worked with the Nineteenth Route Army to import a whopping 150 tons of Persian opium in a single shipment during 1933.[45] A year later, in late 1934 and not long after the collapse of the Nineteenth Route Army's independent government in Fujian, Ye traveled to Taiwan to purchase another 10 million yen worth of Persian opium from the Japanese government "for distribution in South China and also for the manufacturing of narcotic drugs."[46]

It is not likely coincidental that the waves of seizures of A&B Monopoly Persian opium in the Netherlands Indies took off around 1934. According to the terms of his agreement with the Guomindang, which lasted from late 1934 until the summer of 1937, Ye was bound to exclusively supply Fujianese smokers with domestic opium shipped out of Hankou. It seems plausible, given the actual truckloads of Persian opium that Ye owned when he took over this position, that Ye was also supplying smokers in Southeast Asia. Ye Qinghe's competitors in Xiamen were certainly looking to Iran for opium supplies, as in 1936 when Hong Kong customs seized 326 kg of raw Persian opium bound for Xiamen after receiving a confidential tip from Ye's Yumin Company.[47] A few years later during the Japanese occupation of Xiamen, the state opium monopoly also relied extensively on imported Persian opium.[48] At that later stage the drugs were imported into Xiamen via Shanghai, and as the British consul-general in Xiamen believed, "with the assistance of the Japanese naval authorities."[49] In Fujian, where domestic opium (both local and from other parts of China) were widely available, Persian opium was still a sound investment because of the ability of Fujianese smugglers to serve customers in places like Java.

PROHIBITION AND SMUGGLING IN THE US PHILIPPINE ISLANDS

Like Singapore and the Netherlands Indies, the Philippine Islands were home to a large population of Fujianese migrants and a long history of opium consumption, regulation, and taxation. But in contrast to the British and Dutch colonies, which both employed monopolies that more or less encouraged opium use, US colonial rulers in the Philippines established a system of opium suppression on a rapid scale beginning in 1905.[50] This was a tall order in a place with an established opium market and a dense network of shipping and financial connections with south China. Between 1899 and 1903, 1,105,348 pounds of opium had been imported legally into the Philippines, averaging 221,069 pounds per year.[51] By 1908, the final year of legal opium imports, only 50,776 pounds were imported.[52]

US rulers in the Philippines ultimately decided to follow the model the Japanese had undertaken in Taiwan, a system that prioritized opium's eventual prohibition over the gathering of revenue by selling state monopoly opium under black market prices. After the prohibition plan commenced in 1905, legal imports tapered quickly. When opium had been legal during earlier years, the majority of the drug was brought in from the British colonies of Hong Kong and Singapore. The British willingly cooperated with the United States in opium prohibition, unencumbered by the historical baggage that affected British policy towards prohibition in China, and the Colonial Office readily prohibited shipments of opium to the Philippines from British colonies. When prohibition reached its final stage in 1908, colonial authorities estimated that there were 20,000 opium smokers still consuming the drug in the Philippines.[53]

Prohibition in the Philippines created an entirely different set of circumstances for Fujian's opium smugglers from the other jurisdictions with state opium monopolies. The market in Manila was for processed opium paste rather than raw opium, because the drug could not be processed on site without attracting attention. Turning raw opium into paste is a conspicuous operation, it requires space and labor, and is not easily hidden from authorities. The Persian A&B Monopoly opium that flooded the Straits Settlements and Netherlands Indies worked in those places because of preexisting opium-processing infrastructure. This was not the case in the Philippines. Drug runners operating between China and the Philippines largely bought their opium preboiled in Fujian. In 1930, the US government seized a total of 261,671 kg of opium paste in the Philippines, compared with just 15,390 kg of crude opium.[54]

Because all legal channels for opium imports were shut down, the only possible way to get the drug into the Philippines was to smuggle it in. "We are grappling in darkness," wrote a Manila customs officer, "with an unknown quantity of opium floating in the East and which is ready to spurt into the Philippine Islands at any time, like a flow of quicksilver."[55] It was an island of prohibition in a sea of opium, and the people whose lives traversed jurisdictions between the Philippines and Fujian understood the opportunity at hand. As a columnist in Shanghai described it: "Southern newspapers constantly report ingenious attempts by Chinese to import opium into the Philippine Islands. Notwithstanding heavy penalties and a smart detective department, smuggling is rife." In the case that prompted that article, a passenger from Xiamen had been found upon arrival in Manila with $1,000 worth of opium concealed in bundles of onions.[56]

After Fujian plunged into civil war in 1917, the Philippines emerged as one of the most popular destinations for Fujianese opium. In 1920 the US government seized $1,000,000 worth of opium, some of which had been concealed in a shipment of salt fish from Xiamen to Manila, and the rest of which had been found in the ocean off Mindanao attached to floating pieces of wood.[57] In 1925, a police raid on the Hong Kong offices of a Xiamen-based Tong Yue firm found evidence that the firm "had been specializing in shipping prepared opium to the Philippines and Honolulu packed in other cargo, their usual shipments being from 3,000 to 5,000 taels at a time."[58] Customs officials in the Philippines stated that "almost every steamer from Amoy is bringing the contraband."[59]

All but a small few of the seizures in the American customs reports took place during searches of Chinese passengers' baggage on three ships: the SS *Macaria*, the SS *Anking*, and the SS *Susanna II*, which all operated on the direct route between Manila and Xiamen. In one of the largest seizures on record, US customs officials in the Philippines confiscated 3,400 tins of opium on the SS *Susanna II*, a ship that an officer from the Xiamen Post Office called "the most notorious smuggler on the coast."[60] A year later the Manila customs unearthed 2,000 tins of Lion and 555 Brand opium paste hidden in bamboo baskets containing sweet potatoes on the SS *Macaria* arriving from Xiamen.[61] Two years after that customs officials searched the SS *Anking* on its arrival in Manila from Xiamen and found 900 tins of Tongee brand opium paste and 900 tins of Lion brand opium paste in a packing case supposed to contain rice noodles.[62] The League of Nations archive is littered with accounts of smaller seizures on these three ships, almost all involving Fujian's Lion, 555, and Tongee brands, packaged in one-tael (37 gram) tins. Like their contemporaries in Java, an army of small-time smugglers between Fujian and Manila were taking advantage of preexisting shipping networks in foodstuffs and various ordinary produce.

A Fujianese crime boss named José Alindogan was the American government's primary suspect in the import of Xiamen opium into the Philippines during these years. Alindogan's name was tied to some of the largest seizures on record, such as the 1930 confiscation of 2,000 tins of 555 and Lion brands of Xiamen opium weighing a total 71.15 kg discovered on arrival in Manila as part of a shipment consigned to Alindogan.[63] A *New York Times* article on the case called him "the most powerful opium racketeer in the Philippines" and indicated several high-ranking customs and government officials who were accused of collusion in the scheme.[64] As of 1931, authorities in the Philippines had connected the case to ten other major confiscations related to the 555 and Lion brands of Xiamen opium.[65] Fujian's warlord-protected opium market was one side of the equation, and on the receiving end were men like Alindogan and the veritable army of unnamed individuals who performed similar work.

THE SHENZHOU PHARMACY AND FLEETING GLIMPSES OF XIAMEN'S EXPORT SPECIALISTS

At 9 a.m. on a November morning in 1929, police and government officials assembled in Xiamen's Sun Yatsen Park to burn 2,280 pounds of raw Persian opium worth an estimated 200,000 yuan. The officers doused the piles of drugs with gasoline and set them ablaze in order to "sweep away the spread of the opium curse, and express the government's determination in prohibition."[66] The majority of the opium had been found concealed in oil barrels, ready for export. Each of the barrels was affixed with labels reading "The Cheng Xing Company" or simply "Cheng Brand," as well as an opium prohibition bureau stamp. Alongside the barrels were also several wooden chests affixed with stickers marked "C.S.D." and Maritime Customs import certificates. The wooden chests were filled with paper packets of morphine powder.[67]

Three months earlier, a man named Huang Qing'an was arrested for possession of these materials on the neighboring islet of Gulangyu. The Xiamen police had raided Huang's business, the Shenzhou Dispensary (*Shenzhou Yaofang*), and chased him out the back door, down an alley, and into a public toilet.[68] Huang's arrest was unusual, not least because he was a Spanish subject living in Xiamen's foreign concession, Gulangyu, across the harbor from the city proper. The Xiamen police did not usually risk the diplomatic consequences of ferrying over to Gulangyu to arrest a foreign subject. In this case their boldness came from Huang's claims to Spanish protection. After ceding control of the Philippines to the United States in the late 1890s, the Spanish government had shuttered their consulate in Xiamen and delegated responsibility to the French consul in Xiamen to deal with Spanish subjects as he saw fit. Xiamen's police understood this history, and they arrested Huang without waiting for permission from the French consul.

As documented in the preceding sections of this chapter, evidence abounds from across maritime Southeast Asia that points towards Xiamen as an important source for the illicit export of opium out of China. But while newspapers and customs officers in places like Singapore and Manila regularly reported detailed evidence about the arrival of Fujianese opium into those colonies, they offer no information about how that opium departed China and who was managing the export end of the trade. Only very rarely are the smugglers even identified. Finding the people in Xiamen who were engaged in the opium export trade is made even more difficult by the complete lack of interest that the local government displayed in that side of the business. When Chinese government officials and prohibition activists in Fujian took action against the drug trade, they focused on opium's cultivation, import, and distribution. There is an almost complete archival silence about opium exports from China. I was unable to locate a single mention of opium's export from Xiamen in police reports from the 1930s, the Fujian Provincial Archive, or even local Chinese newspapers like the *Minzhong ribao*, *Chang Yan*, and the *Xiamen ribao*, all of which frequently reported on illegal opium transactions in the region.

In contrast to the wealth of evidence on the import and distribution end of the business, Huang's arrest is one of the only scraps of evidence about the people in Xiamen who arranged shipments of opium out of China. All we know for certain about Huang is that he was a pharmacy manager living in Gulangyu with extraterritorial status, who was found in possession of two tons of Persian opium that appeared ready for export. The sources surrounding his case do not explicitly state that he was planning to export the drugs in his possession. It is my belief that the opium was being prepared for export, based on the opium having been imported, repackaged, and packed into oil drums, which was a common method of concealment used by smugglers who sent drugs from Xiamen to places like Singapore.[69]

Supporting this hypothesis is a conspicuous amount of evidence pointing towards the Shenzhou Dispensary having long served as an export specialist for drug traders in Xiamen. As discussed later in this chapter, another Xiamen pharmacist named E. S. Cheong (Zhang Yongshun) was implicated in the smuggling of morphine and cocaine into Southeast Asia.[70] In 1930, the British consul in Xiamen reported that the Shenzhou Pharmacy had been a regular partner of Dr. Cheong.[71] One of Ye Qinghe's subordinates stated that the Shenzhou Dispensary was one of Ye's businesses, which he owned together with a man named Chen Shangcai.[72] This same Chen Shangcai was indeed arrested together with Huang Qing'an in the 1929 raid on the Shenzhou Dispensary.[73] Two years later Chen reappears in local newspapers, named as one of Ye Qinghe's partners in a short-lived bid for the navy's opium distribution monopoly in Xiamen.[74] When Ye took over the Guomindang opium monopoly after 1934, Chen was also a partner.[75] For people like Ye who were known to cash in on the export of drugs out of Xiamen, affiliation with a pharmacy in the foreign concession in Gulangyu would have been an important and useful part of the business model.[76]

Sites like the Shenzhou Pharmacy were key nodes in the transformed global spatiality of the drug trade. The global opium trade by the 1920s was no longer characterized by the long-term historical eastward movement of opium from India to China, and actors like Huang Qing'an were using creative measures like flexible citizenship and medical licensing to facilitate and protect their illicit movement of opium from China westward into the maritime Southeast Asian colonial sphere. Huang was also moving morphine, and as we shall see, pharmacies were crucial sites for the import, production, and movement of drugs like morphine, heroin, and cocaine. This too was part of an evolving reorientation of the spatiality of the drug trade, the reconstitution of new global networks in response to new laws, new technologies, and new regulatory institutions.

Narcotic Alkaloids in the New Global Drug Economy

The laboratory-produced alkaloids known as morphine, heroin, and cocaine were an integral part of the wide-scale expansion of the drug business in early twentieth-century Fujian. As early as 1894 the British consul in Xiamen reported a falling off in local opium imports due to "the growing habit of the people in this consular district to substitute morphia, in the form of pills and injection, for opium smoking."[77] The customs reported a total of 23,722 ounces of morphine, or nearly 21 million doses, imported legally into Xiamen from 1902 until the drug's importation was prohibited in 1909.[78] During this same period, the commissioner of customs also noted that the majority of the trade never made it into customs records. "The bulk of Amoy's supply," wrote the customs officer, "which comes chiefly from Germany, Japan and Great Britain, is smuggled into the port."[79] As of the 1909 International Opium Commission investigation, consumption of morphine in Fuzhou was "reported to be just as great as ever," and the drug was described as "a terrible curse" on the communities of rural Yongchun to the north of Xiamen, where at least eight dealers were known to sell morphine preparations.[80]

These new drugs proliferated throughout the early twentieth century, and by the 1930s, southern Fujianese locales such as rural Hui'an county and Nanri island were littered with morphine houses. "Many of these operations are located within the rice shops of the local marketplaces," states a 1934 newspaper article, "where locals come to engage in friendly intercourse, but rather than opium or tea, they enter and begin preparing their morphine needles . . . Visiting guests, whether or not they are addicts, are invited to shoot up as a display of their respect."[81] Arrest reports and other articles in local newspapers from the 1920s and 1930s confirm this bombastic description of the prominence of morphine in Xiamen and the surrounding area.

Needle and pill drugs were cheap and ubiquitous. Li Liu, a laborer arrested in June of 1936 with three pouches of morphine and two counterfeit banknotes, is reported to have told authorities that "because of the hardships of his profession he hadn't enough money for opium and so switched over to morphine."[82] Other illustrative reports include a 1936 newspaper story about a teenager who was selling pudding at the Xiamen city gate when he was arrested for heroin possession, or the 1934 raid on a Gulangyu opium den that uncovered twelve homemade hypodermic needles.[83] Even Guomindang soldiers, most notoriously those stationed on Nanri Island up the coast from Quanzhou, were reported to be heavy users of needle morphia.[84] In one 1929 case, an informer told the International Anti-Opium Association that Cai Ducheng of Dongshi village in Jinjiang was the head of an operation that manufactured "opium-quitting" pills made of a morphine-cocaine concoction and sold them in the surrounding villages.

The association sent word down to local officials, who dispatched a dozen soldiers to arrest Cai, but were rebuffed by a mob of 500–600 villagers who came to the druggist's aid.[85]

Just as the opium market saw the proliferation of new and competing brands, these years saw the emergence of a wide range of preparations marketed to morphine users. One dealer named Chen Xuying, thirty-six years old, unemployed, and the sole caregiver of a three year-old boy, was arrested in her Jinjiang county home in possession of four hypodermic needles, two "rocks" of morphine, two small packets and one large packet of morphine, one bottle of morphine powder, two packets of opium dross, and two packets of opium.[86] She had opened the door for a twelve-year-old boy, ostensibly sent on an errand to her house by his father, a regular customer of Chen's who possessed an opium-quitting license from the local government intended to gradually wean him off the drug. The man was not satisfied with the amount of drugs allotted him by the state and was also buying morphine from Chen on the sly. The police discovered his habit and coerced him to send his son into Chen's house to help them prove she was dealing morphine. Chen dumped a substantial amount of drugs down the toilet as the police were entering her home, but the remaining evidence was enough to send her to jail.

Cases documenting the arrest of around three dozen people in Hui'an and Jinjiang counties during 1937–1939 offer some of the only remaining records of street-level morphine arrests during an age in which hypodermic and oral use of the narcotic by all accounts pervaded the coastal districts of southern Fujian.[87] The cases give brief outlines of the arrest and prosecution of thirty-one men and five women for use, possession, and sales of morphine. They were all classified as laborers, farmers, or unemployed. Each arrest is accompanied with a list of confiscated items, usually a variety of powdered and liquid forms of morphine, as well as (often homemade) hypodermic needles. The people captured in these records were pulled off the street for doing something that was at that moment as commonplace as smoking opium had been for over a century. The vast majority of the people in these cases (twenty-eight) were given twelve years in jail for morphine use, most often with no other evidence than track marks—the physical traces of hypodermic injection on their bodies.[88] Many of them died in prison.[89]

The arrest records and newspaper articles that have survived offer important evidence about the regional market for these new laboratory-produced drugs. Morphine was widely available to even the unemployed rural poor. Men, women, and children were all involved in the trade, and it was not difficult to get the materials together to become a small-time dealer. People were heavily invested in the morphine business and often violently resistant to government or other outside intervention. And most germane to the argument of this chapter, the wide assortment of varieties of morphine described in the Chen Xuying case was not atypical among other cases from the period.

This was a complex and commercialized market, with different varieties of powdered, paper, liquid, paste, and pill morphia, from an equally diverse range of origins. In November of 1937, two other women from Jinjiang were arrested for dealing an impressive variety of morphia. Zhang Henian was found with ten small packets of wet morphine and seventeen strips of white paper morphine; Xu Jiniang was arrested with twenty-two packets of wet morphine, as well as one bottle of liquid morphine and another 94 grams of morphine, presumably powder.[90] Pills and paper applications were available for consumers who were scared of needles. Different brands circulated to meet a wide range of preferences and taste. It was a new age, and Fujian was once again a central hub in the swirling global circulation of narcotics.

GLOBAL MORPHINE FLOWS AND THE RISE OF JAPAN

The morphine and heroin trade in Fujian arose out of coinciding structural transformations on local, regional, and global scales. Morphine, heroin, and cocaine were all invented, manufactured, and marketed out of Europe during the early years of the trade, morphine having been sold commercially since the German firm Merck put it on the market in 1827. Widespread commercial sales of these new laboratory drugs started to take off during the 1890s and spread quickly across the globe. In China, British and German agents were particularly active in the introduction of morphine, heroin, and cocaine. But around the end of World War I, Japanese drug companies started to manufacture these drugs on a large scale, just as new international drug control systems emerged to cut off European drug manufacturers from consumers in Asia, and just as the chaotic political situation in China opened up opportunities for the emergence of clandestine laboratories for local manufacture.

Some of the best information we have about the early introduction of morphine into China comes from a 1913 letter intercepted by the British gov-

ernment. The author of the letter was a German by the name of Gustav Hoffmann, writing to a potential business partner in China about how to smuggle
narcotics from Europe into Xiamen.[91] The drugs offered by Hoffmann included German morphine and cocaine from Merck and British morphine
from the firms of Winks and Smiths (see Figure 5.5).[92] Hoffmann gave clear
instructions about how European drug manufacturers could arrange consignments of illicit cargo with their Asian customers. He boasted of bringing
regular shipments of morphine and cocaine into Xiamen via Hong Kong
without incident for several years running. He described concealing the drug
in tins of castor oil, margarine, Vaseline; in drums of calcium carbide, caustic soda, and caustic potash; or in casks of aniline salts, naphthalene, Epson
salt, and soda ash. He suggested using the telegraph to send coded messages
and reduce the potential for detection and seizure when passing the customs:
"When cabling kindly mention your telegraphic address and note the code
words—*Cheese* for *Cocaine* and *Margarine* for *Morphia*."[93]

A decade later the British government made another major breakthrough
into the mechanics of the illegal trade, when a Taiwanese merchant was
captured in Hong Kong with a large cargo of European drugs intended
for Xiamen. Tieu Yui Kim, the captured suspect, had personally escorted
the drugs to Hong Kong from Europe in the Japanese-owned SS *Mishima*

FIGURE 5.5: Label for J. A. Wink brand morphine.

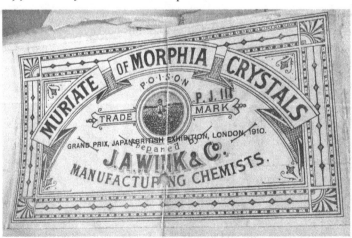

Source: United Nations Archive at Geneva. Reprinted with permission.

Maru, concealed in four cases of furniture. He was captured when customs agents in Hong Kong searched the furniture and discovered 2,500 ounces of cocaine and 2,400 ounces of morphine (approximately 4,375,000 and 2,100,000 doses respectively). The Hong Kong police searched the man's lodgings and uncovered letters and telegrams containing a trove of information, some of which eventually led to the arrest in London of a British merchant named Howard Montague Fogden Humphrey.[94] Humphrey, it was found, had signed a contract with a Xiamen-based firm called Tong Say Brothers in 1922 for exclusive supply of no less than 1,000 pounds of the narcotics annually.[95] According to letters between Humphrey and a man named Loo Ben Tan (another representative of Tong Say) based in Osaka, the drugs were to be sent by Humphrey from Switzerland to Hong Kong, and then brought up to Xiamen by sail.[96]

Despite the large hit to their business, Tong Say and Humphrey were well-enough capitalized that they altered their methods and continued to invest in even larger cargoes of the drugs. Tong Say's managing director in Xiamen wrote to Humphrey in November 1922 explaining that Tieu had made several rookie mistakes that led to the seizure: it was Tieu's first trip to Europe, and on his visits to London and Holland "it was hard for him to keep his action secret on his way home in hotels or with interpreter and carries that caused great suspicion [*sic*]." Tong Say reassured Humphrey that "all the responsibility was under Mr. Tiew. You and our partners are all free . . . We are now arranging for his coming out sooner." Tong Say advised Humphrey to change up their telegraph code, the instructions to which had been confiscated by the Hong Kong police, and to come up with better arrangements to get the drugs to Xiamen, where "we have full power to land when it reaches our ports."[97]

Humphrey responded the next January with a letter planning out his personal delivery of 50,000 ounces of narcotics to Xiamen, suggesting alternative shipping routes (substituting Vladivostok for Hong Kong) and a new telegraph code for the different brands of drugs, including morphine, heroin, and cocaine from Winks, Boehringer & Sohn, and Merck. Humphrey planned to purchase the drugs for £40,000 and believed that the Tong Say group would be able to sell the drugs in China for £120,000.[98] He was arrested in London before he could make the trip.

Like Hoffman's group, the Tong Say-Humphrey network was also importing European drugs into Xiamen, transshipped in Hong Kong. But where the nationality of Hoffmann's partners in China remains unknown, the Humphrey case centers around a Taiwanese firm that maintained offices in Xiamen, Taiwan, and Osaka. A memorandum on the drug trade issued in response to the Humphrey case summarizes a typical arrangement for organizations like Tong Say: a firm in Japan approaches a known European drug company with an offer; "if the offer is accepted, letters of credit are opened through banks having branches both in Japan and in Europe. The drugs are then packed in cases etc., of apparently innocent goods which are shipped to China."[99] Japanese-Taiwanese firms based in Xiamen were establishing a special place in the movement of European drugs through Asia.

These Taiwanese firms were operating on a truly global scale, connecting Europe, the Americas, and Asia in a shadowy web of drugs and money. In a 1926 case, police in the Netherlands Indies discovered two boxes of vests hiding within them a total of 62 kg of morphine and another 27 kg cocaine.[100] The drugs had nominally been ordered by a fictional firm in Havana through a French intermediary firm called Follet & André from the German manufacturer Roessler. The consigner of both shipments was a person named Paul Dubois, who also proved to be fictional, and it was the fictional Dubois who supposedly informed Follet & André to redirect the shipment from Havana to Batavia. Who designed this scheme we cannot know, but the drugs were ultimately confiscated on two Dutch steamships that were being loaded for transport from the Netherlands Indies to Xiamen under consignment of a Taiwanese firm called Lian Bo, whose intermediary in securing the shipment was a Japanese firm in Batavia called Kubo & Company. Strategies like this—layers of subterfuge, dummy companies, and complex transnational networks—enabled Xiamen's Taiwanese drug importers and their global partners to evade the increasingly intrusive international monitoring of the League of Nations drug control institutions the mid-1920s.

Xiamen native Ye Qinghe, while living in Shanghai during the early 1920s, also worked with colleagues in Japan to bring European manufactured drugs into China on Dutch and Japanese steamships. Ye's Gwanho (Yuanhe) and Quanji Companies, both registered at No. 50 Canton Road in Shanghai, had gotten into trouble in 1924 when the Shanghai opium magnate Judah Ezra accused Ye of stealing a huge cargo of Persian opium from him, and the municipal council police raided Ye's business and found the missing opium. Amidst the documentation seized in Ye Qinghe's office in 1924 was a telegraph from Gwanho to the Swiss drug company Hoffman-La Roche referencing the successful shipment of 520 kilos of "M.H.C." (morphine, heroin, cocaine) to China, and requesting information about pricing, telegraph codes, and the potential for the League of Nations to intervene in Hoffman-La Roche's export operations.[101] Like the Kubo & Co. case described above, Gwanho and Hoffman-La Roche used Dutch steamships to bring the drugs from Europe, coded in their telegrams as "Mr. Holland."[102] The documentation seized in Ye's Canton Road office also included dozens of connections to Japan, including several expense reports from hotels in Kobe, lawyer's fees in Japan, and bills from the captain of the Japanese steamer, the SS *Kamagata Maru*.[103]

Ye and the Gwanho company were astute to ask Hoffman-La Roche about the scrutiny of the League of Nations, which succeeded over the course of the 1920s in largely cutting off people like Ye from their connections with the established German and British drug companies represented by Hoffmann, Humphrey, and Follet & André. The broader trend of the 1920s is that China's drug traders were finding more local sources of heroin, morphine, and cocaine. North China had become one of the world's foremost depots for narcotics, and production operations large and small had sprung up in Sichuan, Shanghai, Dalian, Tianjin, Kobe, Osaka, and Taipei (see Figure 5.6).

Ye Qinghe, who by 1934 was being referred to in Shanghai newspapers as a "Morphine King," was a pioneer in this field and an important link between Xiamen and the Shanghai drug market.[104] Several historians have previously noted Ye's involvement with the Sichuanese warlord Fan Shaozheng in manufacturing heroin with domestic Chinese opium, a relationship that is also detailed in an oral history of one of Ye's employees.[105] By the early 1930s Ye had also established the United Dispensary (*guomin yaofang*) in Shanghai's French concession under the same alternate name he later used for his Japanese citizenship papers, Ye Zhensheng.[106] Ye used the legal business of the pharmacy to import the equipment necessary to launch his own heroin factory in the French concession district with the help of two Japanese scientists.

Ye set up his Shanghai heroin factory with a Chinese crew to keep surveillance over the high-priced Japanese scientists until he was able to replicate the process more cheaply.[107] The legitimate operation he used to supply

FIGURE 5.6: Small heroin factory in Shanghai.

Source: United Nations Archive at Geneva. Reprinted with permission.

the factory, the United Dispensary, had multiple direct links to Xiamen, not only through Ye Qinghe, but also through two Xiamen residents that were highly placed in the dispensary's leadership: the company's chairman Lin Youming, who lived in Xiamen's foreign concession on Gulangyu, and another company director Wang Youxiong, the owner of a textile firm in Xiamen proper.[108] As noted in chapter 4, one of Ye's drug factories in Shanghai was raided in 1932 just before his escape back home to Fujian.

Dealers of morphine and heroin in Fujian responded enthusiastically to the new, more local supply-chain opportunities created by Ye and other laboratory operators. European drugs were still coming east—as the 1926 Follet & André case demonstrates—but after the mid-1920s, Japanese, Korean, and Chinese drugs were more widely available, brought down from Shanghai and other ports north of Xiamen, or across the strait from Taiwan. One journalist reported in 1936 that heroin with a retail value of $1.30 an ounce was "smuggled into [Xiamen] from Formosa packed in tins weighing 18 ½ ounces each. The imports have risen from 300 to 500 tins in the past six months, which gives some idea of the expanding market."[109] By the mid-1930s Fujian was also producing its own morphine. The 1936 report listed at least four factories for morphine production in the province, all located in southern Fujian: in Anhai, Hui'an, Zhangzhou, and Xiamen. The Xiamen factory was said to be run and operated by a Taiwanese syndicate under the protection of the Japanese government.

The most prolific and sustained morphine production operation in Fujian was a lineage-based business located in a small town called Zhanglin village in Jinjiang county. Zhanglin is situated on the road between Quanzhou and Xiamen, in the heart of poppy country, with easy access to opium grown in the highly productive districts of Hui'an, Nan'an, Jinjiang, and Tong'an counties. In 1925 a Taiwanese doctor visited the village, realized the opportunity at hand, and partnered with a local man named Zhang Ziyin to set up a morphine factory.[110] Like Ye Qinghe's crew in Shanghai, Zhang Ziyin watched the doctor closely and learned the science and procurement terminology necessary to launch his own morphine business. Zhang's lineage maintained and expanded their morphine operations through the subsequent decades, successfully resisting periodic government raids like when they fought off the 419th Special Brigade in September of 1932.[111] As late as 1949 a Guomindang survey found over forty morphine companies still operating in Zhanglin village, employing 543 people, or 33 percent of the village's population (involving 80 percent of the village's families). The lineage owned 180 bicycles used for the express purpose of delivering morphine around the county.[112]

The story of the morphine trade in Fujian illustrates the transition from an import market supplied by major European drug companies to a more complex marketplace within which swirled a wide array of local and global products. This trend was facilitated perhaps most crucially by the utter lack of an effective government in southern Fujian. People who wanted to import European drugs across Asia looked to entrepreneurs in Fujian to get the drugs through the interstate control system. People who wanted to manufacture these new drugs had an endless supply of raw local and Persian opium in southern Fujian.

The intra-Asian morphine and heroin trade was also dependent on the rise of Japanese power. Evidence from the supply side indicates that Xiamen's drug smugglers worked tirelessly to manipulate the port's location within the Japanese imperial sphere to their advantage. Morphine was brought into Xiamen through Japanese-protected channels, and much of what was manufactured in China was either managed or assisted by people with Japanese protection. Fujian's proximity to the Japanese colony in Taiwan likewise facilitated the flow of drugs into China.

ASIA'S COCAINE "TRAMPOLINE"

Cocaine too flooded coastal Fujian, shipped alongside morphine and heroin from Europe in the early years and later sourced from within Asia. But unlike the trade in opiates, most of the cocaine brought into Fujian was imported, cut, packaged, and reexported to India and Southeast Asia. The port of Xiamen, in the parlance of late twentieth-century narco-capitalism, operated throughout the early twentieth century as a cocaine "trampoline."[113] The term connotes a location within a drug trade route that is valuable purely for its role in clandestine transshipping logistics. Fujian province was loosely regulated, especially when it came to narcotics like cocaine, in an increasingly tightly regulated global environment. Xiamen was a port where people could access a broad menu of drugs from Europe and across Asia and then turn around and board any number of direct and busy steamship lines to a whole continent of places where access to those drugs was restricted.

Cocaine initially became a staple of the Xiamen import-export market in the last years of Qing rule when it was a legal item of trade. The stimulant was first entered into customs records in 1908, when local Fujianese pharmacists and hospitals imported 1,970 ounces. Imports rose to 11,727 ounces in 1909 and then rocketed to 27,578 ounces in the first six months of 1910, after which time the drug became a controlled substance and was removed from the list of legal imports.[114] That year, the single port of Xiamen was responsible for over 98 percent of all of the cocaine imports into Qing treaty ports.[115]

The elevated stature of Xiamen within the Chinese cocaine trade was not due to local consumption, but rather to the ability of locals to effectively and clandestinely serve consumers across maritime Asia. As it turns out, cocaine was not an especially popular drug among the Fujianese. There is very little evidence of cocaine use in and around Xiamen during the early twentieth century, where opium and morphine consumption is well documented. Instead, the evidence surrounding cocaine that does exist points to the Fujianese mercantile community's role in transshipping the drug to the Straits Settlements, Burma, and India. This sustained cocaine smuggling route was made possible, argued one British investigator, because authorities in those places were only on the lookout for drugs coming directly from Europe, and "it is supposed that steamers from [Xiamen] trading to those places will not be suspected of carrying such articles."[116]

There was a well-established market for cocaine in the South and Southeast Asian colonial ports. Interviews conducted by United States investigators in Burma during 1906 describe cocaine being used "a great deal," "to an amazing extent," and "in large quantities."[117] A 1908 article in the *Singapore Free Press* similarly describes Delhi as "the great centre of cocaine smuggling" and goes on to suggest that the drug was being imported from Germany through the post.[118] As historian James Mills has documented, cocaine use spread rapidly across South Asia in the first two decades of the twentieth century, often used as an additive to betel nut paste and consumed across class lines.[119] By 1910, authorities in Burma and the Straits Settlements were sending the British consul in Xiamen "constant complaints" of cocaine smuggling "by the native crews of the steamers which carry on the coolie emigration trade between Amoy and [the Straits Settlements and Burma]."[120] Like the story of opium exports, the circulation of cocaine out of China during these years was facilitated by passenger steamship lines that connected Xiamen directly to markets in the Straits Settlements, Burma, and India.

Cocaine followed a winding route from producer to consumer, and the mysterious Fujitsuru brand of cocaine illustrates the particular role of Fujianese intermediaries in facilitating the trade. Fujitsuru cocaine had long flummoxed British authorities, who were unable to trace the cocaine to any known company. The first major break in the case came with two seizures in Rangoon during the fall of 1928, when the British government confiscated several parcels of Fujitsuru cocaine that were packed alongside some apparently European cocaine, which the British then traced back to a legal consignment of the drug that had been exported from Germany under license to a doctor named E. S. Cheong in Xiamen.[121] In both parcels of confiscated cocaine, there was some authentically German cocaine packed together with other cocaine, which was packaged and stamped with two untraceable labels: those of "The Fujitsuru Brand" and "C.P. Boehringer & Soehne, Mannheun [*sic*]".[122] British authorities determined that the misspelling of "Sohn" and "Mannheim" was evidence that the supplementary German label was a forgery. The cocaine was real, but the label was fake.

So where had the drugs come from? The name Fujitsuru is unmistakably of Japanese origin, but the company itself was a mystery.

E. S. Cheong was a pharmacist in Xiamen with powerful connections. He was an intimate of the father-in-law of Garfield Huang, who was president and founder of the National Anti-Opium Association of China, and a close friend of Wu Liande, who was director of the National Quarantine Service.[123] According to a British investigation, Cheong was also on friendly terms with the Superintendent of Trade in Xiamen, who was the officer in charge of issuing import licenses for controlled substances.[124] Accordingly, he was "the only trafficker" left in Xiamen who still procured his drugs from Europe.[125] The consul's blanket assessment is, at a minimum, illustrative of the broader trend in global cocaine and morphine flows: by the late 1920s, most of Xiamen's drug movers sourced their products from within Asia. Even Cheong's European drugs were packed together with this mysterious (but clearly Asian) Fujitsuru brand of cocaine, boxed up and loaded onto steamships in Xiamen for transit to ports in South and Southeast Asia.

By the late 1920s, Fujitsuru was the most prevalent brand of cocaine in South and Southeast Asia. Between 1924 and 1929, the League of Nations received reports on the seizure of 11,670 ounces of Fujitsuru cocaine from officials in Calcutta, Rangoon, Singapore, Hong Kong, Bengal, Bombay, Hathras, and Penang.[126] If the total amount of cocaine seized by the state represented roughly 5 percent of the total trade (as one revenue officer estimated), then the total amount of Fujitsuru cocaine unloaded into the various colonial ports of South and Southeast Asia would have been around 180,000 ounces, equal to 11,250 pounds or around 315,000,000 doses, each year.[127] It was a trend increasingly viewed as a crisis among British authorities in India and Burma. In response, the Central Board of Revenue in Calcutta dispatched Special Officer James Slattery on a maritime odyssey to try and track down the murky origins of the mystery cocaine brand.

Slattery believed that the drug was Japanese in origin not only because of the name, but also because of the heavy investment in cocaine production by Japanese pharmaceutical companies. "Japan is the only country in the East which manufactures the drug, and cocaine has been discovered in India bearing the labels of recognized Japanese factories," he wrote, "but Japan has always maintained that the Fujitsuru, Elephant and Buddha brands are not of Japanese origin."[128] This was suspicious to Slattery because Japan was home to three large pharmaceutical companies that produced cocaine: the Hoshi Pharmaceutical Company, Koto Seiyaku, and Sankyo. The Hoshi Company had originally purchased land for the cultivation of coca leaves in Peru in 1917, a year after the Ensuiko Sugar Company first initiated experimental coca production in Taiwan.[129] In the 1920s, in order to save money on importing the coca leaf from South America, Japan's pharmaceutical companies set up coca plantations in Taiwan, Iwo Jima, and Okinawa, and also purchased from Dutch growers in Java, who had been cultivating coca there since the 1850s.[130] The Hoshi Seiyaku and Taiwan Shoyaku companies, on a combined 694 acres of land in the Taiwanese interior, produced a total of 700,814 kg of coca leaf between 1927 and1931, about one-fifth of which was transferred to Japan for processing, and the rest was processed into crude cocaine by those companies' factories in Taiwan.[131] The total production of coca leaf in Taiwan during this years was around 150,000 tons per year, which once processed into cocaine would have yielded around seven tons per year.[132]

While Slattery and the League of Nations investigators never found conclusive evidence that the Fujitsuru cocaine was produced with Japanese official knowledge, they had good reason to suspect that Japan's annual reports on cocaine production were concealing leakages of the drug into the Asian marketplace. Both Slattery and independent League of Nations' investigators argued that the figures submitted by Japan to the League showed evidence that raw and partially processed cocaine was disappearing into the black market.[133] In Taiwan, Japanese pharmaceutical companies produced 291 kg in 1927, 819 kg in 1928, then around 800 kg each year for several years thereafter. Local consumption there was estimated at less than 40 kg per year.[134] As one British Home Office official complained, there was a great deal more cocaine being produced than seemed medically necessary.[135] Slattery directly asked the Japanese Home Department to account for the missing cocaine: "Why was there excess manufacture of 337 kilogrammes during [1929], an excess of some 700 kilogrammes in 1928 and of some 850 kilogrammes in 1927; and what has happened to these enormous surplus stocks? Presumably this expensive drug is not manufactured irrespective of demand and allowed to decay on the factory shelves."[136] No satisfactory answer was produced.

As Slattery complained, this mysterious cocaine had to be coming from somewhere, and yet the Fujitsuru, Elephant, and Buddha brands of cocaine "have never been found on a Japanese ship, or in the possession of a Japanese."[137] The Fujitsuru brand of cocaine was exclusively found in southern locations connected directly to Xiamen by passenger steamship.[138] It was never found in northern parts of China or on any Japanese-owned shipping line. "It is a matter of common knowledge," wrote one officer investigating the traffic, "that there is extensive smuggling from Japan into North China, through Shanghai and Tientsin, yet these 'mystery' brands are entirely unknown there."[139] The Fujitsuru cocaine network was a southern affair, built out of southern Fujian's long-standing role as an opium trampoline' for markets in South and Southeast Asia.

On the receiving end of the trade in India and Southeast Asia, Chinese traffickers monopolized the import of Fujitsuru cocaine even to the exclusion of would-be Japanese participants. A professional smuggler told Slattery that in Calcutta the import of cocaine was controlled exclusively by a Chinese woman who had previously resided in Bombay and who had monopolized access to the Peshawari wholesale distributers responsible for selling off the drug within the city.[140] A similar system existed in Bombay, where Chinese middlemen controlled the receipt of cocaine from sailors on incoming steamers and then sold it off to the Rampuri distributers. When Japanese sailors attempted to smuggle known Japanese cocaine brands into Calcutta, they too had to sell their drug to the Chinese traffickers who controlled the import trade.[141]

On the export end of the trade, when the drugs were loaded onto ships in Xiamen, the cocaine business was in the hands of opium, morphine, and cocaine traders who imported drugs from Europe, Japan, and Taiwan for packaging and reexport. In many cases, German and Japanese brand-name cocaine imported by people like E. S. Cheong was doctored locally with inferior Taiwanese product (as well as Novocain, milk powder, and various other powdery white substances) and repackaged for the Southeast Asian and South Asian markets. One journalist reported in 1936 that around 300 tins of "genuine medicinal cocaine" and 1,000 tins of "cheap unrefined cocaine" were smuggled into Xiamen from Taiwan monthly, mostly for refining, packaging, branding, and then finally, reshipment to the "South Seas and Malaysia."[142] Large quantities of cocaine were smuggled from Japan to Xiamen in secret consignments on steamers from the coal ports of Japan, or by steamer or fishing boat down to Keelung in Taiwan and then on small fishing or motorboats across to Xiamen from the southern end of the island.[143] New diesel-engine motorboats began to ply between Taiwan and the mainland in a matter of hours, making smuggling exponentially more difficult to police.

The success of the Asian cocaine industry, and indeed what made the producers and sellers of these drugs so difficult to find, hinged on the ubiquity of counterfeiting practices. There was no Fujitsuru brand, as such. Or perhaps more accurately, there were so many knock-offs and production was so decentralized that identification of the "original" Fujitsuru was irrelevant to the task of prohibition. The first people known to use the brand name were a group of Cantonese residents in Kobe, who almost immediately inspired a rash of more successful copycat operations in Fujian and Guangdong. In one example, a Fujianese resident of Kobe named Wai Kee opened a grocery shop in Xiamen, importing Japanese cocaine through a Taiwanese pharmacist, doctoring the cocaine with 30 percent Novocain, and packaging it into tins for reexport under the Fujitsuru label. The Wai Kee ring was broken up during 1929–1930, but the Fujitsuru cocaine trade continued into the mid-1930s. Kwong Yee Sang and Lee Chick Hong are two other Fujianese who had spent time in Kobe; their names were found in documents seized in a cocaine bust in Rangoon during 1931, detailing over fifty remittances from South and Southeast Asia during 1929–1931.[144]

The labels attached to the Fujitsuru and other mystery cocaine brands (see Figure 5.7) are also a clue that points to Xiamen and the surrounding countryside. Fujian was a notorious and well-established center for the market in counterfeit labels.[145] In 1922, the British consul in Xiamen had lodged complaints about the counterfeit of soap, water bottle, candle, and pharmaceutical labels. Several of the accused counterfeiters had Taiwanese citizenship; many were located in outlying districts beyond Xiamen.[146] The Wai Kee ring had employed a Xiamen-area printer named Lee Lang Kun at the rate of $7 per sheet to print false Koto Seiyaku, Boehringer, and Fujitsuru labels.[147] As the Japanese government consistently told Slattery and League of Nations investigators, the Fujitsuru brand cocaine labels "could not be Japanese because the printing was inferior to that of modern Japanese work."[148] Using his trusty Hanovia Analysis Lamp, Slattery was able to determine a multiplicity of Fujitsuru labels: some with more or less detail on the plumage of the storks, some with more or less clear outlines of the back of the bird, and each hosting an array of different stamped monograms.[149] In a place like Xiamen, the Fujitsuru, false Boehringer, Elephant,

FIGURE 5.7: Fujitsuru and (false) Boehringer cocaine labels.

Source: CO 129-498-14, No. 2, Governor Clementi of Hong Kong to Lieutenant Colonel Amery, August 20, 1926. Reprinted with permission.

and Buddha labels would have been easy to arrange, and counterfeits inspired counterfeits of their own.

The Asian cocaine trade was interlocked with the opium business, especially in terms of personnel and capital. But the story of cocaine highlights a different group of networks, connections, and mechanisms from the example of morphine. Morphine was popular in Fujian, and it could be produced with an agricultural commodity that was grown in Fujian (and generally speaking, widely available). The logistics of procurement and the geography of consumption were entirely different in the cocaine business, which in Fujian was exclusively reliant on importing, repackaging, and then reexporting the drug to the brothels and gambling dens of far-off Singapore,

Rangoon, and Calcutta. The role of the Japanese empire, in terms of procurement, was fundamental to the cocaine business in a way that is less true for the story of opium, morphine, and heroin. Japanese investment in coca production in Java and Taiwan intensified the benefits accrued to Fujianese cocaine traders by virtue of political geography.

Conclusion: Shifting Structures and Profit Opportunities

China's place in the reoriented spatiality of the global drug trade in the early twentieth century has been undertheorized and poorly represented. These were the years of opium's reverse course. Just as a new global consensus was beginning to recognize that China had been victimized by the opium trade, the fragmented former Qing empire was assuming a new role in the global history of narcotics flows as an illicit exporter of opium, morphine, and cocaine into the British, Dutch, and American colonies of maritime Southeast Asia. This transformation, which happened simultaneously and with different logics across several clandestine branches of the drug trade, opens up rich possibilities for sorting out the complex interplay of structure and agency in what was a financial powerhouse of an interstate black marketplace.

The branches of the opium, morphine, and cocaine trades analyzed in this chapter were lucrative because the drugs were cheap in China and expensive in Southeast Asia. The ability of people to smuggle these drugs was made possible by imperially subsidized steamship lines that connected Southeast Asian ports directly to Xiamen. The supply side of the trade was fueled by Fujian's chaotic political situation, where competing warlords encouraged locals to cultivate the opium poppy and purchased large stocks of Persian opium to use as a currency alternative, ignored or failed to suppress local morphine laboratory operations, and failed or declined to adequately control the import of manufactured narcotics from Europe and Japan. The morphine and cocaine trades were additionally facilitated by the proximity of Japanese Taiwan, the rise of Japanese drug companies, and the ability of Fujianese intermediaries to activate Japanese imperial networks to their advantage. The centrality of Japanese imperialism to the success of Fujian's drug traders during this period is the focus of the next and final chapter of this book.

CHAPTER 6

Opium and the Frontier of Japanese Power in South China, 1895–1945

At 3 p.m. on a rainy day in 1936, a Xiamen police officer named Zhang Yongde set out walking on his beat through the city. Zhang had graduated from the police academy the previous March and had recently completed his first year on the job. His route began at the intersection of Siming Road and Sun Yatsen Avenue, then and now the commercial center of the bustling port. He walked past narrow alley entrances, up and down stone staircases between houses, winding through the maze of walkways and alleys that extend from the Siming Road thoroughfare to the wharf at the bottom of the hill.

Zhang was not from Fujian, and Xiamen was proving to be a learning experience for the north Chinese transplant. He particularly resented the numerous and troublesome manifestations of Japanese imperialism in the southern treaty port. This was understandable, given his background. Two years before arriving in Xiamen, on another rainy day, Zhang had learned that seventy-three farmers, including his entire family, were slaughtered by a roving unit of Japanese troops. At the time he was enlisted in an underground militia in Manchuria, and the incident sent Zhang's life into disarray. Rainy days, for Zhang, were associated with painful memories.

As the storm gathered, Zhang ducked under an awning. While he stood there in the shadows, two men dressed in black sprinted down an adjacent alley, chased by a group of a dozen other figures shouting "Stop! Thief!" As the pursuing mob closed in, a gunshot echoed through the rainy alleyways. The men stopped in their tracks. They shuffled backward, uncertain, and then continued their chase around the corner. Zhang drew his police whistle to his lips, cursing that he was tied up in yet another violent robbery case. He blew the signal repeatedly until he heard a response, then drew his handgun from the holster and set off in pursuit of the men.

Zhang found the dwindling group of pursuing men milling in the middle of a long and narrow street, unsure of which direction to continue their chase. The road from end to end had entrances to at least forty small alleyways, all dark, all candidates for the fleeing thieves to have found refuge. Zhang shook his head. He had been introduced to this neighborhood during his first days on the job. It was a poorly lit maze of winding alleyways and an area of the city completely dominated by the resident Taiwanese population. He looked up and saw above each doorway a wooden placard that read "Registered citizen of Japan" (*da Riben jimin*), a clear signal to Chinese police officers like Zhang that the residents and business owners in these buildings were not subject to Chinese law or police intervention.

Zhang chose an alley and considered the possibilities as he walked. There was no way to be certain whether the residents hiding behind these symbols of Japanese citizenship were actually Taiwanese. Many local residents rented the wooden placards from actual Taiwanese people, and others simply made their own counterfeit versions. Inside the shops one was more than likely to find businesses organized around morphine rigs, opium pipes, gambling tables, and sex workers. Surely the thieves had their favorite brothel or opium den in the neighborhood, but Zhang was coming around to the realization that he was unlikely to find the men, and he had no legal recourse if they claimed Japanese protection.

The character of Zhang Yongde is from a short work of fiction published in a 1930s Xiamen periodical.[1] The author of the story was seeking to link up the local story of Japanese imperialism in Xiamen to the national outrage about the Japanese conquest of Manchuria. Zhang's tale ends in bitter disappointment, the officer weeping in the rain outside of a Taiwanese morphine den unable to pursue or arrest men he witnessed in the commission of a crime. "Xiamen is on Chinese soil," he cries out, "it is not the same as Manchuria!" But here in Chinese Xiamen, the narrator tells us, Zhang is just as likely to be subject to the depredations of the "evil" Japanese.

This chapter follows the fictional police officer Zhang Yongde into the alleyways and brothels of urban Xiamen. It traces back the global circulations of opium and powdered narcotics discussed in chapter 5 into the treaty port itself, where local "opium kings" and Taiwanese businessmen ran brothels and opium and gambling dens, and played critical roles in government opium monopoly bureaus and global-scale drug networks. As such, this chapter highlights the particular role of citizenship, extraterritoriality, and Japanese imperialism in the apex years of the opium business in southern Fujian.

Extraterritoriality was the policy that most served to define the terms of China's victimization at the hands of outside imperial powers, and opium is the most potent symbol of that victimization. A common and not inaccurate conception about the history of extraterritoriality in China is that it served as a shield for people to commit drug crimes, that it undermined China's sovereignty and destabilized Chinese society because it normalized lawbreaking and served to increase drug use. The evidence in this chapter does indeed confirm this familiar narrative, but it also expands our understanding of the relationship between opium and empire in China by rereading the history of extraterritoriality from the perspective of the Chinese people who claimed it. Drawing on the tactics of self-preservation and sheltering profits from the state originally discovered by the pioneers of flexible citizenship in British colonial Southeast Asia, small-time dealers and powerful opium magnates across the Fujian littoral became Japanese imperial citizens.

This transformation of the opium business into an industry that was under the protection of Japanese diplomatic and naval authorities had profound consequences for the local Chinese state. The warlord and Guomindang opium prohibition bureaus and poppy tax agencies analyzed in chapter 4 were, by the 1930s, almost exclusively contracted to people under Japanese protection. When Japan finally invaded and took over Xiamen in 1938, the opium business community had already done the work of turning the city into a full-fledged drug colony.

Southern Fujian in the Japanese Imperial Vision

Japan gained control over Taiwan following the first Sino-Japanese War of 1894–1895. Administratively, small areas of Taiwan had been governed by the Qing as a prefecture within Fujian province until 1875, when the entire island was declared a province. Culturally and economically, the western (mainland-facing) half of Taiwan had been closely connected to Fujian for centuries. Xiamen and the neighboring city of Quanzhou were the chief ports of departure for Fujianese migrants to Taiwan, and Hokkien colonists (people of southern Fujianese ancestry) were by the late nineteenth century the majority population of the island. So with one stroke of the treaty brush, Japan found itself with a heavy economic interest in the port of Xiamen and in nominal control of a substantial and highly mobile population of Hokkien subjects with family and commercial ties to southern Fujian. Almost immediately, the port of Xiamen and the southern districts of Fujian assumed a new strategic importance for the expanding Japanese empire.

Before the first Sino-Japanese War, the Meiji government had few diplomatic or commercial investments in Xiamen. After building a consulate in Xiamen during 1875, Japan shuttered the office five years later and hired a British merchant to act as a proxy. In 1887, Japan established a consulate in Fuzhou with jurisdiction over Xiamen.[2] But once Japan gained control over Taiwan in 1895, strategic interest in Fujian increased rapidly. By 1899, the Meiji state was pressuring the Qing to grant Japan its own independent foreign concession near the most desirable part of Xiamen's harbor.[3] That effort remained at a standstill until the Japanese Navy took dramatic action in the summer of 1900, using the ostensible danger presented by the Boxer Uprising in north China as a pretext to try and extract concessions from the Qing government. Never mind that the uprising was a thousand miles away, with no evidence of agitation in Fujian. Suddenly, and without apparent provocation, Japanese troops descended on Xiamen in late August of 1900, setting off a rumor mill of invasion that led to an estimated 100,000 people fleeing from their homes and businesses in the city.[4]

For Chinese, European, and American observers alike, Japan's actions in Xiamen during the Boxer Uprising signaled the dawn of a new era of Japanese influence in southern Fujian. By 1905, the US consul in Xiamen was complaining of Japanese "claims to unusual privileges being made on the ground that this territory opposite Formosa was peculiarly Japan's sphere of influence." He described the expansion of Japanese interests in Xiamen as a "commercial campaign" that was "as well planned as any military campaign . . . In this campaign Japan has been looking more to the future, has had more regard for ultimate advantages, and has paid more attention to the sociological or possibly the political control of the Chinese people, than any other nation."[5] In a report from a few months later, the same consul complained that Japanese-subsidized steamships were driving British and American liners out of the market, and Japanese Buddhist missionaries were roaming the countryside "enrolling the people as converts" by promising them "protection from official or private aggression."[6] Local rumor had it that Japanese officials were scheming to take over the province entirely.[7] As one British consul wrote in 1908, "the whole of this district [Xiamen] swarms with Japanese who are working slowly but surely towards the absorption of the province into the Japanese empire at a propitious moment."[8]

The concerns expressed by the US and British consuls were alarmist and likely rooted in a racist suspicion about the prospects of Japanese power in Asia, but the notion that Japan was seeking "political control" over people in Fujian was not entirely misplaced. During the first three decades of the twentieth century, Japanese consuls in Xiamen enrolled tens of thousands of people with Fujianese ancestry as Taiwanese, and therefore Japanese, citizens.[9] These people were officially known as "registered people," or *jimin* (*sekimin* in Japanese). In this book I follow this convention, referring to them as "registered Taiwanese" wherever possible. Contemporaneous Chinese newspapers and later historians have often referred to them as Japanese-protected *ronin* (Chinese *langren*), as opportunistic mercenaries who were instruments in a wider Japanese plot to destabilize China.[10] It would be a mistake, however, to view these people solely as instruments. They were people who made choices and whose actions had unpredictable consequences.

The *jimin* category originated during the period from May 8, 1895 and ending May 8, 1897, when the Japanese government gave people living in Taiwan two years to either relocate to China or remain in Taiwan and become Japanese imperial citizens. The deadline proved to be the launching point for citizenship questions, rather than the ultimate settlement of the issue. As many as 90 percent of the people Japan registered in Taiwan as "native Taiwanese" were either born in southern Fujian or had families and property in Fujian.[11] People living in China also had innumerable business and personal reasons to come to Taiwan and in so doing were given the opportunity to become Japanese citizens. Many families had property on both sides of the Taiwan Strait. As a 1934 newspaper put it, "the 4,000,000 people of Taiwan are all proficient in the Xiamen dialect, their customs are entirely identical to the customs of southern Fujian."[12] The only reliable way to distinguish a *jimin* was by looking at their passport.

By the time Japanese citizenship emerged as a possibility for people from the southeast coast of China, they and their families and neighbors had over sixty years of experience with registering as colonial subjects of foreign regimes. Aihwa Ong, who wrote the pioneering study of flexible citizenship, describes the late twentieth-century phenomenon of people adopting multiple and shifting citizenships as one that is fundamentally about "strategies to accumulate capital and power."[13] The origins of modern flexible citizenship began during an earlier age of globalization, after the first of the treaties between China and Britain in 1843 created the possibility for British citizenship claims among "Straits Chinese," or people from Guangdong and Fujian who settled or sojourned in British colonial Southeast Asia. The terms of extraterritoriality in China embodied an assumption among the treaty's drafters that the line between British and Chinese people was unquestionably clear. So when the people who traversed between China and Southeast Asia discovered the value of British extraterritorial protection vis-à-vis the Qing state, they created dilemmas for the Qing and British officials stationed in southeast ports like Xiamen. These mid-level officials—not treaty drafters, but treaty implementers—had to figure out what to do with people who spoke, dressed, looked, and to them seemed by all accounts to be Chinese, but who had either been born in or sojourned in the British Straits colonies and could legitimately claim British citizenship.

In Xiamen, the port of departure for around half the migrants to the Straits Settlements, the question did not take long to arise. Unlike the Japanese consuls after 1895, earlier British consular officials in Xiamen were determined to keep the number of British-registered Fujianese low. In large part, the reticence among British consuls on this matter seems to have stemmed from a combination of discrimination and bureaucratic recalcitrance. It made their jobs easier to limit their own liability when it came to people of Chinese descent with claims to citizenship. Framing it as an issue of reputation, one British consul complained in 1851 that the Straits Chinese in Xiamen "sink the character of British subjects entirely."[14] That consul even considered trying to reduce the number of applicants by requiring them to dress in British costume, a policy that was generally agreeable to the sartorially minded Qing bureaucrats.[15]

Throughout the late nineteenth and early twentieth centuries, other British and American consuls were similarly tightfisted when it came to citizenship applicants of Chinese descent. In 1905, the US consul in Xiamen summarized his frustrations on this issue, denying legal support to several people who had spent time in the Philippines, Hawaii, and other American colonial territories. "All these Chinese seem to be 'American' for the business advantage they have here in China," he wrote, "and not for the purpose of returning to the United States or for any patriotic reason."[16] A British officer in Xiamen wrote similarly in 1922 that "ninety nine per cent of these British subjects of Chinese race are Chinese first and British when it suits them . . . the obligation to recognise and protect them against their own natural authorities is the most irksome of the duties of Consular Officers in these southern ports."[17] The number of Chinese people registered in Xiamen's British and American (as well as Dutch and French) consulates was accordingly small. In 1907, nearly seventy years after the port was opened to British commerce, only 42 of 160 registered British subjects in Xiamen were of Chinese ancestry.[18] This number is remarkably low, considering that tens of thousands of people moved back and forth between Fujian and British colonial Southeast Asia each month.

The Japanese approach was different. Once Japanese rule in Taiwan began in 1895, people on both sides of the Taiwan Strait readily availed themselves of the business advantages that came with being Japanese without any obstruction from the Japanese consular officials in Fujian. When the 1897 deadline passed and people living in Taiwan were officially considered Japanese subjects, the number of Taiwanese-registered businesses in Xiamen increased rapidly: there were nine by October of 1897 and eighteen by January 1898.[19] That year there were around 500 Taiwanese *jimin* in the city. By 1917 there were 2,800 passport-holding Taiwanese in Xiamen, up to 6,879 in 1929 and 10,217 by 1937.[20] During the mid-1920s, one observer estimated that an additional 10,000 more had come over from Taiwan and neglected to formally register with the Japanese consulate.[21] No accurate estimates exist for how many local Fujianese *pretended* to be Taiwanese, but by all accounts the number was enormous, probably in the tens of thousands. The standard estimation in the mid-1930s was that there were around 30,000–40,000 people who claimed registered Taiwanese status living permanently in and around Xiamen.[22]

The rapid growth of Xiamen's registered Taiwanese population during the early twentieth century presented the Japanese government with clear strategic advantages in the treaty port. British, American, and Chinese observers were especially concerned with how the Japanese government leveraged the *jimin* situation to impinge on Chinese sovereignty and assume some of the duties and privileges of a governing body on the Chinese mainland. This process began in earnest during 1916, when the Japanese consulate established an independent police force in Xiamen proper "for the control of Japanese-Chinese subjects from Formosa."[23] This was distinct from the joint police force operating in the International Settlement, as it was located not in the Gulangyu foreign concession but across the harbor in the Chinese city, in an office located in a Taiwanese-owned brothel and staffed with nine officers. As the US consul quipped a few years later, "the Japanese consul stated that this police station was for the purpose of controlling the bad Formosan characters, in [Xiamen] city, but no one believed this."[24] Rather, the assumption shared by Chinese and Euro-American critics was that the police force was being used to protect the registered Taiwanese population and their businesses from the local Chinese government. In 1920, the Xiamen Daoyin and anti-opium activist Chen Peigun repeatedly petitioned the Japanese consul and the other foreign representatives to the Gulangyu mixed court that the Japanese police station in Xiamen was a violation of Chinese sovereignty, but the Japanese government refused to abandon the idea.[25]

REGISTERED TAIWANESE AND THE DRUG TRADE

Gaining Taiwanese registration became common sense for many people in Fujian, as there were both legal advantages and tax incentives. The earliest reference of someone leveraging Japanese citizenship in local Xiamen newspapers is from 1903, when members of the Zheng lineage in Longxi county were alleged to have bribed the Japanese consulate in order to procure a *jimin* placard to hang from their door. They had done this, according to the reporter, in order to intimidate local authorities from punishing them for violent actions during a feud with a neighboring lineage.[26] Between April and July of 1913, the new Republican government in Xiamen unsuccessfully sought the repatriation of forty-seven registered Taiwanese for crimes like murder, kidnapping, opening opium dens, robbery, and imitating government officials for the purposes of extortion.[27] In 1926, the Japanese consul in Xiamen explained that harsh military law under the city's warlord administration was partly responsible for the trend of locals seeking Japanese protection, citing a case wherein an impoverished purse snatcher from Jiangxi was sentenced to death by Yang Shuzhuang's naval court.[28] Shelter from Chinese legal institutions during the violent and chaotic warlord era was clearly important to people who sought out Japanese protection.

Much of the attraction of Taiwanese registration stemmed from the financial advantages. Lin Man-Houng has written about the benefits of Japanese imperial citizenship for tea merchants from southern Fujian, who "converted to Japanese nationality to protect their life and property from the depredations of the warlords."[29] As Lin-yi Tseng demonstrates in her study of the large *jimin* population in neighboring Shantou (150 miles down the coast from Xiamen), people with Taiwanese registration used the advantages of Japanese protection to dominate a wide range of industries in that port, including textiles, insurance, tea, and more.[30] The most powerful Taiwanese merchant in Shantou, Luo Bingzhang, had originally risen to prominence by using his Japanese citizenship to evade a provincial ban on the sale of blended liquors.[31] In a similar story from Xiamen, a collection of around ninety registered-Taiwanese brothel owners who founded a Hotel Guild in 1923 had achieved dominance over the city's sex industry, according to the Japanese consul responsible for their protection, due to their ability to avoid paying the local government's "flower tax."[32]

An overwhelming number of registered Taiwanese came to be employed in the vice industry: in brothels, usury, gun-running, and drugs. During the periods when opium was illegal, people with Japanese citizenship could avoid arrest for trading in the drug. When opium was under government monopoly, they could break the monopoly and retain their position of advantage. The commissioner of Maritime Customs described the administrative difficulty posed to Chinese institutions by registered Taiwanese, writing that "the difficulty of penalizing Formosans" for smuggling was "a problem requiring considerable tact." Customs officers found themselves unable to extract fines and conduct confiscations on Taiwanese, "on account of their enjoying extraterritorial rights," and "the search of premises has not been attempted . . . on account of the liability of the customs being involved in diplomatic controversy, as most of the smuggling godowns at Amoy [Xiamen] are owned or under the name of, Formosans."[33]

And so Fujian's opium dens started turning Japanese. In 1916, the Japanese colonial government in Taiwan estimated that only 10–20 percent of the 600 registered Taiwanese in Fuzhou were engaged in lawful business, while the rest had opened opium dens or rented out their status to Chinese citizens.[34] In 1921, Xiamen and the adjacent Heshan district together had over 2,000 opium dens owned by registered Taiwanese or by locals who had rented Taiwanese *jimin* placards to hang over the doors of their businesses.[35] In 1926, the Japanese consul in Xiamen estimated that 2,000 registered Taiwanese were employed in the opium sector.[36] In 1929, the Xiamen police reported that there were over 300 opium dens in the city displaying *jimin* placards on their doors.[37] Early that year, just after the Guomindang announced a new opium prohibition plan, the Japanese consul in Xiamen promulgated a regulation banning Taiwan-registered opium dens in Xiamen. To enforce the rule, the Japanese consul empowered a group of registered-Taiwanese men who were a veritable "who's who" of the city's most prominent opium den and brothel owners, including Lin Gun, Lin Qingcheng, and Wu Tianci.[38] Over a year later, the Fujian Provincial Government was still lobbying the Japanese consul to shut down the city's Taiwan-registered opium dens.[39]

As the 1930s wore on, the phenomenon of Taiwan-registered opium dens reached absurd heights. By 1936, nearly two-thirds of Xiamen's 724 opium dens were legitimately registered as Japanese, though all 724 dens were seen to hang a placard claiming to be under Japanese protection. "In other words, there are 293 opium shops in Amoy which are really Chinese but are illegally using Japanese protection," wrote the American journalist Haldore Hanson. "The police are afraid to attempt any arrests because they do not know which shops are really Formosans and which are not."[40] By that point, it was irrelevant if one was actually registered as Taiwanese; that the possibility existed was enough to keep the local Chinese police from interfering with the drug trade. The short story about the police officer Zhang Yongde that introduced this chapter, published in 1936, is rooted in this context.

Because people with Taiwanese registration could disobey local laws with impunity, they posed a distinct threat to the warlord and Guomindang opium prohibition bureaus that were established to control and profit from the drug trade. Warlords and Guomindang (GMD) officials alike dealt with this threat by hiring Taiwanese *jimin* on as high-level investors and street-level enforcers in their state opium agencies. If Xiamen's registered Taiwanese were going to defy the prohibition and licensing schemes with impunity, it made sense for the local government to offer them a stake in the profits. This trend goes back at least as far as the early 1920, and escalated throughout the subsequent decades. One hundred and twenty Taiwanese *jimin* worked for the Opium Prohibition Inspectorate (the state monopoly) in 1926, when Xiamen was under the control of the GMD Navy and Yang Shuzhuang.[41] As discussed in chapter 4, Ye Qinghe's operation of opium monopolies for the navy in 1931, the Nineteenth Route Army in 1933–1934, and the Guomindang in 1934–1937 were all conducted through joint investment companies formed with major figures in Xiamen's Taiwan Guild. Ye and his Taiwanese partners also hired local *jimin* neighborhood gang leaders as the door-to-door inspectors for the opium monopoly.[42]

In rural areas too, warlords hired wealthy opium merchants from the Xiamen registered Taiwanese community to oversee collection of the poppy tax in hinterland counties. In one prominent example, the warlord rulers of Hui'an county—one of the epicenters of poppy production—hired on the Taiwanese opium den and brothel keeper Lin Gun to operate the opium prohibition inspectorate and collect poppy taxes in 1926.[43] When the warlord Cang Zhiping ruled over Xiamen in the early 1920s he likewise farmed out the lucrative poppy tax in Tong'an and Anhai counties to two former presidents of the Xiamen Taiwan Guild, Zeng Houkun and Yuan Shunyong.[44]

The Japanese consul in Xiamen used the concept of vertical integration to explain why people like Zeng Houkun were able to acquire warlord contracts for the collection of poppy taxes. The consul argued that inland warlords hired prominent Taiwanese opium dealers like Zeng and Lin Gun to collect the poppy tax because they were the most important distributors and exporters in the Xiamen opium market, and it was easier and cheaper for the warlords to have the people already purchasing their opium come collect the tax quotas as well.[45] For Zeng and Lin, the ability to merge prohibition bureau directorships with oversight of a poppy cultivation system meant being able to control both the opium supply chain and the distribution networks.

The son of a Jinjiang tobacco merchant who acquired Taiwanese registration for business purposes, Zeng Houkun managed to maintain his position at the heights of the opium business through the 1920s and 1930s as the war-torn districts surrounding Xiamen shifted hands over and again.[46] Zeng, as discussed in chapter 4, rose up in the poppy tax industry through a deal made with the Zhejiang militarist Cang Zhiping, beginning at least as early as 1921. In 1924, Zeng then took over the poppy tax in Jinjiang, Nan'an, and Hui'an counties after they were subsumed under the control of Fujian's military governor Zhou Yinren.[47] In the autumn of 1926, Zeng experienced some difficulty in meeting the poppy tax quotas in those three counties and was briefly put under house arrest in Nan'an until his associates were able to supply the local warlord Kong Zhaotong with a portion of the missing funds.[48] Undeterred, Zeng continued on in his role as a state-affiliated opium contractor into the early 1930s. He partnered with Ye Qinghe in the first iteration of the Wufeng company during 1931, a joint stock corporation that purchased the license for the naval opium prohibition monopoly in Xiamen.[49] In April 1932, Zeng had again taken over the opium prohibition inspectorate in Xiamen together with a coalition of other registered Taiwanese, hired by the Guomindang Provincial Chairman.[50] When Ye Qinghe returned to Fujian in 1933 to open the second iteration of the Wufeng firm under the auspices of the Nineteenth Route Army's prohibition bureau, the Xiamen office of Wufeng was located inside of one of Zeng Houkun's businesses.[51]

Other than perhaps Ye Qinghe, no single person features more prominently in the history of the southern Fujian opium trade during the 1920s and early 1930s. But Zeng never left the region, as Ye did. Zeng was involved in every angle of the business and state regulation of the opium trade, from the poppy tax, to transport taxes and distribution monopolies. He was integral to the negotiation of power in the city, linking up in various important ways with the Japanese government, the local Chinese government, and the merchants and lineages that had traditionally dominated the city. In 1921, one of Zeng's firms successfully bid on a $1,500,000 contract with the city's warlord government to fill in the foreshore of Yuandang Bay, forever altering the urban landscape of the city. [52] Today most of what had been a bay is now solid land, with a small lake in the middle. In 1926, the Japanese Ministry of Foreign Affairs appointed Zeng to be president of the Xiamen Finance Association, a new institution intended to provide loans and financial services for the city's growing Japanese-protected population.[53] Between 1914 and 1930, Zeng served eleven terms as the president of the city's influential Taiwan Guild.[54] Men like Zeng and the "Eighteen Elder Brothers" described below helped formalize the place of Taiwanese intermediaries at the nexus of opium, finance, and government in Xiamen.

The Local Origins of the Occupation Regime

IT PAID TO BE TAIWANESE: THE EIGHTEEN ELDER BROTHERS

The urban landscape of Xiamen changed dramatically as a result of the Japanese Foreign Ministry's permissive attitude towards imperial citizenship. The Chen, Ji, and Wu lineages and their subsidiary neighborhood gangs who had traditionally dominated a range of industries—including opium, prostitution, and gambling—were displaced or coopted by a loosely affiliated coalition of Taiwanese *jimin* known as the "Eighteen Elder Brothers." The transition in the neighborhoods began in 1905 when a group of Taiwanese migrants started opening gambling dens in Xiamen and registering their businesses with the Japanese consulate.[55] During 1912–1913 a second wave of emigrants came from Taiwan to Xiamen under the aegis of two secret societies.[56] These were the remnants of rival street gangs from Taipei, and they had fled Japanese rule in Taiwan only to seek Japanese protection on the mainland.

The Taiwanese migrants caught on quickly to the advantages of Japanese extraterritorial protection in China. Coffee shops, teahouses, pharmacies, gambling dens, brothels, hotels, opium dens, and restaurants opened up all over the city and countryside, sporting placards that proclaimed them to be under the protection of the Japanese consul.[57] Lin Gun, a younger member of the 1912–13 wave of migrants and relatively unknown gambler, got funds together to launch the Fuxing Hotel (Figure 6.1). This was the first of what became an empire of gambling and opium institutions including the world-famous Butterfly Dance Hall (see Figure 6.2).[58] By the late 1920s, gambling, prostitution, and usury in the seedy neighborhood of Liaozaihou was entirely under his control.[59] Lin had also branched out into contracting with the state for opium services, and in 1926 he simultaneously held the poppy tax rights and the prohibition bureau directorship in Hui'an county.[60] Lin later partnered with Zeng Houkun and Ye Qinghe in the 1931 iteration of the Wufeng company and again between 1934 and 1937 in Ye Qinghe's

FIGURE 6.1: Lin Gun.

Source: Taiwan jinshikan (Who's Who of Taiwan), (Taibei: Taiwan shin minpo sha, 1934), 215.

FIGURE 6.2: Advertisement for Lin Gun's Butterfly Dance Hall.

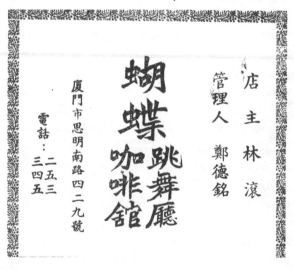

Source: Xiamen shi shanghui tekan (Special issue of the Xiamen Chamber of Commerce Journal), Xiamen: Xiamen Chamber of Commerce, 1940, 163.

Lutong Company, which managed the Guomindang opium monopoly for southern Fujian.[61]

Lin's rise was possibly the most dramatic—he's referred to as the leader of the Eighteen Elder Brothers in later years, reaching an astonishing level of power and capitalization from seemingly humble origins—but other Taiwanese migrants also did remarkably well in the earlier years. Xie Afa took over the central Siming Beilu neighborhood opening a lively gambling and opium joint called the Southeastern Hotel (see Figure 6.3). Li Longxi settled on Siming Nanlu, Zheng Youyi on Jukou Jie (a commercialized historical alley in present Xiamen, see Figure 6.4), and Tang Shouren was known to ride his sedan chair around the Guanzai Nei area of town. "Opium dens outnumbered rice shops, gambling dens outnumbered groceries, and brothels outnumbered hotels," concluded one popular saying.[62] The gangs that maintained these operations were not only large—Lin Gun's supposedly approached 100 members—but also well-armed.

The rising participation of these Taiwanese new arrivals in Xiamen's opium, gambling, and prostitution industries created tensions with the lineages that had traditionally run those businesses. The budding conflict erupted into violence in late 1923, drawing the Chinese police and Japanese Navy into the fray.[63] At the time the feud began, the Zhejiang warlord Cang Zhiping had a tenuous hold on Xiamen.[64] When a bloody feud erupted between the city's Taiwanese contingent and the Wu family, one of Xiamen's oldest and most powerful lineages, Cang backed the Wu and attacked the Taiwanese with a police force that he had built up with muscle from the city's rough-and-tumble underworld, including a well-known local gangster named Li Qingbo.[65] In response, the leadership of Xiamen's Taiwanese Guild organized themselves into a "Self-Defense Force"—with the implicit backing of the Japanese consul. Weeks of street fighting shook the port city. The British landed naval forces for forty-eight hours, and Japanese marines began patrolling the streets to put an end to any anti-Taiwanese behavior.[66]

The dispute between the Wu lineage and the Taiwanese group was temporarily settled in November 1923, after a well-publicized series of banquets and negotiations involving Cang Zhiping and the Japanese consul. By February 1924, however, hostilities flared up again. There was a series of armed robberies, attributed in the Chinese press to the Taiwanese, and attributed by the Taiwanese to local people pretending to be Taiwanese.[67] The gang of an Eighteen Elder Brother named Chen Fensao was widely recognized as

FIGURE 6.3: Xie Afa.

Source: Taiwan jinshikan (Who's Who of Taiwan), (Taibei: Taiwan shin minpo sha, 1934), 84.

FIGURE 6.4: Stone gate to Jukou jie in contemporary Xiamen.

Peter Thilly, 2019

one of the chief perpetrators of armed terror in the city, and the city police launched a second offensive to arrest Chen, which included an attempt to enforce an order for every Taiwanese resident in Xiamen to hand over all weapons in their possession to the Chinese authorities. The confiscation effort was discontinued after the death of at least ten people, according to British sources.[68]

Violence continued to escalate during 1924. Early that year Cang Zhiping lost his footing in Xiamen and was replaced in April by an admiral in the Guomindang Navy named Yang Shuzhuang. Yang appointed Fuzhou native Lin Guogeng to take over Xiamen's police department, and from the outset Lin took an even harder line on the registered Taiwanese than Cang Zhiping had. Lin would later go on to rule Xiamen on behalf of the navy from 1926 until the late 1930s. Xiamen historian Mo Jun writes that during his early tenure as police chief, Lin regularly used torture to force captured members of Chen Fensao's gang to admit they had been born on the mainland and thereby renounce their claims to Japanese protection, giving Lin leave to execute them by public beheading.[69]

A final pitched battle occurred when Lin Guogeng's local forces attacked Chen Fensao's Taiwanese gang at the Juyi Hotel in the Maizaicheng neighborhood during early September of 1924. The Taiwanese group started off well, shooting from an elevated position. The Xiamen police promptly set the place on fire, and Chen's men came running out of the building into direct gunfire.[70] The incident launched a new round of negotiation between the Xiamen authorities and the Japanese consul, and the Japanese Navy again sent troops into the city. During the negotiations, wherein Xiamen's authorities capitulated on nearly every point, the consul reportedly demanded the execution of two police officers who were involved in the attack on Chen Fensao. One was the former gangster Li Qingbo, who had ruled the Caozaian neighborhood underworld prior to serving on the police force. Li was lured into police headquarters on the pretense of an assignment and ambushed and executed. Ma Kunzhen, the other man demanded by the Japanese, died soon after while drunk in a windstorm, a death shrouded in suspicion and innuendo.[71]

The events of 1924 were a turning point in Xiamen's urban history, after which the remaining non-Taiwanese gangs either collapsed or were folded into the expanding empire of the Eighteen Elder Brothers. The message was clear: it paid to be Taiwanese. By 1926, the opium industry in Xiamen was systematically dominated by Taiwanese interests: opium dens, petty sales, and the import and distribution businesses.[72] At the upper reaches of the industry, non-Taiwanese holdouts sought stability in alliances with the new neighborhood bosses. Song Anzai from the Dawang neighborhood and former detective and Guanzainei boss Xu Zhenrun were among the more notorious local figures who survived the sea change; both came to ally themselves with the *jimin* and became sworn brothers with the Taiwanese rising star Lin Gun.[73] Over the years, Lin also gathered a number of police officers into his entourage. Chief of Police Wang Zongshi, Public Security Bureau Chief Lin Hongfei, and another ranking officer were all named among the alleged sworn brothers of Lin Gun, with the later addition of Hu Zhen, a captain in the Japanese police force during the occupation.[74]

As the Eighteen Elder Brothers expanded their financial and political power within Xiamen, they also reached out to hinterland warlords and used their Japanese protection and connections for more than just control of neighborhood vice operations. Lin Gun's Fuxing and Butterfly Hotels, Xie Afa's Southeastern Hotel, and Wang Changsheng's Gongguan Hotel were all well-known fronts for gun and drug trafficking. These four places in particular are singled out by local historians as having hosted an impressive list of Fujianese military and political power holders, from Hui'an, Nan'an, Tong'an, Dehua, Anxi, and Haicheng counties, across the southern Fujianese littoral.[75] Wang Changsheng, known as one of the "literati" among the Eighteen Elder Brothers and often seen wearing the blue robes of a Qing *xiucai* degree-holder, was a particularly important player in the network operating between Xiamen's underworld and the warlords reigning in the countryside. As head of militarist Gao Yi's procurement division, Wang gained the trust of the Japanese and a collection of warlords in counties across Zhangzhou-Quanzhou region and was thereby able to facilitate the flow of guns and narcotics in and out of the city's neighboring districts.[76]

The sea change was complete by the early 1930s. Lin Guogeng, the police captain who had so ferociously attacked Chen Fensao and the Taiwanese during 1924, had worked his way up the ranks from captain of the military police to head of the naval forces in Xiamen. He had also come around to the reality of Taiwanese control over the vice industries within the city. At least three times between 1931 and 1934, in response to new opium plans handed down from Nanjing, Lin Guogeng or his superiors at the provincial naval headquarters in Fuzhou farmed out the Opium Prohibition Infrastructure in southern Fujian to coalitions of Taiwanese investors, including well-known opium den and brothel keepers like Lin Gun. The longest lasting of these endeavors, the 1934–1937 Yumin monopoly, was owned by Ye Qinghe (now registered as a Taiwanese) and key figures in the Eighteen Elder Brothers, Lin Gun and Chen Changfu. Chen Fensao, Lin Guogeng's old nemesis from the 1924 street fights, was appointed to be one of several key street-level monopoly "enforcers."[77] Lin Guogeng's brother was given a lucrative post within the company, as were the relatives of other important figures in the city's naval government.[78]

In early 1936, Lin Guogeng attended a meeting of the Japanese government's newly reestablished "Xiamen Finance Association" (*Xiamen jinrong zuhe*) together with the Japanese consul and a representative of the Taiwan Governor-General's Office.[79] The purpose of the institution, the reason it was created in 1926 and revived in 1935–1936, was to provide cheap loans and other financial services to help continue to build up commercial networks between Xiamen and Southeast Asia within Japanese-protected channels.[80] The Japanese diplomats had doubled down on this institution as part of their "Southern Strategy," an attempt to expand Japanese power in south China and Southeast Asia. The head of the Finance Association the first time around had been Zeng Houkun, poppy tax collector and prominent opium merchant.[81] This time the Japanese consul tapped another "Opium King" for the position, Chen Changfu, a partner Ye Qinghe's Wufeng opium monopoly and sitting president of the city's Taiwan guild.[82] That same month, Chen announced that the Taiwan Guild was drawing up a districting system (*baojia*) for the control of Taiwanese subjects in Xiamen, drawing scathing protest in nationalist periodicals as a breach of Chinese sovereignty.[83] When Japan invaded Xiamen three years later, Chen Changfu would head up the most profitable branch of the occupation government's opium monopoly.

Lin Guogeng, in attendance at this meeting as the top Guomindang authority in Xiamen, was a man who twelve years earlier had been committed to publicly beheading powerful figures in the Taiwanese community. In the meantime, Japan had invaded Manchuria and posed innumerable threats to Chinese sovereignty. But in Xiamen, Lin had hired on his old Japanese-protected enemies within the state prohibition infrastructure, accepting massive quotas of cash in exchange for the rights to revenue collection and market regulation. He had also contracted with Lin Gun, the

Taiwanese opium trafficker and proprietor of the Butterfly Hotel, for control over the southern Fujian salt monopoly, and Lin Gun was suspected by Guomindang authorities in Nanjing to be engaged in salt smuggling from Taiwan.[84] Indeed, Guomindang leadership were well appraised of the activities of Lin Gun and the Eighteen Elder Brothers, and internal Guomindang documents show concern among some officials that the rise of Xiamen's Taiwanese community might facilitate a Japanese invasion of the region.[85] The stark difference between the view from Nanjing and the view from the Xiamen Naval Garrison is illustrated in Lin Guogeng's participation in the meeting of the Japanese-sponsored Finance Association. People like Chen Changfu and Lin Gun had transformed the structure of power and profit within the city, years before the Japanese invasion, and Lin Guogeng understood this.

THE OCCUPATION OF XIAMEN, 1938–1945

On May 12, 1938, Japan began what would be a seven-year occupation of Xiamen.[86] The neighboring islet of Gulangyu, home to the foreign settlement and ruled by an international municipal council, took in around 120,000 refugees from Xiamen proper that month.[87] On June 21, Admiral Miyata and Consul-General Uchida performed a ceremony in Sun Yatsen Park together with representatives of the Taiwan Guild to inaugurate the "Committee for the Preservation of Law and Order," which would soon transform into a municipal government.[88] The Taiwan Guild, a group that for decades had been presided over by "opium kings" like Chen Changfu and Zeng Houkun, was in an ideal position to provide revenue and street-level enforcement for the occupation government. It was in their best interest, as it had been for decades, to build up their business interests by working with the state.

The committee took immediate steps to take over the Xiamen Naval Garrison's opium distribution infrastructure. As League of Nations investigators wrote in 1940, "the establishment of an opium sales monopoly was one of the first steps taken by the Japanese armies in the occupied territories."[89] The Xiamen monopoly was founded in June 1938, when the occupation authorities launched a "public sales depot" (*gongmai ju*) and put Taizhong native Lin Jichuan in charge of overseeing three new government opium companies called Fuyu, Fuhe, and Fuqing.[90] Fuqing was the retail company, in charge of licensing opium dens and dispensaries. Fuhe was a subsidiary company with the function of processing low quality opium and opium by-product into a cheaper product for sale to the city's poor.[91] Fuyu was the largest of the three, and the new government took their cue from their predecessors in the Chinese Navy and contracted the operation of this company out to a former partner in the Yumin Company, longtime Xiamen resident and president of the Taiwan guild Chen Changfu. For the duration of the occupation, Chen would control the manufacture of opium paste in Xiamen. The British government believed that Fuyu was sourcing opium of Persian origin through Shanghai with the assistance of the Japanese Navy.[92] After the war, Lin Jichuan confirmed in his interrogation by the Guomindang that 100,000 yuan of the initial investment money procured by Fuyu was deposited with the Japanese Navy as "promise money," which they used to procure Persian opium in Shanghai for resale to Fuyu.[93]

The monopoly became immensely powerful, as the issuance of licenses for opium paste dispensaries and dens worked as a reward mechanism within the occupation government. There were around twenty opium paste wholesale dispensaries, most of which were licensed to Taiwanese and Chinese figures within the collaboration government. The dispensaries were run by people in the Japanese military such as Chen Mutu, scout for the Japanese Navy and Li Gong, officer in the Japanese Army. They were also owned by long-standing vice industry bosses associated with the Eighteen Elder Brothers like Lin Gun, Lin Zhuge, and Li Liangxi. Municipal officials and *baojia* headmen also got in on the action, along with various people associated with the occupation police department like informant Wang Wenqing, water police officer Zeng Rong, and police officer Gao Shuilong.[94] Chen Changfu, as the head of the powerful Fuyu Opium Company, was also given other administrative roles within the occupation, including leadership roles in state-affiliated banking, construction, and financial institutions.[95]

Licenses for opium dens were more plentiful, numbering somewhere between 130 and 200. Each opium den was required to pay a deposit of $200 to the Fuyu Company in order to acquire the license, and a wave of new dens had opened along the main roads of the city as of 1939.[96] For the larger-scale opium investors who occupied positions of power within the occupation government, owning both dispensaries and opium dens was a way to vertically integrate their businesses and layer profits. People who took advantage of this opportunity included the occupation mayor, Li Sibao, along with the directors of the municipal finance and construction bureaus, Jin Fusheng and Lu Yongchuan.[97] All opium sold from the dispensaries paid a stamp tax of $1.20 per tael, and in 1939 the British government estimated a monthly revenue of $10,000 from the stamp tax alone.[98]

The people invested in the highly capitalized Fuyu Company were not content with supplying the dens and dispensaries within the city of Xiamen, and some evidence also survives of how drugs from the occupied zone were smuggled inland. A 1941 report from a Guomindang-controlled area in Haicheng county just south of Xiamen details one such import scheme, naming four occupation government officials as the responsible parties for three kilograms of *Shiqiu* brand opium confiscated by the Haicheng police.[99] The confiscated opium was packaged in four- and twenty-ounce packets, like the Fuyu monopoly product. A similar case from 1942 names a collective of "local bullies" from Haicheng county, together with the Zheng lineage of Zhongdui village, as key operatives in the running of opium paste from the occupied districts into Haicheng.[100]

Operatives from within occupied Xiamen were also manufacturing morphine and heroin for sale locally and for smuggling into the neighboring districts. This began immediately after the invasion and escalated during the occupation. One newspaper article suggested that the Japanese had started manufacturing morphine on Jinmen and were using "ignorant fishermen" to bring small packages of the drug to various locations along the coast.[101] The next year, Chen Changfu, longtime Eighteen Elder Brother and head of the occupation's Fuyu Opium Company, would put together a 600,000 yen investment to found a morphine company in the city.[102] A 1941 investigation claimed that one of five businesses in Xiamen was an opium shop, most of which also sold morphine and heroin.[103]

The state of all-out war across China after 1938 engendered innumerable opportunities for local Chinese officials from inland locations to deal in drugs and black-market Japanese goods. The desperate need for cash during wartime only made the drug trade more attractive to people with armies to look after. One case from an area to the north of Xiamen—Hua'an and Longxi counties—details how opium manufactured by the occupation government monopoly was smuggled into Shima (a busy port near Quanzhou) and then brought inland by the Hua'an Fuchang firm. The key figure in this operation was a Guomindang battalion commander and director of the county sanitation bureau.[104]

Lineage connections frequently structured the relationship between drugs, money, and military power during this volatile moment. The powerful Xiao lineage of Hui'an county's Puxi village played a role for their district similar to that played by the wayward battalion commander in Hua'an and Longxi. Among the many Fujianese who joined up with the Japanese, Xiao Wenqing was a captain in the military police of the Xiamen occupation government and commander of their First Battalion. In May 1942 he secretly returned home to organize a series of deals involving local rice, Taiwanese sugar, Japanese textiles, as well as morphine and opium produced in Xiamen. His kinsman Xiao Zhuyuan, branch secretary of the Guomindang's Fourteenth District in Hui'an, reportedly "coerced" local merchants into purchasing the contraband sugar. Contraband is cheaper, however, and real coercion might not have been necessary. Another kinsman named Xiao Desheng took charge of distributing the narcotics Xiao Wenqing brought up from Xiamen.[105]

The concepts of "collaboration" and "treason" hardly seem adequate to describe the operations of lineage like the Xiao during this historical moment. Chinese nationalist political and military entities had made efforts to incorporate the village, but these efforts were mediated through the lineage structure. Newspapers and periodicals arrived, speaking of the Japanese as the *enemy* and of people who sell Japanese goods as *traitors*. Some younger, cosmopolitan, or educated members of the lineage may have shared this nationalist outlook. But the lineage had a satellite entity in Taiwan, which had become a Japanese colony. The whole village had profited from this connection for decades. Xiao Zhuyuan (working for the Guomindang) and Xiao Wenqing (working for the Japanese) were the brain trust behind huge illicit consignments of Taiwanese matches, kerosene, opium, and morphine that were the staples of the village economy.[106] Making money, for many people, probably felt like a filial and untreasonous goal.

THE AFTERMATH

When the Japanese occupation of Xiamen ended in September of 1945, the tables turned quickly on those Fujianese who had worked with the Japanese. In the civil war that ensued, Xiamen became a Guomindang stronghold, the site of an intensive state-led effort to identify and punish anyone tainted by association with Japan. An official from one of the Guomindang Army's statistical bureaus, Dai Liangnong, spearheaded the "Third Military

District Xiamen-Taiwan Committee for Processing Hanjian Cases" in October 1945 and set off on a ten-month investigation into 166 people whom his committee deemed guilty of treason during the occupation of Xiamen. The report proceeds from the most important collaborator—the occupation mayor Li Sibao—and includes among the top twenty-five most notorious traitors the Eighteen Elder Brother notables Chen Changfu, Lin Gun, and Chen Fuqi.[107] Drug trading was, to the Committee for Processing Hanjian Cases, a particularly egregious crime. It was not mentioned that several of these very same people had been repeatedly hired to run Guomindang state opium monopolies in previous years.

Many of the most notorious drug traders of the 1930s and 1940s were identified as part of this investigation, though Dai's report is often vague about their actual trial and punishment. Some of them likely remained politically connected and escaped punishment. Others probably fled the country. The infamous gambler and drug lord Lin Gun seems to have been one of the lucky ones. Where the July 1946 report concludes with the line that Lin "is being sent to the Number One Supreme Court to be punished according to law," a journalist two months later wrote that the case against Lin for operating opium and gambling dens during the occupation was dismissed.[108] I have found no evidence of him after this time, even though local newspapers published several exposés about the sordid history of the Eighteen Elder Brothers in the years leading up to 1949.[109]

Many people were indeed arrested, tried, and imprisoned or executed for treason and drug trading during and after the war. Ye Qinghe was executed by the Communist Party in Guangdong during 1944. Li Longxi, a Taiwanese-registered gambling and opium magnate in Xiamen who worked with the collaboration government, was captured by the GMD in Taiwan during the fall of 1947 and brought to Shanghai for trial on charges of collaboration and treason.[110] Chen Fensao, the 1920s street fighter and accused rapist, continued to smuggle drugs into Xiamen after the departure of the Japanese. Like his old compatriot Lin Gun, Chen too seems to have escaped punishment.[111]

A century had passed since the 1830s, when Fujian's opium traders were first singled out as *hanjian* by patriotic elites. In the rush to find people to blame after a humiliating war, central government officials in both the 1840s and 1940s applied the *hanjian* label to Fujianese drug traders who had made money by working with the enemy. But during the interim, especially during the years of opium's de facto legalization, the drug trade had become normalized. The opium business had helped fund the capstone projects of the Self-Strengthening Movement, literally paying for the ironclad ships built in the Fuzhou harbor. For a time, Fujian's opium traders were not charged with obstructing China's quest for wealth and power. This changed after 1906, when patriotic newspapers began publishing articles about Fujianese drug traders and *jimin* (Taiwanese-registered Chinese) with scathing terms, reviving some of the dormant rhetoric from the 1830s and 1840s. But that had largely been a war of words, as the governments that ruled Fujian from 1906–1937 were almost universally dependent on these so-called *hanjian* drug traders for the fiscal security of their regimes. When Japan invaded in 1937, the revenue arm of occupation government was formed out of people who had been operating state opium agencies under earlier Chinese administrations. The only real rupture was a shift in the recipients of the city's opium revenue and a relative lack of prohibitionist rhetoric.

Conclusion: Consequences, Unintended or Otherwise

For the Japanese consular officials assigned to Xiamen, the enrollment of Fujianese as imperial citizens was part of a strategy to gain political and economic influence in China and Southeast Asia.[112] In a 1926 report by the Japanese consul in Xiamen—an internal report not meant for reading outside of the Japanese foreign ministry—the consul states that his policy towards *jimin* was rooted in the goal of recruiting wealthier classes of people to register as Taiwanese, especially business elites with connections to Southeast Asia.[113] What the consul and his contemporaries wanted was jurisdiction over the people who controlled key industries. And opium, after all, was a key industry. The consul portrayed his attitude towards *jimin* involvement in the drug trade as one of tolerant discomfort.[114] The lawlessness, bad press, and consequent loss of prestige that Japan endured by sheltering the people responsible for the drug trade, he suggested, was ultimately outweighed by the potential gains of enlisting Fujianese as Japanese imperial citizens. The extensive networks of Japanese-protected narcotics trade unfolding in north China during these same years suggests that the Japanese Foreign Ministry was, at a minimum, quite comfortable with protecting the rights of drug traffickers in China.[115]

Japanese consuls in Xiamen frequently relied on Taiwanese opium merchants as intermediaries, empowering them to oversee various social and market regulation operations within the Chinese city, and incorporating these wealthy opium investors ever more formally into the umbrella of the Japanese "Southern Strategy." The city's Taiwan Guild operated at the nexus of power in the city, between the local Chinese administration and the Japanese consuls across the harbor in Gulangyu. When the Japanese consuls in 1926 and again in 1935 ordered the creation of Taiwanese "Finance Associations" in in the city, they tapped the community's most prominent opium merchants for leadership roles: Zeng Houkun in the earlier case and Chen Changfu in 1935.[116] This was not a coincidence. Throughout the 1930s, the opium business, commercial capital, and military and political power in southern Fujian were increasingly consolidated under the Japanese-protected community. Reread through this local history, the Japanese invasion of southern Fujian was experienced within the opium business not as a rupture but as a culmination of long-term trends towards the Japanese-protected community's control over the drug's production and distribution.

The Guomindang had sought repeatedly to harness the opium trade, but their representatives in Fujian time and again contracted out each new iteration of the opium regulatory and taxation systems to people over whom they had no jurisdiction or legal recourse. As a consequence, the Chinese authorities in Xiamen were never fully able to control, regulate, and tax the drug trade. In contrast, Japan's opium monopoly in occupied Xiamen was the longest-lasting iteration of an opium control infrastructure that had ever existed in the region until the Chinese Communist Party's consolidation of power in the early 1950s.

Following the Money, Today and in the Past

The history of the opium business told here is a story of evolving business-state interactions during China's transition from an empire to a fragmented republic. It is a story of the modernizing world, about a fast-moving globalized industry that took root within a local political economy. Long-standing negotiations of profit and authority between commercial elites and the state shaped the systems of bribery, informal taxation, and market regulation that first emerged around opium. Businesspeople in late imperial China were accustomed to provide local or regional officials with funding in exchange for leeway and privilege in their business endeavors. Seafaring merchants were also acquainted with a wide range of tax farming systems in Southeast Asia that informed the way they understood and approached formal opium taxation. Opium traders knew that financial success would hinge on collaboration or resistance with the civil and military institutions that appeared before them, and sharing profits with the state was often the common-sense choice.

As opium revenue assumed an ever-growing importance to government coffers, people with experience in the opium business understood the opportunity at hand. The most successful acquired and capitalized on state contracts for opium taxation and regulation. State agents appreciated the enormous cash quotas coming from their partners in the drug trade, and they continued to privatize the authority to regulate and tax opium. The long evolution of tax farming systems into the 1930s clarifies why "prohibition" in early twentieth century entailed the rapid escalation of volume in drug trafficking just as the wider international community was moving steadily towards shutting down the drug trade. Revolutionary armies, warlords, naval garrisons, and in the end, the Japanese occupation all contracted with powerful "opium kings" to run their monopolies and prohibition bureaus and collect their poppy taxes. Drug interests wrangled and harnessed the modernizing state, just as the state was commanding more influence and control in the local arena.

The opium business first came to Fujian over the seas, and it evolved there together with the province's dual identity as maritime frontier and Mediterranean hub. Maritime traders who connected China and Southeast Asia were the ones to arrange opium's transport into China, which they did not in an isolated way but as one of a diversified set of concerns spanning the tea, rice, cotton, and camphor trades. When the drug trade first accelerated and drew negative attention from the central state, Qing officials blamed the wave of smuggling on what they viewed as a categorically untrustworthy frontier population: the *yanhai jianmin*, or treacherous people of the coastal area. At the time, the unfettered illegal drug trade of the 1830s might have seemed to some of those administrators like the culmination of nearly a half century of chaos on the maritime frontier, beginning with the piratical confederations of the Jiaqing era (1796–1820).

In the long view, that early tidal wave of opium smuggling was also a moment of new beginnings, and the ensuing Sino-British conflict brought about a transformation of what the maritime frontier meant in China. Fujian became a place where Chinese and foreign officials negotiated the new treaty system, implemented and worked out practices for international law, citizenship, and territorial boundaries in the new age. Fujian's cosmopolitan, Mediterranean identity likewise took on a new set of meanings, as the people who traversed between China and Southeast Asia learned to navigate the tensions and opportunities created by the evolving nation-state system. Flexible, shifting citizenships enabled entrepreneurs to shelter profits from the state and evade criminal prosecution. Reforms to taxation and regulatory regimes created new patterns of profit-seeking, and Fujian's maritime entrepreneurs carved out a new role shipping drugs out of China and into colonial jurisdictions like the US Philippine Islands, the Dutch Netherlands Indies, and the British Straits Settlements. This reorientation of the global drug trade after World War I was also structured by the rising power of Japan, whose foreign ministry had identified and coveted Fujian's dense trading network with Southeast Asia, and had welcomed Fujian's business community into the imperial umbrella in huge numbers. Treaty ports like Xiamen, Shantou, and Fuzhou became the new frontier of Japanese power in south China, and the epicenter of an imperial, state-affiliated drug trade.

Stories like this about people who sell illegal drugs and cultivate relationships with the government are likely familiar to the reader. Today we even have a unique term, "narco-capitalism," to summarize the systems of production, distribution, and profit accumulation wherein vertically integrated organizations (or coalitions of organizations) maintain large-scale and resilient operations in the production, transport, wholesale, and distribution of illegal narcotics. The term itself is a product of the 1980s, most often used in connection with a collection of violent organizations operating in Mexico and Colombia. The most famous of these organizations is the Guadalajara cartel, which amassed an unfathomable fortune by connecting cocaine producers in Colombia and heroin producers in Mexico with consumers in the United States.[1] Their business model integrated cultivating and manufacturing the drugs, doctoring and packaging those drugs in factories, transporting them across various jurisdictions to the US border, and smuggling the drugs into the US through key *plazas*, or important border crossing sites like Juarez-El Paso and Tijuana-San Diego.

The term "narco-capitalism" evokes a set of patterns within the dynamics of state-society interaction and political economy that resonate with the history told in this book. The opium business in China offers over a century of history of what today has become a familiar dialectic between state building and illicit drug production and trafficking within a global system of prohibition. Southeast China in the early twentieth century became a critical zone of opium production and transshipment within the world drug economy, much like parts of Mexico and Colombia in the late twentieth century. Like the major drug cartels of the present day, many of the opium traders and state actors featured in this book made choices to pursue drug cultivation and revenue operations that would specifically capitalize on pro-hibition in neighboring states. Xiamen was a maritime *plaza*: an interna-tional border crossing where drugs and money changed hands, and a site of heightened contestation over the extralegal regulation of drug transactions.

Contemporary scholarship on narco-capitalism is especially helpful as a guide to recognizing and theorizing the structural limits on our ability to fully research and understand the illegal drug business. This is an industry where secrecy, violence, bribery, and money laundering have been funda-mental to success. It is never possible to fully understand the secret practices that enable successful drug trading, and there is no realistic way to truly quantify the secret flows of drugs and money, today or in the past. As two scholars of the Mexican cartels put it, "it is difficult to measure the total value of the goods and services produced," and, "it is virtually impossible to gauge the contribution of the drug trade and the narco-economy to the capitalist development process in Latin America."[2] How much more true must this be for the more-than-century-old drug trade and narco-economy examined in this book?

Even the most rigorous quantitative reckoning of the opium trade would be fatally flawed. As a consequence, I have instead worked to identify pat-terns of profit and control. My conclusion: the state-business nexus in the Chinese opium trade operated in a way that belies intuitive distinctions be-tween illegal and legal, public and private, bribery and taxation, and revenue and profit. This was true at the beginning, when the great maritime trading lineages of the Fujian littoral negotiated long-lasting systems of informal taxation with coastal authorities. It was true in the age of legal opium, when rising stars in the drug business began purchasing the rights to tax and regulate the drug, assembling armies of uniformed officers to patrol the streets and enforce the rules of trade. And it was true during the opium trade's stunning recrudescence in the early-twentieth-century, when a tight network of Japanese-protected "opium kings" became the go-to contractors for warlord and Guomindang poppy tax collection and opium prohibition bureau directorships, leveraging their foreign status to take over new state agencies designed to control and draw revenue from the opium business.

The question of state participation hovers at the center of "narco-capitalism." Persistent and unstated assumptions about the distinction be-tween public and private confound clear analysis, today and in the past. In part, this is because narco-capitalist success stories hinge on the ability of private business interests to infiltrate, manipulate, or otherwise transform the state. Ye Qinghe, at the helm of "opium prohibition" in Southern Fujian from 1934–1936, was essentially a tax farmer, a private contractor. He was the head of a powerful state agency with the power to regulate and police trade, and yet he was not accountable in any meaningful way to the state that had hired him. He acquired three non-Chinese citizenships over the years, for this specific purpose. He broke his own monopoly in order to supplement his legal drug profits with illegal drug profits. He also seems to have fulfilled the most important part of his contract—the collection of opium revenue for the Guomindang—and he paid over huge sums to various authorities in both legal and illegal ways. The Guomindang in Fujian was an inefficient narco-state: one that viewed opium revenue as essential, but which farmed out taxation and regulation of the drug to people who were made untouchable by a combination of capital, citizenship, mobility, and Japanese protection.[3]

The concept of "narco-capitalism" also signals distinct patterns in labor and ownership that derive from the drug industry's illegality and secrecy. Today and in the past, illegal drug trading is characterized by heightened levels of violence, coercion, and unequal assumption of risk. People have been very willing to kill each other in competition for profits on illegal drugs, and illegal drug businesses normally operate under the constant threat of state punishment. The tragic and ongoing history of drug-related murders in Juárez, Mexico, and the pattern of state-orchestrated drug killings in the Philippines both illustrate the desperate extremes that this dynamic has assumed in the twenty-first century.[4]

The question of who gets killed, imprisoned, or otherwise dealt violence is instructive. In the story told here, people who achieved positions of power were only rarely subjected to violence or punishment. The structural violence inherent to capitalism was, in the opium business, magnified by the intertwined forces of prohibition, illegality, monopoly, and secrecy. As Huang Juezi wrote in 1840, "boat owners are occasionally caught, but they are no more than fearless ruffians. Meanwhile the real investors are safely in their villages, unharmed and with no reason to stop their practices, and thus the problem has grown bigger."[5] It was the day laborers in the opium business who were expected to take on the risk of state punishment and violence. In narco-capitalism, the working poor have their low wages further garnished with a very real risk of physical danger, imprisonment, and even execution.[6]

But if illegal drug trading involves, on the one hand, forms of exploitation that are more violent and harsh than most other industries, it also has created opportunities for rapid capital accumulation that have been attractive to the upwardly mobile small-time investor. Drug trading is now and has been an enticing option for a great many people, despite the risks involved. It can be a rare opportunity for anyone to rapidly accelerate personal capital accumulation, and not just the well-heeled and connected people at the heights of the industry. Small-scale drug dealing is a ubiquitous feature of the modern world, an important field of opportunity for people with upwardly mobile aspirations.

For the working poor, and for people who might be systematically denied other opportunities to improve their economic situation, drug dealing can be especially attractive. This was true in 1870s Fuzhou when tax evaders could earn a month's wages by smuggling a single ball of opium past the customs, and it was true in 1920s Xiamen when a migrant worker leaving China could earn as much as a 900 percent profit margin by concealing tins of opium paste in their luggage and smuggling it into colonial jurisdictions with state-run opium monopolies.[7] Cocaine, according to one recent study, can accumulate as much as a 30,000 percent profit margin from tree to nostril in today's world.[8] Methamphetamines likewise are stunningly profitable. Small-scale drug dealers benefit from this, on the marginal end of course, as compared with the organizations that produce and transport the drugs.

At the heights of the business, extreme rate of profitability in illegal drug trading has profound consequences that are exceptionally difficult to trace out and measure. Money laundering, or the funneling of illicit capital into ancillary businesses that are expected to operate at a loss, is simultaneously the most important and elusive aspect of the drug trade, today and in the past. Where does this money go? And how has this money changed places and institutions? In frontier spaces during recent years, according to geographer Teo Ballvé, "the loads of illicit money laundered through indiscriminate agribusiness development" have turned drug profits into a "strong agent of dispossession and uneven development."[9] As a group of coauthors have recently explained, responding in part to Ballvé's conceptualization, drug traders in Latin America have chosen to launder their money through land purchases with clear goals in mind: the control over large territories enables secrecy in transport and logistics, and it also enables them to adopt the "cover" of cattle ranching, an industry where the entire supply chain can be vertically integrated on a single landholding, subject to minimal state scrutiny.[10] As a consequence, according to this recent scholarship, the drug business has brought private investment to previously neglected regions, acting as "neoliberal pioneers, spreading circuits of capital into new territories: communal, reserved, and public lands."[11]

Insights like this from scholars of the contemporary world signal the potential and value of future research into the relationship between opium capital and development in nineteenth- and early twentieth-century China. In this book, I have succeeded in some cases of "following the money," but the broader impact of opium capital in late nineteenth and early twentieth century remains an open and intriguing field of study. Consider the opium fortunes amassed in the early 1930s by the southern Fujianese warlords Ye Dingguo ($45 million) and Chen Guohui ($66 million). How was this money allocated? Where did it go? How did it affect the way these men ruled over the counties of coastal Fujian? What was the impact on banking, infrastructure, agriculture, and commerce? When their armies were unseated and the Guomindang eventually evicted them from the region, how much money was left, and what became of it?

Other fortunes, many unaccounted for, were even more unimaginable in their scope. Perhaps the greatest opium fortune of them all belonged to the boss of the Shanghai Green Gang, and longtime director of various Guomindang opium prohibition bureaus, Du Yuesheng. In March of 1955, two of Du's sons were deposed by the Communist authorities in Shanghai and outlined their father's collection of 209 separate investments worth a total of 3,458,574,323 yuan (as well as 2,400 *mu* of land). Among the investments were dozens of banks, hotels, railroads, shipping companies, utilities, pharmacies, newspapers, and insurance companies, as well as a long list of businesses that traded in items like pork, textiles, books, noodles, tea, lumber, glass, and tobacco.[12] As historians continue to explore questions of capitalism and commerce during China's modern history, I hope this study can help underscore the centrality of opium capital, even as it has been most often secretly allocated.

Glossary of Chinese Names, Places, and Terms

aiguo limin	愛國利民
Anhai	安海
Anxi	安溪
baojia	保甲
Beiyang	北洋
busai louzhi	補塞漏厄
canjiang	參將
Cai Bixi	蔡碧溪
Cai Ducheng	蔡都成
Cang Zhiping	藏致平
Changle	長樂
Chaozhou	潮州
Chen Changfu	陳長福
Chen Fensao	陳冀掃
Chen Guohui	陳國輝
Chen Jiongming	陳炯明
Chen Shangcai	陳尚彩
Da Qing	大清

danmin	蜑民
da riben jimin	大日本籍民
Dehua	德化
Deng Yanzhen	鄧延楨
diaohan	刁悍
dizhi waihuo	抵制外貨
Du Yanshi	杜彥士
Du Yuesheng	杜月笙
Fuhe	福合
Fujian	福建
fu kezhang	副科長
Funing	福寧
Fuqing	福慶
Fuyu	福裕
Fuzhou	福州
gongmai ju	公賣局
Guankou	關口
Guanzai nei	關仔內
guojia	國家
Guomindang	國民黨
guomin yaofang	國民藥房
Guo Songtao	郭松濤
Guoxingye (Koxinga)	國姓爺
Gulangyu	鼓浪嶼
Haicheng	海澄
hanjian	漢奸
heiyi	黑夷
Heshan	禾山
Hong Buren	洪卜仁
honghui	紅會
huashui	華稅
Huang Juezi	黃爵滋
Huang Lian	黃濂
Huang Qing'an	黃慶安
Huang Tingyuan	黃庭元
Hui'an	惠安
Jianning	建寧

Jiang Ahua	江阿華
jiancha ju	監察局
jianshang	奸商
jiansheng	監生
jiao	郊
jiao	繳
jieji	接濟
jimin	籍民
jimin pai	籍民牌
Jingguo jun	靖國軍
Jinjiang	晉江
Jinmen	金門
jinyan ju	禁煙局
juan	捐
Jukou Jie	局口街
junxiang	軍餉
Kong Zhaotong	孔昭同
kuai	塊
langren (Japanese: ronin)	浪人
laoda	老大
Lianhe	蓮河
liang (taels)	兩
Liaozaihou	寮仔後
lieshen	劣紳
Li chuanzhu	李船主
Li Hongzhang	李鴻章
Li Houji	李厚基
lijia	里甲
lijin	釐金 （厘金）
Li Longxi	李龍溪
Li Qingbo	李清波
Li Shilin	李時霖
Li Sibao	李思寶
Li Zhengchang	李正昌
Lin Hongfei	林鴻飛
Lin Gun	林滾
Lin Guogeng	林國賡

Lin Jichuan	林劑川
Lin Qingcheng	林清埕
Lin Wenwen	林文文
Lin Yi'nen	林依嫩
Lin Youming	林佑明
Liu Kunyi	劉坤一
Longxi	龍溪
Luo Yudong	羅玉東
Lutong	鷺通
Ma Kunzhen	馬坤貞
maiyan jianmin	買煙奸民
Maizaicheng	麥仔埕
Maxiang	馬巷
miaojuan	苗捐
Min	閩
mu	畝
Nan'an	南安
Nanjing (Fujian)	南靖
Nanri	南日
Nantai	南台
neidi liangmin	內地良民
neidi shangshui	內地商稅
paotai	砲台
piaoshui	票稅
Qi Junzao	祁寯藻
Qiying	耆英
Quanji gongsi	全吉公司
Quanzhou	泉州
Rui Que	瑞却
San Quan Mao	三全茂
Shantou	汕頭
Shenbao	申報
Shenhu wan	深滬灣
Shen Jinkang	沈覲康
Shen Ruhan	沈汝瀚
Shenzhou Yaofang	神州藥房
shiba dage	十八大哥

Shi Hou	施猴
Shijiu lujun	十九陸軍
Shi Lang	施琅
Shima	石馬
Shi Saiguang	施塞洸
Shi Shijie	施士洁
Shi Shubao	施叔寶
Shi Tingyang	史廷颺
shuishi tidu	水師提督
Siming Beilu / Nanlu	思明北路/南路
Song Anzai	宋安在
Songshou	松壽
Sun Zhuanlao	孫傳勞
Taiwan gonghui	台灣公會
tehuo	特貨
Tingzhou	汀州
Tong'an	同安
tuyao lijin	土藥厘金
wan buneng xing	萬不能行
Wang Changsheng	王昌盛
Wang Dazhen	王大貞
wangming zhi tu	亡命之徒
Wang Yongquan	王永泉
Wang Youxiong	王友雄
Wang Zongshi	王宗世
wanhui liyuan	挽回利源
Wufeng	五豐
Wu Liande (Wu Lien-te)	伍連德
Wu Tian	吳添
Wu Tianci	吳天賜
xiedou	械鬥
Xiamen (Amoy)	廈門
Xiamen jinrong zuhe	廈門金融組合
Xianyou	仙游
Xiao Wenqing	蕭文慶
Xiao Zhuyuan	蕭祝元
Xie Afa	謝阿發

Xinghua	興化
Xing-Quan-Yong dao	興泉永道
xingzheng jingfei	行政經費
Xu Chongzhi	許崇智
Xu Zhenrun	許振潤
Yakou	衙口
Yang Alü	楊阿律
Yang Shuzhuang	楊淑莊
Yang Xiyuan	楊熙元
yanhai jianmin	沿海奸民
yapian	鴉片
Ye Dingguo	葉丁國
Ye Qinghe / Ye Zhensheng	葉清和 / 葉振聲
yi	夷
Yongchun	永春
Yuanhe (Gwanho)	源和
Yumin	裕閩
Zeng Guofan	曾國藩
Zeng Houkun	曾厚坤
Zhanglin cun	張林村
Zhangpu	漳浦
Zhang Yongshun	章永順
Zhang Zhen	張貞
Zhangzhou	漳州
Zhang Ziyin	張子銀
Zheng Youyi	鄭有義
zhenxing baoye	振興實業
Zhou Kai	周凱
Zhou Yinren	周隱人
zongli yamen	總理衙門
Zuo Zongtang	左宗棠

Notes

Introduction

1. *Junji chu hanwen lufu zhouzhe* (Grand Council Chinese-Language Palace Memorial Copies), Beijing: First Historical Archives, 03-4015-012, DG 21/4/5, hereafter LFZZ. See also *Neige daku dang'an* (Grand Secretariat Archives) 059365, DG 21/2/13 and 059371, DG 20/11/24, hereafter NGDKDA.

2. *Lijin* bureaus as normally discussed in the scholarship are institutions that were not created until 1853, thirteen years after this case took place. What the officials who wrote the memorial on the Red Society were referencing was an older term for merchant surcharges. On the history of *lijin* after 1853, see Luo 2010. For examples of *lijin* as a merchant surcharge in the context of eighteenth-century Chongqing, see Dykstra 2014, 134–136.

3. The porters were given 200 wen per day for their services. LFZZ 03-4015-012, DG 21/4/5.

4. There is an expansive and growing scholarship on global capitalism, with some especially good histories of individual commodities. For tea, Liu 2020; for cotton, see Beckert 2015; for jute, see Ali 2018; for sugar, see Mazumdar 1998 and Mintz 1985; for indigo, see Bose 1993; for coffee, see Topik and Clarence-Smith 2003. For an analysis of labor in opium's production in Bengal, see Bauer 2019.

5. On the late Qing fiscal-military state, see Halsey 2015. My claim in this book is not that opium was the only or even necessarily the most important taxable commodity during these years, just that it formed a substantial portion of the revenue during this period and

was viewed as indispensable in the eyes of the officials at the helm of the Self-Strengthening Movement. As an essential component of the late Qing fiscal military state, then, opium deserves special consideration due to the legal and moral haziness surrounding the drug's trade and revenue collection. For new research that reappraises the taxation of commerce during the late Qing in light of developments during the preceding centuries, see Dykstra 2022.

6. For the British Straits Settlements, Burma, and French Indochina see Kim 2020. For Singapore, see Trocki 1990 and Trocki 1999. For the Netherlands Indies, see Shen 2013.

7. Kim 2020, see especially chapter 1.

8. Ron Po's recent book on Qing maritime policy in the eighteenth century offers an extended explanation of how Qing naval and trade policy on the southeast coast reflects the region's frontier status. See Po 2018, Introduction. On the concept of the Chinese maritime frontier, see also Macauley 2021, Introduction. For a critical survey of the concept of a "Mediterranean" Asian maritime zone, see Sutherland 2003, 1–20. Other examples of scholarship that relates to the concept include Amrith 2015; Deng 2011, 215; Hamashita 2011, 107–139.

9. On the resistance to the Qing conquest in Fujian and the regime of Zheng Chengong (Koxinga), see Hang 2015. One of the more detailed studies of the coastal evacuation in southern Fujian is Chen 2019, 163–180.

10. The Chinese scholarship on Fujian's long history of maritime trade is voluminous. Two now-classics are Lin 1991 and Lan 1999. For English-language scholarship on the subject, the best place to start is Vermeer 1990b; and Ng 1983. A new addition to this scholarly tradition, which bridges the Qing and Republican periods, is Ong 2021.

11. For scholarship on the lineage formation in southeast China, see Faure 2007; Freedman 1958; Szonyi 2002; and Zheng 2001.

12. For social histories of the Heaven and Earth Society (often called the "triads"), see Murray and Qin 1994 and Ownby 1996. On the anti-Qing rituals of these groups, see ter Haar 2000, 449–450.

13. See Antony 2003; Calanca 2010; and Murray 1987.

14. For scholarship on Chinese migration to Southeast Asia and beyond, including critical debates about the utility of the term *diaspora*, see e.g., Chan 2015, 107–128; Shih 2013, 25–42; Kuhn 2008; McKeown 2011, 62–83; Miles 2020; and Wang 1996, 1–15.

15. These shipping networks go back at least as far as the Ming, see Chang 1990, 64–80.

16. The opium import trade before the 1830s is not well documented. The best scholarly treatment is Lin 1985, 62–71. Archival research in Singapore and Netherlands Indies archives could potentially help build out this picture.

17. For the production end of this story, Bauer 2019, 11–15.

18. The most recent book about Jardine Matheson is Grace 2014. Within the historiography from the China field about opium in the 1830s, scholars have done admirable work in excavating the role of British traders and officials, as well as the policy debates and reaction

to opium among Chinese officials, but the Chinese opium merchants themselves are largely absent from the story. See e.g., Morse 1910; Fairbank 1953; Chang 1964; Owen 1968; Fay 1975, 1997. Stephen Platt's recent book about the Opium War stands out among this field as offering a particularly rich tapestry of narratives about the life on the southeast coast of China in the 1830s, though here also the Chinese opium merchants are not a substantive feature of the narrative, see Platt 2018.

19. The impact of this imbalance of trade on state finances is the subject of ongoing scholarly debate. See Lin 2007; Irigoin 2013; He 2007, 63–80; Deng 2008, 320–258; Polachek 1992.

20. See e.g., Chen 2010, 435–445.

21. Ng 1983, 29–30.

22. Szonyi 2017.

23. See e.g., Macauley 2009, 15–17.

24. Ng 1983, 94.

25. Lin 2014, 11–27, see esp. 24–25.

26. The Jardine Matheson Company Archive, Section K1–2, "Extracts from company records," hereafter JM K1–2, May 15, 1837.

27. Zheng Yangwen gestures towards a similar revision of the periodization of opium's legalization, see Zheng 2005, 110, 152–153.

28. Luo 1936, 328.

29. I believe it is a reasonable possibility that the term *lijin* entered the Red Society through local officials extracting their own fees.

30. The classic Chinese work on the lijin is Luo 1936. Newer scholarship on the opium lijin in Chinese include Lin 2016, 31–81; and Zhou 2010, 57–69. The subject is also central to a number of prominent works in the English-language China field, including Bastid 1985, 51–79; Halsey 2015; Kuhn 1970; Mann 1987; and Rowe1984, 1989. On British opposition to lijin taxes and the transit pass system created in response, see Kent 2016, 78–100.

31. For an overview, see Trocki 2011, 89–90; for the example of Siam, see Eoseewong 2005, 108.

32. Carl Trocki has made this argument in several forms, synthesized most concisely in Trocki 2000, 79–104.

33. For a rich case study of a Fujianese *hui* that was involved in the Penang opium farm, see Wong 2016, 600–627.

34. Pong 1987: 121–152.

35. Jonathan Spence was the first to lay this out in stark terms, see Spence 1975, 143–173. See also Zheng 2005, 150–155; Wong 2000, 189–211.

36. See e.g. LFZZ 03-7403-008, GX 32/10/6.

37. The literature on opium prohibition in the early twentieth century is particularly rich. See Baumler 2008; Madancy 2003; Rimner 2018; Slack 2001. See also Kim 2020.

38. Fuzhou's anti-opium organizations are the subject of Madancy 2003.

39. In one of the more famous incidents, reaching the pages of the *New York Times*, a southern Fujianese lineage militia surrounded and attacked a group of soldiers sent to uproot the poppy crop. *North China Herald* January 9, 1909; *New York Times* December 28, 1908.

40. For an overview of poppy taxes on a national level, see Bianco 2000, 292–322.

41. These institutions are also explored in Baumler 2008; Marshall 1976, 19–48; and Slack 2001.

42. See e.g. Kim 2020; Trocki 1990 and 1999. On the United States prohibition of opium in the Philippines after 1908, see Foster 2000, 253–273.

43. There is a growing and exciting scholarship that takes a translocal approach to the history of the Chinese diaspora. See e.g. Chan 2018; González 2017; Keong 2021; Macauley 2016, 755–779; Macauley 2021; Sinn 2014, 220–237; Soon 2020; Zhou 2019.

44. See Rimner 2018.

45. For a thorough introduction to the Japanese pharmaceutical industry during these years, see Yang 2021.

46. Zhou 2005, chapter 6.

47. Lin 2001, 1003–1004.

48. On the enrollment of Fujianese as citizens and the Japanese "southern strategy," see Brooks 2000, 109–121; Wang 2007, 2006, 1–48. See also Ambaras 2018; Peattie 1989, 166–209. See also Keong 2021, chapter 4.

49. For the southwestern provinces before 1850, see Bello 2005. For a brief survey of cultivation and poppy taxes in the twentieth century across China, see Bianco 2000.

50. Chen 1995, 263–298.

51. Celebrated in the first decade of the twentieth century, the Japanese opium monopoly in Taiwan was by the late 1920s coming under criticism from China and the United States for continuing to profit from the drug, see Kingsberg 2013 and Yang 2021.

52. Wu Jierong is a figure who features prominently in Liu 2020, see especially introduction and chapter 7.

53. Dikötter, Laaman, and Zhou 2004; Zheng 2005. See also Spence 1975, for an early example of historicizing opium use.

54. See e.g., Baumler 2007; Madancy 2003; Rimner 2018; Slack 2001.

55. Hong 1983, 47–68.

Chapter 1

1. On the handkerchiefs, see JM B7.10, Reel 505, No. 66, August 30, 1834.

2. JM B2.7, Reel 495, No. 247, February 24, 1839. This case and the sources for this chapter are also discussed extensively in Thilly 2017.

3. JM B2.7, Reel 495, No. 253, March 25, 1839. The "Admiral" likely refers to the *shui-shi tidu*, but could also refer to a number of other naval officers. The "Chu Kang" is also mentioned in JM B2.7, Reel 495, No. 194, May 19, 1838: "An officer called the Chu Kang is

expected to visit this quarter and I hear several brokers have absented themselves."

4. JM B7.5, Reel 525, No. 5, April 20, 1835.

5. The total value of British trade in China during 1833–34 was $49,953,856, see *The Chinese Repository*, Vol. 4, No. 5, 1836, 523.

6. The total scale of the opium trade was almost certainly larger than these statistics indicate. Jardine Matheson figures do not account for the considerable amount of opium imported by the Parsee and American ships that also ventured up to Fujian, nor do they consider the substantial quantities of drug imported on Fujianese ships from Singapore, Lintin, and Chaozhou. Carl Trocki's work indicates that Fujianese direct trade with Singapore during this period was in fact substantial. See chapter 3, "Opium and the Singapore Economy," in Trocki 1990.

7. *Statement of the Claims of the British Subjects* 1840, 25.

8. The following cases from the First Historical Archives in Beijing offer the best detail I have been able to locate on the opium trade in Fujian during these years: LFZZ 03-4007-048, DG 18/10/29; LFZZ 03-4010-021, DG 19/5/25; LFZZ 03-4009-066, DG 19/3/17; LFZZ 03-4011-046, DG 19/6/21; LFZZ 03-4015-029, DG 21/12/18; ZPZZ 04-01-01-0781-053, DG 16/5/19; ZPZZ 04-01-01-0799-001, DG 20/8/24; ZPZZ 04-01-01-0799-011, DG 20/9/23.

9. Huang, Xu, and Qi 1959, 103.

10. YPZZ-MT, Vol. 4.1, No. 4, 291–295.

11. JM B2.7, Reel 495, No. 96, May 11, 1836.

12. YPZZ-MT, Vol. 4.1, No. 4, 291–295.

13. JM B2.7, Reel 495, No. 106, June 25, 1836.

14. JM K1.2, August 3, 1837.

15. The relationship between Shenhu Bay, Taiwan, and Ningbo is described in the most detail in JM B7 5, Reel 525, No. 134, December 18, 1854.

16. See, e.g., JM B2.7, Reel 495, No. 78, February 9, 1836; JM B2.7, Reel 495, No. 181, March 7, 1838.

17. Here I translate *qianzhuang* as "local banks." Contemporaneous translations include "native banks" and "money shops." Guangdong Governor Li Hongbin describes the system in detail in a memorial from January 1832: ZPZZ 04-01-01-0732-021, DG 11/12/14.

18. Historian Lin Renchuan also identifies the rise of the trade in Malwa opium out of Bombay—not controlled by the BEIC—along with increased Qing attention to opium smuggling in the Pearl River Delta, as factors that contributed to the migration of the opium trade to the Fujian coast. Lin 1991, 62–63.

19. JM K1.2, September 8, 1834.

20. Though competitors, Jardine and Dent seem to have seen this expedition as good for their mutual profit. The two firms maintained a tenuous relationship throughout the decade, sometimes colluding in price-fixing schemes, and just as quickly breaking mutual agreements when it suited them. See for example JM B2.7, Reel 495, No. 96, May 11, 1836.

21. Thomas Rees appears throughout the Jardine Matheson archive materials as a rep-

resentative of the competition. For Dent & Company's approximate share of the opium trade, see Fay 1975, 157, 169, 238. His maps along with several drawn by his brother John are held at the British Library, Add MS 16364, A-I and J-R.

22. It was a lie that Lindsay used repeatedly, see e.g., NGDKDA 060742, DG 12/5/12.

23. Lindsay and Gützlaff 1834, 4.

24. JM A7.346, 1832–1833.

25. YPZZ-MT, 291–295.

26. le Pichon 2006, 312.

27. JM B2.7, Reel 495, No. 6, September 6, 1833.

28. One of the two surviving letters from the brokers in Yakou to Captain John Rees is signed in Chinese by three men, Yazhen, Yabo, and Yayang. Yabo is quite possibly the Yabe in question. JM H1.51.2.

29. JM B2.7, Reel 495, No. 10, February 2, 1834.

30. JM K1.2, Extracts from Company Records, September 8, 1834.

31. JM A8.123, No. 123, Occurrences in Chin Chew Bay, March–April 1837.

32. JM B2.7, Reel 495, No. 265, April 21, 1839.

33. As Gützlaff gleefully reported on one such occasion, "Our good captain whipped the mandarins and sent them as naughty boys back to their mothers." JM B2.7, R. 495, No. 18, September 19, 1834.

34. JM B2.7, Reel 495, No. 57, August 20, 1835.

35. See for example two extraordinary documents from the Jardine Matheson Archive wherein members of the Shi Lineage at Yakou wrote letters to Captain Rees, exhorting him to leave Shenhu Bay for a few days because of an impending visit to the area by patrol boats from the Xiamen naval commander-in-chief and Jinmen brigade general. JM.H1 51.01, 1837 and JM.H1 51.2, 1837.

36. See for example, ZPZZ 04-01-01-0772-049, DG 15/4/24; ZPZZ 04-01-01-0762-052, DG 15/6/7.

37. ZPZZ 04-01-01-0759-012, DG 14/8/22.

38. LFZZ 03-4007-048, DG 18/10/29.

39. My conclusion that John and Thomas Rees are "Big and Little Li" from the Qing document is not conjecture. The Jardine Matheson Archive contains two letters from Chinese opium merchants in Yakou village addressed to "Captain Li" (*Li chuanzhu*) and forwarded to William Jardine by John Rees. See JM H1.51.1 and JM H1.51.2, 1837.

40. Shi Saiguang was sentenced to be cashiered from his rank for the crimes of purchasing opium from a foreign ship, opening an opium den, and enticing the sons and brothers of good families to smoke. His partner Shi Chang, who was not protected by *jiansheng* status, was hanged for the same crimes. LFZZ 03-4007-048, DG 18/10/29.

41. My reading here is that officials were incentivized to downplay the scale and significance of illegal activity in their jurisdictions. So in the case of a thriving opium market like the one in Shenhu Bay, officials were inclined to list only the amounts of drugs and money

exactly testified to by the arrested prisoners and not to speculate or gesture towards exactly how much more was being exchanged than was recorded in the memorial.

42. JM B2.7, Reel 495, No. 56, August 12, 1835.

43. On labor relations at the production end of the trade, in India, see Bauer 2019.

44. LFZZ 03-4007-048, DG 18/10/29. Of the three people who started off providing labor and subsequently invested in their own opium, two were arrested and one remained at large (Lin Ji).

45. See the case of Yang Awan, Yang Jindong, Yang Ayi, Yang Shengzhi, and Yang Aqiu. QDGZ-JJC 405002453, DG 18/12/27.

46. Enclosure 2 in FO 228/62, No. 7, Alcock to Davis, Foochow, February 12, 1846.

47. Of the three people who started off providing labor and subsequently invested in their own opium, two were arrested and one remained at large.

48. JM B2.7, Reel 495, No. 69, November 29, 1835.

49. JM B2.7, Reel 495, No. 76, January 21, 1836.

50. JM B2.7, Reel 495, No. 133, January 21, 1837.

51. JM B2.7, Reel 495, No. 99, May 21, 1836.

52. JM B2.7, Reel 495, No. 102, June 15, 1836.

53. Shi, according to his testimony, sold them the drug at an inflated price, cheating the extortionists out of 25 silver when compared with the rate he charged other customers. LFZZ 03-4007-048, DG 18/10/29.

54. QDGZ-JJC 405002453, DG 18.12.27

55. JM B2.7, Reel 495, No. 131, January 2, 1837.

56. JM B2.7, Reel 495, No. 131, January 2, 1837.

57. JM B2.7, Reel 495, No. 132, January 15, 1837.

58. JM B2.7, Reel 495, No. 133, January 21, 1837.

59. JM B2.7, Reel 495, No. 140, March 28, 1837.

60. JM B2.11, Reel 571, No. 166, June 10, 1837.

61. JM B2.7, Reel 495, No. 144, April 22, 1837.

62. JM B2.7, Reel 495, No. 153, July 16, 1837.

63. YPZZ-MT, Vol. 4.1, No. 4, 291–295.

64. LFZZ 03-2677-064, DG 18/12/23.

65. Zheng 2001, 23.

66. Zheng 2001, 11.

67. See Hang 2015 and Ho 2011.

68. Zheng 2001, 217.

69. See for example, Zheng 2001; Ho 2011; Xiao 1986; Vermeer 1990.

70. Ng 1983, 82; Gang Zhao argues that Shi Lang was not interested in opening Fujian to free trade so much as in establishing a system wherein a few wealthy merchants (himself included) could monopolize foreign trade, and that the Kangxi Emperor himself was the primary force behind the "open door" policy of 1684. See Zhao 2013, 92–93.

71. *Qing shilu*, Vol. 119, QL 5.6, p. 748; ibid, Vol. 129, QL 5.10, 884.

72. LFZZ 03-2677-064, DG 18/12/23. These fortifications were not a new phenomenon. Many date to the Ming.

73. Huang, Xu, and Qi 1959, 103.

74. Lamley 1990, 57.

75. Huang, Xu and Qi 1959, 114–118.

76. Huang, Xu and Qi 1959, 114–118.

77. Huang, Xu and Qi 1959, 104.

78. See for example, Lin 1991; Lan 1999; Vermeer 1990; Ng 1983.

79. Vermeer 1990, 8.

80. Members of Zheng He's famous expeditions during the first few decades of the fifteenth century reported finding thousands of Hokkien and Cantonese people living across maritime Southeast Asia, Dreyer 2007, 40, 184.

81. Chang in Vermeer 1990, 64–80.

82. Chang in Vermeer 1990, 64–80.

83. Wills 2011, 24–77.

84. See Antony 2003 and Murray 1987.

85. LFZZ 03-3607-046, DG 19/12/23.

86. On disrepair of the Admiralty's ships in 1839, see LFZZ 03-3607-046, DG 19/12/23. For difficulties in provisioning troops and securing affordable ammunition, see NGHKTB, 02-01-04-20828-004, DG 16/6/5.

87. Another of Shi Lang's sons, Shi Shilun, became a famous civil official who was later canonized in a series of judge stories called *Shi Gong An*, see Hummel 1943–44, 653–655.

88. Huang 2004, 172.

89. During the early Jiaqing reign (in 1801), the Fujian governor-general had arranged for the merchants of Xiamen to contribute $24,000 in silver each year for the purposes of maritime defense, more still than the Qing state's own contribution of $20,000. NGHKTB 02-01-04-20828-004, DG 16/6/5.

90. One way to deal with insufficient funding was to confiscate boats, though those boats were not necessarily confiscated in good condition.

91. YPZZ-MT, Vol. 4.5, No. 6, 98–399.

92. JM B2.7, Reel 495, No. 151, July 9, 1837.

93. *Chouban yiwu shimo: Xianfeng chao*, (Complete Records of the management of Foreign Affairs: Xianfeng reign), (Taipei: Scripta Sinica Database, http://hanchi.ihp.sinica.edu.tw/ihp/hanji.htm.) Hereafter referred to as CBYWSM-DGC, 1–4.

94. CBYWSM-DGC, 1–4.

95. Huang et al. 1959, 102–104.

96. Huang et al. 1959, 130–133. Huang's argument here is not entirely convincing, although Shen was stolidly anti-opium in his own writings, see e.g. YPZZ MT, Vol. 4.1, No. 4, 291–295.

97. ZPZZ 04-01-01-0781-053, DG 16/5/19.

98. LFZZ 03-4009-066, DG 19/3/17.

99. LFZZ 03-4010-021, DG 19/5/25.

100. ZPZZ 04-01-01-0798-008, DG 20/5/4.

101. ZPZZ 04-01-01-00799-024, DG 20/1/16.

102. Huang et al 1959, 106–107.

103. The new regulations include six points: 1. establishment of an *aozong* who will be responsible for monitering ten aojia units, 2. setting up more surviellance points in the remote areas between major ports, 3. reinstating the ban on renting registered boats, 4. dispatching thirteen new warships under the direct authority of the governor-general to keep a watch on the provincial commander's fleet, 5. increasing surveillance on illegal rice shipments, 6. increasing surveillance on illegal weapons possession. *Fujian shengli* 1964, 723–728.

104. Huang, Xu, and Qi 1959, 106–107.

105. Huang, Xu, and Qi 1959, 103.

106. LFZZ 03-3607-046, DG 19/12/23.

107. JM K1–2, May 15, 1837.

108. JM B2.7, Reel 495, No. 133, January 21, 1837.

109. Lin 2014, 24–25; Ng 1983, 94.

110. JM B2.7, Reel 495, No. 253, 3/25/1839.

111. JM B2.7, Reel 495, No. 144, 4/22/1837.

112. "The system which they adopt on shore when they stop trade is this: the elders of the town meet at the Consoo house, and if the voices are against trading with the ships a Gong is beat round the town and chop to that effect and all those are found trading after the Gong is beaten the property is confiscated or a heavy fine." JM B2.7, Reel 495, No. 225, October 11, 1838.

Chapter 2

1. Evidence about this case is from QDGZ-JJC 406000971, XF 1.8.2; and LFZZ 03-4586-002, XF 1.4.9.

2. My speculation here is based on a similarity between the name of the Jardine Matheson shroff and compradore in Fuzhou during the 1850s, A Hee, and the compradore named in the memorial on Yang Alü, Han Axi.

3. Morse, 1919, 556.

4. See FO 228/11, No. 7, Layton to Bonham, January 28, 1850; FO 228/125, No. 21, Sullivan to Bonham, February 20, 1851; FO 228/141, No. 14, Sullivan to Bowring, February 17, 1852; FO 228/171, No. 17, Robinson to Bonham, February 27, 1854; FO 228/188, No. 36, Winchester to Bowring, February 21, 1855; FO 228/211, No, 23, Blackhouse to Bowring, February 27, 1856.

5. See JM B7.1, Reel 465, Nos. 238, 245, 255, 263, 264, 278, 290, 296, 307, 317, 330, 339,

342, 349, (1853); JM B7.1, Reel 466, Nos. 361, 370, 378, 384, 394, 401, 406, 424, 431, 444, 452, 461, (1854); JM B7.1, Reel 466, Nos. 468, 476, 486, 501, 523, 541, 552, 570, 583, 597, 615, 636, (1855); JM B7.1, Reel 466, Nos. 651, 666, 681, 701, 721, 736, 742, 755, 752, 764, 783, 801, 814, (1856); and JM B7.5, Reel 525–526, Nos. 31, 32, 33, 39, 44, 47, 49, 59, 62, 63, 67, 73, 78, 84, 87, 92, 98, 102, 109, 111, 114, 119, 124, 131, 135, 140, 142, 146, 156, 170, 178, 186, 193, 203, 205, 211, 215, 230, 237, 243, 251, 257, 262, 263, 274, 280, 283, 285, 289, 293, 298, 303, 309, 315, 320, 321, 331, 338, 341, 347, 360, 364, 369, 375, 383, 386, 396, 400, 407, 413, 423, 430, 436, 441, 445, 452, 462, 464, 470, 476, 483, 486, 492, 497, 502, 509, 511, 516, 517, 524, 530, 534, 540, 545, 549, 553, 560, 565, 573, 577, (1853–1861).

6. Based off figures from 1853–1855, during which Jardine's representatives at the Fuzhou outer anchorage sold around 750–1,200 chests per year. Dent's sales can be assumed to be approximately equal. See JM B7.11, Reel 507, Nos. 23, 28, 32, 36, 40, 44, 49, 50, 70, 78, 81, 89, 93, 98, 104, 108, 119, 129, 148, 156, 169, 181, 191, 207, 213, 221, 224, 238, 262, 278, 298 and 316, 1853–55

7. On the relationship between the tea trade in Fuzhou and opium shipments up the Min river, see e.g., JM.B7.11, Reel 507, No. 50, September 12, 1853; JM B7.11, Reel 507, No. 103, May 24, 1854.

8. FO 228/52, No. 37, Alcock to Davis, Foochow, June 16, 1845.

9. FO 228/50, No. 33, Lay to Davis, Xiamen, April 19, 1845.

10. Martin 1848, 291–292.

11. See e.g., JM.B7.5, Reel 525, No. 119, September 27, 1854; JM.B7.5, Reel 525, No. 146, March 30, 1855.

12. JM.B7.5, Reel 525, No. 131, November 27, 1854.

13. See e.g., JM.B7.5, Reel 525, No. 15, November 29, 1847; JM.B7.5, Reel 525, No. 24, October 1, 1852; JM.B7.5, Reel 525, No. 140, January 31, 1855.

14. See e.g., JM B7.11, Reel 507, No. 50, September 12, 1853 and JM B7.11, Reel 507, No. 103, May 24, 1854.

15. JM B7.11, Reel 507, No. 316, December 30, 1855.

16. See e.g., FO 228/171, No. 79, Parkes to Bowring, Amoy, November 22, 1854; JM B7.5, Reel 525, No. 185, July 31, 1855; JM B7.5, Reel 525, No. 215, December 23, 1855.

17. See e.g., JM B7.5, Reel 525, No. 140, January 31, 1855.

18. JM B7.1, Reel 466, No. 43, October 18, 1854.

19. FO 228/62, No. 7, Alcock to Davis, Foochow, February 12, 1846.

20. FO 228/62, No. 7, Alcock to Davis, Foochow, February 12, 1846.

21. FO 881/616, No. 4, Enclosure 9, Sir H. Pottinger to the Imperial Commissioner and His Colleagues, August 8, 1843.

22. FO 705/72, No. 3, From H. Gribble at Kowlongsu and Amoy, November 3, 1843.

23. *Canton Press*, Vol. 8, No. 46, November 18, 1843.

24. FO 228/52, No. 65, Alcock to Davis, Foochow, November 21, 1845, 144.

25. Sales at Shenhu and Quanzhuou were comparable. At one point the two firms dis-

cussed dividing sales between the ports, but old rivalries die hard and the firms continued to send ships to both ports. See JM B7.1, Reel 465, No. 35, October 13, 1846.

26. The final sales report from Quanzhou by a Jardine opium ship captain was from Captain Hodge of the *Adventure*, reporting the sale of thirty-three chests of opium during August 1861. See JM B7.5, Reel 526, No. 577, August 26, 1861.

27. See e.g., FO 228/211, No. 41, Morrison to Bowring, Amoy, June 21, 1856.

28. See Fairbank 1953, 243–247; Norton-Kyshe 1898, 189–192.

29. *China Mail*, No. 105, February 18, 1847 and No. 11, May 1, 1845, cited in Fairbank 1953, 243; also reported in *Singapore Free Press and Mercantile Advertiser* March 11, 1847, 3.

30. As reported in the Chinese memorial on the incident. See CBYWSM-DGC, 77.32–35; cited in Fairbank 1953, 244.

31. *Singapore Free Press and Mercantile Advertiser* March 11, 1847, 3.

32. Fairbank 1953, 245.

33. JM B7.5, Reel 525, No. 160, Fitzgibbon, May 7, 1855.

34. JM B7.5, Reel 525, No. 159, May 4, 1855.

35. JM B7 5, Reel 525, No. 163, Fitzgibbon, May 11, 1855.

36. JM B7.1, Reel 466, No. 498, April 27, 1855.

37. FO 228/171, No. 17, Robinson to Bonham, Amoy, February 27, 1854.

38. FO 228/52, No. 37, Alcock to Davis, Foochow, June 15, 1845.

39. One fairly complete year of statistics for this is 1856, see JM B7.1, Reel 466, Nos. 651, 666, 681, 701, 721, 736, 742, 755, 752, 764, 783, 801, 814, 1856.

40. For example, in July of 1856 the Jardine Matheson receiving ship *Pathfinder* sold 42 chests of opium compared with 107 by the Chinese brokers. JM B7.1, Reel 466, No. 742, July 30, 1856.

41. JM B7.1, Reel 466, No. 424, September 8, 1854.

42. Jardine's instructions to the receiving ships in Quanzhou and Shenhu Bay were to charge $10–20 more than the going rate in Xiamen, but they often found it difficult to maintain those prices when dealers in Xiamen started sending drugs to Shenhu and Quanzhou at just a $4–5 dollar markup. See JM B7.5, Reel 525, No. 46, May 14, 1853; JM B7.5, Reel 526, No. 325, June 1, 1857.

43. See e.g. the comment from Jardine Matheson's Captain Fitzgibbon in 1860 that "a good deal of drug is arriving by the Singapore ships." JM B7.1, Reel 468, No. 1333, June 24, 1860.

44. JM B7.1, Reel 466, No. 486, April 5, 1855.

45. See e.g. *Straits Times* May 7, 1850, 4; *Straits Times* May 25, 1852, 4; *Singapore Free Press and Mercantile Advertiser* May 26, 1854, 3.

46. Jardine employees frequently complained about being undersold by local merchants who imported opium from Singapore, see e.g., JM B7.5, Reel 525, No. 263, July 31, 1856 and JM B7.1, Reel 468, No. 1348, August 1, 1860.

47. See Bello 2005 on opium cultivation in the southwest.

48. For information on opium cultivation in Fujian and Zhejiang in the 1820s, see ZPZZ 04-01-01-0721-056, DG 10/10/13; See also FO 228/111, No. 14, Layton to Bonham, Amoy, March 21, 1850.

49. FO 228/111, No. 18, Layton to Bonham, Amoy, April 26, 1850.

50. See LFZZ 03-4015-012, DG 21/4/5, NGDKDA 059365, DG 21/2/13, and NGDKDA 059371, DG 20/11/24.

51. FO 228/52, No. 37, Alcock to Davis, Foochow, June 15, 1845

52. JM.B7.1, Reel 467, No. 1133, May 19, 1859.

53. LFZZ 03-4586-002, XF 1/4/9.

54. JM B7.5, Reel 526, No. 296, January 8, 1857.

55. Ball 1856, 341.

56. Ball 1856, 340.

57. Ball 1856, 342.

58. Ball l856, 348.

59. FO 228/211, No. 41, Morrison to Bowring, Amoy, June 21, 1856; and, FO 228/211, No. 38, Morrison to Bowring, Amoy, June 5, 1856.

60. FO 228/211, No. 41, Morrison to Bowring, Amoy, June 21, 1856.

61. FO 705/70, Pottinger Papers: Letters from Keying, Chinese agent, 1843–44.

62. FO 663/3 [1], No. 12, Xiamen 1844, 34–37.

63. See JM B7.11, Reel 507, No. 11, November 25, 1850; FO 228/114, No. 60, Sinclair to Bonham, Foochow, November 26, 1850; CBYWSM XFC, Vol. 3, No. 109, 105.

64. See e.g., FO 228/128, No. 10, Sinclair to Bonham, Foochow, February 14, 1851.

65. JM B7 11, Reel 507, No. 5, Roose to Matheson, June 12, 1847.

66. FO 228/192, No. 114, Medhurst to Bowring, Foochow, December 17, 1855; FO 228/216, No. 42, Hale to Bowring, Foochow, July 4, 1856.

67. See FO 228/288, No. 58, Medhurst to Bruce, Foochow, June 30, 1860; JM B7 11, Reel 510, No. 1099, November 23, 1860.

68. ZPZZ 04-01-35-0380-031, DG 25.2.16.

69. FO 17/278, Return to an Address to the House of Lords, 12 March 1857: Enclosure 12, Layton to Bonham, January 28, 1850.

70. Tait and Company were especially active in the camphor business. Jardine's agent in Quanzhou at one point said that Tait's opium-camphor exchange system in Quanzhou "is the only thing that keeps the imports from Formosa to this port." JM B7.5, Reel 525, No. 185, July 31, 1855.

71. There seems to have been little fanfare surrounding the opium *lijin* at this stage, though it was to become a controversial issue after 1870 or so, as discussed in chapter 3. I have found no reference to its inauguration in 1857 beyond a terse description in Luo 1936, 330. It is also referenced in FO 682/1992/50, Copy of memo from three anonymous officials to Emperor, detailing tax on opium, 1859.

72. FO 228/236, No. 40, Hale to Bowring, Foochow, May 9, 1857.

73. FO 228/216, No. 53, Medhurst to Bowring, Foochow, August 7, 1856.

74. FO 228/236, No. 40, Hale to Bowring, Foochow, May 9, 1857.

75. FO 228/236, No. 49, Hale to Bowring, Foochow, June 12, 1857.

76. FO 228/236, No. 49, Hale to Bowring, Foochow, June 12, 1857.

77. JM B7.11, Reel 509, No. 539, June 12, 1857.

78. FO 228/288, No. 31, Medhurst to Bruce, Foochow, March 24, 1860.

79. FO 228/233, No. 62, Morrison to Bowring, Amoy, December 4, 1857.

80. JM B7.1, Reel 467, Nos. 927 and 932, Nov-Dec. 1857.

81. FO 228.251, No. 18, Gingell to Bowring, Amoy, March 28, 1858.

82. JM A8.123–2, Circular, April 10, 1858.

83. FO 228/265, No. 18, Morrison to Bowring, Amoy, March 10, 1859.

84. FO 228/265, No. 18, Morrison to Bowring, Amoy, March 10, 1859, Enclosure 1, 2 February 1859.

85. JM B7.1, Reel 467, No. 1169, August 10, 1859.

86. See chapter 3 of this book and Trocki 1990.

87. JM B7.1, Reel 467, No. 1170, August 10, 1859.

88. JM B7.1, Reel 467, No. 1176, August 21, 1859.

89. JM B7.1, Reel 467, No. 1177, August 27, 1859.

90. JM B7.1, Reel 467, No. 1189, September 27, 1859.

91. For full text of the agreement, see JM F1.123, Customs Agreement of Foreign Firms, October 1859.

92. JM F1.123, Customs Agreement for Tax Farming at Xiamen, October 1859.

93. JM C13.15, No. 453, Jardine to Fitzgibbon, October 11, 1859.

94. Kwass 2014.

95. JM A8.118.27, Opium Sales Accounts of the "Harlequin," April 30, 1852.

96. FO 228/251, No. 18, Gingell to Bowring, Amoy, March 28, 1858.

97. JM H5.10, Public Notice from Quanzhou Prefect, June 27, 1859.

98. JM B7.1, Reel 467, No. 1131, Circular, May 18, 1859.

99. JM B7.5, Reel 526, No. 445, Fox to Jardine, August 1, 1859.

100. JM L5.23, Notice from Daotai demanding withdrawal of opium ships from Quanzhou, August 4, 1859.

101. JM B7.5, Reel 526, No. 447, Fox to Jardine, August 9, 1859.

102. JM B7.5, Reel 526, No. 587, Sullivan to Jardine, February 12, 1862.

103. JM B7.5, Reel 526, No. 591, Sullivan to Jardine, April 22, 1862.

104. JM B7.1, Reel 469, No. 1644, Fitzgibbon to Jardine, October 6, 1862.

105. Fairbank 1953, 263.

106. ZPZZ 04-01-35-0380-014, DG 24.2.14.

107. ZPZZ 04-01-35-0380-030, DG 25.2.16.

108. ZPZZ 04-01-35-0380-030, DG 25.2.16.

109. Of course, as is well documented in the scholarship on Shanghai, Fujianese mer-

chants were a dominant force in that port from the mid-nineteenth century on. The point here is that the boats taking goods to areas north of Shanghai no longer needed to pass through Fujian, and merchants who had previously made their living on the coastal trade now had to permanently relocate to Shanghai to continue their participation in it.

110. FO 228/11, No. 7, Layton to Bonham, January 28, 1850.

111. *Chouban yiwu shimo: Xianfeng chao*, (Complete Records of the management of Foreign Affairs: Xianfeng reign), (Taipei: Scripta Sinica Database, http://hanchi.ihp.sinica.edu.tw/ihp/hanji.htm.), 4:153, 143–4. Hereafter CBYWSM-XFC.

112. FO 228/171, No. 63, Parkes to Bowring, September 21, 1854.

113. ZPZZ 04-01-35-0382-018, XF 4.1.28.

114. JM B7.5, Reel 525, No. 47, 28 May 1853; JM B7.1, Reel 465, No. 287, 30 June 1853.

115. *Beida yijiao tiben* (Routine Memorials, Transferred from Peking University), Number One Historical Archives, Beijing, 02-01-02-3036-015, XF 4.12.13. Hereafter BDYJTB.

116. JM B7.1, Reel 465, No. 287, June 25, 1853.

117. *The Times* August 15, 1853.

118. JM G47.1, Market Reports: Amoy, July 31, 1853.

119. JM B7.5, Reel 525, No. 58, Miller to Jardine, August 22, 1853.

120. JM B7.11, Reel 507, No. 217, Williams to Jardine, June 19, 1855.

121. FO 228/251, No. 12, Gingell to Bowring, Amoy, March 17, 1858.

Chapter 3

1. For the official British and Chinese versions of the affair, see FO 17/701, No. 189, Wade to Lord Denby, October 7, 1875; and LFZZ 31507405, GX 2.4.24. On the rumors in the press, see e.g., *Shenbao* June 9, 1875; *North China Herald* June 12, 1875.

2. *North China Herald* June 12, 1875.

3. CMC Film, Reel 5, "Report on Trade in the Port of Foochow for the Years 1874–1875."

4. Great Britain and Public Record Office, Embassy and Consular Archives, China, General Correspondence, Series I, 1834–1930 (PRO F.O. 228), Reel 554, No. 13, July 22, 1875.

5. Luo 1936, 328–330. See also Halsey 2015, chapters 3–4 for an empire-wide view of lijin collection in the post-Taiping years, with a particular focus on the collection of lijin on other items of trade in Shanghai and Jiangsu province.

6. Zuo Zongtang spelled this out in regards to opium cultivation in the northwest, after his transfer out of Fujian, in LFZZ 03-6490-026, GX 7.5.5. For another, later explanation of this logic in 1897, see Mozhen 1998, 354–355.

7. Shen 2005, Vol 2, 403.

8. Compiled from trade reports published by the Chinese Maritime Customs.

9. Inspector General of the Chinese Maritime Customs, "China Maritime Customs Publications, Microfilm," (Washington, D.C: Association for Research Libraries, Center

for Chinese Research Materials), Reel 11, "Annual Returns for 1873, Part II," 74. Hereafter CMC Film.

10. CMC Film, Reel 4, "Report on The Trade at the Port of Amoy, 1865."

11. Trocki 1999, 113.

12. Compiled from IMC Decennial and Annual Reports.

13. Taiwan was governed until 1887 as a prefecture within the Fujian Provincial Administration. The concept of a "reexport" in the administration of the Maritime Customs refers simply to the movement of an imported good from one treaty port to another. Opium imported to Xiamen and then shipped up to Fuzhou would also be considered a reexport, for example.

14. CMC Film, Reel 4, "Report on the Trade at the Port of Amoy for the Year 1870."

15. CMC Film, Reel 5, "Amoy Trade Report for the Year 1874."

16. Martin 1848, 291–292.

17. CMC Film, Reel 17, "Amoy Trade Report for the Year 1886."

18. CMC Film, Reel 4, "Amoy Trade Report for the Year 1870."

19. CMC Film, Reel 8, "Amoy Trade Report for the Year 1881."

20. CMC Film, Reel 8, "Amoy Trade Report for the Year 1881."

21. CMC Film, Reel 4, "Foochow Trade Report for the Year 1864."

22. This percentage is based on the years 1863–1887, prior to the implementation of the Additional Articles of the Chefoo Convention. This new law, implemented in 1887, put the foreign customs in charge of collecting the opium lijin, which further amplified the importance of opium revenue within foreign trade revenue. The issues surrounding lijin are discussed at greater length later in this chapter.

23. For recent English-language studies of the customs, see Brunero 2006 and van de Ven 2014. The now classic Chinese-language study of the customs is Chen, 2002.

24. See e.g. Kent 2016.

25. CMC Film, Reel 5, Service List, August 1, 1876

26. CMC Film, Reel 4, "Return on Trade at the Port of Foochow for the Year 1865."

27. "Ten-Kilometer Railway Tunnel in SE China Completed," *China View*, http://www.newsgd.com/travel/travelnews/200705150010.htm, May 15, 2007, accessed January 8, 2020.

28. Banister 1932, foreword, chapter 3. Also cited in Van de Ven 2014, 83.

29. Tagliacozzo 2005, 82.

30. "Foochow: The Affray with Smugglers," 1875.

31. "Foochow: The Affray with Smugglers," 1875.

32. "Foochow," 1875.

33. "Foochow: The Affray with Smugglers," 1875.

34. The tidewaiter Le Bretton was transferred to Jiujiang, Bisbee to Shanghai, and acting commissioner James Hart went on leave, replaced by a commissioner of full rank, Edward Bangs Drew. There is no official record that they were transferred because of the

incident, but the *North China Herald* speculated as much, and the timing of the transfers seems to confirm that this was the case. The British consul at Pagoda Anchorage, James Carroll, also left abruptly for sick leave in June of 1875, just a few weeks after the murder. CMC Film, Reel 5, Service List, August 1, 1876.

35. Ma 1998, 260; Luo 1936, 330.

36. Luo 1936, 626–627.

37. Luo 1936, 332.

38. Luo Yudong states that lijin collection in Fujian was formally bureaucratic and not farmed out to merchants. Presumably he was writing of the "baihuo" (ordinary product) lijin. Luo 1936, 334.

39. CMC Film, Reel 4, "Report on the Trade at the Port of Amoy for the Year 1870."

40. CMC Film, Reel 4, "Report on Trade at the Port of Foochow for the Year 1867."

41. E.g., *Shenbao* October 15, 1883.

42. CMC Film, Reel 8, "Report on the Trade at the Port of Swatow for the Year 1881."

43. This figure is based off customs reports from 1875, but the number of passengers grew each year.

44. This claim is distilled most forcefully in CMC Film, Reel 5, "Report on Trade in the Port of Foochow for the Years 1874–1875."

45. FO 228/848, Amoy to Peking, January 17, 1887, "Intelligence Report for Quarter ending December 31, 1886."

46. FO 228/824, No. 68, Amoy to Peking, 26 November 1886.

47. *Shenbao* November 2, 1885.

48. *Shenbao* September 22, 1884.

49. FO 228/848, Amoy to Peking, January 17, 1887, "Intelligence Report for Quarter ending December 31, 1886."

50. FO 228/823, No. 24, Amoy to Peking, April 1, 1886.

51. FO 656/17, Return of Criminal Cases in Amoy, 1866.

52. Edwards has also captured the attention of historians Douglas Fix and Terry Bennett, though neither has focused explicitly on his involvement with the opium trade. See Bennett 2010, 154–192; Fix 2016, chapter 8.

53. FO 228/741, No. 1, Amoy to Peking, February 7, 1884, Enclosure: "Mr. Portley's Report on Smuggling Operations Carried on by Edwards, 17 January 1884." Hereafter "Mr. Portley's Report," 1884. See also FO 228/741, No. 5, Amoy to Peking, March 20, 1884, Enclosure 3: "Translation of Proclamation of Chiang, Haifang, 13 March 1884."

54. FO 228/741, No. 1, Amoy to Peking, February 7, 1884.

55. As historian Douglas Fix argues, Edwards's family does possibly have a connection to Maine, though the most compelling evidence indicates that Edwards Sr. was born in Antigua. Fix 2016, 164–165.

56. Bennett 2010, 154–192.

57. "Mr. Portley's Report," 1884.

58. "Mr. Portley's Report," 1884.

59. Fix 2016, 161.

60. FO 228/742, No. 54, Amoy to Peking, October 7, 1884, Enclosure: "US Consul at Singapore to US Consul at Amoy, 12 September 1884."

61. FO 228/741, No. 5, Amoy to Peking, March 20, 1884, Enclosure 3: "Translation of Proclamation of Chiang, Haifang, 13 March 1884."

62. When he was finally arrested, in 1885, it was by the Americans for a charge unrelated to opium smuggling. He had been in an ongoing conflict with the American consul, Goldsborough. See Fix 2016.

63. FO 228/824, No. 68, Amoy to Peking, November 26, 1886.

64. FO 228/848, Separate, Amoy to Peking, January 17, 1887, "Intelligence Report for Quarter ending December 31, 1886."

65. The idea that the drug was changing hands from foreign buyer to Chinese buyer is an oversimplification but represents the way that the taxes were structured. Most of the drug being imported was on Chinese accounts, but these Chinese merchants used foreign shipping to bring the drug in and stored it in foreign-owned warehouses within the treaty ports before paying the lijin. So a more accurate way to put it is that the lijin was paid when it was moved from a foreign jurisdiction to a Chinese jurisdiction.

66. FO 228/848, Separate, Amoy to Peking, January 17, 1887.

67. *Shenbao* September 22, 1884.

68. FO 228/848, Separate, Amoy to Peking, January 17, 1887, "Intelligence Report for Quarter ending December 31, 1886."

69. Lin 2016, table 4.

70. Lin 2016, table 5.

71. In Fujian, 50,000 taels of the monthly opium lijin revenue was earmarked as a "Capital Levy" (京餉), to be sent to Beijing. This lasted at least into the early 1870s. See Shen 2005, vol. 2, 338–340.

72. On the history of smuggling and smuggling prevention, see Thai 2018.

73. Summarized in Zhou 2010, 57–63.

74. See Luo 1936, 330.

75. Under Zuo's recommendation, a French naval officer, Prosper Giquiel, along with imperially appointed commissioner Shen Baozhen, supervised the construction and operation of Fuzhou's modern naval yard, arsenal, and school of naval science. The arsenal (as it was commonly referred to) was constructed at Mawei—Pagoda Anchorage—just outside Fuzhou, the site of Fuzhou's deepwater port. The shipyard constructed fifteen working transport ships and gunboats while Giquel was in charge (through 1874). After Shen Baozhen and his Chinese successors took over management, the arsenal continued to put out nineteen more ships, despite a period of complete destruction and rebuilding in the Sino-French war of 1884–1885. Giquel 1874, 38, 126. Benjamin Elman argues that the Fuzhou Naval Yard is a key example of one of China's major successes in the development

of modern science and technology after 1860, see chapter 10: "Government Arsenals, Science, and Technology after 1860," in Elman 2005.

76. Van de Ven 2014, 119–120.

77. Pong 1987, 124.

78. Shen 2005, vol. 2, 331.

79. Pong 1987, 128.

80. Pong 1987, 132.

81. Pong 1987, 132–133.

82. Zuo remained heavily involved in the Fuzhou Arsenal after his transfer, and in 1872 he successfully petitioned to reduce the monthly transfer of revenue from Fujian to Gansu by 20,000 taels in order to supplement the arsenal's budget. See Shen 2005, vol. 2, 345–349.

83. Luo 1936, 615–616.

84. Lin 2016, table 11.

85. Halsey 2015, 5.

86. Halsey 2015, introduction and 240–241.

87. On Zuo's anti-opium stance in the northwest, see Ma 1998, 277. Regarding the 1881 negotiations, see LFZZ 03-6490-026, GX 7/5/5 and LFZZ 03-6491-017, GX 7/7/4, as well as Zhou 2010, 57–69, see esp. 57–60.

88. Shen's published memorials from his time in Fujian deal with issues surrounding personnel, the purchase of new technology and supplies, and other areas of concern for the head of a naval yard and arsenal. See Shen 1880 and Shen 2005.

89. See e.g., a discussion of the opium stamp tax (*piaoshui*) in 1871 and its insufficiency to cover expenditures, Shen 2005 vol. 2, 331, 335–338.

90. Guo Songtao references Shen's successful actions against opium dens in LFZZ 03-0334-022, GX 3/6/20.

91. Zuo's memorials on the prohibition of opium are exclusively limited to the issue of poppy cultivation in the northwest, see e.g., Ma 1998, 275–276. On the anti-opium stance of Zhang Zhidong, see Liu 1996, 66–67. For Guo Songtao, Ma 1998 includes dozens of documents spanning from the 1870s to the 1880s.

92. Several of Guo's more extensive memorials on opium can be found in Ma 1998, 282–287.

93. Ma 1998, 285.

94. Ma 1998, 305–307.

95. The most detailed information on lijin rates for this period can be found in the Shantou trade reports, e.g., CMC Film Reel 5, "Swatow Trade Report for 1873," and Reel 7, "Swatow Trade Report for 1877."

96. CMC Film, Reel 4, "Report on the Trade at the Port of Amoy for the Year 1866."

97. CMC Film, Reel 4, "Report on the Trade at the Port of Amoy for the Year 1867."

98. CMC Film, Reel 5, "Report on the Trade at the Port of Amoy for the Year 1872."

99. CMC Film, Reel 5, "Report on the Trade at the Port of Amoy for the Year 1873."

100. Liu is vague about his reasons for being unable to increase the lijin before 1880 but cites the difficult coastline and fierce temperament of the locals. See Ma 1998, 305–307.

101. The opium trade in Shantou would not reach this magnitude again until the 1920s, if ever. CMC Film, Reel 7, "Report on the Trade at the Port of Swatow for the Year 1879."

102. CMC Film, Reel 8, "Report on the Trade at the Port of Swatow for the Year 1880."

103. *Shenbao* August 25, 1883.

104. CMC Film, Reel 17, "Amoy Trade Report for the Year 1885."

105. This was reported on extensively in *Shenbao*. See *Shenbao* March 9, 1886; *Shenbao* September 22, 1886.

106. FO 228/855, Shantou to Beijing, April 21, 1887, 20–42. Cai's name was spelled "Ts'ai Po-Ch'i" by the British consul in Shantou.

107. See e.g., Ma 1998, 305–307.

108. Wong 2000, 207.

109. CMC Film, Reel 4, "Report on Trade at the Port of Amoy for the Year 1870."

110. CMC Film, Reel 4, "Report on Trade at the Port of Amoy for the Year 1870."

111. FO 228/848, Separate, Amoy to Peking, January 17, 1887, "Intelligence Report for the year 1886."

112. In other words, after the implementation of the Additional Article, the only way to evade the lijin was to also evade the import tax, like the smugglers had attempted in Blacklock's case. Previously, people like Edwards could also make money selling opium that had paid the import tax but then evaded the lijin.

113. FO 228/848, No. 5, Amoy to Peking, January 31, 1887.

114. CMC Film, Reel 18, "Amoy Trade Report for the Year 1887."

115. FO 228/848, No. 5, Amoy to Peking, January 31, 1887.

116. FO 228/848, No. 5, Amoy to Peking, January 31, 1887.

117. CMC Film, Reel 18, "Foochow Trade Report for 1887."

118. FO 228/862, No. 4, Amoy to Peking, March 23, 1888, "Report on Trade for 1887."

119. "Report on Trade for 1887."

120. Luo 1936, 606.

121. Luo 1936, 332.

122. Ma 1998, 354–355.

123. Zhou 2010, part 3.

124. FO 228/862, No. 5, Amoy to Peking, 25 July 1888, Enclosure: Daotai Lin to Consul Forrest, July 14, 1888.

125. FO 228/862, No. 5, Amoy to Peking, 25 July 1888, Enclosure: Consul Forrest to Daotai Lin, July 24, 1888.

126. FO 228/886, No 4, Amoy to Peking, 20 March 1890.

127. FO 228/886, No. 21, Amoy to Peking, 5 September 1890, Enclosure No. 2, "Proclamation by Wu, Taotai of Amoy. 4th February 1889."

128. FO 228/886, No. 24, Amoy to Peking, 3 October 1890; FO 228/1766, No. 46,

Amoy to Peking, December 1, 1910, Enclosure 7, "Petition from opium shops to consul, Nov. 1910."

129. There is a vast scholarship on opium in nineteenth-century Southeast Asia. Some good places to start: Rush 2014; Trocki 1990 and 2012; Dick, Sullivan, and Butcher 1993; and Wright 2014.

130. Rush 1990, see especially chapter 3.

131. Trocki 2000, 82.

132. Trocki 1990, 76–78.

133. For Hokkien-Teochow competition in the Straits Settlements see Trocki 1990 and Blythe 1969; for Shanghai, see Goodman 1995.

Chapter 4

1. FO 228/1766, No. 32, Amoy to Peking, September 20, 1910, Enclosure 2, "Proclamation of Haifang Ting, 1 September 1910."

2. FO 228/1766, No. 46, Amoy to Peking, December 1, 1910, Enclosure 7, "Petition from opium shops to consul, Nov. 1910."

3. FO 228/1766, No. 46, Amoy to Peking, December 1, 1910, Enclosure 8, "Consul to Taotai."

4. "Petition from opium shops to consul, Nov. 1910."

5. USDS (1910–1929), 893.114, Reel 113, Amoy to Secy. of State, July 20, 1911, "Report: Anti-Opium Society in Amoy."

6. USDS (1910–1929), 893.114, Reel 113, Amoy to Secy. of State, July 20, 1911, "Report: Anti-Opium Society in Amoy."

7. See Baumler 2008; Madancy 2003; Slack 2001.

8. LFZZ 03-7403-008, GX 32/10/6.

9. Trocki 1999, 126. For this data, Trocki cites Lin 1993.

10. "Decennial Report for Amoy, 1902–11," 102.

11. "Decennial Report for Amoy, 1902–11," 102, 344.

12. FO 228/1797, Separate, Amoy to Peking, October 10, 1911.

13. "Decennial Report for Amoy, 1902–11," 104.

14. "Decennial Report for Amoy, 1902–11," 337.

15. FO 228/1766, No. 46, Amoy to Peking, Dec 1, 1910, Enclosure 7, "Petition from opium shops to consul, Nov. 1910."

16. *North China Herald*, December 11, 1903.

17. ZPZZ 04-01-01-1104-038, XT 1/2/24.

18. *Shenbao* October 5, 1908.

19. FO 228/1659, Separate, Amoy to Peking, April 16, 1907.

20. *Shenbao* September 25, 1908.

21. *Shenbao* January 3, 1909.

22. *North China Herald* January 9, 1909; *New York Times* December 28, 1908.

23. *Law Kang Po* October 3, 1903, f1–4.

24. *Law Kang Po* November 8, 1903, f3.

25. *Shenbao* August 26, 1908.

26. FO 228/1724, Separate, Amoy to Peking, October 26, 1909, Enclosure: "Intelligence Report for September Quarter 1909."

27. As Zhou Zifeng notes, even today certain neighborhoods (eg. 石浔街、石浔巷、打铁街、担水巷) in the older districts of Xiamen are occupied by huge proportions of people with the Wu surname. See, Zhou 2005, 245. See also Qiu 1984: 141–147.

28. See e.g., Ji Baizai and Ji Jinru, Zhou 2005, 251.

29. "Wu Chen erxing da xiedou (The great lineage feud of the Wu and Chen surnames)," *Shenbao*, No. 12, Vol. 13675, March 7, 1911.

30. "Wei xian le zhuo junzhuang (County officials dispatched to confiscate weapons)," *Shenbao*, Vol. 12, No. 13838, August 17, 1911.

31. Zhou 2005, 251.

32. FO 228/1757, No. 17, Amoy to HM Peking, May 10, 1910, Enclosure: "Memorandum. Murder of Wang Pu-ch'ih; Sub-prefect Tung T'ing-jui bribed by murderer to hush up the case; Popular indignation and action."

33. FO 228/1589, Separate, Amoy to Peking, April 11, 1905, Enclosure: "Municipal Council Kulangsu. Report for the Year Ending 31st December 1904."

34. Zhou 2005, 248.

35. *Taiwan Hanwen riri xin bao*, December 21, 1906. Cited in Zhou 2005, 249.

36. Inspection Office, or jiancha ju (the consul wrote "Ch'in-ch'a'chu"). FO 228/1724, Separate, Amoy to Peking, October 26, 1909, Enclosure: "Intelligence Report for September Quarter 1909."

37. FO 228/1903, Separate, Amoy to Peking, October 17, 1914, Enclosure: "Intelligence Report for September Quarter 1914."

38. Because of the shifting political landscape during the early-twentieth century, the names of various state and civil organizations like the Anti-Opium Society can be quite confusing. In this chapter, I generally distinguish between the Xiamen Anti-Opium Society, the Fujian Anti-Opium Society (headquartered in Fuzhou), and the National Anti-Opium Society (headquartered in Beijing).

39. Madancy 2003, 99.

40. Madancy 2003, 147.

41. FO 228/1797, No. 29, Amoy to Peking, November 21, 1911.

42. "Report: Anti-Opium Society in Amoy."

43. "Report: Anti-Opium Society in Amoy."

44. "Report: Anti-Opium Society in Amoy."

45. FO 228/1797, No. 27, Amoy to Peking, November 6, 1911.

46. FO 228/1797, No. 29, Amoy to Peking, November 21, 1911.

47. FO 228/1797, No. 29, Amoy to Peking, November 21, 1911.

48. USDS 1910–29, 893.114/43, Reel 113, No. 393, Amoy to Secy. of State, July 13, 1912.

49. USDS 1910–29, 893.114/43, Reel 113, No. 393, Amoy to Secy. of State, July 13, 1912.

50. USDS 1910–29, 893.114/43, Reel 113, No. 393, Amoy to Secy. of State, July 13, 1912.

51. USDS 1910–29, 893.114/87, Reel 113, Amoy to Secy. of State, May 22, 1913.

52. USDS 1910–29, 893.114/92, Reel 113, Amoy to Secy. of State, June 18, 1913.

53. USDS 1910–29, 893.114/104, Reel 113, Amoy to Secretary of State, December 15, 1913, Enclosure 1.

54. USDS 1910–29, 893.114/96, Reel 113, No. 8, Amoy to Peking, July 12, 1913.

55. FO 228/2455, No. 59, F.O. 329/13. Peking to W.C.P., August 21, 1913.

56. FO 228/2455, No. 51, Shanghai 192/13, No. 100, Shanghai to Peking, August 7, 1913.

57. See e.g., *Registry Files 1933–1946*, (League of Nations Archive: Geneva), Box 4822, Sec 12, Doc 1281, Dossier 388: Illicit traffic between USA and China by the Ezra Brothers. Hereafter LON 1933–1946.

58. FO 228/2455, No. 17, To Amoy, July 18, 1913, Enclosure 2 in No. 8 (draft), "Reply of HM Consul at Amoy to the General Anti-Opium Association of Fujian."

59. See marginalia on "Reply of HM Consul at Amoy to the General Anti-Opium Association of Fujian."

60. FO 228/2455, No. 84, Foochow to Peking, July 29, 1913, Enclosure: "Letter from the General Anti-Opium Society of Fukien to Mr. Consul Werner, 14 June 1913."

61. "Letter from the General Anti-Opium Society of Fukien to Mr. Consul Werner, 14 June 1913."

62. *Straits Times* August 22, 1913, 3.

63. FO 228/1903, Separate, Amoy to Peking, July 10, 1914, Enclosure: "Intelligence Report for the June Quarter, 1914."

64. USDS 1910–29, 893.114/81, Reel 113, Amoy to Secy. of State, April 7, 1913.

65. See chapter 8 in Madancy 2003.

66. The $6 figure is from *Straits Times* August 22, 1913, 3.

67. "Decennial Report for Amoy, 1912–21," 153–154.

68. USDS 1910–29, 893.114/192, Reel 113, Foochow to Secretary of State, December 18, 1918.

69. USDS 1910–29, 893.114/192, Reel 113, Foochow to Secretary of State, December 18, 1918.

70. USDS 1910–29, 893.114/232, Reel 114, Foochow to Secretary of State, 19 May 1919.

71. USDS 1910–29, 893.114/283, Reel 114, Amoy to Secretary of State, April 4, 1921, Enclosure: "Memorandum on collection of poppy cultivation taxes in sections of Fukien province near Amoy, 4 April 1921."

72. LON 1919–1927, Box R706, Sec. 12A, Doc. 13272, Dossier 1717, W.R. Williams, "Report from Branch Associations, Fukien Branch, First Annual Report," in Arthur Sowerby, ed., *International Anti-Opium Association, Peking. Report for the Year Ending February 28, 1921*.

73. USDS 1910–29, 893.114/341, Reel 114, Amoy to Secretary of State, November 3, 1921.

74. The story is related in a longer history of the Yakou militia in the 1920s, see Shi 1995, 94–95.

75. *Duli Qingnian*, volume 1, issue 6, 1926, *Minguo qikan ku* (Republican Periodical Database 1911–1949).

76. LON 1919–1927, Sec 12A, Doc 20286x, Dossier 20286, "Letter from International Anti-Opium Association, Peking: Transmitting information regarding opium condition in Fukien Province during the present season, 21 January 1924."

77. Field 1924.

78. FO 371/5306, No. 120, Peking to Foreign Office, March 8, 1920.

79. Lin 1923, 28.

80. USDS 1910–29, 893.114/423, Reel 115, Amoy to Secretary of State, November 24, 1922.

81. FO 228/3281, Dossier 183O, Intelligence Report for December Quarter of 1922, Amoy, January 8, 1923.

82. FO 228/3281, Dossier 183O, Intelligence Report for September Quarter 1923, Amoy, September 27, 1923.

83. *Shenbao* October 27, 1921, 10.

84. LON 1919–1927, Sec 12A, Doc 20286x, Dossier 20286, 1924–29: "Letter from International Anti-Opium Association, Peking: Transmitting information regarding opium condition in Fukien Province during the present season, 21 January 1924."

85. IOR/L/E/7/1373, File 175, E & O 7561/1926, "Opium Cultivation and Traffic in China: An Investigation in 1925–1926 by the International Anti-Opium Association Peking."

86. See Baumler 2008, chapter 6; Slack 2001, chapter 5.

87. The fullest accounting of Xiamen's political history during the period 1911–1938 that I have found is in Hong 1983, 86–88.

88. Zhonghua 1928, 32.

89. "Fujian yanhuo (The Fujian Opium Tragedy)," *Xinmin qianfeng* 6 (1931), 20–21.

90. *Jiancha yuan gongbao* 1932, 95–101.

91. " *Nanyang Siang Pau* June 28, 1932, 14.

92. Wang 1982, 41–59.

93. *Nanyang Siang Pau* June 28, 1932, 14.

94. *Shenbao* August 31, 1907.

95. USDS (1910–1929), 893.114, Reel 113, Amoy to Secy. of State, July 20, 1911, "Report: Anti-Opium Society in Amoy."

96. FO 228/1903, Separate, Amoy to Peking, July 10, 1914, Enclosure: "Intelligence Report for the June Quarter, 1914."

97. "Intelligence Report for the June Quarter, 1914."

98. USDS 1910–29, 893.114/476, Reel 115, Xiamen to Secretary of State, February 8, 1924, Enclosure: "Translation of General Tsang Chih Ping's proclamation regarding es-

tablishment of Special Bureau to deal with suppression of opium and present illegal sale of the drug."

99. FO 228/3281, Dossier 1830, Intelligence Report for December and March Quarters of 1923–4, Amoy, March 13, 1924.

100. LON 1919–1927, Box R784, Sec 12A, Doc 38720, Dossier 33778, "Report to the Council on the Work of the Sixth Session. August 4th to 14th, 1924."

101. "Minsheng zhi jinyan tan (Discussion of Opium Prohibition in Fujian Province)", *Shenbao*, October 27, 1921, 10.

102. "Xiamen yapian guanmai yi kai ju (Government sale of opium in Xiamen has begun)," *Nanyang Siang Pau*, February 29, 1924, 7.

103. FO 262/1585, No. 150, Peking to Foreign Office, March 9, 1923, Enclosure: "Intelligence Report for Foochow, December 1922."

104. "Yi juan liang bao zhi fenzheng (A conflict over one tax with two farmers)," *Nanyang Siang Pau*, May 30, 1924, 7.

105. "Xiamen haijun caizheng wenti jiejue (The Xiamen Naval financial problems solved)," *Shenbao*, 5/19/1924, 7.

106. IOR/L/E/7/1373, File 175, E & O 7561/1926, "Opium Cultivation and Traffic in China: an Investigation in 1925–1926 by the International Anti-Opium Association Peking."

107. *Nanyang Siang Pau* March 22, 1926, 10.

108. *Duli Qingnian* 1926.

109. LON 1919–1927, Box R759, Sec 12A, Doc 20286, Dossier 20286, "Opium Cultivation and Traffic in China: An Investigation in 1925–1926 by the International Anti-Opium Association, Peking."

110. Marshall 1976, 19–48. See especially pp. 20–22. Edward Slack offers a more nuanced and detailed version of the story and ultimately agrees that control over China's opium supply and distribution was a major priority of Chiang Kai-shek's government. See Slack 2001, especially chapter 5.

111. *Heshan jubao* November 1, 1934.

112. *Shenbao* March 9, 1928, 15.

113. *Nanyang Siang Pau* July 20, 1931, 14.

114. The classic account of the Fujian Rebellion is Dorril 1969, 31–53.

115. On the anti-opium reputation of the Nineteenth Route Army, Baumler 2008, 107. A British memorandum forwarded to the League of Nations also described the Nineteenth Route Army as having taken "effective steps to put a stop to the growing of opium in Fukien," before going on to describe Ye Qinghe's sale of Persian opium to the same army, see LON 1933–1946, Box R4868, Sec 12, Doc 1477, Dossier 526, Cultivation of and trade in opium in China during 1932, "Memorandum on opium situation in certain provinces forwarded from the Director of the Opium Traffic and Social Questions Sections to Sir Malcolm Delevingne of the British Home Office, 26 January, 1934."

116. For the relationship between Du and the Nineteenth Route Army during the 1932

Japanese invasion of Shanghai, see Marshall 1976, 33. On Du Yuesheng, including his activities in the state-protected opium trade under the Guomindang, see Martin 1996; Slack 2001, 110–111, 121–125.

117. "Memorandum on opium situation in certain provinces forwarded from the Director of the Opium Traffic and Social Questions Sections to Sir Malcolm Delevingne of the British Home Office, 26 January, 1934."

118. *Shenbao* June 22, 1932, 10. See also SMA Q90-1-921, Lixin huiji shiwu suo guanyu guomin yaofang youxian gongsi zhangmu shencha, daiban qiye zhuce, shangbiao zhuce deng wenjian (Registration forms of the United Dispensary as submitted by the Lixin Accountancy Firm), 1932–1935. Hong Buren names Ye Zhensheng as Ye Qinghe's alias in Hong 1983b 47–68, 65. Jonathan Marshall speculates the reason for the raids on Du Yuesheng's morphine factories in mid-1932 was related to a backlog of unpaid bribes, see Marshall 1976, 34.

119. Hong 1983b, see 53–57. See also *Shenbao* July 13,1932, 15.

120. "The Ezra Case," Elisabeth Smith Friedman Collection, Box 6, Folder 25, George C. Marshall Archives.

121. LON 1933–1946, Box 4887, Sec 12, Doc 11019, Dossier 793, Documents presented to be discussed at the 5th session of the permanent sub-committee on seizures, May 1934, "OCS/Confidential/19. Memorandum on Illicit Traffic in Persian Opium submitted by the Representative of the United States to the Sub-Committee on Seizures on May 16th, 1934."

122. Hong 1983b, 57–60.

123. *Judu yuekan* 1936, 1–5.

124. International Military Tribunal for the Far East, Transcript of Proceedings September 4, 1946, Document 9506, "Report of the United States Attaché at Shanghai," April 20, 1936, 4,824.

125. *Heshan jubao* September 11, 1934.

126. *Heshan jubao* April 21, 1935.

127. Baumler 2008, 186–188.

128. Hong 1983b, 60–62.

129. Hong 1983b, 62–63.

130. Slack 2001, 140–141

131. Hanson 1936, 425.

132. *Judu yuekan* 1936, 1.

133. CO 825/20/6, No. 3, Smuggling of opium from Hong Kong to Amoy, 1936.

134. *Shenbao* March 13, 1937, 10.

135. Hong 1983b, 63.

136. *Shenbao* March 13, 1937, 10.

137. *Nanyang Siang Pau* November 20, 1935.

138. On the Six Year Plan, see Baumler 2008, chapter 7; Slack 2001, conclusion.

139. See *China Weekly Review* July 17, 1937; and *North China Herald* June 30, 1937.

140. Fujian's governor Chen Yi claimed to have been sick and was only just recently informed that Ye Qinghe and Chen Shangcai had converted to Japanese citizenship. Still, other partners in the monopoly (Zeng Houkun, Lin Gun, etc.) were Japanese citizens from the outset. Indeed, a national publication had referred to the operators of the Lutong Company as Japanese protected "hoodlums" (*liumang*) and exposed Ye's conversion to Japanese citizenship a year earlier in 1936. See Academia Historica, Jiang Zhongzheng zongtong wenwu (Materials from President Chiang Kai-shek) 002-090105-00001-236, June 17, 1937; *Judu yuekan* 1936, 1–5.

141. Hong 1983b, 66.

142. See figure A.5 in Kim 2020, 234.

143. On the Guomindang and opium revenue, see Baumler 2008 and Slack 2001; for the CCP opium monopoly in Yan'an, see Chen 1995.

144. IOR/L/E/7/1373, File 175, E & O 7561/1926, "Opium Cultivation and Traffic in China: an Investigation in 1925–1926 by the International Anti-Opium Association Peking."

Chapter 5

1. LON 1919–1927, Box R766, Doc 42774x, Dossier 24297, "Seizures at Hong Kong of raw opium, November 1 1924, and of prepared opium from the SS 'Kutsang.'"

2. LON 1919–1927, Box R759, Sec 12A, Doc 20286, Dossier 20286, 1922–26, "Opium Cultivation and Traffic in China: An Investigation in 1925–1926 by the International Anti-Opium Association, Peking."

3. See Miles 2020, chapter 3.

4. FO 228/1589, Separate, Amoy to Peking, April 11, 1905, Enclosure: "Intelligence Report for Nov. 1904—Jan. 1905,"; Numbers for 1907 compiled from FO 228/1659 and FO 228/1692.

5. FO 228/1903 and FO 228/1941, Intelligence Reports for 1914.

6. Miles 2020, 98.

7. Philippines Census Office 1918, 31.

8. *Fujian qiaopi dang'an wenxian huibian* (Fujian Qiaopi Documents Collection), Vol. 16, ed. Fujian Provincial Archives, (Beijing: Guojia tushu guan chuban she, 2017), "19330810, No. 0379, Siming No. 1 Post Office Monthly Report for July 1933," 451.

9. The following is based on an extensive report by the US Consul in Xiamen, USDS 1910–29, 893.114/293, Reel 114, Xiamen to Secretary of State, April 30, 1921.

10. Kim 2020 provides an overview of the transition to opium prohibition in French Indochina and British Rangoon and Malaya. On the Philippines, see Foster 2000. For the Netherlands Indies, see Rush 1990 and Tagliacozzo 2005.

11. On the history of interstate opium controls during this period, see Rimner 2018.

12. In 1920, for example, one tael of domestic opium in Xiamen cost around $2.50, while the Hong Kong opium monopoly was retailing opium for $15 per tael. See "Hongkong and Opium," *Canton Times* (1919–1920), August 24, 1920, 2.

13. *Straits Times Weekly Issue* September 17, 1889, 8.

14. *Singapore Free Press and Mercantile Advertiser* October 7, 1889, 426.

15. *Singapore Free Press and Mercantile Advertiser* November 19, 1889, 610.

16. Kim 2020, 122.

17. Opium Investigation Committee 1905, 94–95.

18. Opium Investigation Committee 1905, 93–94.

19. Opium Investigation Committee 1905, 93–94.

20. *Straits Times* September 30, 1904, 5.

21. *Eastern Daily Mail and Straits Morning Advertiser* October 5, 1907, 3; *Eastern Daily Mail and Straits Morning Advertiser* October 9, 1907, 3.

22. *Eastern Daily Mail and Straits Morning Advertiser* October 10, 1907, 2.

23. Trocki 2000, 79–105, 98.

24. On the Opium Revenue Reserve Fund, see Kim 2020, chapter 5. The $8 million figure comes from Trocki 2000, 98.

25. *Straits Times* July 2, 1924, 3.

26. *Straits Times* January 26, 1926, 9.

27. *Singapore Free Press and Mercantile Advertiser* June 7, 1926, 12.

28. See Trocki 2000, 98.

29. LON 1928–1932, Box 3170, Doc 2491, Dossier 2491 (3), "List of Seizures communicated to the secretariat. Summary of Illicit Transactions and Seizures reported to the League of nations between July 1st and September 1st, 1931, No. 341."

30. LON 1928–1932, Box 3170, Doc 2491, Dossier 2491 (4), "List of Seizures communicated to the secretariat, Jan 1st to Dec 31st, 1932, Summary of Illicit Transactions and Seizures Reported to the Secretariat of the League of Nations between October 1st and December 31st, 1932."

31. *Straits Times* July 4, 1934, 12.

32. LON 1933–1940, Box 4848, Sec 12, Doc 15391, Dossier 388, "Seizures of Raw and Prepared Opium in the Straits Settlements, Enclosure in Report of May 1938: Photograph showing method of concealment of 'Red Lion' Chandu in drums of 'Caustic Soda.'"

33. Scheltema 1907, 79–112, 104. See also Rush 1990; Shen 2013; Tagliacozzo 2005.

34. Rush 1990, 241.

35. Rush 1990, 242.

36. Scheltema 1907, 244. Cited in Tagliacozzo 2005, 188.

37. LON 1919–1927, Box R768, Doc 48571x, Dossier 24297, "Seizures of opium at Surabaya, 26 August 1925."

38. LON 1928–1932, Box 3170, Doc 2491, Dossier 2491 (1), "List of Illicit Transactions and Seizures Reported to the Secretariat of the League of Nations since November 8th, 1928."

39. LON 1928–1932, Box 3170, Doc 2491, Dossier 2491 (1), "List of Illicit Transactions and Seizures Reported to the Secretariat of the League of Nations since November 8th, 1928."

40. LON 1928–1932, Box 3170, Doc 2491, Dossier 2491 (3), "Summary of Illicit Transactions and Seizures Reported to the League of Nations between October 9th 1930 and March 31st 1931, No. 156."

41. LON 1933–1946, Box 4883, Sec 12, Doc 1389, Dossier 793, "Summary of Illicit Transactions and Seizures Reported to the Secretariat of the League of Nations between April 1st and June 30th, 1935."

42. LON 1933–1946, Box 4883, Sec 12, Doc 1389, Dossier 793, "Summary of Illicit Transactions and Seizures Reported to the Secretariat of the League of Nations between April 1st and June 30th, 1935."

43. LON 1933–1946, Box 4883, Sec 12, Doc 1389, Dossier 793, "Summary of Illicit Transactions and Seizures Reported to the Secretariat of the League of Nations between October 1st and December 31st, 1934."

44. For example, see LON 1928–1932, Box 3170, Doc 2491, Dossier 2491 (1), "List of Seizures communicated to the Secretariat since November 8th, 1928." See also LON 1933–1946, Box 4887, Sec 12, Doc 11019, Dossier 793, "Memorandum on Illicit Traffic in Persian Opium submitted by the Representative of the United States to the Sub-Committee on Seizures on May 16th, 1934."

45. LON 1933–1946, Box 4887, Sec 12, Doc 11019, Dossier 793, "Memorandum on Illicit Traffic in Persian Opium submitted by the Representative of the United States to the Sub-Committee on Seizures on May 16th, 1934."

46. International Military Tribunal for the Far East, Transcript of Proceedings September 4, 1946, Document 9507, "Report of the United States Attaché at Shanghai," November 9, 1934, 4,823.

47. LON 1933–1946, Box 4844–4845, Sec 21, Doc 10051, Dossier 388, "Monthly Seizures: Hong Kong, Seizure of 326 kgs. 445 grs. of Raw Iranian Opium at Hong Kong on February 6th, 1936."

48. CO 859/15/5, 18. F 6848/57/87, "Drug Situation in Amoy," July 8, 1939.

49. CO 859/15/5, 18. F 6848/57/87, "Drug Situation in Amoy," July 8, 1939.

50. The definitive work on US opium policy in the Philippines is Foster 2000, 253–273.

51. Opium Investigation Committee 1905, 165.

52. International Opium Commission, 1909, 26.

53. International Opium Commission 1909, 23.

54. LON 1933–1940, Box R4868, Sec 12, Doc 3465, Dossier 510, 1930–1931, "Annual Reports on Traffic in Opium: Philippines."

55. International Opium Commission 1909, 24.

56. *North China Herald* April 5, 1913, 15.

57. *Los Angeles Times* December 4, 1920.

58. FO 262/1634, Confidential No. 3, Severn to Amery, March 20, 1925.

59. "Valuable Opium Is Seized in Manila," 1920.

60. *Straits Times* May 2, 1929, 12; and *Fujian qiaopi dang'an wenxian huibian* (Fujian

Qiaopi Documents Collection), Vol. 16, "19280930, No. 0333, Xiamen No. 1 Post Office Monthly Report, September 1928," 259.

61. LON 1933–1940, Box R4868, Sec 12, Doc 3465, Dossier 510, 1930–1931, "Annual Reports on Traffic in Opium: Philippines."

62. LON 1933–1946, Box 4883, Sec 12, Doc 1389, Dossier 793, "Summary of Illicit Transactions and Seizures Reported to the Secretariat of the League of Nations between October 1st and December 31st, 1933."

63. LON 1928–1932, Box R3107, Sec 12, Doc 1383, Dossier 157, Jacket 46, "Seizures of Drugs in the United States of America and the Philippine Islands, 24 July 1930, No. 11, 7 Apr 1930."

64. LON 1928–1932, Box R3107, Sec 12, Doc 1383, Dossier 157, Jacket 46, Enclosure to OC 1242: "Filipino Charges Traffic in Opium," *New York Times,* March 17, 1931.

65. LON 1928–1932, Box R3107, Sec 12, Doc 1383, Dossier 157, Jacket 46, "OC 1242, Seizures of Drugs in the United States of America and the Philippine Islands, 24 July 1930, No. 11, 7 Apr 1930."

66. *Nanyang Siang Pau* November 28, 1929, 14.

67. *Nanyang Siang Pau* September 6, 1929, 10.

68. The raid on the Shenzhou dispensary is also mentioned briefly in IOR/R/20/A/3495, File 963, "Report on the investigation of the problem of smuggling cocaine into India from the Far East," 1932; and USDS 1910–29, 893.114 Narcotics/68, Reel 116, Xiamen to Secretary of State, September 4, 1929.

69. See, e.g., *Nanyang Siang Pau* December 27, 1930, 9; FO 262/1634, No. 48, British Embassy Tokyo to Japanese Government, April 17, 1925.

70. Cheong's name was found on two different consignments of cocaine and morphine captured in Rangoon, one in September 1928 and another in October 1929. See CO 825/10/12, F 358/11/87, No. 1768, HM Minister in Peking to HM Principal Secretary of State for Foreign Affairs, December 2, 1930.

71. CO 825/10/12, F162/22/87, No 1, Jones to Lampson, January 8, 1931.

72. Hong 1983, 58.

73. *Nanyang Siang Pau* September 6, 1929, 10.

74. *Nanyang Siang Pau* July 20, 1931, 14.

75. Chen was arrested together with Ye in 1937 for irregularities associated with the operation of the Guomindang "special product" monopoly in southern Fujian. See Academia Historica Online, President Chiang Kai-shek Archive, 002-090105-00001-236, June 17, 1937.

76. For Ye's suspected ties to the cocaine, morphine, and opium trade from Xiamen to British colonial Southeast Asia, "Report on the investigation of the problem of smuggling cocaine into India from the Far East," 1932. For his links to other branches of the export trade, including opium and heroin to the United States, see e.g. LON 1933–1946, Box 4822, Sec 12, Doc 1281, Dossier 388, "Illicit traffic between USA and China by the Ezra Brothers."

77. FO 228/1150, Separate, October 25, 1894.

78. "Decennial Report for Amoy, 1902–1911," 102.

79. "Decennial Report for Amoy, 1902–1911," 102.

80. International Opium Commission 1909, 68–69.

81. *Heshan jubao* March 1, 1935.

82. *Xiamen dabao* June 12, 1936.

83. *Xiamen dabao* May 21, 1936; *Huaqiao ribao* January 31, 1934.

84. *Fujian sheng minzheng ting* (The Fujian Provincial Bureau of Civil Affairs), Fuzhou: Fujian Provincial Archives, 11.7.5174, 1939. Hereafter cited as FPA 11.

85. *Minzhong ribao* May 30, 1929.

86. Personal names in this case have been changed at the request of the staff at the Fujian Provincial Archive. *Zhu Min suijing zhuren gongshu* (The Office of the Pacification Commissioner of Fujian), Fuzhou: Fujian Provincial Archives, 80 (Hereafter FPA 80) 3.462, 1939.

87. FPA 80.3.376, 80.3.378, 80.3.380, 80.3.392, 80.3.409, 80.3.431, 80.3.435, 80.3.438, 80.3.439, 80.3.454, 80.3.457, 80.3.462, 80.3.586, all from 1938, and 80.3.552 from 1939.

88. e.g.. the Ding brothers, see FPA 80.3.409, 1938.

89. e.g., Li Chi and Li Tou, who died of dysentery and tuberculosis in 1936, see FPA 80.3.431, 1937.

90. Personal names in this case have been changed at the request of the staff at the Fujian Provincial Archive. "Wet" (濕), was most likely a paste made from powdered morphine, different from the liquid morphine packaged in bottles. I am uncertain as to the exact nature of paper (白紙) morphine. FPA 80.3 378, 1938.

91. *Haiguan zongshu* (The Maritime Customs Central Office), Fuzhou: Fujian Provincial Archives, 69.1.57, No. 11 Circular from IG Aglen, January 17, 1914. Hereafter cited as FPA 69.

92. FPA 69.1.57, No. 11 Circular from IG Aglen, 17 Jan 1914.

93. FPA 69.1.57, No. 11 Circular from IG Aglen, 17 Jan 1914.

94. The case is detailed in a variety of government and media sources. One of the better reports on the case, including copies of the seized correspondence, is available in the British National Archives (MEPO 3/1044, C-1, No. 7, Central Officer's Special Report, March 26, 1923.). The estimated dosage is based on the British Pharmacopia's response to a request from the *Manchester Guardian* (1901–1959), March 16, 1923, 9–10.

95. Tong Say, or Dongxi, (東西). MEPO 3/1044, No. 11, Exhibit 1, "Agreement between Tong Say Bros. Coy and H.M.F. Humphrey Ltd.," September 6, 1922.

96. FO 262/1585, No. 336, Wellerby to Palairet, August 21, 1923.

97. MEPO 3/1044, No. 11, Exhibit 2, "Letter from Tong Say Bros. Co. to Humphrey," November 7, 1922.

98. MEPO 3/1044, No. 11, Exhibit 5, "Private Code and List of useful phrases to be used in Code," 1923.

99. FO 262/1585, No. 336, Wellerby to Palairet, August 21, 1923, "Memorandum on the Drug Trade."

100. LON 1928–1932, Box 3172, Doc 36570, Dossier 2491, O.C. 1415, "Part played in the illicit traffic by forwarding agents," April 11, 1932.

101. FO 228/3369, Series I, Dossier 526, Opium Vol. XIII, No. 55, Opium Trial, Judgement and Documents Seized, March 17, 1925, "Telegram from Gwanho & Co., 51 Canton Rd. Shanghai. to F. Hoffman-La Roche & Co., Basle."

102. FO 228/3369, Series I, Dossier 526, Opium Vol. XIII, No. 55, Opium Trial, Judgement and Documents Seized, March 17, 1925, "Telegram from Gwanho & Co., 51 Canton Rd. Shanghai. to F. Hoffman-La Roche & Co., Basle."

103. A full list of the documents is provided in the index to FO 228/3369 Series I, Dossier 526, Opium Vol. XIII, No. 55, Opium Trial, Judgement and Documents Seized, March 17, 1925.

104. The article also notes there is a $3,000 reward out for Ye's capture. *North China Herald* September 26, 1934.

105. Dikötter, Laaman, and Zhou 2004, 169; Martin 1996, 141; Wakeman 1995, 264–265; Hong 1983, 47–68.

106. SMA Q90-1-921, Lixin huiji shiwu suo guanyu guomin yaofang youxian gongsi zhangmu shencha, daiban qiye zhuce, shangbiao zhuce deng wenjian (Registration forms of the United Dispensary as submitted by the Lixin Accountancy Firm), 1932–1935; for Ye's use of this name to register as a Japanese citizen, see Hong 1983b, 64.

107. Hong 1983b, 54. The *Shenbao* accounts of the raid on Ye's morphine operations in 1932 also discusses the employment of a Japanese scientist named Nakamura. See e.g., *Shenbao* June 22, 1932, 10.

108. SMA Q90-1-921.

109. Hanson 1936.

110. Xu and Li 1995, 143–146.

111. "Danhe an (Impeachment case)," *Jiancha yuan gongbao*, Chinese Periodical Full-text Database (1911–1949), No. 15, 1932, 95–10.

112. Xu 1992, 137–142.

113. On cocaine "trampoline" between Colombia, Mexico, and the United States, see e.g., Pasternak and Jehl 1989. For an extended discussion of the dynamics in Mexico that supported this system see Allen 2005, chapter 5.

114. "Decennial Report for Amoy, 1902–11," 102.

115. FO 881/10017X, "CHINA: International Opium Conference Proces-Verbaux, 1911–1912."

116. International Opium Commission 1909, 68–69.

117. Opium Investigation Committee 1905, 112–118.

118. *Singapore Free Press and Mercantile Advertiser* November 6, 1908.

119. Mills 2007, 345–362.

120. FO 228/1757, Separate, Tours to Jordan, March 3, 1910.

121. *Straits Times* August 15, 1930.

122. CO 129/498/14, No. 268, Clementi to Amery, October 27, 1926, "Illicit traffic in opium and drugs."

123. CO 825/10/15, F 4294/22/87, July 13, 1931, "Opium monopoly and drug smuggling in China."

124. IOR/R/20/A/3495, File 963, James Slattery, "Report on the investigation of the problem of smuggling cocaine into India from the Far East," 1932. Hereafter Slattery 1932.

125. Slattery 1932.

126. LON 1928–1932, Box 3172, Sec 12, Doc 17523, Dossier 2491, O.C. 1128, "Notes on seizures of manufactured drugs," December 13, 1929.

127. Slattery 1932.

128. Slattery 1932.

129. Karch 1999, 151. See also Yang 2021.

130. Karch 1999, 147, 156.

131. CO 825/13/4, No. 7, Under Secretary of State for Foreign Affairs to Under Secretary of State for the Colonies, October 18, 1932.

132. Karch 1999, 155–156.

133. LON 1928–1934, Box R3252, Sec 12A, Doc 17901, Dossier 1122, "Stocks Discrepancy in Japanese Narcotics Declarations, 1932."

134. CO 825/13/4, No. 5. Under Secretary of State for Foreign Affairs to Under Secretary of State for the Colonies, September 10, 1932.

135. FO 262/1725, No. 522108–2, Malcome Delevingne at Home Office to Under Secretary of State, Foreign Office, July 16, 1929, "Memorandum on Japanese cocaine seized in the Far East."

136. Slattery 1932.

137. CO 129-498-14, No. 2, Governor Clementi of Hong Kong to Lieutenant Colonel Amery, August 20, 1926.

138. With the exception of Hathras, located in the landlocked province of Uttar Pradesh and over 1,300 km inland from Calcutta.

139. CO 129-498-14, No. 2, Governor Clementi of Hong Kong to Lieutenant Colonel Amery, August 20, 1926.

140. CO 323/1091/8, Confidential, F 1635/1446/87, MacKillop to Morris, April 16, 1930.

141. Slattery 1932.

142. Hanson 1936.

143. Hanson 1936.

144. CO 323/1091/8, Confidential, F 1635/1446/87, MacKillop to Morris, April 16, 1930.

145. See e.g., FO 228/1869, Consul Little to H.M. Minister in Peking, January 21, 1913; and FO 228/1903, Consul Turner in Amoy to H.M. Minister Jordan in Peking, July 10, 1914.

146. FO 228/3281, Consul Eastes, October 7, 1922, "Intelligence Report for September Quarter, 1922."

147. Slattery 1932.

148. Slattery 1932.

149. Slattery 1932.

Chapter 6

1. Lin 1936, 26–28.

2. *Xiamen waishi zhi* (Gazetteer of Foreign Affairs in Xiamen) 2001, 10.

3. USDS 1844–1906, Vol. 14, No. 45, Consul Johnson to ASOS Hill, March 14, 1899.

4. USDS 1844–1906, Vol. 14, No. 87, Consul Johnson to ASOS Hill, August 31, 1900.

5. USDS 1844–1906, Vol. 15, No. 10, Anderson to ASOS Loomis, March 20, 1905.

6. USDS 1844–1906, Vol. 15, No. 59, Lupten to ASOS Bacon, November 19, 1905.

7. USDS 1844–1906, Vol. 15, No. 59, Lupten to ASOS Bacon, November 19, 1905.

8. FO 228/1692, Separate, O'Brien-Butler to Jordan, April 15, 1908.

9. According to historian Barbara Brooks, Japan's strategy in south China was "designed to aid the Japanese to build up the presence of colonial citizens in southern China." Brooks 2000, 111. See also Ong 2021, chapter 4.

10. See for example Working Group 1983.

11. Inoue 1993.

12. "Xia Ri lingshu juxing jimin dengji (Japanese consul in Xiamen initiates registration of jimin)," *Shenbao*, June 1, 1934, 12.

13. Ong 1999, 6.

14. FO 228/111, No. 55, Sullivan to Bonham, November 28, 1850.

15. In a mixed case from February 1889, Xiamen's top legal official ruled that a Singapore comprador (Yan Suanshi) living near Xiamen was Chinese, on the grounds that if he were British, he would have worn British clothing and lived in the city. Chen 2009, vol. 1, 201–216.

16. USDS 1844–1906, Vol. 15, No. 9, Anderson to ASOS Loomis, Mar 20, 1905.

17. Emphasis is mine. FO 228/3281, Dossier 1830, Consul A. E. Eastes, July 12, 1922, "Intelligence Report for June Quarter, 1922."

18. FO 228/1659, No. 60, Amoy, December 31, 1907.

19. Wang 2007, 63.

20. Wang and Wu 1996, 143–144.

21. Wang and Wu 1996, 143–144.

22. See e.g., *Shenbao* April 9, 1934, 8; *Shenbao* June 1, 1934, 12. The 40,000 figure comes from *China Press* July 24, 1934, 9. Barbara Brooks cites a number closer to 30,000, see Brooks 2000, 111.

23. FO 228/2007, No. 2, HM Consul in Amoy to HM Minister in Peking, January 29, 1917; and Wang and Wu 1996, 558–572.

24. USDS 1910–29, 893.102AM/26, Reel 98, No. 39, Xiamen to Secy. of State, May 17, 1921.

25. See section on issues relating to Japanese Police force in Xiamen during 1920–23, in Wang and Wu 1996, 558–572.

26. *Law Kang Po* 1903, 30–31.

27. Wang 2010, 132–134.

28. Inoue 1993, 18–19.

29. Lin 2001, 997.

30. Tseng 2014, 68–92.

31. Tseng 2014, 73.

32. Inoue 1993, 18. On the "flower tax" and the taxation and regulation of prostitution in early twentieth-century China, see Carroll 2001, 413–436. See also Hershatter 1997, 204–205.

33. *China and the West*, Reel 219, Summaries of Reports Called for by Circular No. 4926 on the Working of the Preventive Law, July 25, 1935.

34. Wang 2010, 137.

35. *Shenbao* October 27, 1921, 10.

36. Inoue 1993, 20.

37. *Gongjiao zhoukan* 1929, 13.

38. *Nanyang Siang Pau* February 14, 1929, 14.

39. *Nanyang Siang Pau* July 19, 1930, 14.

40. Hanson 1936, 425.

41. Inoue 1993, 11.

42. Hong 1983, 60.

43. *Shenbao* January 30, 1926, 13.

44. FO 228/3281, A.E. Eastes, January 9, 1923, "Intelligence Report for December Quarter 1922."

45. Inoue 1993, 11.

46. Zeng also appears in a recent urban history of Xiamen, see Ong 2021, 117.

47. LON 1919–1927, Sec 12A, Doc 20286x, Dossier 20286, 1924–29, "Letter from International Anti-Opium Association, Peking: Transmitting information regarding opium condition in Fukien Province during the present season, 21 January 1924." A brief history of Zeng's life is available in Working Group 1983, 8. See also *Nanyang Siang Pau* March 22, 1926, 10.

48. See e.g. *Nanyang Siang Pau* September 2, 1926, 10; *Nanyang Siang Pau* October 18, 1926, 10.

49. For the 1931 Wufeng Company, see CO 825/10/15, No. 52, Jones to Lampson, July 9, 1931; and *Nanyang Siang Pau* July 20, 1931, 14. For the 1933 Wufeng Company, see Hong 1983, 58.

50. *Shenbao* April 3, 1932, 6.

51. Hong 1983, 57.

52. FO 228/3281, Eastes, January 13, 1922, "Intelligence Report for December Quarter 1921."

53. The Finance Association seems to have fizzled out at some point in the 1920s and was later revived in the late 1930s under the leadership of Chen Changfu, see below. The regulations of the original association from 1926 can be found at the Japan Center for Asian Historical Records, Ministry of Foreign Affairs, B10074275300, Taisho 15/10/30, herafter JACAR.

54. Working Group 1983, 8.

55. Working Group 1983, 3.

56. The 28 Constellations (二十八宿) and the Martial-Moral Society (武德會). See Working Group 1983, 3 and Lu 1948.

57. The signs read "日籍 x x 洋行" or "大日本籍民 x x 寓", according to Working Group 1983, 15.

58. See, e.g., for a celebratory description in a Singapore newspaper: *Nanyang Siang Pau* September 9, 1935, 11.

59. See Lu 1948 and Working Group 1983, 1–49.

60. *Shenbao* January 30, 1926, 13.

61. *Nanyang Siang Pau* July 20, 1931, 14; Hong 1983, 60.

62. Working Group 1983, 15.

63. Mo 1985, 105–118.

64. Cang had no local support outside of Xiamen: the territory from Zhangzhou to the Guangdong border was held by Chen Jiongming's troops, and Jinmen by the Fujian Navy. The mainland opposite Xiamen was controlled by troops allied with the central government. Quanzhou, Tong'an, and Anhai districts were garrisoned by followers of the Zhili party. See FO 228/3281, Dossier 1830, Consul A.E. Eastes, December 21, 1923, "Political Report for December Quarter, 1923."

65. Working Group 1983, 36.

66. FO 228/3281, Dossier 1830, Consul A. E. Eastes, September 24, 1923, "Political Report for September Quarter, 1923."

67. *Shenbao* February 20, 1924, 11.

68. FO 228/3281, Dossier 1830, Consul Hewlett, March 13, 1924, "Political Report for March Quarter, 1924" and Working Group 1983, 1–49.

69. Mo 1985, 105–118. The beheading claim is repeated in "Xiamen haijun yanzhi taifei (The Xiamen Navy strictly prosecutes Taiwanese bandits)," *Shenbao*, May 26, 1924, 7.

70. Mo 1985, 108; see also FO 228/3281, Dossier 1830, Consul Hewlett, September 18, 1924; *Shenbao* September 15, 1924, 6; *Shenbao* September 22, 1924, 6.

71. Mo 1985, 108.

72. See section on occupations of Taiwanese in Xiamen from Sept. 1926, in Wang and Wu 1996, 148–149.

73. Mo 1985, 105–118.

74. Yao 1986, 48–54 and Working Group 1983, 1–49.

75. Working Group 1983, 30.

76. Lu 1948.

77. Hong 1983, 59.

78. Hong 1983, 61.

79. *Shenbao* December 20, 1935, 9; *Nanyang Siang Pau* February 4, 1936, 18.

80. The organization and bylaws of the 1926 Finance Association are in JACAR B10074275300, August 1926.

81. JACAR B10074275300, August 1926. On the Japanese "Southern Strategy," see Brooks 2000; Wang 2007.

82. *Nanyang Siang Pau* February 4, 1936, 18.

83. *Xian shijie* 1936, 136.

84. AH 002-080200-00180-114, September 18, 1934.

85. See e.g., AH 002-080200-00164-083, May 13, 1934; AH 002-080200-00231-112, June 20, 1935.

86. On the Japanese occupation of Xiamen, see Wang 2006, 35–45; Yao 1986, 55–66.

87. FO 371/23525, Code 10, File 4908, 1939, "Kulangsu Municipal Council Report for the Year Ending 31st December, 1938."

88. Records Created and Inherited by the War Office (hereafter WO) 208/250, Directorate of Military Operations and Intelligence, and Directorate of Military Intelligence, Fitzmaurice to Kerr, June 21, 1938, "Amoy: occupation by Japan, 01 May 1938–30 June 1940."

89. LON 1933–1946, Box R4870, Sec 12, Doc 37540, Dossier 526, October 4, 1940, "Extract from the Report to the Council on the work of the 25th Session of the Advisory Committee on Traffic in Opium and other Dangerous Drugs."

90. Hong and Ye 1985, 91.

91. Hong and Ye 1985, 98.

92. CO 859/15/5, No. 13, Fitzmaurice to Kerr, June 14, 1939. See also *Xiamen kangri zhanzheng dang'an ziliao* 426–429.

93. Wang and Wu 1997 427.

94. Hong and Ye 1985, 93.

95. Third Military District Xiamen-Taiwan Committee 1947, 10–11.

96. CO 859/15/5, No. 13, Fitzmaurice to Kerr, June 14, 1939.

97. Hong and Ye 1985, 93.

98. CO 859/15/5, No. 13, Fitzmaurice to Kerr, June 14, 1939.

99. "Fujian sheng zhengfu weihui xingzheng yuan lingchi chaji yandu (Fujian Provincial Government Assembly and Administrative Yuan Inspect the Opium Crisis)," *Fujian sheng minzheng ting* (The Fujian Provincial Bureau of Civil Affairs), Fuzhou: Fujian Provincial Archives, FPA 11.7.5242 (2), 1941. Hereafter FPA 11.

100. FPA 11.7.5240, No. 10, Haicheng County, MG 31/11/16.

101. *Jiangsheng bao* April 20, 1938.

102. See Wang and Wu 1997 298, cited in Wang 2006, 40.

103. Wang and Wu 1997, 393–395.

104. FPA 11.7.5240, No.12, Hua'an and Longxi Counties, MG 32/1/12.

105. "Fujian shengfu chaji ge xianqu renmin sifan yandu, 1939–43 (Fujian Provincial Government Inspects the Opium Crisis Among Various Counties and People)," FPA 11.7.5240, No. 18, Hui'an County, MG 32/3/10.

106. FPA 68.4.20, Memo No 821, Clerk-in-Charge at Hanjiang to Deputy Commissioner at Fuzhou, June 3, 1935.

107. Third Military District Xiamen-Taiwan Committee 1947, 10–11, 18–19, 23–24.

108. *Xingguang ribao* September 25, 1946.

109. The most extensive was a series of six long articles by Lu 1948.

110. *Xiamen dabao* November 23, 1947.

111. *Jiangsheng Bao* December 19, 1948.

112. My interpretation here is generally shared by Brooks 2000 and Wang 2006 and 2007, who both argue that the enrollment of Fujianese people as Japanese citizens was part of a broader plot to destabilize China. Wang is the most assertive in regards to considering the drug trade a considered element of the plan, rather than its unintended consequence.

113. Inoue 1993, 6–12.

114. The full text of the report has been translated into Chinese and reprinted in Inoue 1993, 6–12,

115. The fullest depiction of the Japanese-protected drug trade in North China is Kingsberg 2013.

116. *Shenbao* December 20, 1935, 9.

Conclusion

1. There is an extensive scholarship on drugs in Latin America, much of which comes from the security studies community. For two overviews of the operations of the Guadalajara cartel, see Grillo 2011 and Watt and Zepeda 2012.

2. Veltmeyer and Petras 2019, 38.

3. For an overview and critique of the concept of a narco-state, see Chouvy 2016, 26–38.

4. For an academic treatment of drug-related murders in the 1990s and early 2000s, see Eisenhammer 2014, 99–109; for the present-day, see Borunda 2020, https://www.elpasotimes.com/story/news/local/juarez/2020/07/30/juarez-mexico-murders-top-1000-drug-violence-despite-covid-19-pandemic/5535755002/; "Philippines' 'War on Drugs,'" Human Rights Watch, accessed August 20, 2020, https://www.hrw.org/tag/philippines-war-drugs.

5. Huang et al. 1959, 106–7.

6. For works that deal with this dynamic, see e.g., Larkins 2011; Muehlmann 2013.

7. Opium retailed by the monopoly in the Straits Settlements retailed in 1929 for 37

262 NOTES TO THE CONCLUSION

Swiss francs per tael (or 17 yuan in Chinese prices), and in the Netherlands Indies for 62 Swiss francs per tael (or 29 yuan). The drug could be purchased in Xiamen for as little as 2–3 yuan per tael. See Kim 2020, 60.

8. Ballvé 2019, 218.

9. Ballvé 2019, 218–219.

10. See also McSweeny et al. 2017, 3–29.

11. McSweeny et al. 2017, 16.

12. "Youguan Du Yuesheng de zhengzhi qingkuang ji touzi qiye danwei de cailiao dihan [Documents relating to Du Yuesheng's political situation and investments]," SMA B5-2-58-16, March 15, 1955.

References

ARCHIVAL SOURCES
Academia Historica: Taipei, Taiwan
AH 002   Jiang Zhongzheng zongtong wenwu (Materials from President Chiang Kai-shek)

British Library: London, England
Add MS   Cartographic items
IOR   India Office Records

CMC Film
Bickers, Robert, and Hans van de Ven, compilers. 2004–2008. *China and the West, the Maritime Customs Service Archive from the Second Historical Archives of China, Nanjing.* Woodbridge, CT: Thomson Gale, Primary Source Microfilm.

Complete Records of the Management of Barbarian Affairs: Daoguang Reign
CBYWSM-DGC   *Chouban yiwu shimo xuanji: Daoguang chao.*Taipei: Scripta Sinica Database. http://hanchi.ihp.sinica.edu.tw/ihp/hanji.htm.

First Historical Archives of China: Beijing, China
BDYJTB   Beida yijiao tiben (Routine Memorials, Transferred from Peking University)
LFZZ   Junji chu hanwen lufu zhouzhe (Grand Council Chinese-Language Palace Memorial Copies)
NGHKTB   Neige huke tiben (Routine Memorials from the Censorate, Office of Scrutiny for the Board of Revenue)

NGXKTB   Neige xingke tiben (Routine Memorials from the Censorate, Office of Scrutiny for the Board of Justice)

SYD   Junji chu dang'an shangyu dang (Grand Council Archives, Record Book of Imperial Edicts and Related Documents)

ZPZZ   Gongzhong hanwen zhupi zouzhe (Chinese-Language Imperially Inscribed Palace Memorials)

Fujian Provincial Archives: Fuzhou, China

FPA 11   Fujian sheng minzheng ting (The Fujian Provincial Bureau of Civil Affairs)

FPA 40   Jiancha yuan Min-Zhe jiancha qu jiancha shi shu (Office of the Fujian-Zhejiang Surveillance Commissioner)

FPA 68   Min haiguan ji xiashu zhiguan (The Fujian Maritime Customs and Out-Port Stations)

FPA 69   Haiguan zongshu (The Maritime Customs Central Office)

FPA 80   Zhu Min suijing zhuren gongshu (The Office of the Pacification Commissioner of Fujian)

FP 87   Fujian sheng gaodeng fayuan (The Fujian Supreme Court)

FPA 89   Fujian sheng baoan chu (The Fujian Provincial Public Security Office)

George C. Marshall Archives: Lexington, Virginia, United States
Elisabeth Smith Friedman Collection

Imperial Maritime Customs (IMC)
Reports and Special Series. Shanghai: Kelly & Walsh.
Decennial Reports, Amoy, 1882–1891, 1892–1901, 1902–1911, 1912–1921.
Decennial Reports, Foochow, 1882–1891, 1892–1901, 1902–1911, 1912–1921.
Decennial Reports, Swatow, 1882–1891, 1892–1901, 1902–1911, 1912–1921.

Japan Center for Asian Historical Records: Tokyo, Japan
JACAR   Diplomatic Archives of the Ministry of Foreign Affairs

Jardine Matheson & Company Archives: Cambridge University Library Department of Manuscripts, Cambridge, England

JM A   Accounting and Related Papers

JM B   In-Correspondence

JM C   Out-Correspondence

JM F   Legal Documents

JM G   Prices Current and Market Reports

JM H   Chinese Documents

JM I   Papers of Other Companies

JM J   Later Bound Correspondence

JM K   Miscellaneous Correspondence

JM L   Miscellaneous Papers

League of Nations Archive: Geneva, Switzerland
LON 1919–1927   Registry Files 1919–1927
LON 1928–1932   Registry Files 1928–1932
LON 1933–1946   Registry Files 1933–1946

National Archives: Kew, England
ADM   Records Created and Inherited by the Admiralty
CO   Records Created and Inherited by the Colonial Office
FO   Records Created and Inherited by the Foreign Office
HO   Records Created and Inherited by the Home Office
WO   Records Created and Inherited by the War Office

Palace Museum: Taipei, Taiwan
NGDKDA   Neige daku dangan (Grand Secretariat Archives)
QDGZ-JJC   Qingdai gongzhong dang'an zouzhe ji junji chu dang zhejian quanwen
yingxiang ziliao ku (Qing Palace and Grand Council Archives Database)

SMA   Shanghai Municipal Archives: Shanghai, China

United States. Department of State Archives, National Archives, College Park, Maryland
USDS (1844–1906)   Despatches from the United States Consuls in Amoy, China. Microfilm
USDS (1849–1906)   Despatches from the United States Consuls in Foochow, China. Microfilm.
USDS (1906–1910)   Records of the United States Department of State Relating to the Internal Affairs of China (The Numerical File). Microfilm.
USDS (1910–1929)   Records of the United States Department of State Relating to the Internal Affairs of China (The Decimal File). Microfilm.

NEWSPAPERS AND PERIODICALS
Canton Press
Canton Register
China Mail
China View
China Weekly Review
*Chinese Repository**
Duli Qingnian
Eastern Daily Mail and Straits Morning Advertiser
El Paso Times
Gongjiao zhoukan
Heshan Jubao
Huaqiao Ribao

Jiancha yuan gongbao
Jiangsheng bao
Judu yuekan
Law Kang Po
Los Angeles Times (1886–1922)
Manchester Guardian (1901–1959)
Minzhong Ribao
Nanyang Siang Pau
New York Times
North China Herald
Shenbao
Singapore Free Press and Mercantile Advertiser (1835–1869)
Straits Times
Straits Times Weekly Issue
Taiwan hanwen riri xin bao
The Times
Xiamen Dabao
Xian shijie
Xingguang ribao
Xinghua
Xinmin qianfeng

PUBLISHED REFERENCES

Ali, Tariq Omar. 2018. *A Local History of Global Capital: Jute and Peasant Life in the Bengal Delta*. Princeton, NJ: Princeton University Press.

Allen, Christian M. 2005. *An Industrial Geography of Cocaine*. London: Routledge.

Ambaras, David. 2018. *Japan's Imperial Underworlds: Intimate Encounters at the Borders of Empire*. Cambridge: Cambridge University Press.

Amrith, Sunil. 2015. *Crossing the Bay of Bengal: The Furies of Nature and the Fortunes of Migrants*. Cambridge, MA: Harvard University Press.

Antony, Robert. 2003. *Like Froth Floating on the Sea: The World of Pirates and Seafarers in Late Imperial South China*. Berkeley: University of California Press.

Ball, B. L. 1856. *Rambles in Eastern Asia, Including China and Manila, During Several Years' Residence*. Boston: James French and Company.

Ballvé, Teo. 2019. "Narco-Frontiers: A Spatial Framework for Drug-Fueled Accumulation." *Journal of Agrarian Change* 19: 211–224.

Banister, T. R. 1932. *The Coastwise Lights of China: An Illustrated Account of the Chinese Maritime Customs Lights Service*. Shanghai: Inspectorate General of Customs.

Bastid, Marianne. 1985. "The Structure of the Financial Institutions of the State in the Late Qing." In *The Scope of State Power in China*, edited by S. R. Schram, 51–79. London: School of Oriental and African Studies.

Bauer, Rolf. 2019. *The Peasant Production of Opium in Nineteenth-Century India*. Leiden: Brill.

Baumler, Alan. 2008. *The Chinese and Opium under the Republic: Worse the Floods and Wild Beasts*. Albany: State University of New York Press.

Beckert, Sven. 2015. *Empire of Cotton: A Global History*. New York: Vintage Books.

Bello, David. 2005. *Opium and the Limits of Empire: Drug Prohibition in the Chinese Interior, 1729-1850*. Cambridge: Harvard University Press.

Bennett, Terry. 2010. *History of Photography in China: Western Photographers, 1861–1879*. London: Quaritch.

Bianco, Lucien. 2000. "The Responses of Opium Growers to Eradication Campaigns and the Poppy Tax, 1907–1949." In *Opium Regimes: China, Britain, and Japan, 1839–1952*, edited by Timothy Brook and Bob Tadashi Wakabayashi, 292–322 (Berkeley: University of California Press).

Blythe, Wilfred. 1969. *The Impact of Chinese Secret Societies in Malaya: A Historical Study*. London: Oxford University Press.

Borunda, Daniel. 2020. "Juárez Murders Top 1,000 as Violence Continues Despite COVID-19 Pandemic." *El Paso Times*, July 30, 2020, https://www.elpasotimes.com/story/news/local/juarez/2020/07/30/juarez-mexico-murders-top-1000-drug-violence-despite-covid-19-pandemic/5535755002/.

Bose, Sugata. 1993. *Peasant Labour and Colonial Capital*. Cambridge: Cambridge University Press.

Brooks, Barbara. 2000. "Japanese Colonial Citizenship in Treaty Port China: The Location of Koreans and Taiwanese in the Imperial Order." In *New Frontiers: Imperialism's New Communities in East Asia, 1842–1953*, edited by Robert Bickers and Christian Henriot. 109–121. Manchester and New York: Manchester University Press.

Brunero, Donna. 2006. *Britain's Imperial Cornerstone in China: The Chinese Maritime Customs Service, 1854–1949*. London: Routledge.

Calanca, Paolo. 2010. "Piracy and Coastal Security in Southeastern China, 1600–1780." In *Elusive Pirates, Pervasive Smugglers: Violence and Clandestine Trade in the Greater China Seas*, edited by Robert Antony. Hong Kong: Hong Kong University Press.

Canton Times.1920. "Hongkong and Opium." August 24, 1920, 2.

Carroll, Peter. 2001. "The Place of Prostitution in Early Twentieth-Century Suzhou." *Urban History* 38, no. 3: 413–436.

Chan, Shelly. 2018. *Diaspora's Homeland: Modern China in the Age of Global Migration*. Durham, NC: Duke University Press.

Chan, Shelly. 2015. "The Case for Diaspora: A Temporal Approach to the Chinese Experience." *Journal of Asian Studies* 74, no. 1: 107–128.

Chang, Hsin-Pao. 1964. *Commissioner Lin and the Opium War*. Cambridge, MA: Harvard University Press.

Chang, Pin-Tsun. 1990. "Maritime Trade and the Local Economy in Ming Fujian." In *The Development and Decline of Fukien Province in the 17th and 18th Centuries*, edited by Eduard B. Vermeer. 64–80. Leiden: Brill.

Chen, Boyi. 2019. "The Coastal Evacuation of Zhangpu County in Early Qing: Borders, Shifting Zones, and Social Change as Seen in Forts and Fortified Villages." *Chinese Studies in History* 52, no. 2: 163–180.

Chen, Shiqi. 2002. *Zhongguo jindai haiguan shi* (History of China's modern maritime customs). Beijing: Renmin Daxue Chubanshe.

Chen, Yung-fa. 1995. "The Blooming Poppy under the Red Sun: The Yan'an Way and the Opium Trade." In *New Perspectives on the Chinese Communist Revolution*, edited by Tony Saich and Hans van de Ven. 263–298. New York: M. E. Sharpe.

Chen, Zhanqi, ed. 2009. *Qingmo minchu tongshang kouan dang'an huibian* (Reproduction of Archival Sources of Foreign Commerce in Chinese Commercial Ports from 1862 to 1915). Beijing: Quanguo tushuguan wenxian suowei zhongxin.

Chen, Zhiping. 2010. "Merchant Lineage in Coastal Jinjiang, Quanzhou Prefecture during the Qing Dynasty." *Frontiers of History in China* 5, no. 3: 435–445.

China Press. 1934. "Authorities Worried by Amoy Ronins." July 24, 1934, 9.

China Weekly Review. 1937. "Notorious Opium King at Foochow Taken into Custody." July 17, 1937.

Chouvy, Pierre-Arnaud. 2016. "The Myth of the Narco-State." *Space and Polity* 20, no. 1: 26–38.

Deng, Kent G. 2011. "Why Shipping 'Declined' in China from the Middle Ages to the Nineteenth Century." In *Shipping and Economic Growth 1350–1850*, edited by Richard W. Unger. Leiden: Brill.

Deng, Kent G. 2008. "Miracle or Mirage? Foreign Silver, China's Economy, and Globalization from the Sixteenth to the Nineteenth Centuries." *Pacific Economic Review* 13, no. 3: 320–358.

Dick, Howard, Michael Sullivan, and John Butcher, editors. 1993. *The Rise and Fall of Revenue Farming: Business Elites and the Emergence of the Modern State in Southeast Asia*. New York: Palgrave Macmillan.

Dikötter, Frank, Lars Laamann, and Zhou Xun. 2004. *Narcotic Culture: A History of Drugs in China*. Chicago: University of Chicago Press.

Dorril, William F. 1969. "The Fukien Rebellion and the CCP: A Case of Maoist Revisionism." *China Quarterly* 37: 31–53.

Dreyer, Edward. 2007. *Zheng He: China and the Oceans in the Early Ming Dynasty, 1405–1433*. New York: Pearson Longman.

Duli Qingnian."1926. Fujian yanhuo jilue—ling yan" (Discussion of the opium curse in Fujian). Vol. 1, issue 6, *Minguo qikan ku* (Republican Periodical Database 1911–1949).

Dykstra, Maura Dominique. 2014. "Complicated Matters: Commercial Dispute Resolution in Qing Chongqing from 1750 to 1911." PhD diss., University of California Los Angeles.

Dykstra, Maura Dominique. 2022. "Growing Up before the Rebellion: Merchant Organization and Local Administration in Chongqing." *Late Imperial China*. Forthcoming in Spring 2022.

Eastern Daily Mail and Straits Morning Advertiser. 1907. "The S.S. Petchaburi Chandu Case." October 5, 1907, 3.

Eastern Daily Mail and Straits Morning Advertiser. 1907. "Importation of Illicit Chandu." October 9, 1907, 3.

Eastern Daily Mail and Straits Morning Advertiser. 1907. "Opium Smuggling." October 10, 1907, 2.

Eisenhammer, Stephen. 2014. "Bare Life in Ciudad Juárez: Violence in a Space of Exclusion." *Latin American Perspectives* 41, no. 2: 99–109.

Elman, Benjamin. 2005. *On Their Own Terms: Science in China, 1550–1900.* Cambridge, MA: Harvard University Press.

Eoseewong, Nidhi. 2005. *Pen and Sail: Literature and History in Early Bangkok.* Translated by Chris Baker. Chiang Mai: Silkworm Books.

Fairbank, John King. 1953. *Trade and Diplomacy on the China Coast, The Opening of the Treaty Ports, 1842–1854.* Cambridge, MA: Harvard University Press.

Faure, David. 2007. *Emperor and Ancestor: State and Lineage in South China.* Stanford, CA: Stanford University Press.

Fay, Peter Ward. (1975) 1997. *The Opium War, 1840–1842.* Chapel Hill: University of North Carolina Press.

Field, Rose C. 1924. "China Again in Grip of Opium and Morphia: Absence of Centralized National Authority Allows Separate Military Governments to Exploit Poppy Raising and Drugs for Tax Revenues—Smuggled Imports Increase." *New York Times,* August 24, 1924.

Fix, Douglas. 2016. "The Global Entanglements of a Marginal Man in Treaty-Port Xiamen." In *Law, Land and Power: Treaty Ports in Modern China,* edited by Robert Bickers and Isabella Jackson. London: Routledge.

Foster, Anne L. 2000. "Prohibition as Superiority: Policing Opium in South-East Asia, 1898–1925." *International History Review* 22, no. 2: 253–273.

Freedman, Maurice. 1958. *Lineage Organization in Southeastern China.* London: University of London, Athlone Press.

Fujian Provincial Archives, ed. 2017. *Fujian qiaopi dang'an wenxian huibian* (Fujian Qiaopi documents collection). Beijing: Guojia tushu guan chuban she.

Fujian shengli (Fujian provincial sub-statutes). 1964. Taiwan wenxian congkan 199. Taipei: Taiwan yin hang.

Fujian yanhai hangwu dang'an (Jiaqing chao) bufen juan (Fujian Maritime Trade Archive, Jiaqing Reign). 2004. Taiwan wenxian xunkan. Xiamen: Xiamen University Press.

Giquel, Prosper. 1874. *The Foochow Arsenal, and its Results, from the Commencement in 1867, to the End of the Foreign Directorate, on the 16th February, 1874. Translated from the French, by H. Lang.* Shanghai Evening Courier.

Gongjiao zhoukan. 1929. "Jimin yance zhi diaocha" (Report on *jimin*-owned opium dens). No. 27, 1929, 13.

González, Fredy. 2017. *Paisanos Chinos: Transpacific Politics among Chinese Immigrants in Mexico.* Berkeley: University of California Press.

Goodman, Bryna. 1995. *Native Place, City, and Nation: Regional Networks and Identities in Shanghai, 1853–1937.* Berkeley: University of California Press.

Grace, Richard J. 2014. *Opium and Empire: The Lives and Careers of William Jardine and James Matheson.* Montreal: McGill-Queen's University Press.

Grillo, Ioan. 2011. *El Narco: Inside Mexico's Criminal Insurgency.* New York: Bloomsbury Publishing.

Halsey, Stephen R. 2015. *Quest for Power: European Imperialism and the Making of Chinese Statecraft.* Cambridge: Harvard University Press.

Hamashita, Takeshi. 2011. "The Lidai Baoan and the Ryukyu Maritime Tributary Trade Network with China and Southeast Asia, the Fourteenth to Seventeenth Centuries." In *Chinese Circulations: Capital, Commodities, and Networks in Southeast Asia*, edited by Eric Tagliacozzo and Wen-chin Chang. 107–139. Durham, NC: Duke University Press.

Hang, Xing. 2015. *Conflict and Commerce in Maritime East Asia: The Zheng Family and the Shaping of the Modern World, c. 1620–1720*. Cambridge: Cambridge University Press.

Hanson, Haldore. 1936. "Fukien Drug Rackets Not Japanese Run." *North China Herald*, vol. 200, issue 3605, September 2, 1936, 425.

He, Liping. 2007. "Yapian maoyi yu baiyin wailiu guanxi zhi cai jiantao" (Reexamining the relationship of the opium trade and silver outflows). 2007. *Shehui kexue zhanxian* 1: 63–80.

Hershatter, Gail. 1997. *Dangerous Pleasures: Prostitution and Modernity in Twentieth Century Shanghai*. Berkeley: University of California Press.

Heshan jubao. 1934. "Heshan gonggao yuexiao siqian liang (The Heshan public sale of opium paste quota is set at 4,000 liang). September 11, 1934.

Heshan jubao. 1934. "Xianfu jinzhong yanmiao, he bu jinmai yapian" (The county government has prohibited poppy cultivation, why have they not prohibited opium sales?). November 1, 1934.

Heshan jubao (The Heshan Ten-Day Report). 1935. "Tezai huibei mafei zhi duliu" (Special report: The spread of morphine in northern Hui'an). March 1, 1935.

Heshan jubao. 1935. "Jinyan tiaoli xianqi suqing chengban tugao jili tuixiao maodun" (Performing the rapid eradication of the Opium Prohibition Laws and increasing the sale of opium paste, a contradiction). April 21, 1935.

Ho, Dahpon. 2011. "Sealords Live in Vain: Fujian and the Making of a Maritime Frontier in Seventeenth-Century China." PhD diss., University of California, San Diego.

Hong, Buren. 1983b. "'Yapian dawang' Ye Qinghe (Ye Qinghe: Opium King)." *Xiamen wenshi ziliao* 5, 47–68.

Hong, Buren. 1983a. *Xiamen difang shi jianggao* (Lecture notes on Xiamen's local history). Xiamen: Xiam,en zonggong hui.

Hong, Ling, and Gengxin Ye. 1985. "Xiamen lunxian qijian de yapian he dubo" (Opium and gambling during the occupation in Xiamen). *Xiamen wenshi ziliao* 8, 91–104.

Huang, Guosheng. 2004. "The Chinese Maritime Customs in Transition, 1750 to 1830." In *Maritime China in Transition: 1750–1850*, edited by Wang Gungwu and Ng Chin-Keong. Wiesbaden: Harrassowitz Verlag.

Huang, Juezi, Naiji Xu, and Sihe Qi. 1959. *Huang Juezi zou shu. Xu Naiji zou yi: he kan* (Collected memorials of Huang Juezi and Xu Naiji). Beijing: Zhonghua shu ju.

Huaqiao ribao. 1934. "Weifa yingye yance ji mafei guan gongbu ju pohuo" (Illegal operation of morphine and opium dens broken up and captured by the public works office). January 31, 1934.

Hummel, Arthur. 1943–1944. *Eminent Chinese of the Ch'ing Period*, vol. II. Washington, DC: United States Government Print Office.

Inoue, Torajirô. 1993. "Xiamen de Taiwan jimin wenti" (Xiamen's *Jimin* problem). In *Min-Tai guanxi dang'an ziliao* (Archival sources on Fujian-Taiwan relations). Xiamen: Lujiang Publishing.

International Opium Commission 1909. *Report of the International Opium Commission, Shanghai, China, February 1 to February 26, 1909.* London: P. S. King and Son.

Irigoin, Maria Alejandra. 2013. "A Trojan Horse in Daoguang China? Explaining the Flows of Silver in and out of China." Economic History working papers, 173/13. London: Department of Economic History, London School of Economics and Political Science.

Jiancha yuan gongbao. 1932. "Tihe Fujian junguan Zhang Zhen, Chen Guohui, He Xianzu, Jin Zhenzhong pingji wuli qiangpo zhongyan an: benyuan wu Guomin zhengfu wen" (Forced opium cultivation by the Fujian militarists Zhang Zhen, Chen Guohui, He Xianzu, and Jin Zhenzhong). 15, 95–101.

Jiangsheng bao. 1938. "Jinmen wokou shixing bo dipi, xiangang wan yunqu citu shenduo, mafei faxian yu Xiashi" (Japanese bandits in Jinmen are stripping the soil, the Hong Kong Maru is shipping out a lot of porcelain clay, and morphine is discovered in Xiamen city). April 20, 1938.

Jiangsheng Bao. 1948. "Chen Fensao du'an shuijing juzhen xun zhong" (The ongoing investigation into Chen Fensao's drug crimes by detectives in the Water Police). December 19, 1948.

Judu yuekan. 1936. "Minnan xiqu yapian zhuanmaiju lutong gongsi yingye gaikuang" (Summary of the operations of the Lutong Company, the state monopoly for south and western Fujian). 96, 1–5.

Karch, Steven B. 1999. "Japan and the Cocaine Industry of Southeast Asia, 1864–1944." In *Cocaine: Global Histories,* edited by Paul Gootenberg, 146–164. London: Routledge.

Kent, Stacie. 2016. "Problems of Circulation in the Treaty Port System." In *Treaty Ports in Modern China: Law, Land, and Power,* edited by Robert Bickers and Isabella Jackson, 78–100. Routledge: Oxon.

Keong, Ong Soon. 2021. *Coming Home to a Foreign Country: Xiamen and the Returned Overseas Chinese, 1843–1938.* Ithaca, NY: Cornell University Press.

Kim, Diana. 2020. *Empires of Vice: The Rise of Opium Prohibition Across Southeast Asia.* Princeton, NJ: Princeton University Press.

Kingsberg, Miriam. 2013. *Moral Nation: Modern Japan and Narcotics in Global History.* Berkeley: University of California Press.

Kuhn, Philip A. 1970. *Rebellion and Its Enemies in Late Imperial China.* Cambridge, MA: Harvard University Press.

Kuhn, Philip A. 2008. *Chinese among Others: Emigration in Modern Times.* Lanham: Rowman & Littlefield.

Kwass, Michael. 2014. *Contraband: Louis Mandrin and the Making of a Global Underground.* Cambridge, MA: Harvard University Press.

Lamley, Harry. 1990. "Lineage Feuding in Southern Fujian and Eastern Guangdong under Qing Rule." In *Violence in China: Essays in Culture and Counterculture,* edited by Jonathan Lipman. Albany: State University of New York Press.

Lan, Daqi. 1999. *Xuannao de haishi: Min dongnan gangshi xingshuai yu haiyang renwen* (The bustling ports: Southeast Fujian's maritime culture and the rise and decline of its port cities). Nanchang: Jiangxi gaoxiao chubanshe.

Larkins, Erica Robb. 2011. "The Spectacular Favela: Narcotrafficking, Policing, and the Commodification of Violence in Rio de Janeiro." PhD diss., University of Wisconsin.

Law Kang Po (A Journal for the Times). 1903. "Affairs of Fujian: Arms Trade in Fuzhou and Zhangzhou." book 3, vol. 39, October 3, 1903, f1–4.

Law Kang Po (A Journal for the Times). 1903. "Affairs of Fujian: Xiamen: Feuding in Quanzhou." book 5, vol. 49, November 8, 1903, f3.

Lin, Chengfen. 1923. "Difang tongxun: qiangpo zhongyan Fujian (Local correspondence: forced poppy cultivation in Fujian)." *Xinghua*, vol. 20, no. 50, 1923, 28, *Minguo qikan ku* (Republican Periodical Database 1911–1949).

Lin, Man-Houng. 1993. "Opium Poppy Cultivation, Interregional Migration, and Late Ch'ing China's Population." Paper delivered at the 1993 International Workshop on Historical Demography: Population History of East Asia, Reitaku University, Japan. January 28–February 3, 1993.

Lin, Man-Houng. 2001. "Overseas Chinese Merchants and Multiple Nationality: A Means for Reducing Commercial Risk (1895–1935)." *Modern Asian Studies* 35, no. 4: 985–1009.

Lin, Man-Houng. 2004. "Late Qing Perceptions of Native Opium." *Harvard Journal of Asiatic Studies* 64, no. 1: 117–144.

Lin, Man-Houng. 2007. *China Upside Down: Currency, Society, and Ideologies, 1808–1856*. Honolulu: University of Hawaii Press.

Lin, Man-Houng. 2016. "Wan Qing de yapian shui, 1858–1906" (Opium taxation in the late Qing, 1858–1906). *Guojia Hanghai* 16: 31–81.

Lin, Na. 1936. "Jimin pai" (registered-citizen placard). *Tongsu wenhua zhengzhi jingji kexue gongcheng banyue kan* 4, no. 5: 26–28.

Lin, Renchuan. 1985. "Qingdai Fujian de yapian maoyi" (The opium trade in Qing dynasty Fujian). *Zhongguo shehui jingji yanjiu* (Xiamen: Fujian xinwen), no. 1: 62–71.

Lin, Renchuan. 1991. *Fujian duiwai maoyi yu haiguan shi* (The history of foreign trade and the maritime customs in Fujian). Xiamen: Lujiang chubanshe.

Lin, Yuju. 2014. "Trade, Public Affairs and the Formation of Merchant Associations in Taiwan in the Eighteenth Century." In *Merchant Communities in Asia, 1600–1980*, edited by Lin Yu-ju and Madeline Zelin, 11–27. London: Routledge.

Lindsay, Hugh Hamilton, and Charles Friedrich August Gützlaff. 1834. *Report of Proceedings on a Voyage to the Northern Ports of China: In the Ship Lord Amherst*. London: B. Fellowes.

Liu, Andrew B. 2020. *Tea War: A History of Capitalism in China and India*. New Haven, CT: Yale University Press.

Liu, Yabin. 1996. "The Origin of Neo-Traditionalism in China: Zhang Zhidong and His *Quanzue Pian* (Exhortation to Learn)." MA thesis, University of Hawai'i at Manoa.

Los Angeles Times. 1920. "Valuable Opium Is Seized in Manila." December 4, 1920.

Lu, Chun, 1948. "Cong shiba dage dao jiaotou haohan, 1–6" (From the 18 elder brothers to true men of the corners, parts 1–6). *Jiangsheng bao*, September 24–29, 1948.

Luo, Yudong. (1936) 2010. *Zhongguo lijin shi* (A history of *lijin* in China). Beijing: shangwu yinshuguan.

Ma, Mozhen, editor. 1998. *Zhongguo jindu shiliao 1749 nian–1949 nian* (Historical sources on drug prohibition in China, 1749–1949). Tianjin: Tianjin renmin chuban she.

Macauley, Melissa. 2009. "Small Time Crooks: Opium, Migrants and the War on Drugs in China, 1819–1860." *Late Imperial China* 30, no. 1: 1–47.

Macauley, Melissa. 2016. "Entangled States: The Translocal Repercussions of Rural Pacification in China, 1869–1873." *American Historical Review* 121, no. 3: 755–779.

Macauley, Melissa. 2021. *Distant Shores: Colonial Encounters on China's Maritime Frontier.* Princeton, NJ: Princeton University Press.

Madancy, Joyce. 2003. *The Troublesome Legacy of Commissioner Lin: The Opium Trade and Opium Suppression in Fujian Province, 1820s to 1920s.* Cambridge, MA: Harvard University Press.

Mann, Susan. 1987. *Local Merchants and the Chinese Bureaucracy, 1750–1950.* Stanford, CA: Stanford University Press.

Marshall, Jonathan. 1976. "Opium and the Politics of Gangsterism in Nationalist China." *Bulletin of Concerned Asian Scholars* 8, no. 3: 19–48.

Martin, Brian. 1996. *The Shanghai Green Gang: Politics and Organized Crime, 1919–1937.* Berkeley: University of California Press.

Martin, R. Montgomery. 1848. *China; Political, Commercial, and Social, in an Official Report to Her Majesty's Government, Vol. II.* London: James Madden.

Mazumdar, Sucheta. 1998. *Sugar and Society in China: Peasants, Technology, and the World Market.* Cambridge, MA: Harvard University Asia Center.

McKeown, Adam. 2011. "The Social Life of Chinese Labor." In *Chinese Circulations: Capital, Commodities, and Networks in Southeast Asia,* edited by Eric Tagliacozzo and Wen-chin Chang. 62–83. Durham, NC: Duke University Press.

McSweeny, Kendra, Nizih Richani, Zoe Pearson, Jennifer Devine, and David J. Wrathall. 2017. "Why Do Narcos Invest in Rural Land?" *Journal of Latin American Geography* 16, no. 2: 3–29.

Miles, Steven B. 2020. *Chinese Diasporas: A Social History of Global Migration.* Cambridge: Cambridge University Press,.

Mills, James. 2007. "Drugs, Consumption, and Supply in Asia: The Case of Cocaine in Colonial India, c. 1900–1930." *Journal of Asian Studies* 66, no. 2: 345–362.

Min-Tai guanxi dang'an ziliao (Archival Sources on Fujian-Taiwan Relations). 1993. Xiamen: Lujiang Publishing,.

Mintz, Sidney. 1985. *Sweetness and Power: The Place of Sugar in Modern History.* New York: Penguin.

Minzhong ribao. 1929. "Anhai dongshi xiang zhi da mafei an" (The great morphine case of Dongshi Village, Anhai). May 30, 1929.

Mo, Jun. 1985. "Xiamen de ge jiaotou liumang (The Hooligans of Xiamen's Various Neighborhoods)." *Xiamen wenshi ziliao* 8: 105–118.

Morse, Hosea Ballou. 1910. *The International Relations of the Chinese Empire.* 3 Vols. London: Longmans, Green and Co.

Muehlmann, Shaylih. 2013. *When I Wear my Alligator Boots: Narco-Culture in the US Borderlands.* Berkeley: University of California Press.

Murray, Dian. 1987. *Pirates of the South China Coast, 1790–1810.* Stanford, CA: Stanford University Press.

Murray, Dian, and Qin Baoqi. 1994. *The Origins of the Tiandihui: The Chinese Triads in Legend and History.* Stanford, CA: Stanford University Press.

Nanyang Siang Pau. 1924. "Xiamen yapian guanmai yi kai ju" (Government sale of opium in Xiamen has begun). February 29, 1924, 7.

Nanyang Siang Pau. 1924. "Yi juan liang bao zhi fenzheng" (A conflict over one tax with two farmers). May 30, 1924, 7.

Nanyang Siang Pau. 1926. "Minnan zhi yanhuo lieshen baoban yanmiao juan" (Evil gentry control the poppy tax amidst the Southern Fujian opium crisis). March 22, 1926, 10.

Nanyang Siang Pau. 1926. "Zeng Houkun you zi jukou zhong" (Zeng Houkun under house arrest). September 2, 1926, 10.

Nanyang Siang Pau. 1926. "Zeng Houkun xinde yuanzhu" (Zeng Houkun receives new help). October 18, 1926, 10.

Nanyang Siang Pau. 1929. "Taiji yanguan xianqi xieye ye" (Taiwan-registered opium dens shut down for a period). February 14, 1929, 14.

Nanyang Siang Pau. 1929. "Gulang pohuo dazong yantu jingguo" (Gulangyu authorities confiscate large amount of opium). September 6, 1929, 10.

Nanyang Siang Pau. 1929. "Zhongshan gongyuan fenshao shenzhou yantu xiangqing" (Situation surrounding the burning of Shenzhou Pharmacy opium in Sun Yatsen Park). November 28, 1929, 14.

Nanyang Siang Pau. 1930. "Sheng jin weihui dui taishi tantu" (Provincial anti-opium official speaks on Taiwan issues). July 19, 1930, 14.

Nanyang Siang Pau. 1930. "Zhishala chuan Zhong souhuo dazong yapian" (Patrol Boat confiscates large amount of opium). December 27, 1930, 9.

Nanyang Siang Pau. 1931. "Jinyan yi" (Opium prohibition, one). July 20, 1931, 14.

Nanyang Siang Pau. 1932. "Heren tingwen zhi minsheng feijun guanzhang zhi zichan" (Frightful news about the personal wealth of the bandit warlords in Fujian). June 28, 1932, 14.

Nanyang Siang Pau. 1935. "Xiamen xianzhuang sumiao" (Sketches of life in Xiamen). September 9, 1935, 11.

Nanyang Siang Pau. 1935. "Yapian dawang Ye Qinghe" (Opium King Ye Qinghe). November 20, 1935.

Nanyang Siang Pau. 1936. "Tairen zushe Xiamen jinrong zuhe" (Taiwanese people establish the Xiamen Finance Association). February 4, 1936, 18.

New York Times. 1908. "Opium Riot in China: Officer and Ten Civilians Killed in Enforcing Edict Against Planting Poppies." December 28, 1908.

Ng, Chin-Keong. 1983. *Trade and Society: The Amoy Network on the China Coast, 1683–1735.* Singapore: Singapore University Press.

Ng, Chin-Keong. 2017. *Boundaries and Beyond: China's Maritime Southeast in Late Imperial Times.* Singapore: National University of Singapore Press.

North China Herald. 1875. "Foochow: The Affray with Smugglers." Vol. 31, issue 0422, June 12, 1875.

North China Herald. 1875. "Foochow." Vol. 34, issue 0436, September 18, 1875.

North China Herald. 1903. "The Use of Opium in China." Vol. 88, issue 1896, December 11, 1903.

North China Herald. 1909. "Late Telegrams." Vol. 27, issue 2161, January 9, 1909.

North China Herald. 1913. "Onions not Onions." Vol. 124, issue 2382, April 5, 1913, 15.

North China Herald. 1934. "Shanghai Law Reports: Rewards Offered by Court." Vol. 192, issue 3503, September 26, 1934.

North China Herald. 1937. "Fukien Opium King Arrested." June 30, 1937.

Norton-Kyshe, James William. 1898. *History of the Laws and Courts of Hongkong, Tracing Consular Jurisdiction in China and Japan and Including Parliamentary Debates, and the Rise, Progress, and Successive Changes in the Various Public Institutions of the Colony from the Earliest Period to the Present Time, Vol. I.* London: T. Fisher Unwin,

Ong, Aiwha. 1999. *Flexible Citizenship: The Cultural Logic of Transnationality.* Durham, NC: Duke University Press.

Ong, Soon Keong. 2021. *Coming Home to a Foreign Country: Xiamen and Returned Overseas Chinese, 1843–1938.* Ithaca, NY: Cornell University Press.

Opium Investigation Committee. 1905. *Report of the committee appointed by the Philippine Commission to investigate the use of opium and the traffic therein and the rules, ordinances and laws regulating such use and traffic in Japan, Formosa, Shanghai, Hongkong, Saigon, Singapore, Burmah, Java, and the Philippine Islands.* United States: Philippine Commission.

Owen, David Edward. 1968. *British Opium Policy in China and India.* Hamden, CT: Archon Books.

Ownby, David. 1996. *Brotherhoods and Secret Societies in Early and Mid-Qing China.* Stanford, CA: Stanford University Press.

Pasternak, Judy, and Douglas Jehl. 1989. "Officials Trace 'Trampoline' Drug Route." *Los Angeles Times*, September 30, 1989.

Peattie, Mark. 1989. "Japanese Treaty Port Settlements in China, 1895–1937." In *The Japanese Informal Empire in China, 1895–1937*, edited by Peter Duus, Ramon Myers, and Mark Peattie, 166–209. Princeton, NJ: Princeton University Press.

Philippines Census Office. 1918. *Census of the Philippine Islands taken under the Direction of the Philippine Legislature in the Year 1918.* Two Volumes. Manila: Bureau of Printing.

Platt, Stephen. 2018. *Imperial Twilight: The Opium War and the End of China's Last Golden Age.* New York: Knopf.

Po, Ron C. 2018. *The Blue Frontier: Maritime Vision and Power in the Qing Empire.* Cambridge: Cambridge University Press.

Polachek, James. 1992. *The Inner Opium War.* Cambridge, MA: Harvard University Press.

Pong, David. 1987. "Keeping the Foochow Naval Yard Afloat: Government Finance and China's Early Modern Defence Industry, 1866–75." *Modern Asian Studies* 21, no. 1: 121–152.

Qing shilu (Historical annals of the Qing dynasty). Taipei: Scripta Sinica Database, http://hanchi.ihp.sinica.edu.tw/ihp/hanji.htm.

Qiu, Ming. 1984. "Xiamen san da xing de chansheng" (The making of Xiamen's three great surnames). *Xiamen wenshi ziliao* 7: 141–147.

Rimner, Steffen. 2018. *Opium's Long Shadow: From Asian Revolt to Global Drug Control.* Cambridge, MA: Harvard University Press.

Rowe, William. 1984. *Hankow: Commerce and Society in a Chinese City, 1796–1889.* Stanford, CA: Stanford University Press.

Rowe, William. 1989. *Hankow: Conflict and Community in a Chinese City, 1796–1895.* Stanford, CA: Stanford University Press.

Rush, James R. 2014. *Opium to Java: Revenue Farming and Chinese Enterprise in Colonial Indonesia, 1860–1910.* Ithaca, NY: Cornell University Press.

Scheltema, J. F. 1907. "The Opium Trade in the Dutch East Indies, I." *American Journal of Sociology* 13, no. 1: 79–112.

Shen, Baozhen. 1880. *Shen Wensu gong zheng shu* (The book of the political memorandums to the throne by Shen Baozhen), Vol. 4–5. Fuzhou: Wushishan.

Shen, Baozhen. 2005. *Shen Wensu chuangong zougao* (Shen Baozhen collected memorials on naval affairs), Vol. 1–2. Beijing: Quanguo tushuguan wenxian weisuo fuzhi zhongxin, Vol 2.

Shen, Yanqing. 2013. *Heyin zhimin zhengfu yapian shuishou zhengce ji qidui zhaowa huaren shehui de yingxiang (From Opium Farm System to Opium Régie: A Study of Opium Policy in Netherlands East Indies and its Impact on Chinese Society in Java).* Xiamen: Xiamen University Press.

Shenbao. 1883. "Min zhong jinshi" (Recent news from central Fujian). August 25, 1883.

Shenbao. 1883. "Min zhong youyin." (News from central Fujian) October 15, 1883.

Shenbao 1884. "Xiamen suolu" (News from Xiamen). September 22, 1884.

Shenbao. 1885. "Tai-Xia zalu" (News from Taiwan and Xiamen). November 2, 1885.

Shenbao. 1886. "Yangyao jianli" (Opium lijin reduced). March 9, 1886.

Shenbao. 1886. "Xiamen linyao" (Recent news from Xiamen). September 22, 1886.

Shenbao. 1907. "Min shang yuanjiao jukuan baoban yan'gao zhuanmai" (Fujian merchant proffers large sum to monopolize opium paste distribution). August 31, 1907.

Shenbao. 1908. "Xiamen siyun junhuo an yijie" (Resolution of the arms smuggling case in Xiamen). August 26, 1908.

Shenbao. 1908. "Songdu dianchi zhong yingsu" (Governor Song prohibits poppy cultivation). September 25, 1908.

Shenbao. 1908."Mindu dianchi jinzhong yingsu" (Fujian governor prohibits poppy cultivation). October 5, 1908.

Shenbao. 1909. "Tong'an guan min xiedou qingxing" (Officials and people in Tong'an to deal with lineage feuding). January 3, 1909.

Shenbao. 1911. "Wu Chen erxing da xiedou" (The great lineage feud of the Wu and Chen surnames). March 7, 1911.

Shenbao. 1911. "Wei xian le zhuo junzhuang" (County officials dispatched to confiscate weapons). August 17, 1911.

Shenbao. 1921. "Minsheng zhi jinyan tan" (Discussion of opium prohibition in Fujian province). October 27, 1921, 10.

Shenbao. 1924. "Xiamen Hui'an lühu gongmin dianqing jinyan" (The Hui'an Guild in Shanghai requests help in opium prohibition). January 30, 1926, 13.

Shenbao. 1924. "Xiamen Zhong-Ri jiaoshe kuada" (Sino-Japanese relations get worse in Xiamen). February 20, 1924, 11.

Shenbao. 1924. "Xiamen haijun caizheng wenti jiejue" (The Xiamen Naval financial problems solved). May 19, 1924, 7.

Shenbao. 1924. "Xiamen haijun yanzhi taifei" (The Xiamen Navy strictly prosecutes Taiwanese bandits). May 26, 1924, 7.

Shenbao. 1924. "Xiamen junjing yanbu Taifei" (The Xiamen military and police arrest Taiwanese bandits). September 15, 1924, 6.

Shenbao. 1924. "Xiamen Chen-Wu chuanhu zhi xiedou" (Feud between the Chen and Wu boatmen in Xiamen). September 22, 1924, 6.

Shenbao. 1928. "Jiangsu jinyan zongju xiaoxi" (News about the Jiangsu Opium Prohibition Bureau). March 9, 1928, 15.

Shenbao. 1932. "Judu hui kangzheng minsheng yapian gongmai" (Anti-Opium Society resists the public sale of opium in Fujian province). April 3, 1932, 6.

Shenbao. 1932. "Ye zai liaoyang yuan beigou" (Ye captured at the Sino-Foreign Clinic). June 22, 1932, 10.

Shenbao. 1932. "Sizao yapian daiyongpin panzui" (Prosecution for private manufacture of opiate products). July 13, 1932, 15.

Shenbao. 1934. "Xiamen Tairen xingjie ju'an" (The great Taiwanese robbery case in Xiamen). April 9, 1934.

Shenbao. 1934. "Xia Ri lingshu juxing jimin dengji" (Japanese consul in Xiamen initiates registration of jimin). June 1, 1934, 12.

Shenbao. 1935. "Tairen zushe Xiamen jinrong zuhe" (Taiwanese create the Xiamen Finance Association). December 20, 1935, 9.

Shenbao. 1937. "Wei zuzhi qitu zaimin xiangxiao daiwu" (The Puppet Group in Fujian is unloading substitute products). March 13, 1937, 10.

Shi, Guangrong. 1995. "Yakou xiangtun xiaomie jing zhe liangjun" (The Yakou village militia defeated the Zhejiang and Jingguo armies). *Jinjiang wenshi ziliao* 1–5: 94–95.

Shi, Lang. 1959. *Jinghai ji shi* (Record of the pacification of the seas), Taiwan wencian congkan. Taipei: Taiwan yinhang.

Shih, Shu-mei. 2013. "Against Diaspora: The Sinophone as Places of Cultural Production." In *Sinophone Studies: A Critical Reader*, edited by Shu-mei Shih, Chien-hsin Tsai, and Brian Bernards. 25–42. New York: Columbia University Press.

Singapore Free Press and Mercantile Advertiser. 1847. "China." March 11, 1847, 3.

Singapore Free Press and Mercantile Advertiser. 1889. "Saturday, October 5, 1889." October 7, 1889, 426.

Singapore Free Press and Mercantile Advertiser 1889. "Perak News." November 19, 1889, 610.

Singapore Free Press and Mercantile Advertiser. 1908. "Illicit Sale of Cocaine in India." November 6, 1908.

Singapore Free Press and Mercantile Advertiser. 1926. "Opium Seized on Jardine Steamer." June 7, 1926, 12.

Sinn, Elizabeth. 2014. "Pacific Ocean: Highway to Gold Mountain, 1850–1900." *Pacific Historical Review* 83, no. 2: 220–237.

Slack, Edward. 2001. *Opium, State, and Society: China's Narco-Economy and the Guomindang, 1924–1937*. Honolulu: University of Hawai'i Press.

Soon, Wayne. 2020. *Global Medicine in China: A Global History*. Stanford, CA: Stanford University Press.

Spence, Jonathan. 1975. "Opium Smoking in Ch'ing China." In *Conflict and Control in Late Imperial China*, edited by Frederic Wakeman and Carolyn Grant. 143–173. Berkeley: University of California Press.

Statement of the Claims of the British Subjects Interested in Opium Surrendered to Captain Elliot at Canton for the Public Service. 1840. London: Pelham Richardson.

Straits Times Weekly Issue. 1889. "Government Gazette, 18th September." September 17, 1889, 8.

Straits Times. 1904. "Sensational Opium Case." September 30, 1904, 5.

Straits Times. 1913. "China and Opium." August 22, 1913, 3.

Straits Times. 1924. "Government Monopolies." July 2, 1924, 3.

Straits Times. 1926. "Huge Chandu Seizure." January 26, 1926, 9.

Straits Times. 1929. "Manila's Opium Seizure." May 2, 1929, 12.

Straits Times. 1930. "Traffic in Illicit Drugs." August 15, 1930.

Straits Times. 1934. "Fresh Hauls of Chandu." July 4, 1934, 12.

Sutherland, Heather. 2003. "Southeast Asian History and the Mediterranean Analogy." *Journal of Southeast Asian Studies* 34, no. 1: 1–20.

Szonyi, Michael. 2002. *Practicing Kinship: Lineage and Descent in Late Imperial China.* Stanford: Stanford University Press.

Szonyi, Michael. 2017. *The Art of Being Governed: Everyday Politics in Late Imperial China.* Princeton, NJ: Princeton University Press.

Tagliacozzo, Eric. 2005. *Secret Trades, Porous Borders: Smuggling and States Along a Southeast Asian Frontier, 1865–1915.* New Haven, CT: Yale University Press,.

Taiwan jinshikan (Who's who of Taiwan). 1934. Taibei: Taiwan shin minpo sha.

ter Haar, Barend. 2000. *Ritual and Mythology of the Chinese Triads: Creating an Identity.* Leiden: Brill.

Thai, Philip. 2018. *China's War on Smuggling: Law, Economic Life, and the Making of the Modern State, 1842–1965.* New York: Columbia University Press.

Thilly, Peter. 2017. "Opium and the Origins of Treason: The View from Fujian." *Late Imperial China* 38, no. 1: 155–197.

Third Military District Xiamen-Taiwan Committee for Processing *hanjian* [Han traitor] Cases. 1947. *Mintai hanjian zuixing jishi* (A record of the punishment of Fujianese and Taiwanese *hanjian*). Xiamen: Xiamen jiangsheng wenhua chuban she.

Topik, Steven, and William Gervase Clarence-Smith, editors. 2003. *The Global Coffee Economy in Africa, Asia, and Latin America, 1500–1989.* Cambridge: Cambridge University Press.

Trocki, Carl. 1990. *Opium and Empire: Chinese Society in Colonial Singapore, 1800–1910.* Ithaca, NY: Cornell University Press.

Trocki, Carl. 1999. *Opium, Empire and the Global Political Economy: A Study of the Asian Opium Trade, 1750–1950.* Oxon: Routledge.

Trocki, Carl. 2000. "Drugs, Taxes, and Chinese Capitalism in Southeast Asia." In *Opium Regimes: China, Britain, and Japan, 1839–1952*, edited by Timothy Brook and Bob Tadashi Wakabayashi, 79–105. Berkeley: University of California Press.

Trocki, Carl. 2011. "Opium as a Commodity in the Chinese Nanyang Trade." In *Chinese*

Circulations: Capital, Commodities, and Networks in Southeast Asia, edited by Eric Tagliacozzo and Wen-chin Chang, 84–106. Durham, NC: Duke University Press.

Tseng, Lin-Yi. 2014. "A Cross-Boundary People: The Commercial Activities, Social Networks and Travel Writings of Japanese and Taiwanese Sekimin in The Shantou Treaty Port, 1895–1937." PhD diss., City University of New York.

van de Ven, Hans. 2014. *Breaking with the Past: The Maritime Customs Service and the Global Origins of Modernity in China*. New York: Columbia University Press.

Veltmeyer, Henry and James Petras. 2019. "Dynamics of Narco-Capitalism." In *Latin America in the Vortex of Social Change: Development and Resistance Dynamics*, edited by Henry Veltmeyer and James Petras. London: Routledge.

Vermeer, Eduard. 1990a. "The Decline of Hsing-Hua Prefecture in the Early Ch'ing." In *The Development and Decline of Fukien Province in the 17th and 18th Centuries*, edited by Eduard B. Vermeer. Leiden: Brill.

Vermeer, Eduard B., editor. 1990b. *The Development and Decline of Fukien Province in the 17th and 18th Centuries* Leiden: Brill.

Wakeman, Frederic. 1995. *Policing Shanghai 1927–1937*. Berkeley: University of California Press.

Wang, Fangwen, and Wu Yangrong, editors. 1996. *Jindai Xiamen shewai dang'an shiliao* (Historical sources of foreign affairs in modern Xiamen). Xiamen: Xiamen University Press.

Wang, Fangwen, and Wu Yangrong, editors. 1997. *Xiamen kangri zhanzheng dang'an ziliao* (Archival sources from Xiamen on the war of resistance against Japan). Xiamen: Xiamen University Press.

Wang, Gungwu. 1996. *Sojourners and Settlers: Histories of Southeast Asia and the Chinese*. Honoloulu: University of Hawai'i Press.

Wang, Lianmao. 1982. "Chen Guohui feibu de dongshan zaiqi ji qi huo Quan zuixing" (The Chen Guohui Bandit Army's resurgence in the Eastern Mountains and their terrorizing criminal actions on Quanzhou). *Quanzhou Wenshi* 1: 41–59.

Wang, Xuexin. 2006. "Taiwan heibang jimin yu riben duihua yapian moulüe, 1895–1945 (The Taiwan-Registered Underworld and the Japanese Opium Plan in China)." *Guoshi guan xueshu jikan* 9: 1–48.

Wang, Xuexin. 2007. "Riben duihua nanjin zhengce yu Taiwan jimin zhi yanjiu, 1895–1945" (The study of Japan's southern advance policy on China and registered Taiwanese: 1895–1945). PhD diss., Xiamen University.

Wang, Xuexin, editor. 2010. *Rizhi shiqi jimin yu guoji shiliao huibian* (Collected sources on registered people and national registration during the Japanese colonial period). Taipei: guoshiguan Taiwan wenxian guan.

Watt, Peter, and Roberto Zepeda. 2012. *Drug War Mexico: Politics, Neoliberalism and Violence in the New Narcoeconomy*. New York: Zed Books.

Wills, Jr., John E. 2011. "Maritime Europe and the Ming." In *China and Maritime Europe 1500–1800: Trade, Settlement, Diplomacy, and Missions*, edited by John E. Wills, Jr. Cambridge: Cambridge University Press.

Wong, R. Bin. 2000. "Opium and Modern Chinese State-Making." In *Opium Regimes:*

China, Britain, and Japan, 1839–1952, edited by Timothy Brook and Bob Tadashi Wakabyashi, 189–211. Berkeley: University of California Press.

Wong, Yee Tuan. 2016. "Hokkien Merchants and the Kian Teik Tong: Economic and Political Influence in Nineteenth Century Penang and Its Region." *Frontiers of History in China* 11, no. 4: 600–627.

Working Group for the Compilation of Historical Sources on the Japanese-Registered *ronin* of Xiamen. 1983. "Xiamen riji langren jishu (The Japanese-Registered *ronin* of Xiamen)." *Xiamen wenshi ziliao* 2: 1–49.

Wright, Ashley. 2014. *Opium and Empire in Southeast Asia: Regulating Consumption in British Burma*. New York: Palgrave Macmillan.

Xiamen dabao. 1936. "Kuli gong da mafei zhen yi da ershi bao (A coolie worker shoots morphine, is arrested with one needle and twenty bags). June 12, 1936.

Xiamen dabao. 1936. "Shoushou hailuoyin" (Heroin confiscation). May 21, 1936.

Xiamen dabao. 1947. "'Shiba dage' toumu Li Longxi jiehu" ('Eighteen elder brother headman' Li Longxi transferred to Shanghai)." November 23, 1947.

Xiamen shi shanghui tekan (Special issue of the Xiamen Chamber of Commerce journal). 1940. Xiamen: Xiamen Chamber of Commerce.

Xiamen waishi zhi (Gazetteer of Foreign Affairs in Xiamen). 2001. Xiamen: Xiamen waishi zhi bianji weiyuan hui.

Xian shijie. 1936. "Zhongguo yu riben: si, zousi: ritai langren qiangduo zousi huo xiaguan yuan beiou shoushang tai" (China and Japan: four, smuggling: smuggling and robbery among Japanese-Taiwanese ronin, and the injury of a Xiamen customs officer). Vol. 1, no. 3, 136.

Xiao, Guojian. 1986. *Qing chu qianhai qianhou Xianggang zhi shehui bianqian* (Social change in Hong Kong before and after the early Qing coastal evacuation policy). Taibei: Taiwan Shangwu.

Xingguang ribao. 1946. "Hanjian Cai Peichu panxing shi'er nian, Chen Ji Lin Gun wuzui" (Hanjian Cai Peichu sentenced to twelve years, Chen Ji and Lin Gun found not guilty). September 25, 1946.

Xinmin qianfeng. 1931. "Fujian yanhuo" (The Fujian opium tragedy). 6, 20–21.

Xu, Jinjie, and Li Jiancheng. 1995. "Yapian da benying—Zhanglin cun (The great opium garrison—Zhanglin village)." *Jinjiang wenshi ziliao* 1–5: 143–146.

Xu, Liangshao. 1992. "Jinjiang jindu ji (Record of opium prohibition in Jinjiang)." *Jinjiang wenshi ziliao* 14: 137–142.Yang, Timothy M. 2021. *A Medicated Empire: The Pharmaceutical Industry and Modern Japan*. Ithaca, NY: Cornell University Press.

Yao, Ziqiang. 1986a. "Xiamen shi de jingcha jiguan yange, wanqing zhi minguo shiqi, 1906–1949" (The development of the Xiamen Police Department, from the late Qing to the Republican period, 1906–1949). *Xiamen wenshi ziliao* 11: 48–54.

Yao, Ziqiang. 1986b. "Xiamen lunxian shiqi de riwei jingcha jiguan, 1938.5–1945.9 (The Japanese "puppet" police of the Xiamen occupation period)." *Xiamen wenshi ziliao* 11: 55–66.

Yapian zhanzheng zai min tai shiliao xuanbian (Fujian-Taiwan Opium War Materials). Fuzhou: Fujian renmin chuban she, 1982. Abbreviated as YPZZ-MT.

Zhao, Gang. 2006. "Reinventing China: Imperial Qing Ideology and the Rise of Modern Chinese National Identity in the Early Twentieth Century." *Modern China* 32, no. 1: 3–30.

Zhao, Gang.. 2013. *The Qing Opening to the Ocean: Chinese Maritime Policies, 1684–1757.* Honolulu: University of Hawaii Press.

Zheng, Yangwen. 2005. *The Social Life of Opium in China.* Cambridge: Cambridge University Press.

Zheng, Zhenman. 2001. *Family Lineage Organization and Social Change in Ming and Qing Fujian,* Translated by Michael Szonyi. Honolulu: University of Hawai'i Press,.

Zhonghua, Guomin judu hui, ed. 1928. *Zhongguo yanhuo nianjian* (Almanac of the Chinese opium curse). Shanghai: Zhongguo Guomin judu hui.

Zhou, Taomo. 2019. *Migration in the Time of Revolution: China, Indonesia, and the Cold War.* Ithaca, NY: Cornell University Press.

Zhou, Yumin. 2010. "Qingji yapian lijin shuilü yange shulue" (The evolution of the Qing-era opium lijin tax rate). *Zhongguo jindai shi* 2: 57–69.

Zhou, Zifeng. 2005. "Jindai Xiamen chengshi fazhan shi yanjiu, 1900–1937" (A study of the urban history of Xiamen, 1900–1937). PhD diss., Xiamen University.

Index

67–68, 69–72, 86, 93; in warlord era, 15, 138–139, 151, 195. *See also* Brokers

Opium business, relations with state: arrests, 31–32, 33, 35–36, 37–38, 47, 50, 67; collaboration, 36–39, 45, 46–47; crackdowns, 30, 47–48, 49; evolution, 4, 9, 208–209, 211–213, 214; fees, 37–39, 50, 51, 56, 77, 88, 115–116; future research, 217; investigations, 24, 42, 46–47; under Japanese occupation, 204–208, 209–210; lack of enforcement, 56, 57, 58, 62–63; lineage networks and, 8; regulations, 119–120, 122; tensions, 11, 56–57; warehouses, 113. *See also* Bribery; Prohibition efforts; State revenues; Taxes; Tax farming

Opium consumption: efforts to reduce, 87, 122; in Fujian, 58, 59, 124–125, 130–131, 145, 151; increases, 90, 125; by officials, 129; in Philippines, 162; in Singapore, 156; in Xiamen, 58, 90, 124–125, 130–131. *See also* Opium market; Prohibition efforts

Opium dens and shops: in Fuzhou, 9, 58; under Japanese occupation, 205; in Nanjing, 106; in Netherlands Indies, 157; owners, 34–35; revenues, 90; shutting down, 106, 130; Taiwan-registered, 194–195, 197, 199, 202; taxes and fees, 90, 119, 130, 138; in Xiamen, 9, 90, 114–116, 119–120, 124–125, 130, 138, 194

Opium kings, 13, 15–16, 151, 212, 214. *See also* Chen Changfu; Lin Gun; Ye Qinghe; Zeng Houkun

Opium market in China: demand, 4, 7, 65, 111; prices, 91, 124, 153, 250n12, 261–262n7. *See also* Opium consumption

Opium poppies, *see* Poppy cultivation

Opium prohibition bureaus, *see* Prohibition bureaus

Opium taxes, *see* Taxes, opium; Tax farming

Opium trade: Chinese exports, 123; Chinese ships, 66; coastal (1832–1839), 23–39, 50–51; de facto legalization, 4, 10, 81–82, 86, 88–91, 103, 117, 208–209; early, 4, 6–7, 16, 26, 58; expansion, 4, 5–6, 7–9, 26–31; in Republican period, 131; value, 23, 88–89; volumes, 32–33, 57–58, 65, 88–89, 103, 229n6. *See also* British firms; Exports; Indian opium; Opium business

Opium War (1839–1842), 1, 8, 49, 79. *See also* Treaty of Nanjing

Opium War (1856–1860; Arrow War), 82. *See also* Treaty of Tianjin

Pathfinder, 68–69, 235n40

Pearl River delta, 5, 27, 30, 31, 229n18. *See also* Guangdong province; Lintin

Penang: cocaine imports, 178; opium smuggling into, 155; steamship traffic, 152

Peninsular & Oriental (P&O) Steam Navigation Company, 89, 99

Persian opium: A&B Monopoly, 159, 160 (fig.), 161, 162; confiscated, 146, 164; imports, 122, 153, 205; smuggled, 13, 143, 144, 145, 159–161

Pharmaceutical companies, 14, 169, 173, 178–179

Pharmacies, 164–166, 173–174, 178

Philippines: Chinese diaspora, 152–153, 161, 163, 191; drug prohibition efforts in twenty-first century, 215; opium consumption, 162; opium imports, 162–164; opium prohibition, 117, 161–164; steamship traffic, 152–153, 163; tax farming, 116; under US rule, 153, 161–164. *See also* Southeast Asia